THE AMERICAN ECONOMY

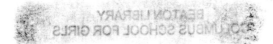

ISSN 1554-4400

THE AMERICAN ECONOMY

Kim Masters Evans

INFORMATION PLUS® REFERENCE SERIES
Formerly Published by Information Plus, Wylie, Texas

GALE
CENGAGE Learning™

Detroit • New York • San Francisco • New Haven, Conn • Waterville, Maine • London

GALE
CENGAGE Learning™

The American Economy

Kim Masters Evans

Kepos Media, Inc., Paula Kepos and Janice Jorgensen, Series Editors

Project Editors: Kathleen J. Edgar, Elizabeth Manar, Kimberly McGrath

Rights Acquisition and Management: Robyn Young

Composition: Evi Abou-El-Seoud, Mary Beth Trimper

Manufacturing: Cynde Lentz

For product information and technology assistance, contact us at
Gale Customer Support, 1-800-877-4253.
For permission to use material from this text or product,
submit all requests online at **www.cengage.com/permissions.**
Further permissions questions can be e-mailed to
permissionrequest@cengage.com

Cover photograph: Image copyright Karen Struthers, 2011. Used under license from Shutterstock.com.

While every effort has been made to ensure the reliability of the information presented in this publication, Gale, a part of Cengage Learning, does not guarantee the accuracy of the data contained herein. Gale accepts no payment for listing; and inclusion in the publication of any organization, agency, institution, publication, service, or individual does not imply endorsement of the editors or publisher. Errors brought to the attention of the publisher and verified to the satisfaction of the publisher will be corrected in future editions.

Gale
27500 Drake Rd.
Farmington Hills, MI 48331-3535

ISBN-13: 978-0-7876-5103-9 (set)   ISBN-10: 0-7876-5103-6 (set)
ISBN-13: 978-1-4144-4854-1   ISBN-10: 1-4144-4854-6

ISSN 1554-4400

This title is also available as an e-book.
ISBN-13: 978-1-4144-7525-7 (set)
ISBN-10: 1-4144-7525-X (set)
Contact your Gale sales representative for ordering information.

Printed in the United States of America
1 2 3 4 5 6 7 15 14 13 12 11

TABLE OF CONTENTS

whether this trade imbalance is good or bad for the U.S. economy. Major trade agreements, the International Monetary Fund and the World Bank, economic sanctions, and the increasing trend toward global free trade, or globalization, are also highlighted in this chapter.

PREFACE

The American Economy is part of the *Information Plus Reference Series*. The purpose of each volume of the series is to present the latest facts on a topic of pressing concern in modern American life. These topics include the most controversial and studied social issues of the 21st century: abortion, capital punishment, care for the elderly, crime, the environment, health care, immigration, minorities, national security, social welfare, women, youth, and many more. Even though this series is written especially for high school and undergraduate students, it is an excellent resource for anyone in need of factual information on current affairs.

By presenting the facts, it is the intention of Gale, Cengage Learning to provide its readers with everything they need to reach an informed opinion on current issues. To that end, there is a particular emphasis in this series on the presentation of scientific studies, surveys, and statistics. These data are generally presented in the form of tables, charts, and other graphics placed within the text of each book. Every graphic is directly referred to and carefully explained in the text. The source of each graphic is presented within the graphic itself. The data used in these graphics are drawn from the most reputable and reliable sources, such as from the various branches of the U.S. government and from private organizations and associations. Every effort has been made to secure the most recent information available. Readers should bear in mind that many major studies take years to conduct and that additional years often pass before the data from these studies are made available to the public. Therefore, in many cases the most recent information available in 2011 is dated from 2008 or 2009. Older statistics are sometimes presented as well, if they are landmark studies or of particular interest and no more-recent information exists.

Even though statistics are a major focus of the *Information Plus Reference Series*, they are by no means its only content. Each book also presents the widely held positions and important ideas that shape how the book's

subject is discussed in the United States. These positions are explained in detail and, where possible, in the words of their proponents. Some of the other material to be found in these books includes historical background, descriptions of major events related to the subject, relevant laws and court cases, and examples of how these issues play out in American life. Some books also feature primary documents or have pro and con debate sections that provide the words and opinions of prominent Americans on both sides of a controversial topic. All material is presented in an even-handed and unbiased manner; readers will never be encouraged to accept one view of an issue over another.

HOW TO USE THIS BOOK

The U.S. economy in the 21st century is enormous and extremely complicated. Workers, employers large and small, consumers, the equities markets, the U.S. government, and the world economy are constantly interacting with each other to affect the U.S. economy and, through it, each other. The U.S. economy produces and consumes raw materials, services, manufactured goods, and intellectual property in vast amounts. This book describes the size and scope of the U.S. economy, explains how it functions, and examines some of the challenges it faces, such as inflation, government regulation, outsourcing, and corporate scandals.

The American Economy consists of 10 chapters and 3 appendixes. Each chapter is devoted to a particular aspect of the U.S economy. For a summary of the information covered in each chapter, please see the synopses provided in the Table of Contents. Chapters generally begin with an overview of the basic facts and background information on the chapter's topic, then proceed to examine subtopics of particular interest. For example, Chapter 6: U.S. Businesses explains the different legal structures of businesses and the advantages and disadvantages of each structure. Then, the role of small businesses and big business (i.e., large corporations) in the economy is examined. The chapter includes a discussion of the crisis that lasted from late 2007 to mid-2009 in the financial industry and discusses the factors that led to the economic contraction and their consequences. Detailed data are presented on the economic performance of businesses in recent years. Also discussed are the different types of federal agencies that oversee U.S. businesses and the effects of government deregulation. This is followed by a discussion of monopolies and monopsonies and why these entities are considered unfair in business competition. The chapter ends with a discussion of some of the corporate scandals that have made headlines, including the public furor over large bonuses that have been handed out at financial corporations also receiving taxpayer bailout money. Readers can find their way through a chapter by looking for the section and subsection headings, which are clearly set off from the text. They can also refer to the book's extensive index, if they already know what they are looking for.

Statistical Information

The tables and figures featured throughout *The American Economy* will be of particular use to readers in learning about this topic. These tables and figures represent an extensive collection of the most recent and valuable statistics on the U.S. economy—for example, graphics cover the spending habits of the typical consumer, employment in manufacturing and service industries, the gross domestic product, the trade deficit, and consumer debt levels. Gale, Cengage Learning believes that making this information available to readers is the most important way to fulfill the goal of this book: to help readers understand the issues and controversies surrounding the U.S. economy and reach their own conclusions.

Each table or figure has a unique identifier appearing above it, for ease of identification and reference. Titles for the tables and figures explain their purpose. At the end of each table or figure, the original source of the data is provided.

To help readers understand these often complicated statistics, all tables and figures are explained in the text. References in the text direct readers to the relevant statistics. Furthermore, the contents of all tables and figures are fully indexed. Please see the opening section of the index at the back of this volume for a description of how to find tables and figures within it.

Appendixes

Besides the main body text and images, *The American Economy* has three appendixes. The first is the Important Names and Addresses directory. Here, readers will find contact information for a number of government and private organizations that can provide further information on aspects of the U.S. economy. The second appendix is the Resources section, which can also assist readers in conducting their own research. In this section, the author and editors of *The American Economy* describe some of the sources that were most useful during the compilation of this book. The final appendix is the index. It has been greatly expanded from previous editions and should make it even easier to find specific topics in this book.

ADVISORY BOARD CONTRIBUTIONS

The staff of Information Plus would like to extend its heartfelt appreciation to the Information Plus Advisory Board. This dedicated group of media professionals provides feedback on the series on an ongoing basis. Their comments allow the editorial staff who work on the project to continually make the series better and more user-friendly. The staff's top priority is to produce the highest-quality and most useful books possible, and the Information Plus Advisory Board's contributions to this process are invaluable.

The members of the Information Plus Advisory Board are:

- Kathleen R. Bonn, Librarian, Newbury Park High School, Newbury Park, California
- Madelyn Garner, Librarian, San Jacinto College, North Campus, Houston, Texas
- Anne Oxenrider, Media Specialist, Dundee High School, Dundee, Michigan
- Charles R. Rodgers, Director of Libraries, Pasco-Hernando Community College, Dade City, Florida
- James N. Zitzelsberger, Library Media Department Chairman, Oshkosh West High School, Oshkosh, Wisconsin

COMMENTS AND SUGGESTIONS

The editors of the *Information Plus Reference Series* welcome your feedback on *The American Economy*. Please direct all correspondence to:

Editors
Information Plus Reference Series
27500 Drake Rd.
Farmington Hills, MI 48331-3535

CHAPTER 1
THE U.S. ECONOMY: HISTORICAL OVERVIEW

It is not what we have that will make us a great nation;
it is the way in which we use it.

—Theodore Roosevelt, 1886

The workings of the U.S. economy are complex and often mysterious, even to economists. At its simplest, the economy runs on three major sectors: consumers, businesses, and government. (See Figure 1.1.) Consumers earn money and exchange much of it for goods and services from businesses. These businesses use the money to produce more goods and services and to pay wages to their employees. Both consumers and businesses fund the government sector, which spends and transfers money back into the system. The banking system plays a crucial role in the economy by providing the means for all sectors to save and borrow money. Finally, there are the stock markets, which allow consumers to invest their money in the nation's businesses—an enterprise that further fuels economic growth for all sectors. Thus, the U.S. economy is a circular system based on interdependent relationships in which massive amounts of money change hands. The historical developments that produced this system are important to understand because they provide key information about what has made the U.S. economy such a powerful force in the world.

DEFINING THE U.S. ECONOMY

The term *market economy* describes an economy in which the forces of supply and demand dictate the way in which goods and resources are allocated and what prices will be set. The opposite of a market economy is a *planned economy*, in which the government determines what will be produced and what prices will be charged. In a market economy, producers anticipate what products the market will be interested in and at what price, and they make decisions about what products they will bring to market and how these products will be produced and priced. Market economies foster competition among businesses, which

typically leads to lower prices and is generally considered beneficial for both workers and consumers. By contrast, a planned economy is directed by a central government that has a far greater degree of influence over prices and production, as well as a tighter regulation of industries and manufacturing procedures. The United States has a mixed economy, which combines aspects of a market economy with some central planning and control of a planned economy to create a system that has both a high degree of market freedom and regulatory agencies and social programs that promote the public welfare.

This mixed economy did not develop overnight. It has evolved over more than two centuries and has been shaped by American experiences at various times with hardship, war, peace, and prosperity.

COLONIAL TIMES

When European colonists first came to the New World, they found a vast expanse of land inhabited by Native Americans. Many of the first colonies were business ventures called charter companies that were financed by wealthy English businessmen and landowners. The colonies were granted limited economic and political rights by the king of England. After profits proved to be disappointing, many of the investors turned over the companies to the colonists themselves. These actions were to have far-reaching consequences on the shape of the United States. Christopher Conte and Albert R. Karr note in *The U.S. Economy: A Brief History* (October 2001, http://usa.usembassy.de/etexts/oecon/chap3.htm) that "the colonists were left to build their own lives, their own communities, and their own economy—in effect, to start constructing the rudiments of a new nation."

At first, the colonists were preoccupied with merely surviving. Eventually, they engaged in commerce with Europe by exploiting the natural resources of their new homeland. The main agricultural products of the colonies

FIGURE 1.1

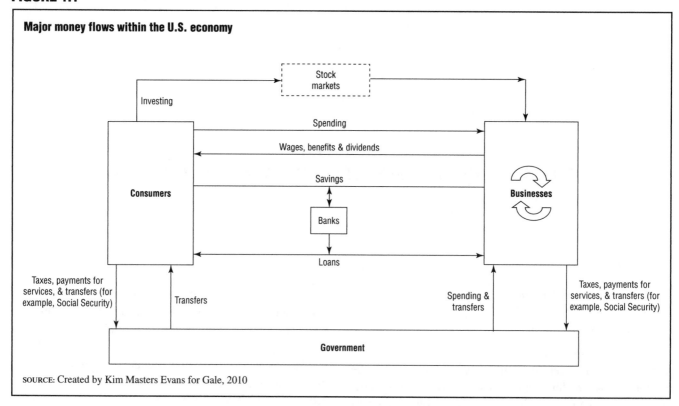

Major money flows within the U.S. economy

SOURCE: Created by Kim Masters Evans for Gale, 2010

were tobacco, wheat, rye, barley, rice, and indigo plant. Other important exports were animal furs, products from fish and whales, and timber. Shipbuilding became a major industry in New England.

Political and Industrial Revolution

Frustrated with the political and economic interference of England, the colonists banded together to forge a new nation: the United States of America. The push for independence from Great Britain, which culminated in the Revolutionary War (1775–1783), was driven by economic and political motivations, including the desire for greater self-governance and tax relief.

In 1776 a book was published in England that would have long-reaching effects on the new United States. The Scottish economist Adam Smith (1723–1790) wrote *An Inquiry into the Nature and Causes of the Wealth of Nations.* The book was remarkable for many reasons. It discussed economic principles in a common sense, nonmathematical manner and argued that the forces of supply and demand affect prices and wages. It criticized the restrictions and regulations common in European countries, and it advocated free and open trade within and between countries and the abolishment of wage and price controls. Smith believed that an "invisible hand" was guiding workers seeking to better their private finances, which in turn helped nations achieve prosperity. In other words, people who work hard for their own gain unconsciously contribute to national

wealth. The principles of a competitive marketplace with little government interference were adopted by the new United States and dominated the nation's economic policy for more than a century.

During the late 1700s Great Britain and the newly formed United States underwent a major social and economic change from agriculture to industry. The Industrial Revolution saw the introduction of the steam engine, the cotton gin, and other machines capable of increasing production while decreasing human labor. Farming, in particular, became much less labor intensive, freeing up people to pursue other forms of employment. Over the next century the United States changed from an agrarian-based nation to one in which the majority of income was generated by manufacturing, trade, and business that provided services to consumers. (See Figure 1.2.)

THE 1800S: EXPANSION AND CIVIL WAR

The 1800s were a period of enormous growth for the United States in terms of territory, population, and economic might. The Northeast developed thriving industries, and cities swelled with hundreds of thousands of European immigrants. Even though the South remained largely rural and agricultural, mechanical innovations, such as the cotton gin, changed the region's focus. Cotton became a major crop and was exported to textile mills in the North and overseas. Much of the economic success of the South was based on the use of slave labor.

FIGURE 1.2

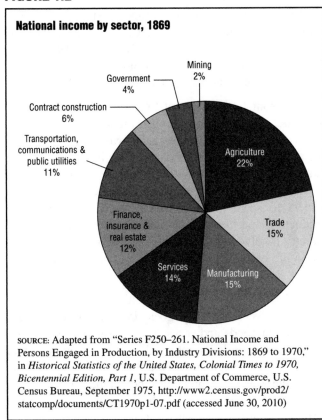

National income by sector, 1869

Mining 2%

Government 4%

Contract construction 6%

Transportation, communications & public utilities 11%

Finance, insurance & real estate 12%

Services 14%

Agriculture 22%

Trade 15%

Manufacturing 15%

SOURCE: Adapted from "Series F250–261. National Income and Persons Engaged in Production, by Industry Divisions: 1869 to 1970," in *Historical Statistics of the United States, Colonial Times to 1970, Bicentennial Edition, Part 1*, U.S. Department of Commerce, U.S. Census Bureau, September 1975, http://www2.census.gov/prod2/statcomp/documents/CT1970p1-07.pdf (accessed June 30, 2010)

Deep divisions arose between factions in the North and South on the morality of slavery and associated political and economic issues, which led to the devastating American Civil War in 1861. By the time the war ended in 1865, the factories of the Northeast had become extremely important in fueling the U.S. economy.

The Gilded Age

In 1873 the American writer Mark Twain (1835–1910) cowrote with his neighbor Charles Dudley Warner (1829–1900) the novel *The Gilded Age: A Tale of To-day*, which describes an American society in which unscrupulous businessmen and corrupt politicians pursue quick fortunes at the expense of the common people. Indeed, the decades following the Civil War were characterized by scandals involving high-level politicians making money from crooked business deals and by an unprecedented boom in business. The resulting social atmosphere was one of decadence among the upper classes contrasted with poverty and labor unrest among the lower classes.

The U.S. government had a hands-off approach to business regulation, a tactic described by the French term *laissez faire* (leave alone or "do as you please"). It was generally believed that the government should not interfere in economic affairs but should instead allow supply and demand and competition to operate unfettered, resulting in a free market.

The Gilded Age is notable for a growth in corporations. A corporation is a legally defined entity that may receive financial support from many investors but is treated as an individual under the law. A corporation is granted a state charter including specific rights, privileges, and liabilities. This type of business organization became popular during the late 1800s. It allowed people to invest in businesses without taking on all the responsibilities and risks of being a business owner. State charters limited the liability of individual investors, who were paid dividends in proportion to their share of investment in the corporation.

Some corporations grew through mergers or by buying out the companies of their competitors. Then they developed a business structure called a trust, in which the component companies were managed by a small group of people called a board of trustees. These corporations controlled nearly all the business in their respective industries, a condition known as monopolization. The public feared that trusts squelched competition that helped keep prices in check. In 1890 Congress passed the Sherman Antitrust Act. Its stated purpose was "to protect trade and commerce against unlawful restraints and monopolies." However, due to court challenges, the law was not successfully applied until the early 1900s.

Panics and Depressions

In economic terms a panic is a widespread occurrence of public anxiety about financial affairs. People lose confidence in banks and investments and want to hold onto their money instead of spending it. This can lead to a severe downturn, or depression, in the economic condition of a nation. The U.S. economy suffered from panics and depressions even during the booming growth of the 1800s. Economists argue about the exact definitions of panics and depressions, but in general it is agreed that panics and/or depressions occurred in the United States in 1819, 1837, 1857, 1869, 1873, and 1893.

The crises were triggered by a variety of factors. Common problems included too much borrowing and speculation by investors and poor oversight of banks by the federal government. Speculation is the buying of assets on the hope that they will greatly increase in value in the future. During the 1800s many speculators borrowed money from banks to buy land. Huge demand caused land prices to increase dramatically, often above what the land was actually worth in the market. Poorly regulated banks extended too much credit to speculators and to each other. When a large bank failed, there was a domino effect through the industry, which caused other banks and businesses to fail.

A panic or depression results in a downward economic spiral in which individuals and businesses are afraid to make new investments. People rush to withdraw their money from banks. As panic spreads, banks demand that borrowers pay back money, but borrowers may lack the funds to do so. Consumers are reluctant to spend money, which negatively affects businesses. Demand for products goes down, and prices must be lowered to move merchandise off of shelves. This means less profit for business owners. To reduce their costs, businesses begin laying off employees and do not hire new employees. As more people become unemployed or fearful about their jobs, there is even less spending in the marketplace, which leads to more business cutbacks and so forth. The cycle continues until some compelling change takes place to nudge the economy back into a positive direction.

THE 20TH CENTURY BEGINS

The early 20th century was a time of social and political change in the United States. Public disgust at the corruption and greed of the Gilded Age encouraged the movement called progressivism. Progressives promoted civic responsibility, worker's rights, consumer protection, political and tax reform, "trust busting," and strong government action to achieve social improvements. The Progressive Era greatly affected the U.S. economy because of its focus on improving working conditions for average Americans. Successes for the progressives included child labor restrictions, improved working conditions in factories, compensation funds for injured workers, a growth surge in labor unions, federal regulation of food and drug industries, and the formation of the Federal Trade Commission to oversee business practices.

Some people viewed the progressive movement as an attack on capitalism and a prelude to socialism. The U.S. economy was first described as "capitalist" by the German political theorist Karl Marx (1818–1883), who used the term to describe an economy in which a small group of people control the capital, or money available for investment, and, by extension, control the power within the economy. A common criticism of capitalism was that it favored profits over the well-being of workers. Marx advocated a socialist system in which wealth and property were not held by a few individuals but were equally distributed among all workers under a heavily planned economy. The socialist movement gained some momentum during the Progressive Era, thanks in large part to its ties to organized labor. However, socialism soon faded as a serious challenge to U.S. capitalism.

Despite its laissez-faire attitude, the federal government took two actions in 1913 that were to have long-lasting effects on the U.S. economy:

- Establishment of the Federal Reserve System to serve as the nation's central bank, furnish currency, and supervise banking

- Ratification of the 16th Amendment to the U.S. Constitution authorizing the collection of income taxes

World War I and Inflation

World War I erupted in Europe in August 1914. The United States entered the conflict in April 1917 and was engaged until the war ended in November 1918. Even though the nation spent only 19 months at war, the U.S. economy underwent major changes during this period.

It is sometimes said that "war is good for the economy" because during a major war the federal government spends large amounts of money on weapons and machinery through contracts with private industries. These industries hire more employees, which reduces unemployment and puts more money into the hands of consumers to spend in the marketplace. This increase in production and hiring also benefits other businesses not directly involved in the war effort. On the surface, these economic effects appear positive. However, major wars almost always result in high inflation rates.

Inflation is an economic condition in which the purchasing power of money goes down because of price increases in goods and services. For example, if a nation experiences an inflation rate of 3% in a year, an item that cost $1.00 at the beginning of the year will cost $1.03 at the end of the year. Inflation causes the "value" of a dollar to go down over the course of the year. In general, small increases in inflation occur over time in a healthy growing economy because demand slightly outpaces supply. Economists consider an inflation rate of 3% or less per year to be tolerable. During a major war the supply and demand ratio becomes distorted. This occurs when the nation produces huge amounts of war goods and far fewer consumer goods, such as food, clothing, and cars. This lack of supply and anxiety about the future drive up the prices of consumer goods, making it difficult for people to afford things they need or want.

During World War I the federal government intervened in private industry to support war needs and exert some control over supply and demand dynamics. Agencies were created to oversee the production of war goods, food, fuel, and nonmilitary ships. Even though the government tried to impose some level of price control in the food and fuel industries, inflation still occurred. According to the U.S. Census Bureau, in *Historical Statistics of the United States, Colonial Times to 1970, Bicentennial Edition, Part 1* (September 1975, http://www2.census.gov/prod2/statcomp/documents/CT1970p1-01.pdf), the prices for many consumer goods nearly doubled between 1915 and 1920. Figure 1.3 shows the average annual inflation rate from 1914 to 1924. The inflation rate was unusually high from 1916 to 1920, peaking at 18% in 1918. Wartime inflation was particularly hard on nonworking citizens, such as the elderly and the sick, because there were no large government programs in place at that time to assist needy people.

A lasting legacy of World War I was the assumption of large amounts of debt by the federal government to fund the

FIGURE 1.3

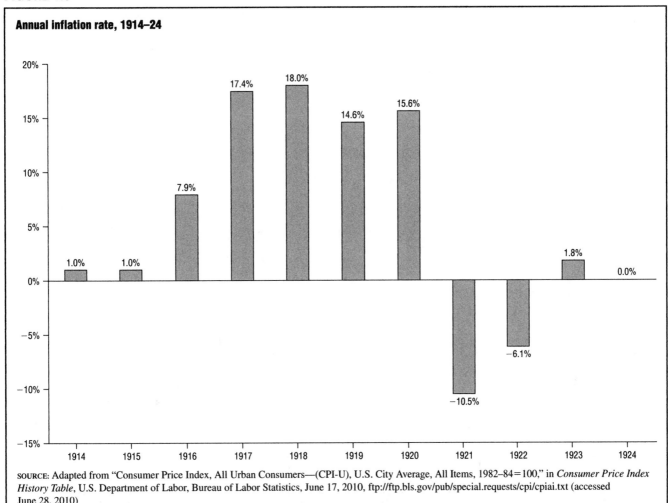

Annual inflation rate, 1914–24

war effort. Figure 1.4 shows the enormous differences that occurred between government spending and revenues (receipts) during the war years. In 1919 government spending peaked at nearly $18.5 billion, whereas revenues for that year were just over $5 billion. The government made up the difference by borrowing money. One method used was the selling of Liberty bonds. Bonds are a type of financial asset—an IOU that promises to pay back at some future date the original purchase price plus interest.

The Roaring Twenties

The Roaring Twenties began with a whimper; there was a severe economic downturn in 1921. However, this crisis was followed by several years of robust economic growth. Mass production and the availability of electricity led to huge consumer demand for household appliances. Installment plans became a popular means for middle-class Americans to purchase expensive long-lasting (durable) goods such as refrigerators, washing machines, and automobiles.

Americans also began spending more money on entertainment. They bought radios and went in large numbers to see motion pictures and baseball games. For many people, the automobile became a necessity, rather than a luxury. Booming car sales boosted the petroleum and housing markets and allowed city dwellers to move to the suburbs.

However, the prosperity of the 1920s was not shared by all Americans. During World War I demand for agricultural goods had skyrocketed, particularly in Europe. Overoptimistic farmers borrowed heavily to pay for tractors and other farm equipment, only to see food prices plummet during the 1920s when supply outpaced demand. Financial problems in the agricultural industry directly affected many Americans. In addition, banks in rural areas were stressed by farmers who were unable to pay back loans. The agricultural crisis was accompanied by downturns in the coal mining and railroad industries that affected many workers.

During the late 1920s the stock market became a major factor in the U.S. economy. Investors were richly rewarded, as stocks increased dramatically in value. Many people took out loans from banks to pay for stock or purchased stock by "buying on margin." In this arrangement an investor would make a small down payment (as little as

FIGURE 1.4

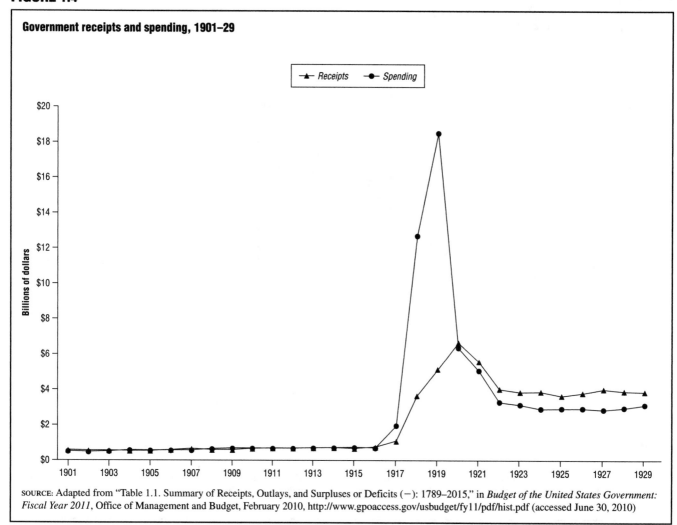

Government receipts and spending, 1901–29

SOURCE: Adapted from "Table 1.1. Summary of Receipts, Outlays, and Surpluses or Deficits (−): 1789–2015," in *Budget of the United States Government: Fiscal Year 2011*, Office of Management and Budget, February 2010, http://www.gpoaccess.gov/usbudget/fy11/pdf/hist.pdf (accessed June 30, 2010)

10%) on a stock purchase. The remainder of the balance would be paid (in theory) by the future increase in the stock value. Buying on margin was widely practiced by optimistic investors of the time. In "The Crash and the Great Depression" (2000, http://us.history.wisc.edu/hist102/lectures/textonly/lecture18.html), Stanley K. Schultz of the University of Wisconsin states that "by 1929, much of the money that was invested in the stock market did not actually exist."

Black Tuesday: October 29, 1929

On October 29, 1929, the stock market crashed. For months, President Herbert Hoover (1874–1964) and other influential people had warned that there was too much speculation in the stock market and that stock prices were higher than the actual worth of the companies. In the fall of 1929 investors began to get nervous. On Thursday, October 24, there was a selling frenzy as people tried to get rid of stocks they thought might be overvalued. The day was dubbed "Black Thursday." The following day the market rebounded somewhat, and stock prices climbed back upward. However, this recovery was short lived.

On Tuesday, October 29, panic selling took place all day. Stock values dropped dramatically. The drawback to buying on margin was that if a stock value went down by a certain amount, the lender would make a margin call by asking the buyer for more cash up front. If the margin buyer could not pay, the lender sold the stock to recoup the money. As "Black Tuesday" progressed, desperate margin buyers paid lenders all their cash in savings in hopes of saving their stock for the expected recovery, but no recovery came. As stock values fell further, lenders demanded more money. By the end of the day, many margin buyers had lost their life savings and their stock. Those who managed to hold on to their stock found it was worth only a fraction of its former value.

According to Harold Bierman Jr. of Cornell University, in "The 1929 Stock Market Crash" (February 5, 2010, http://eh.net/encyclopedia/article/Bierman.Crash), the U.S. stock market lost 90% of its value between 1929 and 1932.

The Great Depression

The U.S. economy suffered a devastating downturn following the stock market crash. The depression was so

FIGURE 1.5

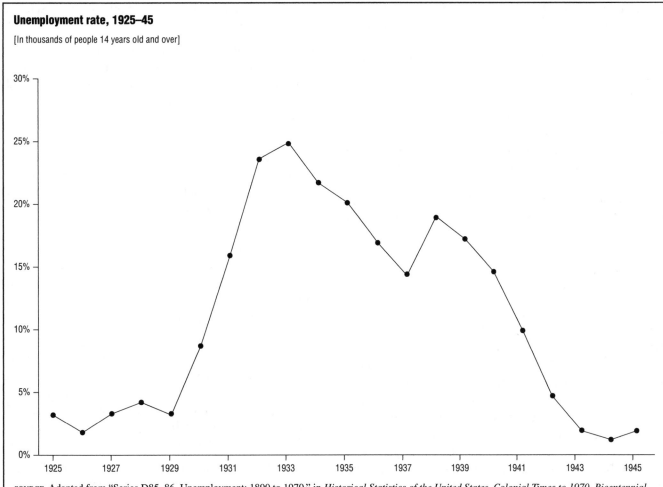

Unemployment rate, 1925–45

[In thousands of people 14 years old and over]

SOURCE: Adapted from "Series D85–86. Unemployment: 1890 to 1970," in *Historical Statistics of the United States, Colonial Times to 1970, Bicentennial Edition, Part 1*, U.S. Department of Commerce, U.S. Census Bureau, September 1975, http://www2.census.gov/prod2/statcomp/documents/CT1970p1-05 .pdf (accessed June 30, 2010)

deep and lasted so long—more than a decade—that it is called the Great Depression.

Historically, economic depressions had been short downturns with limited consequences. They were temporary dips in an overall trend of American prosperity. The Great Depression was a completely different experience. It brought long-term unemployment and hardship to millions of people. The unemployment rate soared from 3.2% in 1929 to 24.9% in 1933. (See Figure 1.5.) It remained more than 10% throughout the 1930s. The public lost confidence in the stock market, the banking system, and big business.

Like all previous depressions, this one included a downward cycle in which businesses reduced spending and production and laid off employees. Unemployed workers and those fearful of losing their jobs cut back on spending, which forced businesses to lay off more people. The economy underwent deflation—a condition where a lack of money among consumers depresses demand and pushes prices downward. Lower prices for agricultural and industrial goods hurt farmers and businesses, particularly

those with high debt. Consumers also had assumed high levels of debt during the 1920s.

The Great Depression was aggravated by a crisis in the banking industry. Some banks had invested heavily in the stock market using their depositors' money or lent large amounts of money to stock market investors. These banks failed after the crash, and the depositors lost their savings. Fear of further failures caused so-called bank runs, in which large numbers of depositors rushed to withdraw their money at the same time. This caused more bank failures, which perpetuated the cycle. In addition, some economists believe that the banking market became oversaturated during the 1920s with underfunded and loosely regulated banks that lent money too easily. These institutions were already financially troubled before the crash and could not survive the stress.

The United States' Great Depression was felt worldwide, particularly in other industrialized countries. By the 1920s the United States played a major role in world commerce by exporting and importing large amounts of goods and investing money in foreign businesses. A prolonged downturn in U.S. production, spending, and investing, combined with the banking crisis, had international consequences. Europe, in particular, suffered financially as it struggled to recover from the devastation of World War I.

The New Deal

When the Great Depression began, the laissez-faire attitude still dominated political opinion. Some economists, including Andrew W. Mellon (1855–1937), who served as the secretary of the treasury from 1921 to 1932, advised President Hoover not to interfere. Mellon took the traditional viewpoint that supply and demand factors would eventually equilibrate and that the economy would recover on its own. Hoover was not convinced. He tried a variety of tax adjustments, asked industry not to cut wages, and pushed for public works projects. However, the depression only deepened.

By 1932 Americans were ready for a change in leadership. Franklin D. Roosevelt (1882–1945), the governor of New York, promised "a new deal" for the nation. He was elected in a landslide victory and developed a government that acted aggressively in economic affairs. The New Deal included a wide variety of programs that were intended to bring relief to suffering Americans, revive farming and business, and reform the stock market and banking industry. After nearly 80 years, economists still argue about whether the New Deal was actually "a good deal" for the nation. They all agree, however, that it was a turning point in U.S. economic history.

Some New Deal programs did not survive court challenges. For example, the National Industrial Recovery Act of 1933 encouraged companies within industries to form alliances and set prices and wages. The companies that participated were exempt from antitrust laws that ordinarily would have forbidden such collusion. In 1935 the U.S. Supreme Court ruled that the law was unconstitutional. The Agricultural Adjustment Act of 1933 paid farmers to reduce production. It was thought that lower supply would raise prices and improve the living conditions of farmers. In 1936 the Supreme Court invalidated parts of the act. However, the payment of farm subsidies became a permanent component of U.S. economic policy.

Other legacies of the New Deal Era include:

- Federal Securities Act (1933)—regulated the selling of investment instruments (such as stock) to ensure that buyers are better educated about their purchases and to prevent fraudulent practices

- Glass-Steagall Banking Act (1933)—separated the commercial and investment banking industries and established the Federal Deposit Insurance Corporation to safeguard depositors' money

- Securities Exchange Act (1934)—regulated the stock exchanges and created the U.S. Securities and Exchange Commission

- National Labor Relations Act (1935)—guaranteed the right of employees in most private industries to organize, form labor unions, and bargain collectively with their employers; it also established the National Labor Relations Board

- Social Security Act (1935)—established a program to provide federal benefits to the elderly and to assist the states in providing for "aged persons, blind persons, dependent and crippled children, maternal and child welfare, public health, and the administration of their unemployment compensation laws"

Government employment programs under the Public Works Administration, the Works Project Administration, and the Civilian Conservation Corps put people to work building roads, dams, bridges, airfields, and post offices and developing national parks for tourism.

Perhaps the greatest legacy of Roosevelt's New Deal was the new role of the federal government as a manipulator of economic forces and a provider of benefits to the needy. This change in U.S. policy was seen as a wise and compassionate move by some people and as a dangerous shift toward socialism by others. In U.S. history the New Deal is considered the birth of big government.

By 1940 the unemployment rate was 14.6%. (See Figure 1.5.) Even though the rate was down from a peak of 24.9% in 1933, it was still high by historical standards. The hardship suffered by many Americans had been softened by nearly a decade of New Deal programs, but the country was still gripped by the Great Depression. It was going to take a war to bring an end to the Depression.

World War II

Even though the United States officially entered World War II in 1941, it had been gearing up its war industries for more than a year. This experience of mobilization (converting civilian industries to produce military goods) proved to be invaluable. The federal government established a host of agencies to oversee wartime production, labor relations, and prices. Efforts were made to avoid the huge inflation increase that had occurred during World War I. Rationing (tight controls over how much of an item a person can use or consume in a certain amount of time) was instituted on some goods to prevent dramatic price increases. Overall, these efforts were successful. Figure 1.6 shows the annual rates of inflation experienced in the United States from 1940 to 1950. Inflation spiked during the early years of the war and immediately after but was not consistently high over the decade.

Businesses rushed to increase production and hire workers to produce the goods needed for the war effort.

FIGURE 1.6

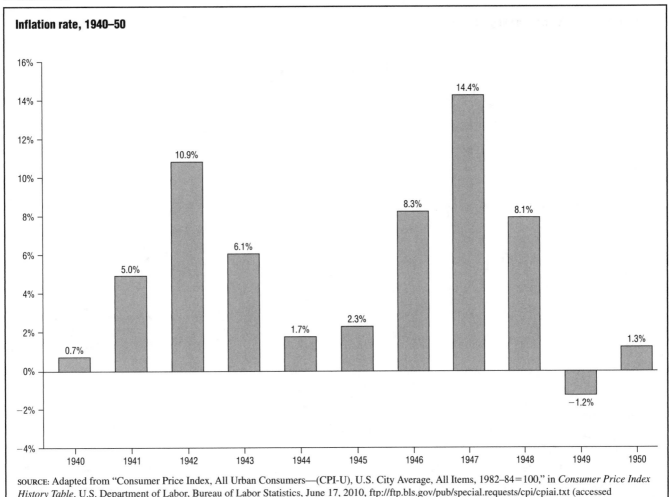

Inflation rate, 1940–50

SOURCE: Adapted from "Consumer Price Index, All Urban Consumers—(CPI-U), U.S. City Average, All Items, 1982–84=100," in *Consumer Price Index History Table*, U.S. Department of Labor, Bureau of Labor Statistics, June 17, 2010, ftp://ftp.bls.gov/pub/special.requests/cpi/cpiai.txt (accessed June 28, 2010)

Unemployment dropped dramatically and wages went up, particularly for workers in low-skilled factory jobs. Laborers found themselves in high demand and joined labor unions in record numbers to consolidate their power and seek better working conditions.

World War II was an expensive endeavor for the United States. However, it was believed that the stakes were so high that the war had to be won at any cost. As shown in Figure 1.7, government spending during the war far outpaced revenues. By 1945 the government was spending around $90 billion per year and taking in revenues around half this amount. Once again, the difference was made up by borrowing.

Keynesian Economics

The Great Depression shook many peoples' beliefs in the laissez-faire approach to economics that was advocated by Smith in the 18th century. During the 1930s and 1940s different approaches to capitalism began to receive serious attention. One of the most famous economists of the time was John Maynard Keynes (1883–1946). Keynes was a British expert on the application of economic theory to real-world problems. He published several influential books, including *The Economic Consequences of the Peace* (1919) and *General Theory of Employment, Interest, and Money* (1936). In the latter book, Keynes advocated strong government intervention in the economy as a remedy for the ongoing economic depression.

Politicians of the 1930s were not completely convinced by Keynes's arguments, particularly in regards to government spending. Maintaining a balanced federal budget was considered so sacred that the Hoover and Roosevelt administrations were reluctant to veer far from that precedent. However, following World War II it appeared obvious that huge government spending had helped fuel recovery from the Great Depression. Keynes's theories on capitalism, unemployment, and business cycles became highly regarded, and he is credited with inventing macroeconomics. This is a big-picture approach that measures broad trends in an economy, such as employment and inflation, and the way these trends interact. In contrast, microeconomics analyzes the economy on a smaller scale—for example, by studying the supply and

FIGURE 1.7

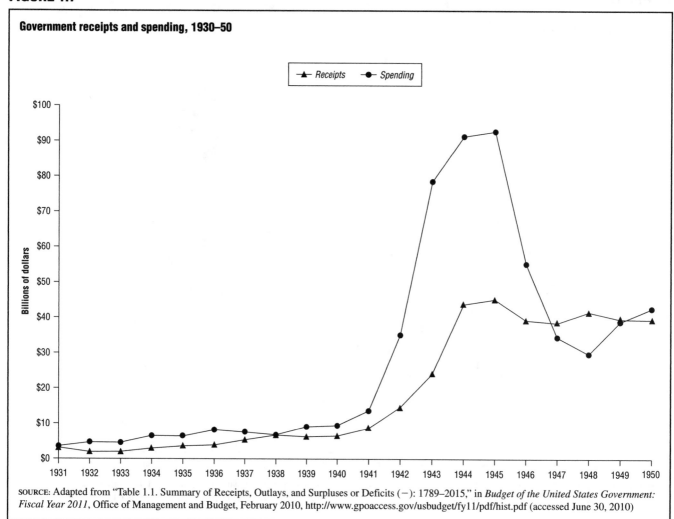

Government receipts and spending, 1930–50

SOURCE: Adapted from "Table 1.1. Summary of Receipts, Outlays, and Surpluses or Deficits (−): 1789–2015," in *Budget of the United States Government: Fiscal Year 2011*, Office of Management and Budget, February 2010, http://www.gpoaccess.gov/usbudget/fy11/pdf/hist.pdf (accessed June 30, 2010)

demand factors at work in individual markets or industrial segments.

Keynesian economics became the operating principle of the U.S. government during the post–World War II era. Even though Keynes had his critics, and his methods have been revised over time, he is considered by many to be the father of the mixed economy system that is still being used in the United States.

The National Income and Product Accounts

One innovation of the 1940s was the National Income and Product Accounts (NIPAs), which are compilations of national economic data. Before that time there was a lack of comprehensive macroeconomic data on the nation's inputs and outputs, such as labor and production of goods and services. This problem became apparent during the Great Depression, when the Hoover and Roosevelt administrations were forced to make decisions based on fragmented and incomplete data on the nation's financial condition. As a result, the U.S. Department of Commerce asked researchers at the National Bureau of Economic Research (NBER) at the University of New York to estimate national income

(e.g., wages, profits, and rent). Development of the NIPAs was overseen by the Commerce Department's Division of Economic Research, which evolved into the modern Bureau of Economic Analysis.

During World War II the federal government began compiling another macroeconomic measure called the gross national product (GNP). The GNP is the amount in dollars of the value of final goods and services produced by Americans over a particular time period. It is calculated by summing consumer and government spending, business and residential investments, and the net value of U.S. exports (exports minus imports).

The GNP provides a valuable tool for tracking national productivity over time. By the end of the 1940s an entire set of NIPAs had been developed to report macroeconomic data on the state of the U.S. economy.

A Postwar Spending Spree

Following World War II many U.S. industries demobilized from producing military goods and returned to producing consumer goods. Well-paid workers who had

FIGURE 1.8

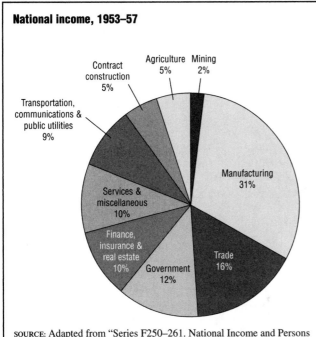

National income, 1953–57

SOURCE: Adapted from "Series F250–261. National Income and Persons Engaged in Production, by Industry Divisions: 1869 to 1970," in *Historical Statistics of the United States, Colonial Times to 1970, Bicentennial Edition, Part 1*, U.S. Department of Commerce, U.S. Census Bureau, September 1975, http://www2.census.gov/prod2/statcomp/documents/CT1970p1-07.pdf (accessed June 30, 2010)

been frustrated by wartime shortages were ready to spend money. Returning soldiers received government incentives to buy houses and start businesses. Postwar euphoria drove a spending spree and a baby boom.

New industries in aviation and electronics arose after World War II. Many existing industries underwent consolidation and growth as corporations merged into giant conglomerates. Figure 1.8 shows the national income that was produced by the business sector from 1953 to 1957. Manufacturing accounted for 31% of the national income during this period.

Dwight D. Eisenhower (1890–1969) was president from 1953 to 1961. His administration is associated with a growing economy that experienced low inflation rates and general prosperity. However, the prosperity of the 1950s was not shared equally in American society. Once again, farmers found themselves in trouble due to overproduction. An oversupply of agricultural goods meant lower prices (and lower profits). Agriculture became increasingly an industry in which large factory farms run by corporations were able to survive, whereas many smaller farmers could not compete.

Minority populations (largely African-American) also suffered financial hardship during this era. Figure 1.9 shows the dramatic difference between the unemployment rates for whites and minorities during the postwar decades. By the mid-1950s unemployment among minorities was twice as high as it was among white workers, a disparity that lingered well into the 1960s. It was in this atmosphere that the civil rights movement gained in strength and urgency. In 1954 segregation was ruled unconstitutional by the U.S. Supreme Court. The following year the African-American seamstress and activist Rosa Parks (1913–2005) was arrested in Alabama for refusing to move from the "white" section of a public bus. This incident spurred a bus boycott and ultimately brought Martin Luther King Jr. (1929–1968) and other leaders of the movement to national prominence.

The Cold War, Korea, and Vietnam

The United States left World War II in sound economic shape. By contrast, all other industrialized nations had suffered great losses in their infrastructure, financial stability, and populations. As a result, the United States was able to invest heavily in the postwar economies of Western Europe and Japan, with the hope of instilling an atmosphere that was conducive to peace and the spread of capitalism. U.S. barriers to foreign trade were relaxed to build new markets for U.S. exports and to allow some war-ravaged nations to make money selling goods to American consumers.

The Soviet Union had been a wartime ally of the United States, but relations became strained after the war. The Soviet Union had adopted communism following a period of revolution and civil war from 1917 to the early 1920s. During World War II the Soviet Union "liberated" a large part of eastern Europe from Nazi occupation. Through various means the Union of Soviet Socialist Republics (USSR) assumed political control over these nations. The USSR had been largely industrialized before World War II and quickly regained its industrial capabilities. It soon took a major role in international affairs, placing it in direct conflict with the only other superpower of the time: the United States. A cold war began between the two rich and powerful nations that had completely different political, economic, and social goals for the world.

The Cold War was fought mostly by politicians and diplomats. A direct and large-scale military conflict between U.S. and Soviet forces never occurred. Regardless, an expensive arms race began in which both sides produced and stockpiled large amounts of weaponry as a show of force to deter a first strike by the enemy. In addition, both sides provided financial and military support to countries around the world in an attempt to influence the political leanings of those populations. Communist China joined the Cold War during the 1950s and often partnered with the USSR against U.S. interests.

By the 1950s the United States was embroiled in two Asian conflicts over communism: the Korean War (1950–1953) and the Vietnam War (1954–1975). In both wars the United States chose to fight in a limited manner without

FIGURE 1.9

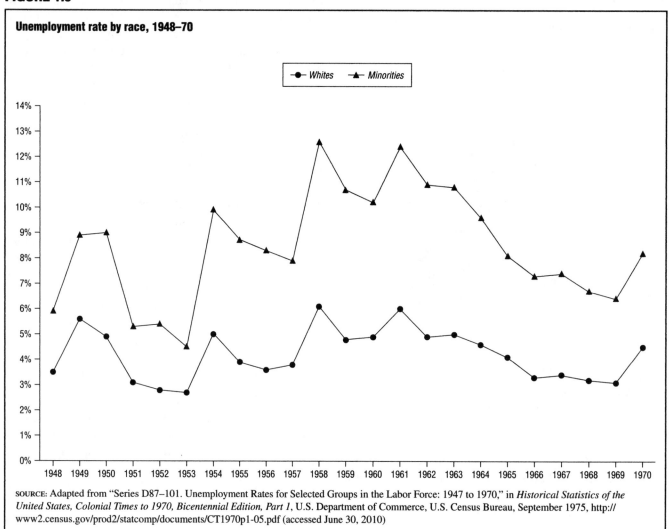

Unemployment rate by race, 1948–70

● Whites ▲ Minorities

SOURCE: Adapted from "Series D87–101. Unemployment Rates for Selected Groups in the Labor Force: 1947 to 1970," in *Historical Statistics of the United States, Colonial Times to 1970, Bicentennial Edition, Part 1*, U.S. Department of Commerce, U.S. Census Bureau, September 1975, http://www2.census.gov/prod2/statcomp/documents/CT1970p1-05.pdf (accessed June 30, 2010)

using its arsenal of nuclear weapons or engaging Chinese or Soviet troops directly for fear of sparking another world war. Unlike World War II, full-scale mobilization of U.S. industries was not required for these wars. Instead, a defense industry developed during the Cold War to supply the U.S. military on a continuous basis with the arms and matériels it needed.

Figure 1.10 shows the percentage of the national budget that was devoted to national defense from 1940 to 1970. Spending on national defense soared during World War II and then declined dramatically following the war's end. However, military spending quickly climbed again as the Cold War intensified during the early 1950s and remained above 40% for nearly two decades.

The Birth of the Modern Federal Reserve

The nation's central bank—the Federal Reserve System—was formed in 1913 to furnish currency and supervise financial institutions. Gradually, it took on other roles that affected the amount of money circulating in the United States and the interest rates charged by banks

FIGURE 1.10

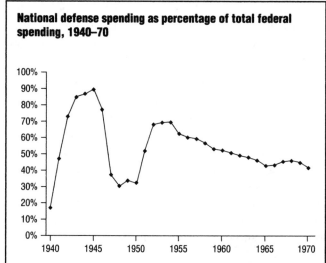

National defense spending as percentage of total federal spending, 1940–70

SOURCE: Adapted from "Table 1.1. Summary of Receipts, Outlays, and Surpluses or Deficits (−): 1789–2015," and "Table 3.1. Outlays by Superfunction and Function: 1940–2015," in *Budget of the United States Government: Fiscal Year 2011*, Office of Management and Budget, February 2010, http://www.gpoaccess.gov/usbudget/fy11/pdf/hist.pdf (accessed June 30, 2010)

to their customers. The Federal Reserve System consists of 12 regional banks located around the country and is overseen by a seven-member board of governors headquartered in Washington, D.C.

The Federal Reserve was designed to be as independent as possible from political pressures from both the U.S. president and Congress. This safeguard was included to prevent the Federal Reserve from having to bow to demands for short-term economic fixes requested by politicians seeking reelection. The Federal Reserve was charged with taking a long-term approach to economic policy for the good of the nation as a whole.

Robert L. Hetzel and Ralph F. Leach explain in "After the Accord: Reminiscences on the Birth of the Modern Fed" (*Economic Quarterly*, vol. 87, no. 1, Winter 2001) that from its inception until the early 1950s, the Federal Reserve was influenced by the policies of the U.S. Department of the Treasury. During the late 1940s Federal Reserve and Treasury officials disagreed about how best to handle the large debt that was accumulated by the United States during World War II. This conflict led to a new agreement, or accord, between the two agencies about the roles of each in the U.S. economy. This accord is considered the birth of the modern Federal Reserve, an organization that has grown to exert great power in the U.S. economy.

The chairman of the board of governors at the time of the accord was William McChesney Martin Jr. (1906–1998). Martin was a dynamic leader who maintained his post for nearly two decades. Under his leadership the Federal Reserve assumed greater control over the nation's financial policies. This control was exercised primarily by influencing interest rates on loans. Lowering interest rates encouraged borrowing, which put more money into circulation for spending or investing. However, if demand outpaced supply, price inflation became a problem. The Federal Reserve would respond by raising interest rates to make borrowing less attractive and dampen demand. Martin reportedly summed this up by saying, "You have to take away the punch bowl when the party is warming up." His policy proved to be fruitful during the prosperous decades of the 1950s and 1960s.

The 1960s: Social Upheaval and Economic Growth

The 1960s were a time of social and economic change for the United States. The decade began with the election of President John F. Kennedy (1917–1963), who promised to ensure economic growth and address growing social problems within the United States. In 1963 Kennedy's efforts were cut short by his assassination. Lyndon B. Johnson (1908–1973) took over as president and dramatically enlarged the federal government and its role in socioeconomic affairs. Johnson's administration initiated large-scale programs for the needy, including the health care programs Medicare (for the elderly) and Medicaid (for the

poor), jobs programs, federal aid to schools, and food stamps for low-income Americans. The so-called War on Poverty and the escalating war in Vietnam proved to be extremely expensive. At the same time, the United States was pursuing a costly (but ultimately successful) endeavor to land astronauts on the moon before the end of the decade.

Consumer and government spending drove the nation's GNP during the 1960s. However, inflation became a problem (as it often does in a fast-growing economy) in the late 1960s. At the macroeconomic level, there was too much money in the hands of consumers, which resulted in consumer demand that was higher than supply. In *Consumer Price Index* (August 13, 2010, ftp://ftp.bls.gov/pub/special.requests/cpi/cpiai.txt), the U.S. Bureau of Labor Statistics (BLS) notes that by 1970 the inflation rate had reached 5.7%.

According to the NBER, in "US Business Cycle Expansions and Contractions" (August 2, 2010, http://www.nber.org/cycles.html), the United States left the 1960s having experienced the longest continuous stretch of positive GNP growth in history—from the first quarter of 1961 to the last quarter of 1969. However, high inflation was about to become a major problem.

The 1970s: Stagflation and Energy Crises

"Stagflation" is a word coined during the 1970s to describe an economy suffering stagnant growth, high inflation, and high unemployment all at the same time. This combination of economic problems was unprecedented in U.S. history. Previously, high inflation had occurred when the economy was growing quickly, such as during World War II, and high production had meant high employment levels. By contrast, economic downturns were associated with higher unemployment but lower inflation (and even deflation). These relationships had been considered natural and certain.

The 1970s were unique because both unemployment and inflation were high, by historical standards. The economist Arthur Okun (1928–1980) coined the term *discomfort factor* to describe this condition. His discomfort factor, which became popularly known as the Misery index, is computed by summing the unemployment rate and the inflation rate. Figure 1.11 shows the annual Misery index calculated from 1968 to 1983. Beginning in 1974 each rate exceeded 5%.

There were three presidents during the 1970s: Richard M. Nixon (1913–1994), Gerald R. Ford (1913–2006), and Jimmy Carter (1924–). Each tried a variety of measures to stem stagflation, but none was considered effective. By 1980 the Misery index had climbed to 21%. (See Figure 1.11.)

FOREIGN OIL AND COMPETITION. The United States' economic problems were aggravated by its dependence on foreign oil and competition from foreign industries. In

FIGURE 1.11

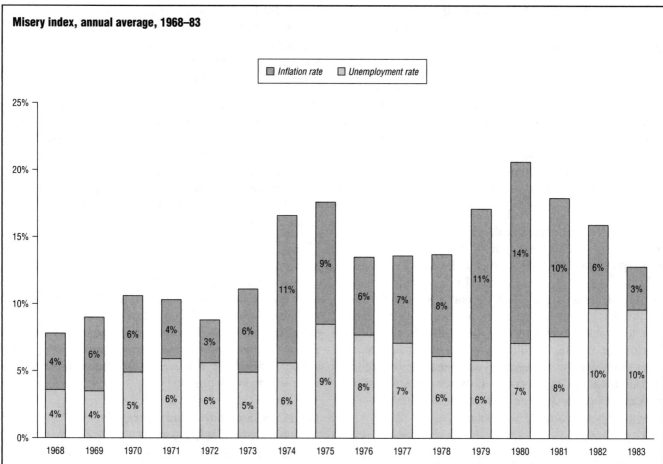

Misery index, annual average, 1968–83

SOURCE: Adapted from "Consumer Price Index, All Urban Consumers—(CPI-U), U.S. City Average, All Items, 1982–84=100," in *Consumer Price Index History Table*, U.S. Department of Labor, Bureau of Labor Statistics, June 17, 2010, ftp://ftp.bls.gov/pub/special.requests/cpi/cpiai.txt (accessed June 28, 2010); and "1. Employment Status of the Civilian Noninstitutional Population, 1940 to Date," in *Labor Force Statistics from the Current Population Survey*, U.S. Department of Labor, Bureau of Labor Statistics, January 2010, http://www.bls.gov/cps/cpsa2009.pdf (accessed June 28, 2010)

1973 the Middle Eastern members of the Organization of the Petroleum Exporting Countries halted oil exports to the United States in retaliation for U.S. support of Israel. The oil embargo lasted five months. When shipments resumed, the price of oil had dramatically increased. Americans faced high prices, long lines, and shortages at the gas pumps. Figure 1.12 shows that the average retail price of gasoline surged from $0.36 per gallon in 1972 to $1.35 per gallon in 1981. During the late 1970s a revolution in oil-rich Iran brought a second wave of shortages to U.S. energy supplies.

The energy crisis of the 1970s had a ripple effect throughout the U.S. economy, causing the prices of other goods and services to increase. Lower profits and uncertainty about the future caused businesses to slow down and reduce their workforces. At the same time, U.S. industries in steel, automobiles, and electronics endured stiff foreign competition, particularly from Japan. Small energy-efficient Japanese cars became popular in the United States. By 1980 gasoline cost nearly $1.25 per gallon, which was three and a half times the price in 1972. (See Figure 1.12.)

U.S. carmakers struggled to compete, having always relied on consumer demand for large automobiles—which were now considered "gas guzzlers."

DEREGULATION. One of the measures that President Carter used to combat stagflation was deregulation. For decades, certain U.S. industries had been given government immunity from market supply and demand factors. The railroad, trucking, and airline industries were prime examples. Companies in these industries were guaranteed rates and routes and were allowed to operate contrary to antitrust laws. In 1978 the airline industry was deregulated. The result was that airlines began to compete with each other over fares and routes, and new companies entered the industry. Some of the large, well-established companies were unable to compete in the new environment and went out of business. However, demand increased as prices came down and flying became available to many more Americans. By 1980 deregulation had been completed or was under way for the railroad, trucking, energy, financial services, and telecommunications industries.

FIGURE 1.12

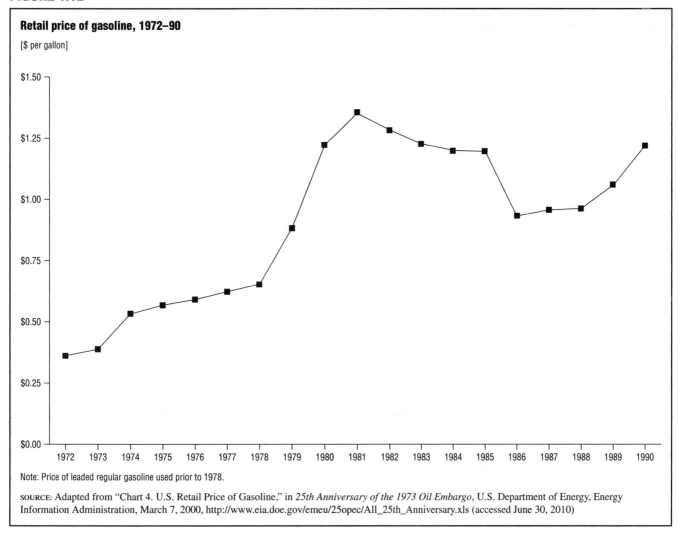

Retail price of gasoline, 1972–90

[$ per gallon]

Note: Price of leaded regular gasoline used prior to 1978.

SOURCE: Adapted from "Chart 4. U.S. Retail Price of Gasoline," in *25th Anniversary of the 1973 Oil Embargo*, U.S. Department of Energy, Energy Information Administration, March 7, 2000, http://www.eia.doe.gov/emeu/25opec/All_25th_Anniversary.xls (accessed June 30, 2010)

The 1980s: Recession and Reaganomics

In November 1980 the American people elected Ronald Reagan (1911–2004) as the new president. Inflation was at 14% that year, which was incredibly high for a peacetime economy. (See Figure 1.11.) Unemployment was at 7%, meaning that millions of people were unemployed and faced with rapidly increasing prices in the marketplace. The economic situation was dire, and drastic measures were required to turn the economy around.

SLAYING THE INFLATIONARY DRAGON. In late 1979 President Carter had appointed a new chair of the Federal Reserve board of governors, Paul A. Volcker (1927–), who promised to "slay the inflationary dragon." Volcker began by tightening the nation's money supply. This had the effect of making credit more difficult to obtain, which drove up interest rates. The government knew that rising interest rates would probably trigger a production slowdown (a recession) that would push unemployment even higher. It was a trade-off that policy makers during the previous decade had been unwilling to accept.

Volcker forged ahead with his policies, and by the early 1980s interest rates had reached historical highs. Figure 1.13 shows that the prime loan rate (the interest rate that banks charge their best customers) peaked at 21.5% in December 1980. According to the Federal Home Loan Mortgage Corporation, in "30-Year Conventional Mortgage Rate" (August 3, 2010, http://research.stlouisfed.org/fred2/data/MORTG.txt), in 1981 the average interest rate for a conventional 30-year mortgage soared to nearly 18.5%, the highest rate ever recorded.

The lack of credit caused a business slowdown—a reduction in GNP growth (or recession). As expected, the recession put more people out of work. Unemployment climbed at first, averaging 10% in 1982 and 1983, but then began to decline. (See Figure 1.11.) By the end of the decade it was down around 5%. According to the BLS, in *Consumer Price Index*, the inflation rate dropped from a high of 13.5% in 1980 to 4.8% by 1989. Even though the spike in unemployment had been painful for Americans, the inflationary dragon was finally dead.

FIGURE 1.13

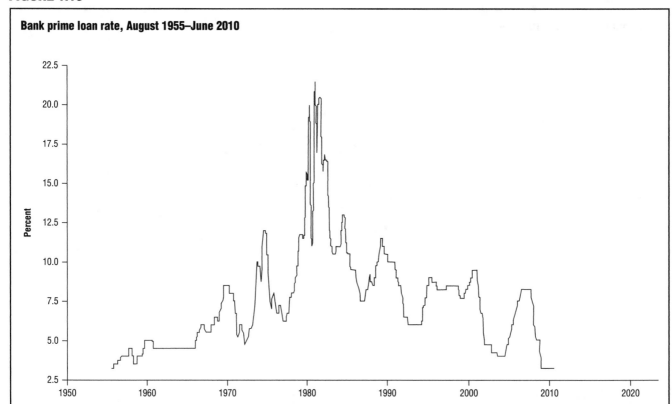

Bank prime loan rate, August 1955–June 2010

SOURCE: "Bank Prime Loan Rate (WPRIME)," in *Economic Data—FRED®: Bank Prime Loan Rate*, Federal Reserve Bank of St. Louis, July 27, 2010, http://research.stlouisfed.org/fred2/graph/fredgraph.pdf?&chart_type=line&graph_id=&category_id=&recession_bars=Off&width=630&height =378&bgcolor=%23B3CDE7&graph_bgcolor=%23FFFFFF&txtcolor=%23000000&ts=8&preserve_ratio=true&fo=ve&id=WPRIME&transformation =lin&scale=Left&range=Max&cosd=1955-08-10&coed=2010-07-21&line_color=%230000FF&link_values=&mark_type=NONE&mw=4&line_style =Solid&lw=1&vintage_date=2010-07-29&revision_date=2010-07-29&mma=0&nd=&ost=&oet=&fml=a (accessed July 29, 2010)

REAGANOMICS. When Reagan took office in 1981, he brought a new approach to curing the nation's financial woes: supply-side economics. Traditionally, the government had focused on the demand side—the role of consumers in stimulating businesses to produce more. Reagan preferred economic policies that directly helped producers. In "Supply Side Economics" (2005, http://www.auburn.edu/~johnspm/gloss/supply_side), Paul M. Johnson of Auburn University describes the philosophy this way: "Supply-side policy analysts focus on barriers to higher productivity—identifying ways in which the government can promote faster economic growth over the long haul by removing impediments to the supply of, and efficient use of, the factors of production."

One of the cornerstones of supply-side economics is reducing taxes so that people and businesses have more money to invest in private enterprise. Reagan enacted tax cuts through two pieces of legislation: the Economic Recovery Tax Act of 1981 and the Tax Reform Act of 1986. The result was a much lower number of tax brackets (the various rates at which individuals are taxed based on their income), a broader tax base (wealth within a jurisdiction that is liable to taxation), and reduced tax rates on income and capital gains (the profit made from selling an investment, such as land).

At the same time, Reagan pushed for greater national defense spending as part of his "peace through strength" approach to the Soviet Union and for selective cuts in social services spending. However, no cuts were made to the largest and most expensive programs within the social services budget. The combination of all these factors resulted in high federal deficits during the 1980s. In other words, the federal government was spending more than it was making each year. As shown in Figure 1.14, the federal deficits of the mid-1980s were more than three times what they had been during the mid-1970s. According to the article "U.S. Debt Past $1 Trillion" (*New York Times*, October 23, 1981), the national debt (the sum of all accumulated federal deficits since the nation began) reached $1 trillion in 1981.

The 1990s: Sparkling Economic Performance

The 1990s were a time of phenomenal economic growth for the United States. President George H. W. Bush (1924–) took office in 1989 and served until 1993. Bush had been elected in large part because of his promise not to raise taxes. During his presidential campaign he famously said, "Read my lips: No new taxes." However, the promise was not one he could keep, given the economic realities of

FIGURE 1.14

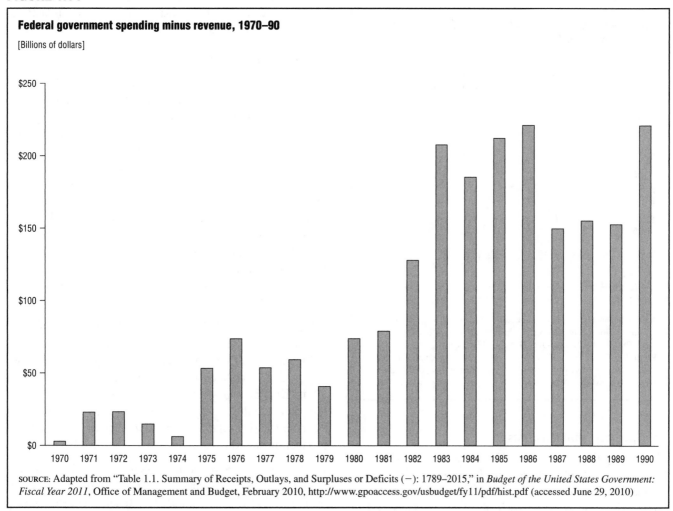

Federal government spending minus revenue, 1970–90

[Billions of dollars]

SOURCE: Adapted from "Table 1.1. Summary of Receipts, Outlays, and Surpluses or Deficits (−): 1789–2015," in *Budget of the United States Government: Fiscal Year 2011*, Office of Management and Budget, February 2010, http://www.gpoaccess.gov/usbudget/fy11/pdf/hist.pdf (accessed June 29, 2010)

the time. During the late 1980s there had been a severe financial crisis in the savings and loan industry, which had been recently deregulated. A series of unwise loans and poor business decisions left most of the industry in shambles and necessitated a government bailout. At the same time, the government faced rapidly rising expenditures on health care programs for the elderly (Medicare) and the needy (Medicaid). Bush reluctantly agreed to a tax increase, a move that was politically damaging. In 1992 he lost his reelection bid to the Arkansas governor Bill Clinton (1946–), who was reelected in 1996.

Joseph Tracy, Henry Schneider, and Sewin Chan indicate in "Are Stocks Overtaking Real Estate in Household Portfolios?" (*Current Issues in Economics and Finance*, vol. 5, no. 5, April 1999) that, overall, the 1990s were a period of peace and prosperity for the United States: the Cold War ended when the Soviet Union disintegrated into individual republics; technological innovations, particularly in the computer industry, helped push the economy to new heights; and sterling business success led to robust investor confidence in the stock markets. Figure 1.15 shows the portion of household assets that were invested in

real estate and corporate equity (stocks) from 1945 to 1998. Even though real estate was the preferred investment through nearly all of this period, the 1990s witnessed tremendous increases in the holdings of corporate equity by the average American. In the mid-1980s the average household had only 10% of its assets in corporate equity. By 1998 this percentage had reached nearly 30%, roughly equal to the percent held in real estate. The Dow Jones Industrial Average is a stock market index—a measure used by economists to gauge the value (and performance) of the stock of 30 large companies. Between the late 1970s and the late 1990s the index soared from around 1,000 points to 11,000 points—reflecting the tremendous value gained by these companies during this period.

The combination of low interest rates, low unemployment, and high investment rates and business growth combined to greatly expand the U.S. economy. According to the article "Excerpts from Federal Reserve Chairman's Testimony" (*New York Times*, January 21, 1999), Alan Greenspan (1926–), the chair of the Federal Reserve board of governors, described this expansion as "America's sparkling economic performance."

FIGURE 1.15

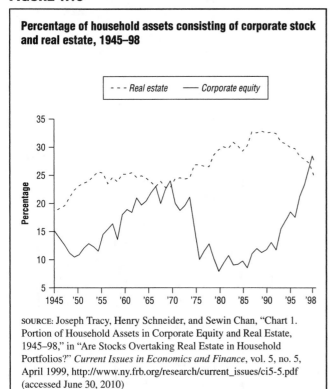

Percentage of household assets consisting of corporate stock and real estate, 1945–98

SOURCE: Joseph Tracy, Henry Schneider, and Sewin Chan, "Chart 1. Portion of Household Assets in Corporate Equity and Real Estate, 1945–98," in "Are Stocks Overtaking Real Estate in Household Portfolios?" *Current Issues in Economics and Finance*, vol. 5, no. 5, April 1999, http://www.ny.frb.org/research/current_issues/ci5-5.pdf (accessed June 30, 2010)

The Internet Bubble Bursts

During the late 1990s the stock market witnessed tremendous growth, driven in large part by investor enthusiasm for Internet-related businesses. Access to the Internet became widespread in the United States and in much of the developed world, which created many new market opportunities for entrepreneurs. Investors enthusiastically poured money into the stock of these new businesses. The National Association of Securities Dealers Automated Quotation System (NASDAQ) is a U.S.-based stock market on which the stock of many technology companies is traded. The NASDAQ composite index is a measure of the performance of many of the stocks on NASDAQ. In 1990 the index was less than 500. In early 2000 it peaked above 4,000 during the height of the Internet stock craze. Many of the stocks had become overvalued, and their high prices could not be sustained based on the actual financial results that the companies were producing. What followed was a sharp market correction, as investors sold off many Internet-based stocks and prices plummeted. By late 2002 the NASDAQ composite index was around 1,200, from which it slowly began to climb again.

In economics a bubble is a phenomenon in which investors overzealously invest (speculate) in a particular commodity or market sector that becomes overvalued. Excitement about possible gains overrules frank analysis of the underlying financial factors. What frustrates investors and analysts alike is that the very existence of a bubble is not evident until after the fact, when the bubble has burst and much value has been lost in the investments and the businesses involved.

The Great Recession

During the early years of the first decade of the 21st century the United States endured the September 11, 2001, terrorist attacks, the outbreak of wars in Afghanistan and Iraq, corporate scandals, devastating hurricanes, and a slump in the stock market. Nevertheless, the overall economy remained robust, as evidenced by relatively low unemployment rates, moderate rates of inflation, and growth in the nation's production. National production is tracked through a numerical measure called the gross domestic product (GDP). The GDP is similar to the GNP described earlier, but the GNP includes production of U.S. companies outside the United States, whereas the GDP considers only production of U.S. companies within the United States.

The nation's GDP is considered a key measure (or metric) of how the economy is doing. The GDP is expected to increase over time, for example, from quarter to quarter. If the GDP stagnates or declines, then the economy is ailing. Declining GDP means that businesses are producing less. Because they need less workers, unemployment rises. As noted earlier, the term *recession* refers to a national production slowdown.

In "Determination of the December 2007 Peak in Economic Activity" (December 11, 2008, http://www.nber.org/cycles/dec2008.html), the NBER officially defines a recession as "a significant decline in economic activity spread across the economy, lasting more than a few months, normally visible in production, employment, real income, and other indicators. A recession begins when the economy reaches a peak of activity and ends when the economy reaches its trough [lowest point]." According to the NBER, the U.S. economy reached a peak in December 2007 and then went into a recession.

The NBER (September 20, 2010, http://www.nber.org/cycles/sept2010.pdf) notes that its analysis of national economic data indicates that the recession ended in June 2009. In total, the recession spanned a total of 18 months, making it the longest lasting recession since World War II. The NBER also points out that the recession's end does not mean that "the economy has returned to operating at normal capacity," only that a recovery began to occur. In fact, the organization notes that "economic activity is typically below normal in the early stages of an expansion, and it sometimes remains so well into the expansion."

There have been many recessions in U.S. history; most were short and unremarkable. The exception is, of course, the Great Depression. The economic downturn that occurred from December 2007 to June 2009 was so deep and so damaging that many economists have dubbed it "the great recession." Its contributing factors and consequences are described briefly here and in detail in the following chapters.

THE HOUSING MARKET COLLAPSES. The root cause of the great recession was a bursting bubble—this time in the housing industry. As shown in Figure 1.13, the United States experienced historically low interest rates during the early years of the first decade of the 21st century. This spurred demand throughout the housing industry, which pushed housing prices upward. Homes in many areas of the country began to appreciate (rise in value) at an unprecedented rate. Investors eagerly bought houses and sold them a short time later for a higher price. Many banks and financial institutions became caught up in the frenzy and lowered their normally strict loan standards. They introduced new types of mortgages in which payments were low at first and then quickly rose over a certain period. Eager home buyers, especially first-time buyers, entered into these agreements without adequately considering the consequences to their personal finances.

In late 2005 and early 2006 the housing bubble burst. Overspeculation had pushed home prices above sustainable levels. Demand suddenly plummeted and homes depreciated (lost value) in many areas of the country. Homeowners began defaulting (ceasing making payments) on their loans, which put extreme pressure on mortgage lenders. The lenders were forced to foreclose (take legal possession of) on the homes that had been defaulted and then sell them at a loss. The construction industry, which had rushed to build new homes in response to the high demand, was economically devastated by the sudden collapse. The bursting housing bubble was bad enough on its own, but the problem was aggravated by certain actions taken by the financial industry.

THE FINANCIAL INDUSTRY FALTERS. Mortgages are an asset (something with value) to the company that holds them. Oftentimes, companies will bundle mortgages together and sell these bundles to investors. During the late 1990s and the early years of the first decade of the 21st century large investment companies came up with new and riskier ways to trade bundled mortgages. For one thing they invented a type of insurance contract called the credit default swap. The traditional insurance industry is heavily regulated by the U.S. government. Companies that insure assets against loss must prove that they have sufficient collateral (typically cash or other assets with immediately obtainable and verifiable worth) to cover any losses that do occur. Credit default swaps were not regulated because they were not insurance policies in the traditional sense. As a result, financial corporations were using swaps they owned as "collateral" for swaps they were issuing to each other and to investors.

As noted earlier, many mortgage lenders lowered their standards during the boom in the housing market. This greatly increased the risk that the mortgage holders would default. The investors who bought these bundled mortgages were either unaware or overlooked the risk they were assuming by buying the investments. When the housing bubble burst, mortgage defaults quickly soared and the value of the bundled mortgages plummeted. Panicked investors tried to redeem their credit default swaps, but the swaps were not backed by enough real currency and proved nearly worthless. Major banks and investment corporations, which are the backbone of the U.S. financial industry, suffered huge losses. Some failed, whereas others were rescued by enormous inflows of cash from the U.S. government. As of September 2010, the so-called bailout of troubled financial companies had cost American taxpayers more than $1 trillion.

THE LINGERING EFFECTS OF THE GREAT RECESSION In one sense the U.S. economy is a machine, as depicted in Figure 1.1. Money is the fuel for the machine because it flows from one component to another and keeps the machine operating. However, in reality the U.S. economy is driven by hope, faith, and confidence. When businesses and consumers are worried about the future, they hold onto their money rather than spend or invest it. Businesses hire fewer people and lay off employees, and consumers do not buy as much, which hurts business profitability. The longer this downward spiral lasts, the more serious the damage is to both the economy and consumers.

As noted earlier, a recession officially ends when the economy reaches its lowest point and then begins to recover. However, full recovery can be a slow process. Even though the great recession officially ended in June 2009, many of its damaging effects still lingered as of September 2010. Two of these problems—high unemployment and continuing fallout from the housing bubble burst—were particularly troublesome for the American people. As a result, public opinion polls conducted well into 2010 indicated deep pessimism about the country's economy and future. The great recession was particularly long and deep; thus, returning the United States to a strong and thriving economic condition was expected to be a long process.

CHAPTER 2
ECONOMIC INDICATORS AND PUBLIC PERCEPTIONS

Because the U.S. economy is so large and complex, it is difficult to assess its overall health at any given time. Economists use a variety of numerical measures to analyze and track macroeconomic factors, such as employment and production. (Macroeconomics is an analysis of the overall economy using information such as unemployment, inflation, production, and price levels.) These economic indicators are widely broadcast in the media and are the subject of much analysis by leaders in government, industry, and the financial markets. The American public tends to gauge the health of the economy based on other factors, including their own personal and community-wide experiences and expectations.

ECONOMIC INDICATORS

Economists gauge the strength of the economy using data on wages, spending, saving, unemployment, and the production and consumption of goods and services. Some of these data are called economic indicators because they provide key information about the macroeconomic condition of the country. One example is the National Income and Product Accounts that are compiled by the Bureau of Economic Analysis (BEA) under the U.S. Department of Commerce. The U.S. Census Bureau, the U.S. Department of Labor, and some private organizations also publish key economic indicators. (See Table 2.1.)

Three of the most important and telling economic indicators are the gross domestic product, the consumer price index, and the unemployment rate.

Gross Domestic Product

The gross domestic product (GDP) measures in dollars the total value of U.S. goods and services newly produced or newly provided during a given time period. It is calculated and published by the BEA and is one of the most important and accurate ways the government tracks the health of the economy. The GDP can be

calculated in different ways. One method is the expenditure approach. It sums all the spending that takes place during a specified time period on final goods and services that are newly produced or newly provided. The components of this calculation are:

- Consumption—the amount spent by consumers on final goods and services. This includes food, clothing, household appliances, and so on, and payments for medical care, haircuts, dry cleaning, and other types of services. One major item not included in this category is the purchase of residential housing, which is considered an investment, rather than a consumption expense.

- Investment—this category has three components. One is the amount spent by businesses on assets they will use to provide goods and services (e.g., new machines and equipment, warehouses, software, and company vehicles). Also included are changes in the value of business inventories. This amount can be positive or negative. Residential housing is the third component of the investment category.

- Government expenditures—the amount spent by the government (local, state, and federal) on final goods and services. This category does not include transfer payments to the public (such as Social Security and unemployment compensation) because these expenditures do not represent goods or services purchased.

- Net exports—the difference between the value of U.S. exports and imports. In other words, net exports equal the amount that foreigners paid for American goods minus the amount that Americans spent on foreign goods. If the United States exports more than it imports, this value will be positive. If the country imports more than it exports, this value will be negative.

It should be noted that the GDP counts only the final value paid for goods and services, not the value of

TABLE 2.1

Key economic indicators for U.S. economy

Economic indicator	Description	Website
Gross domestic product	Value of goods and services produced in a given time period	http://www.bea.gov/national/index.htm#gdp
Personal income and outlays	Personal income, disposable personal income, and personal consumption expenditures.	http://www.bea.gov/national/index.htm#personal
Corporate profits	Corporate profits based on current production.	http://www.bea.gov/national/index.htm#corporate
Fixed assets	Net stocks, depreciation, and investment for private residential and nonresidential fixed assets.	http://www.bea.gov/national/index.htm#fixed
Balance of payments (international transactions)	Quarterly trade in goods, services, income, unilateral transfers, and financial assets.	http://www.bea.gov/international/index.htm#bop
Consumer price index	Monthly changes in the prices paid by urban consumers for a representative basket of goods and services.	http://www.bls.gov/cpi/
Producer price index	Group of indexes that measure the average change over time in the prices received by U.S. producers of goods and services	http://www.bls.gov/ppi/
Unemployment rate	Number of unemployed people divided by total labor force. Based on monthly survey.	http://www.bls.gov/cps/lfcharacteristics.htm#unemp
Monthly retail trade	Survey of companies that sell merchandise and related services to final consumers.	http://www.census.gov/retail/
Monthly wholesale trade	Survey of companies that are primarily engaged in merchant wholesale trade in the U.S.	http://www.census.gov/wholesale/index.html
Consumer confidence index	Consumers' assessment of economic conditions based on monthly surveys of a representative sample of 5,000 U.S. households.	http://www.conference-board.org/data/consumerdata.cfm
Leading economic index	Index based on vendor performance, stock prices, consumer expectations, manufacturers' new orders, manufacturing hours, interest rate spread, building permits, claims for unemployment insurance, and real money supply.	http://www.conference-board.org/data/bci.cfm
ISM report on business	Economic activity in many manufacturing and nonmanufacturing industries based on orders, production, employment, supplier deliveries, imports, prices, and inventories.	http://www.ism.ws/ISMReport/

SOURCE: Created by Kim Masters Evans for Gale, 2010

intermediate transactions. For example, the value of steel sold by a steel company to an automaker is not counted. The value of the car made from the steel is counted when the car is sold in the marketplace. To be counted in the GDP, a product must be new. The sales of used items are not included.

COMPARISON WITH THE GROSS NATIONAL PRODUCT. Before 1991 the U.S. government relied on an economic indicator called the gross national product (GNP) to measure U.S. productivity. The GNP is calculated the same way that the GDP is calculated, except that the GNP includes the contribution of U.S. production in foreign countries (e.g., an American-owned factory in Mexico). The GDP includes only production occurring within the boundaries of the United States.

NOMINAL VERSUS REAL GDP. Economists refer to GDP values as being nominal (based on current dollar values) or real (based on inflation-adjusted dollar values). Consider a simple example in which a nation's only production is 1,000 identical new cars produced and sold each year. Assume this nation suffers from inflation, meaning that the price charged and paid for each car increases each year. A graph of this nation's GDP would go upward, indicating that production increases each year, while actually it is just the price of the cars that is increasing.

To remedy this problem, economists adjust the actual GDP values (nominal values) to account for inflation.

The adjusted values are called the real GDP values. They are useful for comparing GDP changes over time. Figure 2.1 shows the real GDP values for the U.S. economy from 1929 to 2009. These values were calculated assuming that a dollar had the exact same value over time—the value it had in 2005.

Figure 2.2 shows the annual percentage change in the real GDP from 1994 to 2009. In general, GDP growth of 2% to 4% per year is considered optimal for the U.S. economy. The real GDP did not grow at all from 2007 to 2008 and decreased by 2.6% between 2008 and 2009, reflecting the poor state of the economy.

Consumer Price Index

The consumer price index (CPI) provides a measure of price changes in consumer goods and services over a specific period. Each month the U.S. Bureau of Labor Statistics (BLS), a division of the Department of Labor, calculates the purchase price of a fixed "basket" of thousands of goods and services commonly purchased for consumption by U.S. households. These purchases are divided into eight major categories:

- Food and beverages—at-home and away-from-home consumption

- Housing—includes rent of primary residence or owners' equivalent rent

- Apparel

FIGURE 2.1

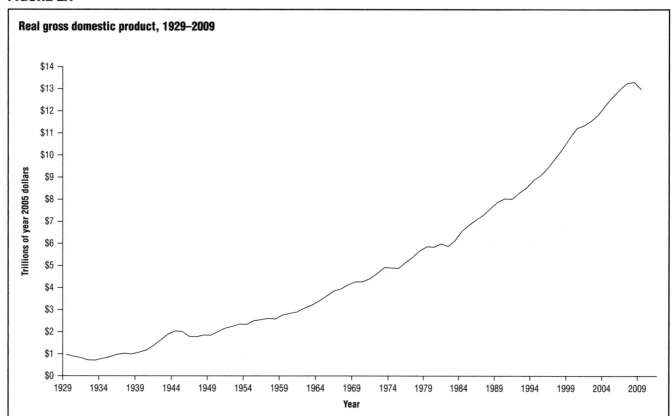

Real gross domestic product, 1929–2009

SOURCE: Adapted from "Table 1.1.6. Real Gross Domestic Product, Chained Dollars," in *National Income and Product Accounts*, U.S. Department of Commerce, Bureau of Economic Analysis, June 25, 2010, http://www.bea.gov/national/nipaweb/TableView.asp?SelectedTable=6&ViewSeries=NO&Java =no&Request3Place=N&3Place=N&FromView=YES&Freq=Year&FirstYear=1929&LastYear=2009&3Place=N&AllYearsChk=YES&Update =Update&JavaBox=yes (accessed June 28, 2010)

FIGURE 2.2

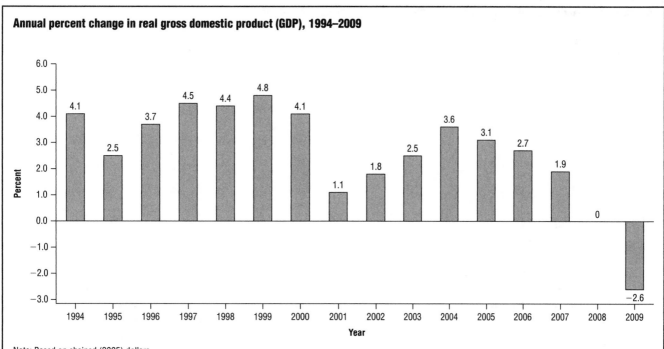

Annual percent change in real gross domestic product (GDP), 1994–2009

Note: Based on chained (2005) dollars

SOURCE: Adapted from "Table 7. Real Gross Domestic Product: Percent Change from Preceding Year," in *National Income and Product Accounts: Gross Domestic Product: Second Quarter 2010 (Advance Estimate); Revised Estimates: 2007 through First Quarter 2010*, U.S. Department of Commerce, Bureau of Economic Analysis, July 30, 2010, http://www.bea.gov/newsreleases/national/gdp/2010/pdf/gdp2q10_adv.pdf (accessed August 2, 2010)

- Transportation—includes insurance payments

- Medical care

- Recreation—includes pet expenses

- Education and communication—includes computer software

- Other goods and services—haircuts, cigarettes, funeral expenses, and so on

The basket price includes sales and excise taxes paid on goods purchased. Payments for income taxes and investments, such as stocks and bonds, are not included.

An index is a useful tool for comparing changes over time. The index for the basket price for a selected time period is arbitrarily set to 100. This is the reference index. All other basket prices are compared with the reference index using this equation: index = (basket price/reference basket price) × 100. Therefore, a graph of CPI data over time does not show the actual prices paid for the baskets but a series of index numbers useful for determining price changes. Figure 2.3 shows the average annual CPI from 1913 to 2009. It uses the time period of 1982 to 1984 as the reference time period for which the CPI value is arbitrarily set to 100.

Percent changes in price between two years can be determined based on the difference in index values. For example, according to the BLS, in *Consumer Price Index*

(August 13, 2010, ftp://ftp.bls.gov/pub/special.requests/cpi/cpiai.txt), the average CPI was 124 in 1989. By 2009 it had risen to 214.5—a difference of 90.5 index points. Dividing 90.5 by 124 and multiplying by 100 provides a percentage difference of 73%. On average, prices increased by 73% over this 20-year period.

The data presented in Figure 2.3 are for urban households. According to the BLS, in "Frequently Asked Questions (FAQ)" (June 28, 2010, http://www.bls.gov/cpi/cpifaq.htm), the urban CPI (CPI-U) represents the buying habits of approximately 87% of the U.S. population. The BLS also calculates a CPI for urban dwellers employed in clerical or wage occupations, which are a subset of people included in the CPI-U. This subset represents approximately 32% of the U.S. population. Besides the national average, the BLS publishes CPI data for specific regions of the United States and for dozens of metropolitan areas.

CALCULATING AVERAGE ANNUAL INFLATION RATES FROM THE CPI. Price inflation can be defined as the increase in price over time of a fixed basket of goods and services. Thus, the CPI provides economists with a tool for quantifying inflation rates. The percent change in CPI from year to year is the inflation rate for that year. Figure 2.4 shows the average annual inflation rate for the U.S. economy for each year from 1915 to 2009 based on CPI-U data. In *Consumer Price Index*, the BLS states that

FIGURE 2.3

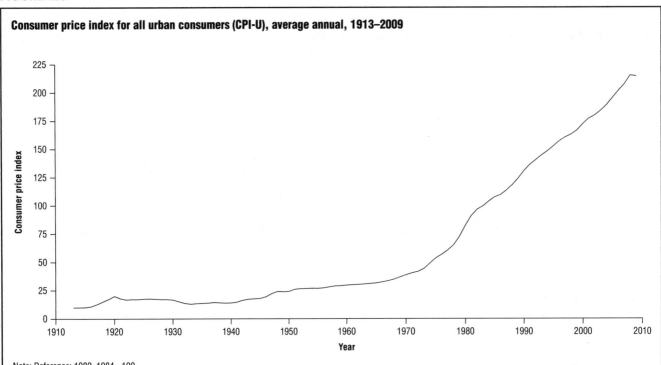

Consumer price index for all urban consumers (CPI-U), average annual, 1913–2009

Note: Reference: 1982–1984=100

SOURCE: Adapted from "Consumer Price Index, All Urban Consumers—(CPI-U), U.S. City Average, All Items, 1982–84=100," in *Consumer Price Index History Table*, U.S. Department of Labor, Bureau of Labor Statistics, June 17, 2010, ftp://ftp.bls.gov/pub/special.requests/cpi/cpiai.txt (accessed June 28, 2010)

FIGURE 2.4

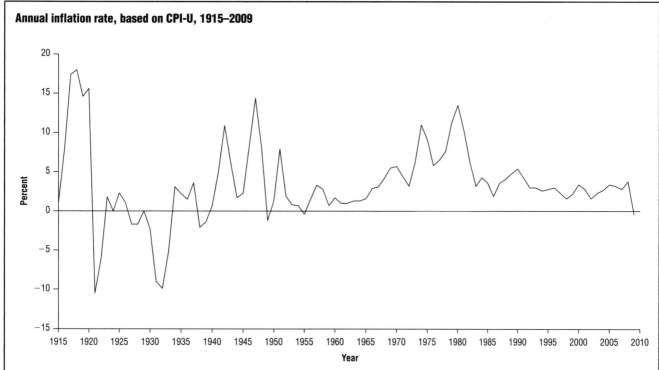

Annual inflation rate, based on CPI-U, 1915–2009

SOURCE: Adapted from "Consumer Price Index, All Urban Consumers—(CPI-U), U.S. City Average, All Items, 1982–84=100," in *Consumer Price Index History Table*, U.S. Department of Labor, Bureau of Labor Statistics, June 17, 2010, ftp://ftp.bls.gov/pub/special.requests/cpi/cpiai.txt (accessed June 28, 2010)

the average CPI-U for 2007 was 207.3 and for 2008 was 215.3. The inflation rate was ([215.3−207.3]/207.3) × 100 = 3.9%. This means that, on average, the price of consumer goods and services increased by 3.9% between 2007 and 2008. It also means that the purchasing power of a dollar decreased during this period. For example, an item that cost $1.00 in 2007 cost nearly $1.04 in 2008.

In general, annual inflation rates of 2% to 3% are considered signs of a healthy growing economy where demand slightly outpaces supply. Larger inflation rates can be worrisome. The U.S. economy has suffered from double-digit inflation rates due to the effects of the world wars and during the 1970s and early 1980s.

From a macroeconomic standpoint, the average annual inflation rate of 3.9% from 2007 to 2008 appears to be higher than "normal" for a healthy economy. However, 2008 was a very unusual year. Not only did it begin to feel the effects of the so-called great recession but also it featured a midyear swing in CPI-U values. This can be seen in Figure 2.5, which shows monthly CPI-U values from January 2008 to June 2010. The values climbed steeply in early 2008, and then plummeted through the remainder of the year. In "Inflation in 2008 Slowest since 1954" (*Wall Street Journal*, January 16, 2009), Brian Blackstone explains that the inflationary trend during the first half of 2008 was driven by sharply rising fuel prices. High fuel prices pushed up the

prices for other goods and services, primarily due to higher transportation and heating and cooling costs. However, Blackstone notes that the price of oil dropped by approximately 75% between July and December 2008. The deepening financial crisis in the country also spurred consumers to spend less money (i.e., overall demand decreased). As a result, the monthly CPI-U increased from 211.1 in January 2008 to 220 in July 2008, and then it sharply decreased to 210.2 in December 2008.

Another way to look at annual inflation rates is on a December-to-December basis. According to the BLS, in *Consumer Price Index*, the annual inflation rate calculated from December 2007 to December 2008 was only 0.1%, which was the lowest annual inflation rate recorded in more than five decades. Thus, for the year as a whole consumers experienced only a tiny increase in prices.

During 2009 the CPI-U began to climb again. (See Figure 2.5.) Even though the index rose throughout the year, the monthly values were generally lower than those recorded during 2008. The result was an average annual inflation rate of −0.4% when comparing 2008 to 2009. The last time the United States experienced a negative average annual inflation rate was in 1955. (See Figure 2.4.) In fact, negative inflation rates have occurred very rarely since the Great Depression. A negative inflation rate indicates deflation, which is a downward trend in

FIGURE 2.5

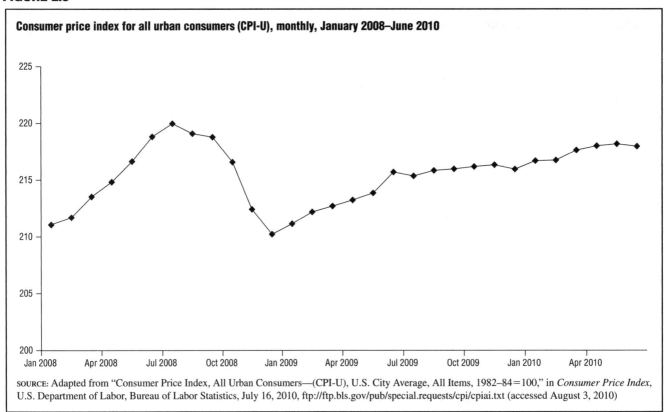

Consumer price index for all urban consumers (CPI-U), monthly, January 2008–June 2010

SOURCE: Adapted from "Consumer Price Index, All Urban Consumers—(CPI-U), U.S. City Average, All Items, 1982–84=100," in *Consumer Price Index*, U.S. Department of Labor, Bureau of Labor Statistics, July 16, 2010, ftp://ftp.bls.gov/pub/special.requests/cpi/cpiai.txt (accessed August 3, 2010)

prices. Once again, looking at the annual inflation rate on a December-to-December basis provides a different viewpoint on how prices changed during 2009. According to the BLS, the annual inflation rate calculated from December 2008 to December 2009 was 2.7%, which was well within the "normal" range.

Unemployment Rate

The U.S. government calculates the nation's unemployment rate for a given time period by dividing the number of unemployed people by the total labor force (unemployed plus employed people). The employment status of people is determined based on responses by the public to a monthly government survey called the Current Population Survey (CPS). The CPS is administered by the Census Bureau for the BLS. According to the BLS, in "How Is the Unemployment Rate Related to Unemployment Insurance Claims?" (March 4, 2004, http://www.bls.gov/cps/uiclaims.htm), the survey is administered to more than 60,000 households per month.

The BLS counts people as being unemployed if they meet all the following criteria:

- Do not have a job
- Have actively looked for work in the previous four weeks
- Are currently available for work

The BLS does not consider active-duty military personnel or institutionalized workers (such as prison inmates) to be in the labor force. In addition, some Americans are neither employed nor unemployed under the BLS definitions and thus are not in the labor force. The most obvious examples are patients in long-term care facilities and retirees. Many students and stay-at-home parents also fall into this category.

Figure 2.6 shows the annual U.S. unemployment rate from 1925 to 2009. For years through 1947, the rate is calculated based on people aged 14 years and older. Because of the passage of child labor laws, the unemployment rate for years following 1947 includes only people aged 16 years and older. The unemployment rate soared during the Great Depression, reaching nearly 25% in 1933. More typically, it has ranged between 3% and 8%. During the early 1980s the unemployment rate was nearly 10%, its highest rate since the 1930s. From the mid-1990s to 2008 it hovered between 4% and 6%, which is generally considered to be a reasonable range for a healthy economy. In 2009 the unemployment rate increased sharply. The BLS (January 2010, http://www.bls.gov/cps/cpsa2009.pdf) notes that the rate reached 9.3% in 2009—the highest value in more than two decades.

Critics believe the BLS data are not representative of the nation's actual unemployment rate because the data do not include people who become discouraged and quit actively looking for work.

FIGURE 2.6

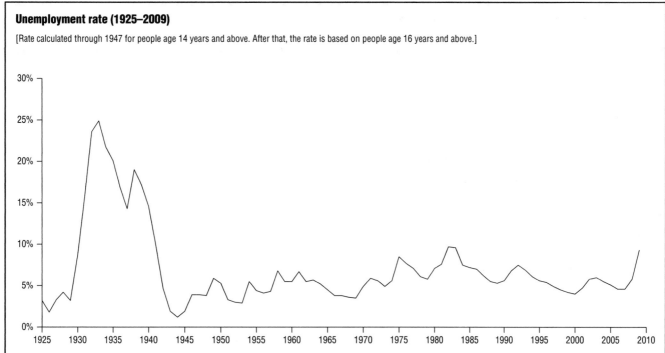

Unemployment rate (1925–2009)

[Rate calculated through 1947 for people age 14 years and above. After that, the rate is based on people age 16 years and above.]

SOURCE: Adapted from "Series D85–86. Unemployment: 1890 to 1970," in *Historical Statistics of the United States, Colonial Times to 1970, Bicentennial Edition, Part 1*, U.S. Department of Commerce, U.S. Census Bureau, September 1975, http://www2.census.gov/prod2/statcomp/documents/CT1970p1-05 .pdf (accessed April 4, 2008), and "1. Employment Status of the Civilian Noninstitutional Population, 1940 to Date," in *Labor Force Statistics from the Current Population Survey*, U.S. Department of Labor, Bureau of Labor Statistics, January 2010, http://www.bls.gov/cps/cpsa2009.pdf (accessed June 28, 2010)

THE NUMERICAL STATE OF THE U.S. ECONOMY

Government and industry statistics on the state of the U.S. economy are released with varying frequency. Some economic indicators are published monthly, whereas others are published quarterly. Three government agencies—the BLS, the BEA, and the Census Bureau—publish updated economic indicators regularly.

The BLS: Unemployment, Wages, and Prices

The BLS publishes *U.S. Economy at a Glance*, which includes statistics gathered by the agency on unemployment, wages, prices, and other economic factors. Table 2.2 shows data that were available at the end of June 2010.

The unemployment rate in June 2010 was 9.5%. (See Table 2.2.) The rate had dropped slightly from earlier months. It peaked at 9.9% in April 2010. Comparison with the historical unemployment chart in Figure 2.6 shows that the rates from January to June 2010 are high rates for postdepression America.

The BLS (August 2010, http://www.bls.gov/ces/) also tracks changes in nonfarm payroll employment and average hourly earnings. These data are based on monthly surveys that are administered to approximately 140,000 businesses and government agencies as part of the bureau's Current Employment Statistics program. About 125,000 jobs were lost in June 2010. (See Table 2.2.) This

was the first recorded loss of jobs for any month during 2010. In fact, more than 1 million jobs were added during the first five months of the year. The average hourly wage for employees on private nonfarm payrolls was $22.53 in June 2010, up slightly from $22.45 in January. Note that some data in Table 2.2 are considered preliminary and may change after further analysis by the BLS.

The CPI-U declined by 0.1% from May to June 2010. (See Table 2.2.) Monthly movements in the CPI-U were very slight for the first six months of 2010, ranging from −0.2% to 0.2% per month.

There are three other indexes reported by the BLS:

- Producer price index (PPI)—a family of indexes that measure changes over time in the selling prices received by the makers and providers of goods and services. The PPI has risen dramatically from its reference value of 100 in 1982. (See Figure 2.7.) The PPI shows a dramatic downturn in 2008. In 2009 the PPI began increasing again. The PPI decreased by 0.5% from May to June 2010. (See Table 2.2.) PPI values for the first six months of 2010 varied from −0.5% to 1.3%. PPI values can differ from CPI values because of factors such as taxes and distribution costs.

- U.S. import price index (MPI)—indicates monthly changes in the prices of nonmilitary goods and services imported to the United States from the rest of the

TABLE 2.2

U.S. Department of Labor economic indicators, January–June 2010

United States—monthly data	Jan 2010	Feb 2010	Mar 2010	Apr 2010	May 2010	June 2010
Data series						
Unemployment rate[a]	9.70	9.70	9.70	9.90	9.70	9.50
Change in payroll employment[b]	14	39	208	313	433[h]	−125[h]
Average hourly earnings[c]	22.45	22.48	22.48	22.50	22.55[h]	22.53[h]
Consumer price index[d]	0.20	0.00	0.10	−0.10	−0.20	−0.10
Producer price index[e]	1.30	−0.50	0.80[h]	−0.10[h]	−0.30[h]	−0.50[h]
U.S. import price index[f]	1.20	−0.10	0.40	1.10	−0.50[g]	−1.30[g]

[a]In percent, seasonally adjusted. Annual averages are available for not seasonally adjusted data.
[b]Number of jobs, in thousands, seasonally adjusted.
[c]Average hourly earnings for all employees on private nonfarm payrolls.
[d]All items, U.S. city average, all urban consumers, 1982–84=100, 1-month percent change, seasonally adjusted.
[e]Finished goods, 1982=100, 1-month percent change, seasonally adjusted.
[f]All imports, 1-month percent change, not seasonally adjusted.
[g]Revised
[h]Preliminary

United States—quarterly data	1st quarter 2009	2nd quarter 2009	3rd quarter 2009	4th quarter 2009	1st quarter 2010
Data series					
Employment cost index[a]	0.4	0.4	0.4	0.4	0.6
Productivity[b]	0.9	7.6	7.8	6.3	2.8

[a]Compensation, all civilian workers, quarterly data, 3-month percent change, seasonally adjusted.
[b]Output per hour, nonfarm business, quarterly data, percent change from previous quarter at annual rate, seasonally adjusted.

SOURCE: Adapted from "United States," in *Economy at a Glance*, U.S. Department of Labor, Bureau of Labor Statistics, July 28, 2010, http://data.bls.gov/eag/eag.us.htm (accessed July 29, 2010)

world. The MPI decreased by 1.3% from May to June 2010. (See Table 2.2.) The BLS also tracks an export price index as part of its International Price Program.

- Employment cost index (ECI)—tracks quarterly changes in nonfarm civilian business labor costs based on a national compensation survey. It includes wages, salaries, and employer costs for employee benefits. The ECI increased by 0.6% from the fourth quarter of 2009 to the first quarter of 2010. (See Table 2.2.)

Finally, the BLS includes in *U.S. Economy at a Glance* a measure of national productivity (or efficiency). This number is a quarterly estimate of the change in output per hour of nonfarm businesses. It is calculated by comparing the amount of goods and services produced with the inputs that were used to produce them. According to the BLS, productivity increased by 2.8% from the fourth quarter of 2009 to the first quarter of 2010. (See Table 2.2.)

The BEA: The GDP, Income, Savings, and Profits

The BEA publishes *Overview of the Economy*, which includes the latest agency statistics for the GDP, corporate profits, personal income and savings, and other economic factors. It should be noted that until they are dubbed "final," these statistics are estimates and are frequently revised by the BEA as new data become available.

REAL GDP. Figure 2.8 shows the quarterly changes in the real GDP for the second quarter of 2006 to the second quarter of 2010. The real GDP grew between 0.9% and

3.2% per quarter through the end of 2007 and then declined sharply. The negative values for much of 2008 and for the first two quarters of 2009 represent a substantial downturn from past performance. The worst showing was in the fourth quarter of 2008, when the real GDP declined by 6.8% from the previous quarter. In the press release "Gross Domestic Product: Fourth Quarter 2008 (Final)" (March 26, 2009, http://www.bea.gov/newsreleases/national/gdp/2009/pdf/gdp408f.pdf), the BEA reports that the real GDP for that quarter was negatively affected by sharp decreases in consumer spending, exports, business spending on equipment and software, and residential investment in housing.

During the third quarter of 2009 the real GDP slowly rebounded by showing an increase of 1.6% from the previous quarter. (See Figure 2.8.) The fourth quarter was especially robust with a 5% increase. Overall, the real GDP declined by 2.6% in 2009. (See Figure 2.2.) The real GDP had a 3.7% gain in the first quarter of 2010 and a 2.4% gain in the second quarter. (See Figure 2.8.) Even though these values represent historically good growth, there was a troubling downward trend from 5% to 3.7% to 2.4%. As of September 2010, it remained to be seen whether the real GDP would continue to decline, or perhaps stabilize and even increase.

NOMINAL GDP. The BEA reports that the nominal GDP (GDP in current dollars) was $14.1 trillion in 2009. A breakdown by component is detailed in Table 2.3. The four major components of the GDP are shown graphically

FIGURE 2.7

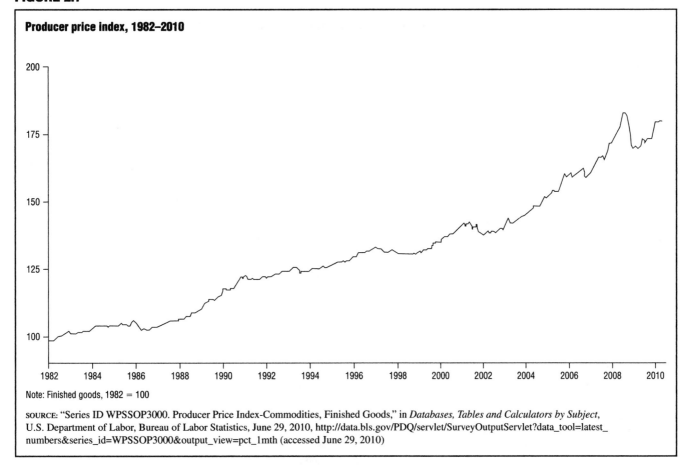

Producer price index, 1982–2010

Note: Finished goods, 1982 = 100

SOURCE: "Series ID WPSSOP3000. Producer Price Index-Commodities, Finished Goods," in *Databases, Tables and Calculators by Subject*, U.S. Department of Labor, Bureau of Labor Statistics, June 29, 2010, http://data.bls.gov/PDQ/servlet/SurveyOutputServlet?data_tool=latest_numbers&series_id=WPSSOP3000&output_view=pct_1mth (accessed June 29, 2010)

in Figure 2.9. Personal consumption expenditures (PCE) accounted for $10 trillion of the GDP in 2009. This is consumer spending on goods and services. Services accounted for more than half of PCE, totaling close to $6.8 trillion. Housing and utilities was the largest single service component, accounting for nearly $1.9 trillion of the total. Health care costs were the second-largest component, at over $1.6 trillion. Spending on nondurable goods amounted to $2.2 trillion. Expenditures for durable goods totaled just over $1 trillion. The BEA explains in *A Guide to the National Income and Product Accounts of the United States* (September 2006, http://www.bea.gov/national/pdf/nipaguid.pdf) that durable goods are "tangible commodities that can be stored or inventoried and that have an average life of at least 3 years." Nondurable goods are classified as "all other tangible commodities that can be stored or inventoried."

Gross private domestic investments totaled nearly $1.6 trillion in 2009. The vast majority of this total ($1.4 trillion) was devoted to nonresidential (business) investments in structures, equipment, and software. Residential fixed investments totaled $352.1 billion. The contribution from the change in private inventories was −$127.2 billion.

Government spending and investment amounted to just over $2.9 trillion. State and local governments accounted

for more than half of this total. Net exports were a negative contributor to the GDP in 2009 because the value of imports ($2 trillion) was greater than the value of exports ($1.6 trillion).

PERSONAL INCOME AND SAVINGS. The BEA also tracks changes in personal income and its disposition. Personal income includes wages and salaries (the largest component), wage and salary supplements (e.g., employer contributions to private pension funds on behalf of employees), rental income, proprietors' income (earned by entrepreneurs, small businesses, and farmers), and interest and dividend income. Most of the data are based on private and government payrolls. In the press release "Personal Income and Outlays: June 2010" (August 3, 2010, http://www.bea.gov/newsreleases/national/pi/2010/pdf/pi0610.pdf), the BEA notes that personal income increased by less than 0.1% in June 2010. By comparison, personal income grew between 0.1% and 0.4% per month during the previous five months.

Disposable personal income (DPI) is the amount of income received by people after taxes are subtracted. In other words, the DPI is the income available to people for spending or saving. According to the BEA, the DPI increased by less than 0.1% in June 2010, compared with a range of 0.1% to 0.5% during the previous five months.

FIGURE 2.8

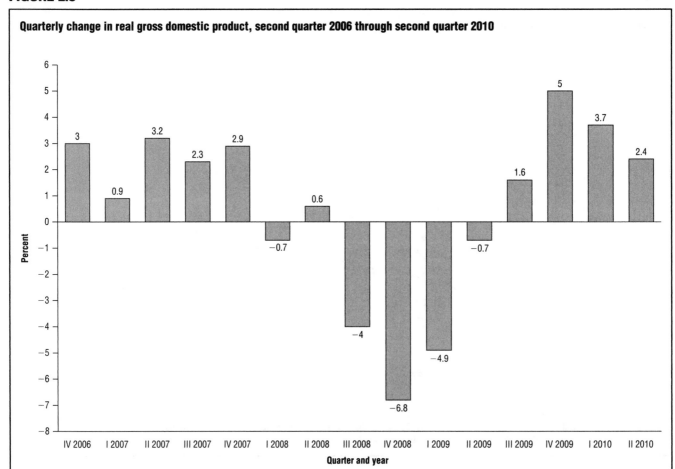

Quarterly change in real gross domestic product, second quarter 2006 through second quarter 2010

SOURCE: Adapted from "Table 1. Real Gross Domestic Product and Related Measures: Percent Change from Preceding Period," in *National Income and Product Accounts: Gross Domestic Product: Second Quarter 2010 (Advance Estimate); Revised Estimates: 2007 through First Quarter 2010*, U.S. Department of Commerce, Bureau of Economic Analysis, July 30, 2010, http://www.bea.gov/newsreleases/national/gdp/2010/pdf/gdp2q10_adv.pdf (accessed August 2, 2010)

Personal savings (DPI minus personal outlays) was $725.9 billion in June 2010, up from $713.9 billion in May 2010.

CORPORATE PROFITS. The BEA reports in the press release "Gross Domestic Product: First Quarter 2010 (Third Estimate)" (June 25, 2010, http://www.bea.gov/newsreleases/national/gdp/2010/pdf/gdp1q10_3rd.pdf) that corporate profits from current production increased by $116.9 billion during the first quarter of 2010 after increasing by $108.7 billion in the fourth quarter of 2009.

PUBLIC PERCEPTION OF THE ECONOMY

The government's various economic indicators provide a picture of the overall condition of the U.S. economy. In reality, the state of the nation's economy is a reflection of the financial condition of the hundreds of millions of individuals and businesses that contribute to it. Thus, economic conditions at the national level can be quite different from those experienced by people at the regional and local levels.

Regional and Local Economies

Part of microeconomics study involves the economic health of various geographical regions and communities. (Microeconomics is an analysis of the behavior of economic units such as companies, industries, or households.) A regional economy can be an area as small as a neighborhood or as large as a group of states with climate, geography, industry, or culture in common. The relative strength of a regional economy reflects broader national trends. For example, in the late 19th and early 20th centuries—with the economy of the American South in shambles after the Civil War (1861–1865)—northern cities attracted millions of workers to their rapidly growing industrial centers, such as the steel mills of Pittsburgh, Pennsylvania, and the car factories of Detroit, Michigan. Later, as the population migrated elsewhere, this region became known as the Rust Belt. Similarly, in the late 20th century western states experienced substantial growth with the rise of the computer industry, thanks in large part to Microsoft, which is headquartered in Seattle, Washington, and the dot-com companies centered in California's Silicon Valley. Other

TABLE 2.3

Components of gross domestic product (GDP), 2009

[Billions of current dollars.]

	2009
Gross domestic product	**14,119.0**
Personal consumption expenditures	10,001.3
Goods	3,230.7
Durable goods	1,026.5
Motor vehicles and parts	319.7
Furnishings and durable household equipment	248.1
Recreational goods and vehicles	317.5
Other durable goods	141.1
Nondurable goods	2,204.2
Food and beverages purchased for off-premises consumption	777.9
Clothing and footwear	322.2
Gasoline and other energy goods	303.7
Other nondurable goods	800.4
Services	6,770.6
Household consumption expenditures (for services)	6,511.8
Housing and utilities	1,876.3
Health care	1,623.2
Transportation services	290.1
Recreation services	378.8
Food services and accommodations	603.6
Financial services and insurance	813.8
Other services	925.9
Final consumption expenditures of nonprofit institutions serving households	258.9
Gross output of nonprofit institutions	1,058.1
Less: Receipts from sales of goods and services by nonprofit institutions	799.2
Gross private domestic investment	1,589.2
Fixed investment	1,716.4
Nonresidential	1,364.4
Structures	451.6
Equipment and software	912.8
Information processing equipment and software	530.7
Computers and peripheral equipment	80.0
Software	260.2
Other	190.4
Industrial equipment	150.4
Transportation equipment	76.4
Other equipment	155.4
Residential	352.1
Change in private inventories	−127.2
Farm	3.8
Nonfarm	−131.1
Net exports of goods and services	−386.4
Exports	1,578.4
Goods	1,063.1
Services	515.3
Imports	1,964.7
Goods	1,587.8
Services	376.9
Government consumption expenditures and gross investment	2,914.9
Federal	1,139.6
National defense	771.6
Consumption expenditures	664.1
Gross investment	107.5
Nondefense	368.0
Consumption expenditures	323.0
Gross investment	45.0
State and local	1,775.3
Consumption expenditures	1,424.4
Gross investment	351.0

TABLE 2.3

Components of gross domestic product (GDP), 2009 [CONTINUED]

[Billions of current dollars.]

	2009
Addenda:	
Final sales of domestic product	14,246.3
Gross domestic purchases	14,505.4
Final sales to domestic purchasers	14,632.7
Gross domestic product	14,119.0
Plus: Income receipts from the rest of the world	629.8
Less: Income payments to the rest of the world	483.6
Equals: Gross national product	14,265.3
Net domestic product	12,257.9

SOURCE: Adapted from "Table 3A. Gross Domestic Product and Related Measures," in *National Income and Product Accounts: Gross Domestic Product: Second Quarter 2010 (Advance Estimate); Revised Estimates: 2007 through First Quarter 2010*, U.S. Department of Commerce, Bureau of Economic Analysis, July 30, 2010, http://www.bea.gov/newsreleases/national/gdp/2010/pdf/gdp2q10_adv.pdf (accessed August 2, 2010)

FIGURE 2.9

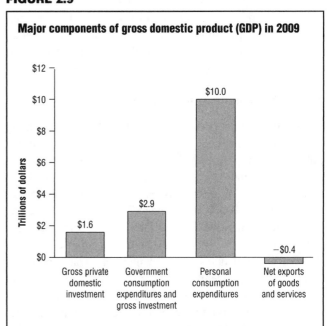

Major components of gross domestic product (GDP) in 2009

SOURCE: Adapted from "Table 3A. Gross Domestic Product and Related Measures," in *National Income and Product Accounts: Gross Domestic Product: Second Quarter 2010 (Advance Estimate); Revised Estimates: 2007 through First Quarter 2010*, U.S. Department of Commerce, Bureau of Economic Analysis, July 30, 2010, http://www.bea.gov/newsreleases/national/gdp/2010/pdf/gdp2q10_adv.pdf (accessed August 2, 2010)

major economic regions of the United States include the Farm Belt of the Great Plains and the Sun Belt states of the South and Southwest, with warm climates that make them popular tourist destinations and strong agricultural regions.

When a region or community experiences a serious economic downturn—such as in the upper Midwest, when the auto and steel manufacturers started losing ground to foreign competitors, or in the Farm Belt, with the rise of agribusiness and the subsequent demise of the small family farm—its citizens often fall into a cycle of unemployment and poverty, leading federal and local governments and private nonprofit organizations to step in to offer assistance.

The Role of the Individual in the Economy

Almost every aspect of American life is influenced by, and further influences, the economy. Whether a person drives or flies during his or her next vacation, how he or she will pay for college and save for retirement, what advertisements he or she sees, what movies he or she watches, and what magazines he or she reads all involve making economic decisions, which then affect the way the economy functions. If a person works or plans to work, that person is a small but important part of the economy. Likewise, every time an individual buys goods or saves money, he or she is participating in economic activity.

Economists maintain that the better off the economy is, the better its participants will be. In a healthy economy people tend to have more job security, earn more money, and are able to increase opportunities for themselves and their family—thus improving their overall quality of life. By contrast, in an unstable, bad economy—such as during the Great Depression and during recessions—people are less certain of the future, face increasing pressures at work and may lose their job, and have less flexibility in being able to pay for goods and services, which in turn affects trends in employment, interest rates, the cost of living, the money supply, and all other aspects of the economy, on both the macro and micro levels.

Public Opinion about the Economy

PROBLEMS FACING THE COUNTRY. The Gallup Organization is a U.S.-based firm that conducts frequent public opinion polls to gauge the mood and attitudes of the American people on a variety of subjects. In July 2010 Gallup asked Americans to name "the most important problem facing this country today." The responses receiving the most mentions during the poll are listed in Table 2.4. "Economy in general" was the top response, cited by 31% of respondents. Unemployment/jobs was mentioned by 22% of respondents. Other economically related problems that were cited include the high cost of health care (7% of respondents), the federal budget deficit and federal debt (6%), fuel/oil prices (5%), and "lack of money" (3%).

Figure 2.10 summarizes Gallup polls dating back to 2001 for the net percentage of respondents mentioning some aspect of the economy as the country's most important problem. In July 2010, 64% of respondents mentioned some aspect of the economy as the top problem. The percentage peaked above 80% in early 2009. Before 2008 (the first full year of the great recession) the percentage ranged from approximately 20% to 50%.

THE PUBLIC RATES THE ECONOMY. Since 1992 Gallup has asked poll participants to provide their assessment of the overall economic condition of the country by rating it as "excellent," "good," "only fair," or "poor." Table 2.5 shows the results of this survey for July 2010. Only a small percentage of respondents (2%) rated the economy as

TABLE 2.4

Public opinion about the most important problem facing the United States, July 2010

WHAT DO YOU THINK IS THE MOST IMPORTANT PROBLEM FACING THIS COUNTRY TODAY?

Top 10 mentions

	% Mentioning
Economy in general	31
Unemployment/jobs	22
Dissatisfaction with government/Congress/politicians; poor leadership; corruption; abuse of power	11
Immigration/illegal aliens	7
Poor healthcare/hospitals; high cost of healthcare	7
Natural disaster response/relief	7
Federal budget deficit/federal debt	6
Fuel/oil prices	5
Wars/war (nonspecific)/fear of war	4
Lack of money	3
Ethics/moral/religious/family decline; dishonesty	3
Situation/war in Afghanistan	3
Education/poor education/access to education	3
Situation/war in Iraq	3

SOURCE: Frank Newport, "What do you think is the most important problem facing this country today?" in *Economy Dominates as Nation's Most Important Problem*, The Gallup Organization, July 14, 2010, http://www.gallup.com/poll/141275/Economy-Dominates-Nation-Important-Problem.aspx (accessed August 2, 2010). Copyright © 2010 by The Gallup Organization. Reproduced by permission of The Gallup Organization.

"excellent." A higher number (10%) described the economy as "good." Nearly four out of 10 (38%) said the economy was "only fair" and 50% described it as "poor." When asked about the direction of the economy, 27% of respondents said the economy is "getting better," whereas 66% said the economy is "getting worse."

Gallup has historically used the responses to these two questions to calculate its own economic indicator called the Gallup Economic Confidence Index (GECI). As shown in Table 2.5, the GECI for July 2010 was −39. Figure 2.11 shows weekly aggregates of the GECI based on Gallup polls dating back to 2008. The results indicate that the GECI reached its lowest level (−65) in late 2008.

Another respected indicator of the nation's economic mood is the Consumer Confidence Index (CCI), which is maintained by the Conference Board Inc., a nonprofit business organization that was founded in 1916. The CCI is calculated from the responses to monthly surveys of 5,000 U.S. households. The respondents are asked to rate the state of the existing economy and its likely direction over the next six months. In "Consumer Confidence Improves" (August 31, 2010, http://www.conference-board.org/data/consumer confidence.cfm), the Conference Board reports that the CCI was 53.5 in August 2010, up from 51 the previous month. An arbitrary baseline value of 100 is assigned to the year 1985. According to the Federal Reserve Bank of New York, in "Consumer Surveys" (September 7,

FIGURE 2.10

Percentage of Americans mentioning the economy as the nation's most important problem, 2001–10

PERCENTAGE OF AMERICANS MENTIONING THE ECONOMY AS THE NATION'S MOST IMPORTANT PROBLEM

Selected trend—January 2001-present

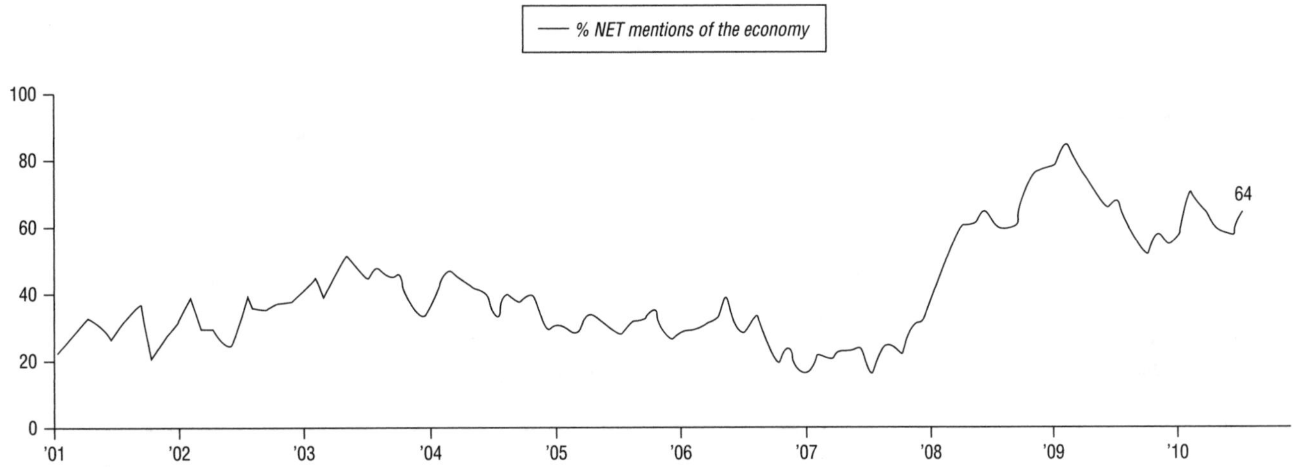

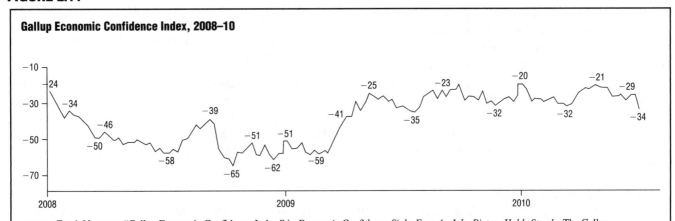

SOURCE: "Percentage of Americans Mentioning the Economy As the Nation's Most Important Problem," in *Most Important Problem*, The Gallup Organization, July 2010, http://www.gallup.com/poll/1675/Most-Important-Problem.aspx (accessed August 2, 2010). Copyright © 2010 by The Gallup Organization. Reproduced by permission of The Gallup Organization.

TABLE 2.5

Public opinion on the state of the economy and the economic outlook, July 2010

Perceptions of current economy and economic outlook

	Current economy				Direction of economy		
	% Excellent	% Good	% Only fair	% Poor	% Getting better	% Getting worse	Economic Confidence Index
Jul 3–6, 2010	2	10	38	50	27	66	−39

SOURCE: Frank Newport, "Perceptions of Current Economy and Economic Outlook," in *Economic Confidence Sinks Even As Jobs Picture Holds Steady*, The Gallup Organization, July 8, 2010, http://www.gallup.com/poll/141185/Economic-Confidence-Sinks-Even-Jobs-Picture-Holds-Steady.aspx (accessed July 9, 2010). Copyright © 2010 by The Gallup Organization. Reproduced by permission of The Gallup Organization.

FIGURE 2.11

Gallup Economic Confidence Index, 2008–10

SOURCE: Frank Newport, "Gallup Economic Confidence Index," in *Economic Confidence Sinks Even As Jobs Picture Holds Steady*, The Gallup Organization, July 8, 2010, http://www.gallup.com/poll/141185/Economic-Confidence-Sinks-Even-Jobs-Picture-Holds-Steady.aspx (accessed July 9, 2010). Copyright © 2010 by The Gallup Organization. Reproduced by permission of The Gallup Organization.

FIGURE 2.12

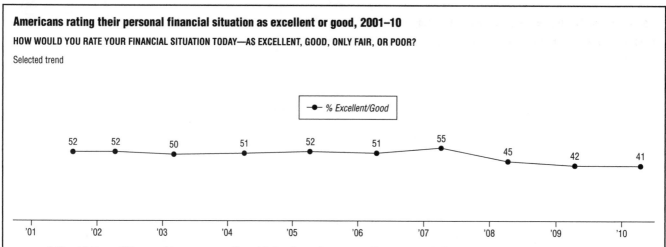

Americans rating their personal financial situation as excellent or good, 2001–10

HOW WOULD YOU RATE YOUR FINANCIAL SITUATION TODAY—AS EXCELLENT, GOOD, ONLY FAIR, OR POOR?

Selected trend

SOURCE: Jeffrey M. Jones, "How would you rate your financial situation today—as excellent, good, only fair, or poor?" in *Americans Remain down about Their Financial Situations*, The Gallup Organization, April 22, 2010, http://www.gallup.com/poll/127493/Americans-Remain-Down-Financial-Situations.aspx (accessed June 29, 2010). Copyright © 2010 by The Gallup Organization. Reproduced by permission of The Gallup Organization.

2010, http://www.newyorkfed.org/research/directors_charts/econ_fin.pdf), the CCI hovered above 100 from early 2006 to late 2007 and then plummeted to around 25 in early 2009. By mid-2009 the CCI had recovered to around 50 and fluctuated near that level through August 2010.

Thomson Reuters and the University of Michigan provide economic indicators based on their monthly Survey of Consumers. In "Consumer Confidence Tumbles" (July 30, 2010, https://customers.reuters.com/), Richard T. Curtin, the director of the program, reports that the Index of Consumer Sentiment was 67.8 in July 2010, down from 76 the previous month. The computed index is compared with a benchmark level of 100 arbitrarily set for the first quarter of 1996. According to the Federal Reserve Bank of New York, the index was above 80 from the 1990s to late 2007. By early to mid-2008 it plunged below 60 and then fluctuated between 60 and 70 through August 2010.

PERSONAL FINANCIAL SITUATION. As part of *Gallup Poll Social Series: Economy and Personal Finance*, pollsters have asked Americans to rate their financial situation as "excellent," "good," "only fair," or "poor." Figure 2.12 shows that only 41% of respondents reported an "excellent" or "good" financial situation in 2010. Polls conducted between 2001 and 2007 show that more than half of Americans considered their financial situation to be "excellent" or "good." The percentage began falling in 2008 as economic conditions worsened in the country.

When asked if their financial situation is "getting better" or "getting worse," 40% of poll participants in 2010 said their financial situation is "getting worse," whereas 39% said it is "getting better." (See Figure 2.13.) Between 2001 and 2007 about half of the respondents polled each

year reported an improving financial situation. In 2008 the value dropped to only 32%.

In July 2010 Gallup asked poll participants to name "the most important financial problem" facing their family. The results are shown in Table 2.6. The most commonly cited problem at 13% was lack of money/low wages. Other problems ranking in the top five included unemployment/loss of job (11%), too much debt/not enough money to pay debts (11%), health care costs (10%), and the cost of owning or renting a home (8%).

The Great Recession's Effect on Activities and Perceptions

As noted in Chapter 1, the great recession officially lasted from December 2007 to June 2009. This did not mean that the economy returned to normal in June 2009, only that a recovery began to occur. Chapters 3, 4, and 7 address the major economic activities that changed due to the great recession—that is, data indicate that Americans spent less money, took on less debt, and saved more money, respectively, during the recession and, in some cases, for many months after its official end.

Some researchers also believe that other behaviors were affected by the great recession. For example, media outlets reported that marriage, divorce, and birth rates all dropped due to the recession. However, it should be noted that it is difficult to tie modern societal trends to specific economic causes.

In "Births, Marriages, Divorces, and Deaths: Provisional Data for 2009" (*National Vital Statistics Reports*, vol. 58, no. 25, August 27, 2010), the National Center for Health Statistics (NCHS) reports that the U.S. marriage rate was 7.3% in 2007, 7.1% in 2008, and 6.8% in 2009.

FIGURE 2.13

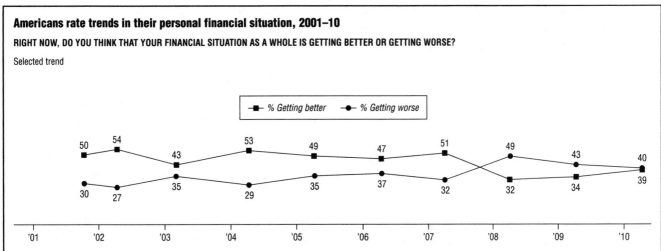

Americans rate trends in their personal financial situation, 2001–10

RIGHT NOW, DO YOU THINK THAT YOUR FINANCIAL SITUATION AS A WHOLE IS GETTING BETTER OR GETTING WORSE?

Selected trend

SOURCE: Jeffrey M. Jones, "Right now, do you think that your financial situation as a whole is getting better or getting worse?" in *Americans Remain down about Their Financial Situations*, The Gallup Organization, April 22, 2010, http://www.gallup.com/poll/127493/Americans-Remain-Down-Financial-Situations.aspx (accessed June 29, 2010). Copyright © 2010 by The Gallup Organization. Reproduced by permission of The Gallup Organization.

TABLE 2.6

Polling results on most important financial problem of U.S. families, July 2010

WHAT IS THE MOST IMPORTANT FINANCIAL PROBLEM FACING YOUR FAMILY TODAY? [OPEN-ENDED]

Recent trend:	July 8–11, 2010 %
Lack of money/low wages	13
Unemployment/loss of job	11
Too much debt/not enough money to pay debts	11
Healthcare costs	10
Cost of owning/renting a home	8
High cost of living/Inflation	6
College expenses	5
Retirement savings	5
Taxes	4
Lack of savings	3
Stock market/investments	3
State of the economy	2
Energy costs/oil and gas prices	2
Interest rates	1
Social security	1
Transportation/commuting costs	1
Controlling spending	*
Other	3
None	20
No opinion	4

SOURCE: Adapted from "What is the most important financial problem facing your family today? [OPEN-ENDED]," in *Economy*, The Gallup Organization, 2010, http://www.gallup.com/poll/1609/Economy.aspx#1 (accessed August 5, 2010). Copyright © 2010 by The Gallup Organization. Reproduced by permission of The Gallup Organization.

Likewise, the divorce rate dropped from 3.6% in 2007 to 3.5% in 2008 to 3.4% in 2009. As a result, there were media reports that marriage and divorce rates had dropped due to the great recession, presumably because weddings and divorces are expensive endeavors. However, marriage and divorce rates have been declining for years. For example, the NCHS reports in "Births,

Marriages, Divorces, and Deaths: Provisional Data for 2003" (*National Vital Statistics Report*, vol. 52, no. 22, June 10, 2004) and in "Births, Marriages, Divorces, and Deaths: Provisional Data for 2006" (*National Vital Statistics Report*, vol. 55, no. 20, August 28, 2007) that the U.S. marriage rate decreased from 8.2% in 2001 to 7.3% in 2006. Likewise, the divorce rate declined from 4% in 2001 to 3.6% in 2006. Both drops occurred over relatively prosperous years in the U.S. economy and reflect even longer-term trends dating back several decades. Thus, it is difficult to determine with any certainty that the declines that occurred during 2008 and 2009 were specifically related to the great recession.

Gretchen Livingston and D'Vera Cohn of the Pew Research Center report in "U.S. Birth Rate Decline Linked to Recession" (April 6, 2010, http://pewsocialtrends.org/pubs/753/american-birth-rate-decline-linked-to-recession) that U.S. birth rates "began to decline in 2008 after rising to their highest level in two decades, and the decrease appears to be linked to the recession." The previously mentioned NCHS reports provide the following birth rates (i.e., number of live births per 1,000 total U.S. population):

- 2001—14.1% birth rate
- 2002—13.9% birth rate
- 2003—14% birth rate
- 2004—14% birth rate
- 2005—14% birth rate
- 2006—14.3% birth rate
- 2007—14.3% birth rate
- 2008—13.9% birth rate
- 2009—13.5% birth rate

Livingston and Cohn claim that a state-by-state analysis of the 2008 and 2009 data indicates "a strong association" between declining birth rates and "key economic indicators including changes in per capita income, housing prices and share of the working-age population that is employed across states."

As noted earlier, polls conducted between 2008 and 2010 show that Americans are very concerned about the state of the economy and their own financial situation. Poor economic conditions associated with the great recession also bred deep pessimism about the future among some demographic groups. In *A Balance Sheet at 30 Months: How the Great Recession Has Changed Life in America* (June 2010, http://pewsocialtrends.org/assets/pdf/759-recession.pdf), the Pew Research Center reports the results of polls it conducted during May 2010 about various economic issues.

The Pew Research Center asked Americans if they believe that their children will enjoy a "better" or "worse" standard of living when their children become the same age as the current age of the poll respondents. Overall, 45% of the respondents said their children will enjoy a "better" standard of living. This value is down from 61% recorded in 2002. However, the researchers note that there were broad differences in opinion on this question in the May 2010 poll based on respondent age, race, and political affiliation. Younger adults (i.e., those under the age of 30 years) were much more optimistic about the future. Nearly two-thirds (64%) of them expect their children to have a "better" standard of living, compared with only 35% of

respondents aged 50 years and older. Likewise, African-Americans (69%) and Hispanics (64%) indicated much more optimism than did whites (38%) on this issue. More than half (55%) of Democrats said their children would enjoy a "better" standard of living, whereas only 37% of Republicans felt this way.

Overall, the Pew Research Center finds that Democrats, minorities, and younger adults are much more upbeat about the nation's current and future economic state than are Republicans, whites, and older adults. The researchers believe this optimism is driven by the confidence that Democrats, minorities, and younger people have in President Barack Obama (1961–; an African-American Democrat). They point out that during the administration of George W. Bush (1946–; a white Republican) the reverse situation was true, in that Republicans and whites were more optimistic about the economy. The researchers note that the optimism of Democrats during the great recession is surprising because "they have lower incomes and less wealth and have suffered more job losses during the recession." In addition, the polls indicate that Democrats, African-Americans, and younger people are more upbeat about the economy in general and their own personal finances "regardless of whether they have had difficulty paying their bills, making mortgage or rent payments; getting or paying for medical care; or have had to cut spending during the recession." The researchers conclude "in an age of highly polarized politics, Democrats and Republicans differ not only in their values, attitudes and policy positions, but, increasingly, in their basic perceptions of reality."

CHAPTER 3
THE AMERICAN CONSUMER

The use of money is all the advantage there is in having money.

—Benjamin Franklin, *Poor Richard's Almanack* (1737)

Americans love to spend money, and their aggressive spending helps fuel both the U.S. and global economies, as imported goods are widely available and popular in the U.S. market. In fact, consumer spending (which is called personal consumption expenditures [PCE]) is the single largest contributing factor to the nation's gross domestic product (GDP; the total market value of final goods and services produced within an economy in a given year). High consumer spending rates produce a ripple effect that spreads across many other macroeconomic sectors, including employment, wages, corporate profits, and interest rates.

The so-called great recession that began in late 2007 witnessed a downturn in consumer spending. In the press release "National Income and Product Accounts: Gross Domestic Product: Second Quarter 2010 (Advance Estimate)" (July 30, 2010, http://www.bea.gov/newsreleases/national/gdp/2010/pdf/gdp2q10_adv.pdf), the Bureau of Economy Analysis (BEA) reports that the PCE grew by 2.4% between 2006 and 2007. Over the following year the PCE dropped by 0.3%. In 2009 the PCE was down 1.2% compared with 2008. As a result, the U.S. GDP was stagnant in 2008 and decreased by 2.6% in 2009. However, the PCE began growing again in late 2009. It was up by 2% and 0.9% in the third and fourth quarters, respectively, of 2009 and up by 1.9% and 1.6% in the first and second quarters, respectively, of 2010. Thus, Americans were beginning to return to their prerecession spending habits.

THE RISE OF THE CONSUMER CULTURE
World War II

World War II (1939–1945) is generally credited with lifting the United States out of the Great Depression (the period of economic disaster that lasted from 1929 through the early 1940s). The urgent need for weapons, tanks, planes, and other war goods led the government to invest heavily in getting the nation's factories running again, especially after the United States joined the war in late 1941. When the war ended in 1945, many factories were converted into facilities to manufacture civilian products such as appliances and automobiles, for which demand was especially high after the war.

RATIONING AND THE WAR PRODUCTION BOARD. During the war citizens were encouraged to exercise restraint in spending to conserve materials for the war effort. Some items were temporarily banned from public use; for example, platinum was declared a "strategic metal" to be used only in the manufacture of military goods, so its use in jewelry making was halted. The government also established rationing (tight controls over how much of an item a person can use or consume in a certain amount of time). All citizens were issued coupon books for rationed items every six months; once they used up their coupons for the month, they had to wait until the next month to buy more rationed goods. Coffee, sugar, meat, butter, and canned vegetables were rationed, as were gasoline, rubber, silk, fuel oil, and other goods, all of which were used for military purposes. Victory gardens became common as the government encouraged Americans to grow their own vegetables rather than buy them.

In 1942 the War Production Board (WPB) was created to oversee production programs for war-related commodities. The WPB's first move was to halt all American automobile production and order car factories to produce only planes, tanks, firearms, diesel engines, and military trucks. Producers of other consumer goods were also ordered to join the war effort. For example, a domestic housewares company called International Silver converted its manufacturing facilities to the production of military goods such as surgical instruments, machine gun clips, and gasoline bombs. To conserve materials needed to clothe soldiers and make other fabric items for the war effort, the WPB regulated every aspect of U.S. clothing design. Silk stockings were banned, so women drew seams on the backs of their legs to simulate them. To conserve fabric, the WPB mandated that dresses and skirts be made shorter and that men's suits have narrower lapels and pants with no cuffs. Women's two-piece bathing suits became popular because they used less fabric than one-piece suits.

The Postwar Boom

When the war came to an end in 1945, Americans were divided about becoming consumers again. Some were excited to begin spending, while others were reluctant. To help create jobs for the tens of thousands of soldiers returning from the war and to build on the country's newfound economic prosperity, the government, businesses, and marketing firms began a campaign to stir up consumer activity. Spending was promoted as a civic duty and an expression of patriotism rather than as a personal indulgence. A postwar baby boom also changed Americans' perspective on spending.

Growing families purchased bigger houses, many of which were built in the suburbs. The suburban population shift was accompanied by a growth in shopping centers, supermarkets, and car ownership. According to Alonzo L. Hamby of Ohio University, in *Outline of U.S. History* (2005, http://www.america.gov/media/pdf/books/historytln .pdf#popup), the annual production of automobiles quadrupled between 1946 and 1955. Air conditioning and television became widely available after the war. Air conditioning spurred migration from the Northeast and Midwest to the Southeast and Southwest. By the end of the 1950s three-fourths of all American families owned at least one television set. Television advertising reached a large audience and promoted more consumer spending.

THE COLD WAR: BEATING COMMUNISM BY SHOPPING. By the late 1940s the Cold War (a decades-long period of political tension between the United States and the former Soviet Union that began just after World War II and ended in the early 1990s) was well under way. To contrast the U.S. open market system with Soviet socialism—under which private ownership was generally disallowed—U.S. politicians argued that widespread ownership of more possessions would create greater social equality, thereby proving the superiority of the market system. Therefore, consumer spending acted as a function of the drive to defeat communism.

HOMEOWNERSHIP. Foremost on the list of items that many Americans wanted was new housing, and the ideal housing, according to the standards of the time, was a mass-produced single-family home in the suburbs. Lizabeth Cohen of Harvard University explains in "The Landscape of Mass Consumption" (February 2003, http://www.nthpo sition.com/landscapeofmass.php) that residential housing construction after the war occurred at rates never before seen in the United States. This increase in housing con-

struction was bolstered by the federal government, which helped veterans buy homes with guaranteed loans and connected the new suburbs to cities with an immense system of federally built highways. Between 1947 and 1953 the number of people living in the suburbs increased by 43%, and by 1960, 62% of Americans owned their own home.

AUTOMOBILES. Homeownership generated the need for many items, but few had more far-reaching effects than the automobile. With such a large proportion of Americans living in the suburbs, the ability to commute to work and shopping centers became essential, so a family car went from being a luxury to being a necessity during the 1950s. This necessity led to the birth of the American car culture.

Car ownership led to more travel, which spawned more business opportunities. Fast-food restaurants allowed people to eat in their cars. Motels (motor hotels) provided inexpensive places to stay (and park cars) overnight. Convenience stores sprang up along the new highways, encouraging drivers to stop and shop while they were on the road. Even the camping and outdoor industry saw a rush to its products, as Americans purchased campers and other outdoor equipment and took to the road for family vacations. In *What We Work for Now: Changing Household Consumption Patterns in the Twentieth Century* (December 2001), Jerome Segal, Cynthia Pansing, and Brian Parkinson state that by 1950, 60% of U.S. households had a car and that transportation-related expenses accounted for $1 out of every $7 spent by the typical U.S. household.

TELEVISION. Along with the widespread ownership of automobiles, the introduction of television into daily U.S. life represented one of the most important social, economic, and technological changes of the 20th century. Television was promoted as a social equalizer that would, again, prove the superiority of U.S. capitalism over Soviet communism. With such unprecedented access to information, U.S. citizens were predicted to achieve equality across all classes and social groups. Lyn Spigel explains in "Television" (Mary Kupiec Cayton and Peter W. Williams, eds., *Encyclopedia of American Cultural and Intellectual History*, 2001) that in 1948 about 2% of U.S. households had a television. By 1960 approximately 90% of U.S. households were equipped with at least one television.

CONTEMPORARY CONSUMER SPENDING

The U.S. Bureau of Labor Statistics (BLS) tracks consumer spending and publishes the results in two different formats. PCE data are used on a quarterly basis to calculate the nation's GDP. The PCE is based on aggregate data (data summed to represent the entire population). The BLS also publishes an annual Consumer Expenditure Survey that estimates the consumer spending of an average U.S. household during a given year.

TABLE 3.1

Annual percent change in the urban Consumer Price Index (CPI-U) for selected expenditure categories, December to December, 2002–09

Percent change from previous December

Item and group	December							
	2002	2003	2004	2005	2006	2007	2008	2009
Expenditure category								
All items	2.4	1.9	3.3	3.4	2.5	4.1	0.1	2.7
Food and beverages	1.5	3.5	2.6	2.3	2.2	4.8	5.8	−0.4
Housing	2.4	2.2	3.0	4.0	3.3	3.0	2.4	−0.3
Apparel	−1.8	−2.1	−0.2	−1.1	0.9	−0.3	−1.0	1.9
Transportation	3.8	0.3	6.5	4.8	1.6	8.3	−13.3	14.4
Medical care	5.0	3.7	4.2	4.3	3.6	5.2	2.6	3.4
Recreation*	1.1	1.1	0.7	1.1	1.0	0.8	1.8	−0.4
Education and communication*	2.2	1.6	1.5	2.4	2.3	3.0	3.6	2.4
Other goods and services	3.3	1.5	2.5	3.1	3.0	3.3	3.4	8.0
Special aggregate indexes								
Energy	10.7	6.9	16.6	17.1	2.9	17.4	−21.3	18.2
All items less energy	1.8	1.5	2.2	2.2	2.5	2.8	2.4	1.4
All items less food and energy	1.9	1.1	2.2	2.2	2.6	2.4	1.8	1.8
Commodities less food and energy commodities	−1.5	−2.5	0.6	0.2	−0.1	0.1	−0.6	3.0
Energy commodities	23.7	6.9	26.7	16.7	6.1	29.4	−40.5	46.5
Services less energy services	3.4	2.6	2.8	2.9	3.7	3.3	2.7	1.4

*Indexes on a December 1997=100 base.

SOURCE: Adapted from Malik Crawford et al., eds., "Table 26. Historical Consumer Price Index for All Urban Consumers (CPI-U): U.S. City Average, by Commodity and Service Group and Detailed Expenditure Categories," in *CPI Detailed Report, Data for June 2010*, U.S. Department of Labor, Bureau of Labor Statistics, July 16, 2010, http://www.bls.gov/cpi/cpid1006.pdf (accessed July 28, 2010)

One economic indicator that is extremely relevant to consumer spending is the inflation rate based on the consumer price index (CPI). The BLS explains in *Consumer Price Index* (August 13, 2010, ftp://ftp.bls.gov/pub/special.requests/cpi/cpiai.txt) that the average annual inflation rate based on the CPI for all urban consumers (CPI-U) was −0.4% from 2008 to 2009, which indicates that prices decreased between these two years. However, the annual inflation rate calculated from December 2008 to December 2009 was 2.7%. Thus, consumers experienced a 2.7% increase in the price of goods and services between December 2008 and December 2009.

Table 3.1 lists the annual percent change in the CPI-U for all items and specific categories of items from 2002 to 2009 on a December-to-December basis. These numbers represent annual inflation rates. The overall inflation rate of 2.7% in 2009 for all items was exceeded by the rates for transportation (14.4% increase), other goods and services (8% increase), and medical care (3.4% increase). In addition, the increase of 18.2% in the special aggregate index for energy greatly exceeded the overall inflation rate. According to the BLS, in "How BLS Measures Price Change for Household Fuels in the Consumer Price Index" (August 19, 2009, http://www.bls.gov/cpi/cpifachf.htm), the energy index includes fuel and utility costs that fall under the housing category and motor fuel costs that fall under the transportation category.

Components of the CPI-U that experienced lower rates of inflation than the overall rate of 2.7% were education and communication (2.4%), apparel (1.9%), housing (−0.3%), food and beverages (−0.4%), and recreation (−0.4%). (See Table 3.1.) Likewise, the special aggregate index for all items less food and energy showed a 1.8% increase from December 2008 to December 2009.

Figure 3.1 shows 12-month changes in the CPI-U for all items and for all items less food and energy from June 2000 to June 2010. The inflation rate peaked in mid-2008 in excess of 5.5%. This means that, on average, prices for all items increased by 5.5% between mid-2007 and mid-2008. However, the inflation rate for all items less food and energy for this period was closer to 2%. This indicates that food and energy were the primary culprits in price volatility between 2007 and 2008. In general, this also holds true on a historical basis. Figure 3.1 shows that the inflation rates for all items less food and energy fluctuated much less than the rates for all items between June 2000 and June 2010. This fluctuation can also be seen in Table 3.1, which indicates significant volatility on an annual average basis for energy items (particularly energy commodities) compared with food and beverages.

Personal Consumption Expenditures

In 2009 the nation's PCE totaled $10 trillion. (See Table 3.2.) Major PCE categories include durable goods, nondurable goods, and services. In *A Guide to the National Income and Product Accounts of the United States* (September 2006, http://www.bea.gov/national/pdf/nipaguid.pdf), the BEA defines durable goods as "tangible

FIGURE 3.1

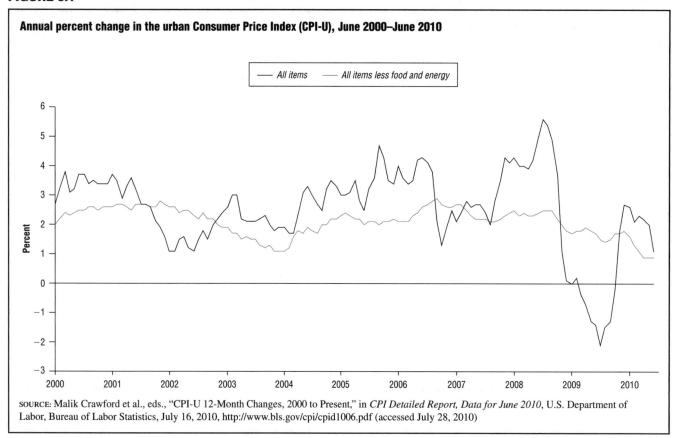

Annual percent change in the urban Consumer Price Index (CPI-U), June 2000–June 2010

SOURCE: Malik Crawford et al., eds., "CPI-U 12-Month Changes, 2000 to Present," in *CPI Detailed Report, Data for June 2010*, U.S. Department of Labor, Bureau of Labor Statistics, July 16, 2010, http://www.bls.gov/cpi/cpid1006.pdf (accessed July 28, 2010)

commodities that can be stored or inventoried and that have an average life of at least 3 years." Nondurable goods are considered "all other tangible commodities that can be stored or inventoried." Note that housing is listed under services. This category includes rent paid by renters and the estimated equivalent of rent for owner-occupied houses (in other words, the amount of money the owner occupants would have paid if they had been renting the space from someone else).

Services accounted for the largest major component of the PCE in 2009, totaling nearly $6.8 trillion. (See Table 3.2.) Housing and utilities ($1.9 trillion) and health care ($1.6 trillion) were the two largest components of services spending. Americans spent more than $2.2 trillion on nondurable goods in 2009. Roughly one-third ($77.9 billion) of this amount was devoted to food and beverages purchased for consumption elsewhere. Another $1 trillion was spent on durable goods, such as motor vehicles and furniture. Note that PCE data are based on industry information. In other words, the BLS estimates consumer spending by calculating the final value of goods and services sold by businesses.

Consumer Expenditure Survey

As of September 2010, the most recent Consumer Expenditure Survey (CE) data were for 2008. CE data are compiled based on consumer-supplied information. Pur-

chase diaries are sent to sample households around the country. Participants record their everyday purchases and expenses in the diaries. Periodic interviews are conducted to collect diary information and quiz participants about their finances and spending habits. CE data are collected from households (called "consumer units") that are representative of the civilian noninstitutional population of the United States (i.e., people not in the military and not in institutions, such as prisons or long-term care facilities).

According to the BLS, the average U.S. household spent $50,486 in 2008. (See Table 3.3.) The largest components were housing ($17,109), transportation ($8,604), and food ($6,443). It should be noted that the housing component does not include mortgage principal payments because they are considered repayment of a loan, rather than a consumer expense. Thus, CE data underreport the true cost of housing for Americans with mortgages.

The BLS notes that the average consumer unit in 2008 included 2.5 people and had a pretax annual income of $63,563. (See Table 3.3.) Most of the consumer units (66%) owned their home.

The CE results provide detailed data on American spending habits. For example, participants break down food purchases as to meal location (at home or away from home). The 2008 survey indicates that the average household spent $2,698 eating out. (See Table 3.3.) Each house-

TABLE 3.2

Personal consumption expenditures, by major type of product, 2009

[Billions of dollars]

Personal consumption expenditures (PCE)	**10,001.3**
Goods	3,230.7
Durable goods	1,026.5
Motor vehicles and parts	319.7
Furnishings and durable household equipment	248.1
Recreational goods and vehicles	317.5
Other durable goods	141.1
Nondurable goods	2,204.2
Food and beverages purchased for off-premises consumption	777.9
Clothing and footwear	322.2
Gasoline and other energy goods	303.7
Other nondurable goods	800.4
Services	6,770.6
Household consumption expenditures (for services)	6,511.8
Housing and utilities	1,876.3
Health care	1,623.2
Transportation services	290.1
Recreation services	378.8
Food services and accommodations	603.6
Financial services and insurance	813.8
Other services	925.9
Final consumption expenditures of nonprofit institutions serving households (NPISHs)[a]	258.9
Gross output of nonprofit institutions[b]	1,058.1
Less: Receipts from sales of goods and services by nonprofit institutions[c]	799.2
Addenda:	
PCE excluding food and energy[d]	8705
Energy goods and services[e]	518.4
Market-based PCE[f]	8,758.5
Market-based PCE excluding food and energy[f]	7,462.7

Note: NPISH = Non-profit institutions serving households.
[a]Net expenses of NPISHs, defined as their gross operating expenses less primary sales to households.
[b]Gross output is net of unrelated sales, secondary sales, and sales to business, to government, and to the rest of the world; excludes own-account investment (construction and software).
[c]Excludes unrelated sales, secondary sales, and sales to business, to government, and to the rest of the world; includes membership dues and fees.
[d]Food consists of food and beverages purchased for off-premises consumption; food services, which include purchased meals and beverages, are not classified as food.
[e]Consists of gasoline and other energy goods and of electricity and gas.
[f]Market-based PCE is a supplemental measure that is based on household expenditures for which there are observable price measures. It excludes most imputed transactions (for example, financial services furnished without payment) and the final consumption expenditures of nonprofit institutions serving households.

SOURCE: Adapted from "Table 2.3.5. Personal Consumption Expenditures by Major Type of Product," in *National Income and Product Accounts: All NIPA Tables*, U.S. Department of Commerce, Bureau of Economic Analysis, July 30, 2010, http://www.bea.gov/national/nipaweb/ TableView.asp? SelectedTable=65&ViewSeries=NO&Java=no&Request3Place=N&3Place =N&FromView=YES&Freq=Year&FirstYear=1970&LastYear= 2009&3Place=N&Update=Update&JavaBox=no (accessed August 2, 2010)

hold averaged $116 per year for reading materials and $1,046 per year for educational expenses. Another $444 per year was spent on alcohol and $317 per year on tobacco products and smoking supplies. The average U.S. household reported donating $1,737 in cash to charitable causes.

HISTORICAL TRENDS IN CONSUMER SPENDING

Expenditures for some components making up the PCE have changed dramatically over time. Figure 3.2 shows spending on durable goods, nondurable goods, housing and utilities, and health care as a percentage of the total PCE for 1970, 1980, 1990, 2000, and 2009. These categories have historically been the four largest components of the PCE.

The data show that the percentage of the PCE dedicated to housing and utilities remained relatively steady between 1970 and 2009. (See Figure 3.2.) A slight downward trend is evident in the percentage spent on durable goods over time. A much more dramatic decrease is seen in the percentage of the PCE devoted to nondurable goods—from 35% in 1970 to 22% in 2009. A percentage decrease in one component making up the PCE means a percentage increase in one or more of the other components. For example, the percentage of the PCE devoted to health care more than doubled from around 7% in 1970 to 16% in 2009.

Food and Energy Price Volatility

Over the short term, food and energy prices can vary tremendously. Food prices are dependent on a variety of factors, including weather conditions (which affect growing costs), transportation and processing costs, and subsidies paid to farmers by the government that influence supply and demand ratios. Energy prices, particularly for oil, are affected by political and economic factors in the Middle East. Because of the volatile nature of food and energy prices, these costs are not included in the economic indicator called the core inflation.

FOOD PRICES. One component of the PCE that has historically become more affordable over time is food. The U.S. Department of Agriculture (USDA; June 11, 2010, http:// www.ers.usda.gov/Briefing/CPIFoodAndExpenditures/Data/ Expenditures_tables/table7.htm) has calculated food prices as a percentage of personal disposable income on an annual basis since 1929. Personal disposable income is also known as after-tax income or take-home pay. During the early 1930s the average U.S. household spent nearly a quarter of its disposable income on food. By the 1960s the percentage had fallen to around 15% and continued to decrease. In 2009 U.S. consumers spent around 9.5% of their disposable income on food. Enormous gains in agricultural productivity and crop yields have been responsible for decreasing the price of food.

In *CPI Detailed Report, Data for July 2010* (August 17, 2010, http://www.bls.gov/cpi/cpid1007.pdf), the BLS provides CPI-U values for food on a December-to-December basis from 2002 to 2009. These values are as follows:

- 2002—1.5%
- 2003—3.6%
- 2004—2.7%
- 2005—2.3%
- 2006—2.1%

TABLE 3.3

Consumer expenditure survey results, 2006–08

Item	2006	2007	2008	Percent change 2006–07	2007–08
Number of consumer units (in thousands)	118,843	120,171	120,770	—	—
Income before taxes	$60,533	$63,091	$63,563	—	—
Averages:					
Age of reference person	48.7	48.8	49.1	—	—
Number of persons in consumer unit	2.5	2.5	2.5	—	—
Number of earners	1.3	1.3	1.3	—	—
Number of vehicles	1.9	1.9	2.0	—	—
Percent homeowner	67	67	66	—	—
Average annual expenditures	$48,398	$49,638	$50,486	2.6	1.7
Food	6,111	6,133	6,443	0.4	5.1
Food at home	3,417	3,465	3,744	1.4	8.1
Cereals and bakery products	446	460	507	3.1	10.2
Meats, poultry, fish, and eggs	797	777	846	−2.5	8.9
Dairy products	368	387	430	5.2	11.1
Fruits and vegetables	592	600	657	1.4	9.5
Other food at home	1,212	1,241	1,305	2.4	5.2
Food away from home	2,694	2,668	2,698	−1.0	1.1
Alcoholic beverages	497	457	444	−8.0	−2.8
Housing	16,366	16,920	17,109	3.4	1.1
Shelter	9,673	10,023	10,183	3.6	1.6
Utilities, fuels, and public services	3,397	3,477	3,649	2.4	4.9
Household operations	948	984	998	3.8	1.4
Housekeeping supplies	640	639	654	−.2	2.3
Household furnishings and equipment	1,708	1,797	1,624	5.2	−9.6
Apparel and services	1,874	1,881	1,801	0.4	−4.3
Transportation	8,508	8,758	8,604	2.9	−1.8
Vehicle purchases (net outlay)	3,421	3,244	2,755	−5.2	−15.1
Gasoline and motor oil	2,227	2,384	2,715	7.0	13.9
Other vehicle expenses	2,355	2,592	2,621	10.1	1.1
Public transportation	505	538	513	6.5	−4.6
Healthcare	2,766	2,853	2,976	3.1	4.3
Entertainment	2,376	2,698	2,835	13.6	5.1
Personal care products and services	585	588	616	0.5	4.8
Reading	117	118	116	0.9	−1.7
Education	888	945	1,046	6.4	10.7
Tobacco products and smoking supplies	327	323	317	−1.2	−1.9
Miscellaneous	846	808	840	−4.5	4.0
Cash contributions	1,869	1,821	1,737	−2.6	−4.6
Personal insurance and pensions	5,270	5,336	5,605	1.3	5.0
Life and other personal insurance	322	309	317	−4.0	2.6
Pensions and Social Security	4,948	5,027	5,288	1.6	5.2

SOURCE: "Table A. Average Annual Expenditures of All Consumer Units and Percent Changes, Consumer Expenditure Survey, 2006–08," in *Consumer Expenditures in 2008*, U.S. Department of Labor, Bureau of Labor Statistics, March 2010, http://www.bls.gov/cex/csxann08.pdf (accessed July 1, 2010)

- 2007—4.9%

- 2008—5.9%

- 2009—−0.5%

The CPI-U values for 2007 and 2008 were historically high. Ronald Trostle of the USDA's Economic Research Service reports in *Fluctuating Food Commodity Prices: A Complex Issue with No Easy Answers* (November 2008, http://www.ers.usda.gov/AmberWaves/November08/PDF/FoodPrices.pdf) that the higher food prices were due to a variety of factors, including rising costs for food commodities (such as grains and vegetable oils), fluctuating oil prices, demand for biofuels (such as corn-based ethanol), and increasing demand for food in developing countries.

During 2009 the CPI-U for food plummeted to −0.5%. According to the Economic Research Service, in "Food Price Outlook, 2010" (August 25, 2010, http://www.ers.usda.gov/briefing/cpifoodandexpenditures/consumerpriceindex.htm), lower prices in 2009 were primarily the result of decreased demand during the great recession.

ENERGY EXPENDITURES AND PRICES. Nondurable energy goods accounted for $303.7 billion of the PCE in 2009. (See Table 3.2.) This category does not include electricity and gas for household operation, which fall under services. Nondurable energy goods include products such as gasoline, other motor fuels, and lubricants. The BLS indicates in *CPI Detailed Report, Data for July 2010* that the CPI-U values for motor fuels (including gasoline) fluctuated wildly from 2002 to 2009. The values on a December-to-December basis are as follows:

- 2002—24.6%

- 2003—6.8%

FIGURE 3.2

Personal consumption expenditure components, selected years 1970–2009

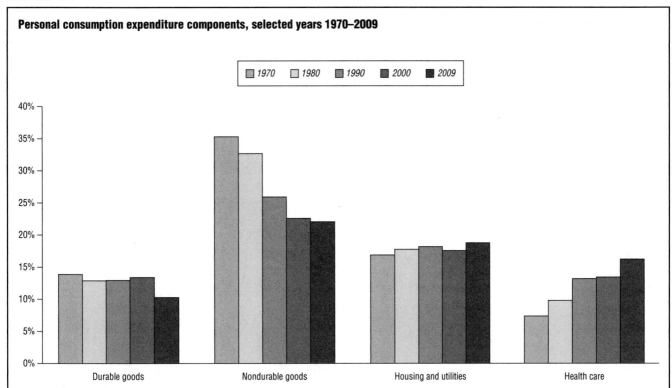

SOURCE: Adapted from "Table 2.3.5. Personal Consumption Expenditures by Major Type of Product," in *National Income and Product Accounts Tables: All NIPA Tables*, U.S. Department of Commerce, Bureau of Economic Analysis, July 30, 2010, http://www.bea.gov/national/nipaweb/TableView .asp?SelectedTable=65&ViewSeries=NO&Java=no&Request3Place=N&3Place=N&FromView=YES&Freq=Year&FirstYear=1970&LastYear=2009& 3Place=N&Update=Update&JavaBox=no (accessed August 2, 2010)

- 2004—26.1%
- 2005—16.2%
- 2006—6.4%
- 2007—29.5%
- 2008—−42.2%
- 2009—50.7%

GASOLINE PRICES. Figure 3.3 graphs the weekly average retail price of a gallon of regular gasoline in the United States from August 1990 to June 2010. The price hovered between $1.00 and $1.50 per gallon from 1990 to about 2003 and then began to increase dramatically. In mid-2008 consumers paid around $4.00 per gallon—the highest price on record. By the end of 2008 the price was back down to around $1.60 per gallon. It began to rise again, and as of June 28, 2010, the price was $2.71 per gallon.

Figure 3.4 illustrates that the average retail price of $2.84 for a gallon of regular-grade gasoline in the United States in May 2010 had four contributing components:

- Crude oil price—64%
- Federal and state taxes—14%
- Distribution and marketing costs—13%
- Refining costs—9%

Thus, the cost of crude oil accounts for nearly two-thirds of the retail price of gasoline. Crude oil is sold by the barrel, with each barrel containing 42 U.S. gallons (158.9 L). During the 1990s the average worldwide price for crude oil was around $20 per barrel. (See Figure 3.5.) In mid-2008 the price peaked at $140 per barrel. Over the next six months the price declined to less than $40 per barrel, which was an unprecedented drop. Throughout 2009 and early 2010 the price climbed back up to around $80 per barrel.

THE COST OF MEDICAL CARE

As noted earlier, the PCE proportion devoted to health care more than doubled from 7% in 1970 to 16% in 2009. (See Figure 3.2.) Health care expenses accounted for $1.6 trillion of the PCE in 2009. (See Table 3.2.)

Table 3.4 shows the CPI-U for medical care on a December-to-December basis from 2002 to 2009. Overall, medical care prices increased by 2.6% to 5% per year during this period. The CPI-U for medical care in 2009 was 3.4%, slightly higher than the overall inflation rate of 2.7% (See Table 3.1.) Health care inflation during 2009 was driven largely by price increases in hospital and related services (up 7.1%), prescription drugs (up 4.4%), and nursing homes and adult day services (up 3.6%). The lowest

FIGURE 3.3

Price of regular conventional gasoline, August 1990–June 2010

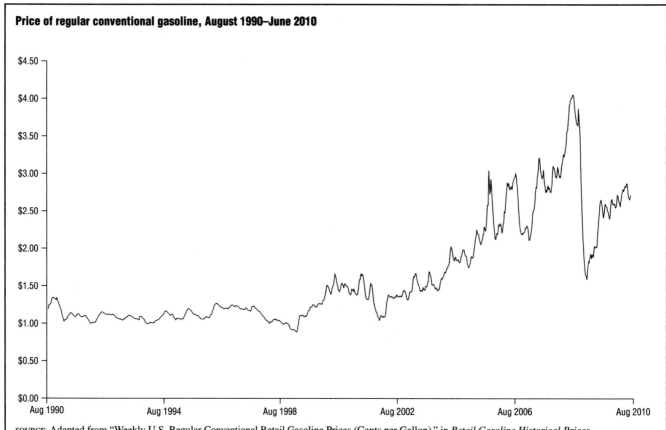

SOURCE: Adapted from "Weekly U.S. Regular Conventional Retail Gasoline Prices (Cents per Gallon)," in *Retail Gasoline Historical Prices*, U.S. Department of Energy, Energy Information Administration, June 28, 2010, http://www.eia.doe.gov/oil_gas/petroleum/data_publications/wrgp/mogas_history.html (accessed July 1, 2010)

FIGURE 3.4

Breakdown of retail price for a gallon of regular gasoline, May 2010

What we pay for in a gallon of regular gasoline (May 2010)

Retail price: $2.84/gallon

Taxes	14%
Distribution & marketing	13%
Refining	9%
Crude oil	64%

SOURCE: "What We Pay for in a Gallon of Regular Gasoline (May 2010)," in *Gasoline and Diesel Fuel Update*, U.S. Department of Energy, Energy Information Administration, July 2010, http://tonto.eia.doe.gov/oog/info/gdu/gaspump.gif (accessed July 29, 2010)

FIGURE 3.5

Average world price of crude oil, 1975–2010

Weekly all countries spot price FOB weighted by estimated export volume

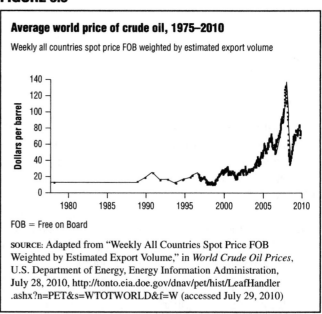

FOB = Free on Board

SOURCE: Adapted from "Weekly All Countries Spot Price FOB Weighted by Estimated Export Volume," in *World Crude Oil Prices*, U.S. Department of Energy, Energy Information Administration, July 28, 2010, http://tonto.eia.doe.gov/dnav/pet/hist/LeafHandler.ashx?n=PET&s=WTOTWORLD&f=W (accessed July 29, 2010)

inflation rates were seen in costs for eyeglasses and eye care (up 1.7%), care for invalids and the elderly at home (up 1.6%), and health insurance (down 3%).

Comparison of the medical care CPI-U values in Table 3.4 with the CPI-U values for all items in Table 3.1 from 2002 to 2009 reveals that medical care inflation outpaced overall inflation in each of these years. In other words, medical care prices have been increasing at a

TABLE 3.4

Annual percent change in the urban Consumer Price Index (CPI-U) for medical care expenditure categories, December to December, 2002–09

Percent change from previous December

Item and group	December							
	2002	2003	2004	2005	2006	2007	2008	2009
Expenditure category								
Medical care	5.0	3.7	4.2	4.3	3.6	5.2	2.6	3.4
Medical care commodities	3.1	2.1	2.2	3.7	1.8	2.7	1.6	3.3
Medicinal drugs[e]								
Prescription drugs	4.5	2.5	3.5	4.4	1.9	3.3	1.5	4.4
Nonprescription drugs[e]								
Medical equipment and supplies[e]								
Medical care services	5.6	4.2	4.9	4.5	4.1	5.9	3.0	3.4
Professional services	3.3	2.8	4.0	3.8	2.6	4.2	3.0	2.5
Physicians' services[c]	3.2	2.3	4.0	3.1	1.7	4.1	2.9	2.5
Dental services[c]	4.5	4.4	4.9	5.7	5.0	5.8	3.7	3.2
Eyeglasses and eye care[d]	−.3	1.5	2.9	3.1	2.0	1.5	.3	1.7
Services by other medical professionals[c, d]	3.6	2.3	2.5	2.5	3.1	3.1	3.8	1.8
Hospital and related services[c]	9.8	6.4	5.2	5.1	6.1	8.1	5.4	7.1
Hospital services[c, f]	10.1	6.4	5.2	5.2	6.2	8.3	5.9	7.7
Inpatient hospital services[a, c, f]	9.4	5.7	5.6	5.3	6.8	7.6	5.7	7.7
Outpatient hospital services[a, c, d]	12.7	6.6	4.5	5.0	5.2	9.9	5.6	8.2
Nursing homes and adult day services[c, f]	4.4	5.8	3.5	3.5	5.0	4.8	3.2	3.6
Care of invalids and elderly at home[b]	—	—	—	—	3.1	3.4	1.6	1.6
Health insurance[b]	—	—	—	—	6.4	8.8	−3.5	−3.0

—Data not available.
Note: Index applies to a month as a whole, not to any specific date.
[a]Special index based on a substantially smaller sample.
[b]Indexes on a December 2005=100 base.
[c]This index series was calculated using a Laspeyres estimator. All other item stratum index series were calculated using a geometric means estimator.
[d]Indexes on a December 1986=100 base.
[e]Indexes on a December 2009=100 base.
[f]Indexes on a December 1996=100 base.

SOURCE: Adapted from Malik Crawford et al., eds., "Table 26. Historical Consumer Price Index for All Urban Consumers (CPI-U): U.S. City Average, by Commodity and Service Group and Detailed Expenditure Categories," in *CPI Detailed Report, Data for June 2010*, U.S. Department of Labor, Bureau of Labor Statistics, July 16, 2010, http://www.bls.gov/cpi/cpid1006.pdf (accessed July 28, 2010)

faster pace than overall prices in the economy. Medical inflation is blamed, in part, on technological advances in medicine that have increased expenses associated with the diagnosis and treatment of patients.

Analysts often talk about health care expenditures as a percentage of the GDP. As shown in Figure 3.6, during the early 1980s U.S. medical care expenditures accounted for just 8% of the GDP. Over the following decade the percentage grew to around 11% and remained near that level until 2000. Since then, medical care expenditures have accounted for an ever larger fraction of the GDP, reaching 13.8% at the end of the second quarter of 2010—the highest percentage on record.

Another measure of medical care expenditures is made by the U.S. Department of Health and Human Services' Centers for Medicare and Medicaid Services (CMS). According to the CMS (June 7, 2010, https://www.cms.gov/NationalHealthExpendData/02_NationalHealthAccountsHistorical.asp#TopOfPage), the National Health Expenditure Accounts (NHEA) are "the official estimates of total health care spending in the United States." The data are considered compre-

hensive because they include not only costs for goods and services but also the costs of public health activities, the administration of government health care programs, private insurance, and research and related investments in health care. As of September 2010, the latest NHEA data were for 2008. Total health expenditures in 2008 were $2.3 trillion. This represented 16.2% of the nation's GDP that year.

The CMS uses historical data, information about planned government spending on health, and sophisticated computer models to predict the national health care expenditures for future years. As shown in Table 3.5, the national health care expenditures were projected to be $2.6 trillion in 2010. The costs were expected to increase annually, reaching $4.7 trillion by 2019.

Health Insurance Coverage

The Agency for Healthcare Research and Quality (AHRQ) is a division of the Department of Health and Human Services. The AHRQ conducts large-scale surveys of medical care recipients and providers as part of its Medical Expenditure Panel Survey (MEPS; http://www.meps.ahrq.gov/), which provides detailed data and reports on medical utilization and expenditures. As of September 2010, comprehensive MEPS data were available for the first half of 2009.

The AHRQ (http://www.meps.ahrq.gov/mepsweb/data _stats/summ_tables/hc/hlth_insr/2009/alltables.pdf) estimates that 81.5% of the U.S. civilian noninstitutionalized population of 300.5 million people had some kind of health insurance coverage during the first half of 2009. Thus, 18.5% of that population group (or 55.6 million people) did not have health insurance. Only a very small percentage (0.8%) of people aged 65 years and older were believed to be uninsured. This age group is widely cov-ered by Medicare (a health insurance program operated by the federal government). Thus, analysts are most interested in the insurance status of people under the age of 65 years. Table 3.6 provides detailed information from the AHRQ study about the U.S. civilian noninstitutionalized population under the age of 65 years during the first half of 2009. Twenty-one percent (or 55.2 million people) of this population was believed to be uninsured. Approximately one-third (33.6%) of the uninsured were aged 35 to 54 years. Other substantial proportions included young adults aged 19 to 24 years (16.3%) and children and teens under the age of 18 years (15.8%). Overall, more males (54.8%) than females (45.2%) were uninsured.

The AHRQ also assessed insurance coverage by racial and ethnic identity. Just over half (51%) of the uninsured population was white. (See Table 3.6.) Hispanics or Latinos accounted for the next largest contingent, at 29%. African-Americans made up 13.6% and Asians and Pacific Islanders accounted for 4.4% of the uninsured population in early 2009. Combining the racial, ethnic, and sex characteristics indicates the following three largest groups among the uninsured:

- White males—27.7%

- White females—23.3%

- Hispanic or Latino males—16.8%

Among people aged 16 to 64 years, those who had never been married (38%) were more likely to be uninsured than those who were married (33.2%), divorced (10.4%), separated (3.5%), or widowed (1.6%). The South had the largest percentage (42.4%) of the uninsured, whereas the Northeast had the lowest percentage (12.8%). The vast majority (87%) of the uninsured population reported their health status to be excellent (29.8%), very good (30%), or good (27.2%). Another 10.2% reported their health to be fair, and 2.8% said their health was poor.

THE COST OF LIVING

The nontechnical term *cost of living* refers to the cost of basic necessities to U.S. households, such as food, clothing, and shelter. Even though many factors affect the prices of these commodities, one economic factor has

FIGURE 3.6

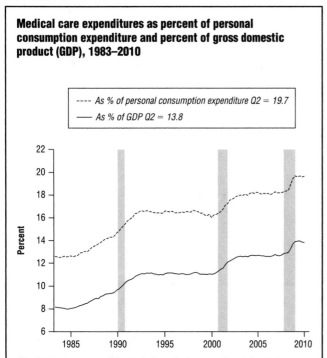

Medical care expenditures as percent of personal consumption expenditure and percent of gross domestic product (GDP), 1983–2010

Note: Medical care expenditures include medical care goods, which include prescription and nonprescription drugs, internal and respiratory over-the-counter drugs, and nonprescription equipment and supplies, and medical care services which include hospitals, physician, dental, eyecare, and services by other medical professionals.

SOURCE: "Medical Care Expenditures," in *U.S. Economy and Financial Markets*, Federal Reserve Bank of New York, July 30, 2010, http://www.newyorkfed.org/research/directors_charts/econ_fin.pdf (accessed August 2, 2010)

TABLE 3.5

Projected national health care expenditures, 2010–19

Calendar year	2010	2011	2012	2013	2014	2015	2016	2017	2018	2019	Total, 2010–2019
NHE (in trillions)	$2.6	$2.8	$2.9	$3.1	$3.3	$3.6	$3.8	$4.1	$4.4	$4.7	$35.3

NHE = National health care expenditures

SOURCE: Richard S. Foster and Stephen K. Heffler, "The following table provides the updated NHE projections with the two adjustments described above," in *Updated and Extended National Health Expenditure Projections, 2010–2019*, U.S. Department of Health and Human Services, Centers for Medicare & Medicaid Services, June 29, 2009, http://www.cms.gov/NationalHealthExpendData/downloads/NHE_Extended_Projections.pdf (accessed July 2, 2010)

TABLE 3.6

Characteristics of uninsured persons under age 65, as of first half of 2009

Population characteristics	Total population in thousands	Percent distribution of population	Percent uninsured	Percent distribution of uninsured population
Total[a]	262,756	100.0	21.0	100.0
Age in years				
Under 4	16,783	6.4	9.9	3.0
4–6	12,273	4.7	8.4	1.9
7–12	24,575	9.4	11.8	5.2
13–17	20,932	8.0	15.1	5.7
Total under 18	74,564	28.4	11.7	15.8
18	4,113	1.6	25.5	1.9
19–24	24,300	9.2	37.0	16.3
25–29	21,024	8.0	34.8	13.2
30–34	19,283	7.3	24.4	8.5
35–54	85,000	32.3	21.9	33.6
55–64	34,472	13.1	17.0	10.6
Sex				
Male	130,923	49.8	23.1	54.8
Female	131,834	50.2	19.0	45.2
Race/ethnicity				
Total Hispanic or Latino	44,678	17.0	35.9	29.0
Total black, single race	33,301	12.7	22.6	13.6
Total white, single race	165,703	63.1	17.0	51.0
Total Asian/Pacific Islander, single race	12,401	4.7	19.5	4.4
Total other races/multiple races	6,674	2.5	17.0	2.1
Race/ethnicity and Sex				
Hispanic or Latino male	23,138	8.8	40.0	16.8
Black male, single race	15,689	6.0	24.5	7.0
White male, single race	82,637	31.5	18.5	27.7
Asian/Pacific Islander male, single race	6,059	2.3	20.2	2.2
Other races/multiple race male	3,400	1.3	18.6	1.1
Hispanic or Latino female	21,540	8.2	31.5	12.3
Black female, single race	17,612	6.7	20.9	6.6
White female, single race	83,066	31.6	15.5	23.3
Asian/Pacific Islander female, single race	6,342	2.4	18.8	2.2
Other races/multiple race female	3,274	1.2	15.4	0.9
Marital status[b]				
Married	100,913	38.4	18.2	33.2
Widowed	3,086	1.2	27.8	1.6
Divorced	21,201	8.1	27.0	10.4
Separated	5,201	2.0	37.4	3.5
Never married	66,876	25.5	31.5	38.0
Census region				
Northeast	46,675	17.8	15.1	12.8
Midwest	57,475	21.9	18.0	18.7
South	96,021	36.5	24.4	42.4
West	62,585	23.8	23.1	26.2
Perceived health status, under age 65				
Excellent	95,513	36.4	17.2	29.8
Very good	80,534	30.7	20.6	30.0
Good	59,433	22.6	25.2	27.2
Fair	20,663	7.9	27.1	10.2
Poor	6,371	2.4	24.6	2.8

Note: Percent distributions may not add to 100 because of rounding.
[a]Total includes persons with unknown perceived health status and marital status.
[b]For individuals age 16 and over. Excludes unknown marital status. As a result, percents do not sum to 100.

SOURCE: Table 4. Total Population and Uninsured Persons under Age 65: Percent by Selected Population Characteristics, United States, First Half of 2009," in *Medical Expenditure Panel Survey: Table 1-5. Complete Set of Health Insurance Coverage Series in PDF Format, First Half of 2009*, U.S. Department of Health and Human Services, Centers for Medicare and Medicaid Services, Agency for Healthcare Research and Quality, 2010, http://www.meps.ahrq.gov/mepsweb/data_stats/summ_tables/hc/hlth_insr/2009/alltables.pdf (accessed July 29, 2010)

played a major role in recent decades: inflation. Because of inflation, the cost of living increases each year as the prices of necessities become more expensive. The CPI is the economic indicator commonly used to gauge changes in inflation and the cost of living.

A cost of living adjustment (COLA) is an adjustment made to wages or benefits to compensate consumers for the effects of inflation. Historically, the government has applied annual COLAs to increase the amounts paid out to recipients of certain benefits, such as Social Security and food stamps.

Public concern about various financial matters, April 2010

PLEASE TELL ME HOW CONCERNED YOU ARE RIGHT NOW ABOUT EACH OF THE
FOLLOWING FINANCIAL MATTERS, BASED ON YOUR CURRENT FINANCIAL
SITUATION—ARE YOU VERY WORRIED, MODERATELY WORRIED, NOT TOO
WORRIED, OR NOT WORRIED AT ALL?

	% Worried	% Not worried
Not having enough money for retirement	66	32
Not being able to pay medical costs of a serious illness/accident	61	37
Not being able to maintain the standard of living you enjoy	54	45
Not being able to pay medical costs for normal healthcare	48	48
Not having enough to pay your normal monthly bills	44	54
Not being able to pay your rent, mortgage, or other housing costs	38	56
Not having enough money to pay for your children's college	36	25
Not being able to make the minimum payments on your credit cards	24	58

SOURCE: Frank Newport, "Please tell me how concerned are you right now about each of the following financial matters, based on your current financial situation—are you very worried, moderately worried, not too worried, or not worried at all?" in *Americans No Less Worried about Healthcare Costs*, The Gallup Organization, May 7, 2010, http://www.gallup.com/poll/127727/Americans-No-Less-Worried-Healthcare-Costs.aspx (accessed July 2, 2010). Copyright © 2010 by The Gallup Organization. Reproduced by permission of The Gallup Organization.

These increases are designed to help people keep up with the rising cost of living due to inflation.

The COLA for Social Security recipients is calculated on the CPI for urban wage earners and clerical workers (CPI-W) from the third quarter of one year to the third quarter of the next year. In "Frequently Asked Questions about the 2010 Cost-of-Living Adjustment" (January 26, 2010, http://www.socialsecurity.gov/cola/2010/2010faqs.htm), the Social Security Administration notes that there was no increase in the CPI-W from the third quarter of 2008 to the third quarter of 2009. As a result, monthly Social Security benefits payable during 2010 did not increase.

PUBLIC OPINION ON CONSUMER ISSUES

The Gallup Organization conducts many polls that question Americans about their consumer habits and concerns. In April 2010 pollsters asked Americans to rate their level of concern about their ability to pay certain costs based on their "current financial situation." Nearly two-thirds (66%) of respondents were worried about having enough money for their retirement years. (See Table 3.7.) Nearly as many (61%) were worried about being able to pay the medical costs associated with a serious illness or accident. Slightly more than half (54%) were concerned about maintaining the standard of living that they currently enjoy.

The Gallup Organization finds that concern about medical costs has been growing for nearly a decade, long before the onset of the great recession. Half of those asked in 2001 were very or moderately concerned about being

able to pay their medical costs in the event of a serious illness or accident. (See Figure 3.7.) By 2010 this percentage had gradually increased to 61%. Americans have been slightly less worried about being able to pay medical costs for "normal healthcare." In 2001, 44% said they were very or moderately worried about this scenario, and in 2010, 48% of respondents were worried.

CONSUMER SPENDING, JOB CREATION, AND INTEREST RATES

Consumer spending is essential to economic growth in the United States and is greatly affected by two things: employment and interest rates, which are interdependent factors in the economy. Historically, when interest rates have been lower, people have spent more money, which has in turn stimulated the job market. When people have steady and dependable work, they are more likely to spend money, which also adds jobs to the economy.

Consumer buying choices can also stimulate—and even shift—job growth among industries. The higher the demand is for certain products and services, the more growth those industries will experience. The goods and services that are purchased by the consumer are called final goods; those that are used in the production of final goods are called intermediate goods. Demand for both final and intermediate goods leads to expansion in their respective industries, which in turn adds jobs to the economy.

Interest Rates and Spending

Interest rates are determined by the Board of Governors of the Federal Reserve System, which is the central bank of the United States. The Federal Reserve sets the federal funds rate (the interest rate banks charge for overnight loans to each other), which then influences the prime rate (the rate that banks charge their best customers; the prime rate is usually set at about three percentage points above the federal funds rate). From there, creditors set competitive rates for lending money to consumers. When interest rates are high, consumer spending (particularly for high-priced items such as cars and houses) tends to slow down because the cost of borrowing money is higher. Lower interest rates stimulate the economy because consumers can afford to borrow more at lower rates. This is particularly true for housing. As noted in Chapter 2, interest rates on home mortgages were historically low during the 1990s and the early years of the first decade of the 21st century.

In economics, to liquefy an asset means to exchange it for cash or to extract cash out of it. The cash is then available to spend or save. For many American families their most valuable asset is their home. People liquefy their home wealth by turning the equity they have built up in their homes into cash. Equity is the proportion of a home's

FIGURE 3.7

Percentage of public very or moderately concerned about being able to pay their medical costs, 2001–10

HOW CONCERNED ARE YOU RIGHT NOW ABOUT EACH OF THE FOLLOWING FINANCIAL MATTERS, BASED ON YOUR CURRENT FINANCIAL SITUATION—ARE YOU VERY WORRIED, MODERATELY WORRIED, NOT TOO WORRIED, OR NOT WORRIED AT ALL?

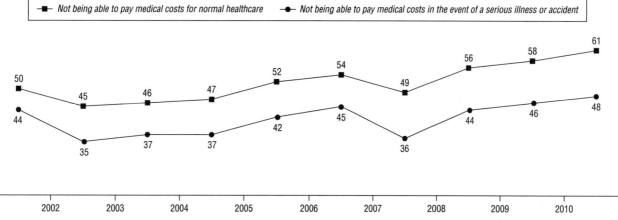

SOURCE: Frank Newport, "How concerned are you right now about each of the following financial matters, based on your current financial situation—are you very worried, moderately worried, not too worried, or not worried at all?" in *Americans No Less Worried about Healthcare Costs*, The Gallup Organization, May 7, 2010, http://www.gallup.com/poll/127727/Americans-No-Less-Worried-Healthcare-Costs.aspx (accessed July 2, 2010). Copyright © 2010 by The Gallup Organization. Reproduced by permission of The Gallup Organization.

mortgage value that a homeowner has paid off and actually owns. A cash down payment can be one component of equity. In addition, there are the monthly mortgage payments, which include both an interest payment and a principal payment. The interest payments represent a bonus or profit for the lender. Over the life of the mortgage the principal payments pay off the original mortgage amount. They also are a major component of the equity that accrues (builds up over time). Another way that equity increases is through appreciation (increase in value). Traditionally, homes have been considered a good investment because they appreciate over time.

There are two primary ways in which homeowners liquefy their home wealth. First, homeowners who sell their home for more than they paid for it reap a cash profit. They can then use that money toward the purchase of another home, spend it in other ways, or save or invest it. Homeowners can often borrow the equity they have built up in their home. These loans are called second mortgages, refinances, or home equity loans, and they become very popular when interest rates are low. During the 1990s and the early years of the first decade of the 21st century U.S. homeowners took advantage of rising property values and low interest rates by liquefying billions of dollars in equity from their homes. Economists believe that some of this money was pumped back into the economy in the form of consumer spending (i.e., consumption of goods and services).

Alan Greenspan and James Kennedy explain in *Sources and Uses of Equity Extracted from Homes* (March 2007, http://www.federalreserve.gov/pubs/feds/2007/200720/200720pap.pdf) that "there is broad agreement in the literature that housing wealth supports consumption; however, there is considerable disagreement as to the magnitude of the effect." They calculate that the cash extracted from home equity between 1991 and 2005 averaged $530 billion per year. The majority of this cash (approximately two-thirds) was from sales of existing homes. The remaining one-third was from equity-based loans. The researchers rely on respected surveys conducted by the University of Michigan and by industry groups, such as the National Association of Realtors and the American Bankers Association, to determine how the liquefied equity was used by homeowners. They point out that these data are self-reported by survey participants and are only available for certain transactions. Greenspan and Kennedy estimate that Americans who liquefied their equity by selling their home and then purchased another home used their equity as follows:

- Applied the equity to the next home purchase—87% of the total cash

- Spent the equity on PCE—7% of the total cash

- Invested the equity or otherwise used it—6% of the total cash

In regards to equity-based loans transacted between 1991 and 2005, Greenspan and Kennedy estimate that approximately one-third of the cash was used by homeowners to pay nonmortgage debt (e.g., credit card debt). Another one-third of the cash likely went toward home improvements. Approximately one-fourth of the lique-fied equity is believed to have been spent on PCE. The remainder was used for investment purposes or for other uses.

Thus, low interest rates spur consumer spending, which helps drive up the nation's GDP. However, low interest rates are not always good for individual finances or the economy because they lead to more debt in the form of home equity loans, car loans, and credit cards. The problems associated with this debt will be discussed in detail in Chapter 4.

CHAPTER 4
PERSONAL DEBT

Beautiful credit! The foundation of modern society.

—Mark Twain and Charles Dudley Warner, *The Gilded Age: A Tale of To-day* (1873)

He who goes a borrowing, goes a sorrowing.

—Benjamin Franklin, *Poor Richard's Almanack* (1757)

Personal debt has both good and bad effects on the U.S. economy. Americans borrow money to buy houses, cars, and other consumer goods. They also take out loans to pay for vacations, investments, and educational expenses. All of this spending helps businesses and boosts the nation's gross domestic product (the total market value of final goods and services produced within an economy in a given year). As long as debt is handled prudently, it can be a positive economic force. However, some Americans take on too much debt and get into financial difficulties. Debt becomes a problem on a macroeconomic scale when people must devote large amounts of their disposable income (after-tax income or take-home pay) to repaying loans instead of spending or investing their money.

During the late 1990s and the first half of the first decade of the 21st century Americans took on massive amounts of mortgage debt as a housing boom swept the nation. When the boom ended, many people found themselves unable (or unwilling) to repay the loans. This produced a widespread financial crisis that affected the economy as a whole. The United States sank into the so-called great recession, an economic slowdown that officially lasted from December 2007 to June 2009. The latter month represents the time when the economy quit contracting and began expanding (recovering). Americans' debt declined dramatically during the great recession and continued to decrease through late 2009 and early 2010. As of September 2010, it was unclear whether this trend would continue once the economy fully recovered or whether Americans would return to their pre-recession borrowing habits.

HISTORICAL DEVELOPMENTS

For centuries religious teachings about making and taking loans affected societal attitudes about the appropriateness of personal debt. The promise to repay a loan was considered a sacred pledge; thus, violating such an agreement was morally reprehensible. The Bible and the Koran (the sacred text of Islam) include scriptures that were interpreted as prohibiting the charging of excessive interest (or even any interest) on loans that were made to certain groups of people. Likewise, granting or assuming debt oftentimes aroused disapproval. In William Shakespeare's (1564–1616) play *Hamlet*, which was first performed around 1600, one of the characters advises: "Neither a borrower, nor a lender be."

English common law allowed for imprisonment of debtors who could not repay their debts. This practice carried over to the fledgling United States. In fact, Robert Morris (1735–1806), one of the signers of the Declaration of Independence, was later imprisoned in Philadelphia for failing to repay personal debt. The use of debtors' prisons in the United States was gradually phased out during the 1800s because of changing societal attitudes and the enactment of bankruptcy laws.

David A. Skeel Jr. explains in *Debt's Dominion: A History of Bankruptcy Law in America* (2001) that federal bankruptcy laws were passed in the United States in 1800, 1841, and 1867. However, each law was in force for only a few years before being repealed. Legislators had a difficult time drafting bills that were considered fair to both creditors and debtors. In 1898 a more workable law was passed that became the foundation for modern bankruptcy law.

As the 20th century progressed, social taboos about personal debt diminished in the face of growing consumer demand for immediate access to goods. The General Motors Acceptance Corporation (the financial arm of the automobile company General Motors Corporation) was established in 1919 to allow Americans to borrow money to acquire new automobiles. The venture proved to be wildly successful and inspired other companies to enter the credit business. During the 1920s middle-class Americans seized on the opportunity to use credit to buy newly available durable (long-lasting) goods, such as appliances. Installment loans became a popular financing method. During the 1950s the first all-purpose credit cards were introduced. Over the next few decades their use became commonplace, representing a major shift in American buying habits and attitudes about the acceptability of debt.

During the latter half of the 20th century Congress passed a number of laws that were designed to protect consumers from unscrupulous lending practices. The first major piece of legislation was the Consumer Credit Protection Act of 1968. It requires lenders to be forthright and clear about the terms and conditions of loans that they make.

CATEGORIES OF DEBT

Economists divide personal debt into two broad categories: investment debt and consumer debt. Money borrowed to buy houses and real estate is considered investment debt. Because most property appreciates (increases in value) over time, the debt assumed to finance its purchase will likely be a wise investment. Likewise, money borrowed to start a business or pay for a college education can bring financial benefits. All of this assumes that the investment was a wise one and that the short-term costs of the debt can be borne. By contrast, consumer debt is assumed purely for consumption purposes. The money is spent to gain immediate access to goods and services that will not appreciate in value (and will likely lose value) over time to help offset the costs of the debt.

Credit falls into two other categories: nonrevolving credit and revolving credit. Nonrevolving loans require regular payments of amounts that will ensure that the original debt (the principal) plus interest will be paid off in a particular amount of time. They are also known as closed-end loans and are commonly used to finance the purchase of real estate, cars, and boats or to pay for educational expenses. Nonrevolving loans feature predictable payment amounts and schedules that are laid out in amortization tables. The term *amortize* is derived from the Latin term *mort*, which means "to kill or deaden." An amortization schedule details how a loan will be gradually eliminated (killed off) over a set period. Revolving debt is a different kind of arrangement in which the debtor is allowed to borrow against a predetermined total amount of credit and is billed for the outstanding principal plus interest. The loans typically require regularly scheduled minimum payments, but not a set time period for repaying the entire amount due. Credit card loans are the primary example of revolving debt.

Loans can also be secured or unsecured. A secured loan is one in which the borrower puts up an asset called collateral to lessen the financial risk of the loaner. If the borrower defaults (fails to pay back the loan), the loaner can seize the collateral and sell it to recoup some or all of the money that was lent. Mortgages on homes and property and loans on cars, boats, motor homes, and other goods of high value are typically secured loans. In all these cases the collateral can be legally repossessed by the loaners. Unsecured loans are not backed by collateral. They are granted solely on the good financial reputation of the borrower. Credit card debts and debts owed to medical practitioners and hospitals are the major types of unsecured debts.

HOUSEHOLD DEBT SERVICE

The Federal Reserve System, the national bank of the United States, compiles an economic indicator called the household debt service ratio (DSR). The DSR is the ratio of household debt payments to disposable personal income. It indicates the estimated fraction of disposable income that is devoted to payments on outstanding mortgage and consumer debt.

As shown in Figure 4.1, the DSR steadily increased between 1994 and 2007. It peaked at nearly 14% in late 2007 and then declined dramatically. By the first quarter of 2010 the DSR was around 12.5%. This means that by the end of the first quarter of 2010 Americans as a whole were spending 12.5% of their disposable income on their debt.

INTEREST RATES

One of the chief factors affecting the amount of debt that people assume is the amount of interest charged on loans. Banks and other financial institutions charge interest to make money on lending money. The interest rate charged must be low enough to tempt potential borrowers, but high enough to make a profit for lenders. In general, commercial lenders base their interest rates on the rates charged by the Federal Reserve. Lower interest rates encourage consumers to borrow money.

The Federal Reserve makes short-term loans to banks at an interest rate called the discount rate. If the Federal Reserve raises or lowers the discount rate, then banks adjust the federal funds rate, which is the rate they charge each other for loans. This affects the prime rate, the interest rate banks charge their best customers (typically large corporations), which in turn affects the rates on other loans. Figure 1.13 in Chapter 1 shows the bank prime loan rate from August 1955 to June 2010. The rate varied widely over time from less than 5% in 1955 to more than 20% in the early to mid-1980s. Since 1990 the prime rate has consistently remained below 10% and temporarily dipped below 5% during the first half of the first decade of the 21st century.

When a loan is granted, the creditor sets terms that specify whether the interest rate to be paid will be fixed or variable. A fixed interest rate remains constant throughout

FIGURE 4.1

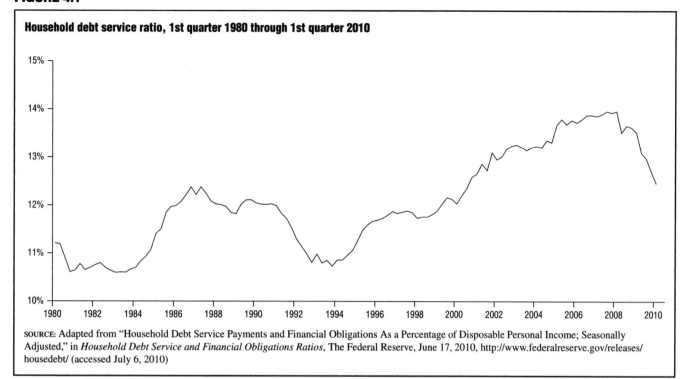

Household debt service ratio, 1st quarter 1980 through 1st quarter 2010

SOURCE: Adapted from "Household Debt Service Payments and Financial Obligations As a Percentage of Disposable Personal Income; Seasonally Adjusted," in *Household Debt Service and Financial Obligations Ratios*, The Federal Reserve, June 17, 2010, http://www.federalreserve.gov/releases/housedebt/ (accessed July 6, 2010)

the life of the loan. A variable rate changes and is typically tied to a publicly published interest rate, such as the prime rate. For example, a loan can be made with the stipulation that the interest rate charged each month will be one percentage point higher than the prime rate. As the prime rate changes, so will the interest rate on the loan and the borrower's monthly payments.

Table 4.1 shows the tremendous difference between loans with differing interest rates and repayment periods. A $100,000 mortgage with a 30-year fixed interest rate of 5% will result in $193,300 being paid over the lifetime of the loan. The same $100,000 loan at 10% interest will cost $315,900. Loans for new cars typically have a repayment period of three to five years. A 7% fixed interest car loan for $20,000 paid over three years results in a total payment of $22,200. The same loan spread over five years will end up costing $23,800. Thus, the shorter loan period results in a much lower overall payout for the car. However, the trade-off to the borrower for a shorter loan period will be higher monthly payments. Borrowers must consider the financial consequences of monthly payments and interest rates to get a loan they can afford in the short and long term.

MORTGAGES

For most Americans a mortgage is the largest personal debt they will ever incur. In 2009 the outstanding household home mortgage debt totaled $10.3 trillion. (See Table 4.2.) Mortgage debt is a form of investment debt because real estate usually increases in value. Thus,

TABLE 4.1

Interest payments for particular loans

Interest rate	Years of loan	Amount borrowed (principal)	Total interest paid*	Total principal + interest paid*
5%	30	$100,000	$93,300	$193,300
10%	30	$100,000	$215,900	$315,900
15%	30	$100,000	$355,200	$455,200
5%	15	$100,000	$42,300	$142,300
10%	15	$100,000	$93,400	$193,400
15%	15	$100,000	$151,900	$251,900
7%	3	$20,000	$2,200	$22,200
7%	4	$20,000	$3,000	$23,000
7%	5	$20,000	$3,800	$23,800

*Rounded to nearest $100

SOURCE: Created by Kim Masters Evans for Gale, 2010

assuming mortgage debt is generally considered a sensible economic move, as long as the payments are well matched to the borrower's income and ability to pay. During the second half of the first decade of the 21st century the U.S. housing market suffered a deep financial crisis. In many cases real estate did not appreciate in value, but depreciated (decreased in value). The causes and consequences of this crisis will be explained later in the chapter. First, it is necessary to understand some basic information about mortgages and how the mortgage market operates.

Mortgage loans have been in use in Europe for centuries, developing along with private ownership of land. In modern times a mortgage represents a lien, or binding

TABLE 4.2

Household home mortgage debt outstanding, 1975–2009

[In billions of dollars]

	Households home mortgage
1975	459.0
1976	517.0
1977	603.0
1978	708.6
1979	826.7
1980	926.5
1981	998.2
1982	1,031.1
1983	1,116.2
1984	1,242.8
1985	1,449.6
1986	1,648.3
1987	1,827.9
1988	2,054.2
1989	2,259.5
1990	2,488.8
1991	2,667.0
1992	2,840.0
1993	2,998.7
1994	3,165.3
1995	3,318.9
1996	3,523.8
1997	3,739.3
1998	4,040.6
1999	4,416.3
2000	4,798.4
2001	5,305.4
2002	6,009.9
2003	6,894.4
2004	7,835.3
2005	8,874.3
2006	9,865.0
2007	10,538.5
2008	10,496.9
2009	10,334.4

Note: Data shown are on an end-of-period basis.

SOURCE: Adapted from "D.3 Debt Outstanding by Sector," in *Federal Reserve Statistical Release Z.1: Flow of Funds Accounts of the United States, Flows and Outstandings, First Quarter 2010*, The Federal Reserve, June 10, 2010, http://www.federalreserve.gov/releases/z1/Current/z1.pdf (accessed July 6, 2010)

charge, against a piece of property for the payment of a debt. In other words, the loan is granted on the condition that the property can be claimed by the loaner (creditor) in the event the borrower defaults. If the loan is satisfactorily paid, full ownership of the property is granted to the borrower. Loaners use a process called underwriting to assess the creditworthiness of potential mortgage borrowers.

Mortgage Underwriting Standards

A home mortgage is a very large loan, usually totaling $100,000 or more, for which the repayment period may be several decades. Mortgage agreements are complex legal documents that bind lenders and borrowers to do certain things. Lenders typically charge borrowers fees (e.g., application fees, home appraisal fees, and so on) to originate a mortgage. In addition, lenders that hold the mortgages they originate will earn money from the interest payments that the borrowers make each month.

If a borrower quits paying on a mortgage, the lender can take possession of the home through a legal process called foreclosure and resell the home to someone else. However, this requires a significant investment of time and resources by the lender. In addition, foreclosed homes are typically sold at a loss. Thus, it is in a lender's best interest to issue mortgages to borrowers highly likely to repay the loans. As a result, lenders use specific underwriting standards to screen potential borrowers. There are four important factors that lenders take into consideration: documentation of the borrower's income and assets, the borrower's credit score, the borrower's debt ratio, and the loan-to-value ratio of the mortgage.

DOCUMENTATION OF INCOME AND ASSETS. Lenders typically require mortgage applicants to provide documentation of their income and assets. Many workers receive regular paychecks from their employer. These applicants provide the lender with paperwork showing the amount and timing of their salary or wages. The length of time the applicant has had the same job is also important to the lender. Some people are self-employed. They typically have to provide the lender with copies of their income tax returns or other documents for proof of income.

Borrowers must also supply written documentation of their assets. These assets usually include cash in bank accounts, savings bonds, stocks or other investments with value, and real estate or vehicles for which the loans have already been paid off.

CREDIT SCORE. A credit score is a numerical rating of a person's creditworthiness based on his or her past history of managing credit. According to Malgorzata Wozniacka and Snigdha Sen, in "Credit Scores: What You Should Know about Your Own" (November 23, 2004, http://www.pbs.org/wgbh/pages/frontline/shows/credit/more/scores.html), credit scoring began during the late 1950s with companies called credit bureaus that collected information about the credit history and general reputation of individuals. In 1971 Congress passed the Fair Credit Reporting Act. Wozniacka and Sen note that the law "established a framework for fair information practices to protect privacy and promote accuracy in credit reporting."

As of September 2010, there were several companies that compiled credit scores. The three major U.S. credit bureaus are Experian, TransUnion, and Equifax. Each company has its own scoring system and maintains a record called a credit report for each individual in its database. Anyone who has ever taken out a loan of any type (including credit cards) from a commercial entity, such as a bank, department store, or auto dealership, most likely has a credit report on file. Lenders regularly update the credit bureaus about the loan payment histories of borrowers, such as whether or not the borrowers make their loan payments on time and in full. Other sources that can influence credit scores are utilities, medical service providers, landlords and leasing agents, and companies with which consumers establish contracts to pay for goods or services, such as cell phone companies.

Fair Isaac Company (now known as FICO) is a financial company that was founded during the 1950s. Over the decades it has developed statistical models that are widely used by the credit bureaus to determine credit scores. A credit score calculated using FICO software is called a FICO score. The FICO method is highly regarded in the credit industry. Thus, FICO scores are relied on by many major financial institutions as reliable measures of the creditworthiness of customers. According to FICO, in "What's in Your FICO Score" (2010, http://www.myfico .com/CreditEducation/WhatsInYourScore.aspx), a FICO score generally depends on the following elements:

- Payment history—35%

- Amounts owed—30%

- Length of credit history—15%

- New credit (i.e., recently opened accounts)—10%

- Types of credit used—10%

In "What's Not in Your FICO Score" (2010, http:// www.myfico.com/CreditEducation/WhatsNotInYourScore .aspx), FICO notes that federal law prohibits the use of information on a person's race, religion, color, national origin, sex, marital status, or age in credit scores.

There are some general guidelines about what FICO scores mean to lenders. In "FICO Credit Scoring" (August 6, 2010, http://www.mbda.gov/blogger/financial-education/ fico-credit-scoring), the U.S. Department of Commerce's Minority Business Development Agency indicates that FICO scores range from 375 to 900 points, with higher scores indicating better creditworthiness. People with higher scores are more likely to be granted credit and to receive better credit terms (e.g., lower interest rates) than people with lower scores. Typically, a score of at least 680 is required to get the best (or prime) credit terms. People with scores lower than about 620 are said to have "subprime" (less than prime) creditworthiness. If they are granted credit, they may be charged a high interest rate by the lender because they are "risky" borrowers who are less likely than "prime" borrowers to repay a loan.

DEBT RATIO. A borrower's debt ratio can be calculated in different ways. One ratio results from dividing total assets (or total income) by total debt. Another example is a ratio of monthly debt payments to all monthly obligations. For example, a borrower's monthly obligations might include utility payments, car and student loan payments, and contract payments, such as for cell phone service. A borrower who already has substantial monthly obligations will find it difficult to also make mortgage payments.

LOAN-TO-VALUE RATIO. A loan-to-value (LTV) ratio is calculated by dividing the amount of a mortgage loan by the value of the home to be purchased. For example, a borrower seeking an $80,000 mortgage to buy a $100,000 home would have an LTV ratio of 0.8. The borrower would have to pay in cash the difference between the purchase price and the mortgage amount—in this case $20,000. This is called a down payment on the home purchase. Historically, mortgage lenders have been reluctant to loan the full purchase price of a home. A borrower who defaults on a mortgage and loses the home through foreclosure also loses the down payment that he or she made when the home was purchased. Thus, a down payment has long been considered by lenders a good sign that the borrower will faithfully make the mortgage payments.

Risk Classifications

Lenders use the results of the underwriting process to classify mortgages into different risk categories, depending on the creditworthiness of the borrower and the likelihood that the person will repay the loan.

As noted earlier, prime loans feature better (lower) interest rates than subprime loans. Nonprime loans are for people who do not qualify for prime mortgages for various reasons—poor or short credit history, lack of assets, low income or inability to prove income, and so on. Nonprime loan holders are more likely than prime loan holders to default on their loans. As a result, lenders charge higher interest rates on nonprime loans because of the greater risk associated with them.

Some lenders further classify nonprime loans as nearprime or subprime. In *The Rise in Mortgage Defaults* (November 2008, http://www.federalreserve.gov/pubs/ feds/2008/200859/200859pap.pdf), Christopher Mayer, Karen Pence, and Shane M. Sherlund point out that these classifications are not strictly or uniformly defined in the mortgage industry. However, near-prime mortgages are generally for borrowers with "minor credit quality issues" or those "who are unable or unwilling to provide full documentation of assets or income." People buying a home as an investment, rather than to live in the home, might also be considered near-prime borrowers because investors are more likely than owner-occupiers to default on mortgage loans. (Investors buy homes with the expectation that the properties will appreciate in value. If this happens, they can resell the homes in a relatively short period for more than they originally paid and make a profit.) Subprime mortgages are for borrowers posing the greatest risk of nonpayment. This classification is typically assigned due to lender concerns about the borrower's credit history, income, assets, debt ratios, and/or lack of documentation.

Mortgage Interest Rates: Fixed and Adjustable

A fixed-rate mortgage charges a set interest rate over the entire lifetime of the loan, typically 30 years. Figure 4.2

FIGURE 4.2

Interest rate on conventional 30-year fixed mortgage, April 1971–June 2010

SOURCE: Adapted from "Contract Rate on 30-Year, Fixed-Rate Conventional Home Mortgage Commitments," in *Federal Reserve Statistical Release: H.15. Selected Interest Rates—Historical Data*, The Federal Reserve, July 27, 2010, http://www.federalreserve.gov/Releases/H15/data/Monthly/H15_MORTG_NA.txt (accessed July 28, 2010)

shows the average annual interest rate charged on a 30-year fixed mortgage from April 1971 to June 2010. Comparison to Figure 1.13 in Chapter 1 shows that fixed mortgage rates mirror the ups and downs of the prime rate. One feature of a fixed-rate mortgage is that the monthly payment remains the same throughout the lifetime of the loan.

Creative financing terms introduced by creditors since the late 1990s have led to many alternatives to the conventional 30-year fixed-rate mortgage. One alternative is a shorter loan period, for example, 15 years, instead of 30 years. Another option is an adjustable-rate mortgage (ARM). ARMs feature variable interest rates (and consequently variable monthly payments) over the life of the loan. An ARM rate is typically tied to a published benchmark rate called an index rate. Low index rates during the first half of the first decade of the 21st century enticed many home buyers to take on ARMs instead of fixed-rate mortgages. Lenders may offer discount (or teaser) rates even lower than the index rate during the early months or years of the ARM repayment period. This translates into extra low monthly payments for an initial period, followed by much higher payments as the ARM matures.

Some creditors offer mortgages that allow homeowners to make interest-only payments for a short initial portion of the loan period. This is followed by a longer period of much higher monthly payments. A similar product is the payment-option mortgage, which allows homeowners to make small minimum payments for an initial short period. Short-term payment schedules requiring one large balloon payment are also offered in some mortgage products.

Mortgage arrangements with changeable monthly payments and balloon payments can pose a financial problem for homeowners who overestimate their ability to meet the costs of the mortgage. Figure 4.3 illustrates how monthly payments can vary significantly between different types of mortgages on a $200,000 home. The buyer assuming a fixed-rate 30-year mortgage at 6% interest pays $1,199.10 per month for the entire lifetime of the loan. The 5/1 ARM is a common ARM arrangement in which the initial interest rate remains fixed for five years and then begins to fluctuate with the index rate. In this example, the buyer pays a discounted rate of 4% during the first five years of the ARM. This translates to a monthly mortgage payment of $954.83. In year six the monthly payment is tied to a 6% ARM rate, and the monthly payment jumps to $1,165.51. In year seven the ARM rate increases to 7%; consequently, the monthly payment increases to $1,389.51. Two other types of mortgages depicted in Figure 4.3—a 5/1 ARM with interest-only payments and a payment-option mortgage—both feature large increases in monthly payments after the initial low-rate period.

Refinancing Mortgages

Most home mortgages cover long periods—up to 30 years. However, interest rates can change dramatically in the short term, rising and falling in response to macroeconomic factors. Home buyers who assume mortgages during times of high interest rates can ask creditors to refinance (adjust the mortgage terms) when interest rates go down. Basically, refinancing entails drawing up a new mortgage contract on a property. Because mortgage contracts are complicated legal documents, creditors usually charge fees to refinance mortgages. Thus, homeowners must weigh the long-term benefits of a reduced interest rate against the expense of refinancing fees.

During the first decade of the 21st century interest rates trended downward, making mortgage refinancing popular. This was particularly true for consumers who had purchased homes during the 1980s, when interest rates were extremely high by historical standards.

Refinancing frequently results in lower monthly payments for the homeowner because of the lower interest rate and because refinancing is commonly performed after at least several years of payments have been made on the original loan. This frees up the borrowers' money for consumer spending, investing, or saving. However, refinances conducted with a long payment period will keep the homeowner in mortgage debt for a longer period than originally anticipated. Some homeowners opt for a shorter loan payback period when they refinance. For example, consider a homeowner who has been paying for five years on a fixed-rate 30-year mortgage. There are 25 years left in the repayment period. Refinancing at a much lower interest rate with a new 15-year payback period may not decrease the monthly payment, but it will reduce by 10 years the amount of time the homeowner will be in mortgage debt.

Home Equity Loans

Real estate tends to appreciate in value. Thus, a property can increase in value above the amount that was originally borrowed to pay for it. For example, imagine a homeowner who bought a house in 2000 for $100,000 with a 30-year fixed-rate mortgage. After making mortgage payments for several years, the homeowner discovers that the principal due on the loan has dropped to $90,000, but the property has increased in value to $140,000. The difference between the amount of principal owed (the outstanding loan balance) and the value of the property is $50,000 and is called home equity. Home equity is an asset that can be borrowed against. Basically, homeowners can liquefy (turn into cash) the equity they have built up in their homes.

As noted in Chapter 3, during the 1990s and the first half of the first decade of the 21st century U.S. homeowners took advantage of rising property values and low interest rates to liquefy billions of dollars in equity from their homes. Alan Greenspan and James Kennedy calculate in *Sources and Uses of Equity Extracted from Homes* (March 2007, http://www.federalreserve.gov/pubs/feds/2007/200720/200720pap.pdf) that the cash extracted from home equity between 1991 and 2005 averaged $530 billion per year. Approximately two-thirds of this total was from sales of existing homes. The remaining one-third was due to equity-based loans. Greenspan and Kennedy estimate that the vast majority (87%) of the liquefied equity from home sales was used by Americans toward the purchase of their next home. The remaining 13% was spent or invested. They believe that one-third of the cash from equity-based loans was applied toward nonmortgage debt (e.g., credit card debt). Another one-third was likely spent on home improvements, and the remainder was spent on other purchases or invested.

Economists are encouraged by the use of home equity loans for home improvements. This type of spending is considered an investment because it adds value to the home. Many homeowners choose to use home equity loans to repay other debt. Because mortgage loans typically have lower interest rates than other loans, this exchange is beneficial. In addition, the interest paid on mortgage loans is tax deductible for most Americans, whereas interest paid on other types of loans is not deductible. Thus, conversion of "bad" types of debt (such as credit cards) to mortgage debt has favorable consequences.

FIGURE 4.3

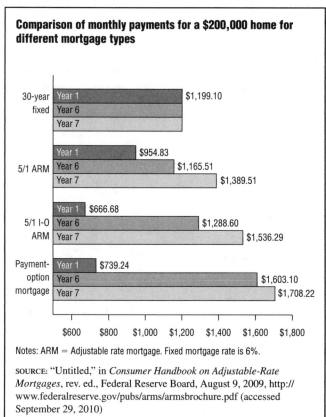

Comparison of monthly payments for a $200,000 home for different mortgage types

Notes: ARM = Adjustable rate mortgage. Fixed mortgage rate is 6%.

SOURCE: "Untitled," in *Consumer Handbook on Adjustable-Rate Mortgages*, rev. ed., Federal Reserve Board, August 9, 2009, http://www.federalreserve.gov/pubs/arms/armsbrochure.pdf (accessed September 29, 2010)

However, some economists worry that homeowners who use home equity loans to pay off bad kinds of debt may succumb to temptation and run up bad debt again. This could put them in a dire financial situation. They will no longer have their home equity to fall back on if their new debts become more than they can afford, and they might have to default on their loans. Home equity loans, like all mortgage loans, are secured by property. Thus, defaulting on a home equity loan can result in the loss of the home by the owner.

Foreclosures, Defaults, and Delinquencies

Foreclosure is a legal process in which a lender takes possession of the collateral (i.e., the home) of a borrower who has stopped paying on a mortgage loan. The borrower is said to be in default, meaning that the borrower has failed to abide by the legally binding mortgage agreement. Typically, lenders grant borrowers up to 90 days to "catch up" on late mortgage payments. After that 90-day period, the foreclosure process begins. Mortgage loans on which borrowers have not made a payment for at least 90 days are said to be "seriously delinquent."

The Secondary Market for Mortgages

Mortgage loans represent an investment for lenders. Mortgages will provide income well into the future as the loan payments (including interest) are paid by the borrowers. As a result, mortgages are commodities that are purchased by investors. This is known as the secondary mortgage market. In general, individual mortgages are bundled together and sold on the stock market. This process is called securitization. The packages are known as mortgage-backed securities or mortgage-based securities. Both are abbreviated MBS.

The original lenders are often eager to sell mortgages on the secondary market to obtain cash that they can use to make new loans. Companies purchase MBS products because mortgages have historically been considered relatively safe investments that will provide regular income in the future. Of course, the secondary buyers are trusting that the original lenders used good underwriting practices and only lent money to people who are very likely to keep making their mortgage payments. If borrowers default on mortgages that are within MBS packages, the MBS investors suffer a financial loss.

The Federal Government's Role in Mortgages

There are two types of mortgages in common use: conventional mortgages and government-underwritten mortgages. Conventional mortgages are loans made by nongovernmental businesses, such as banks and finance companies. Government-underwritten mortgages are insured by a federal, state, or local government agency.

Because high rates of homeownership are considered good for the U.S. economy, the government has taken an active role in the mortgage market. Mortgage terms have changed dramatically since the early 1930s. At that time home buyers could borrow only up to half of a property's market value (i.e., an LTV ratio of 0.5). A typical repayment plan included three to five years of regular payments and then one large balloon payment of the remaining balance. According to the Federal Housing Administration (FHA; September 6, 2006, http://www.hud.gov/offices/hsg/fhahistory.cfm), these terms discouraged many potential homeowners. As a result, the homeownership rate stood at around 40%.

During the 1930s the federal government introduced a variety of initiatives to boost a housing industry that was devastated by the Great Depression and increase homeownership. These efforts were focused on encouraging the supply side of the mortgage industry. They benefited consumers by enhancing the availability and flexibility of home mortgages. For example, amortization schedules covering 15 years or more became common and balloon payments were eliminated—both of these changes made it much easier for consumers to afford houses. Following World War II the Veteran's Administration (VA; now known as the U.S. Department of Veterans Affairs) began offering mortgages on favorable terms to returning veterans. Postwar economic prosperity and relatively low interest rates led to a housing boom. As shown in Figure 4.4, the nation's homeownership rate was around 64% during the mid-1980s. It climbed to a record high of 69.4% in 2004 and then began to decline. As of the second quarter of 2010, the homeownership rate was 66.9%.

FIGURE 4.4

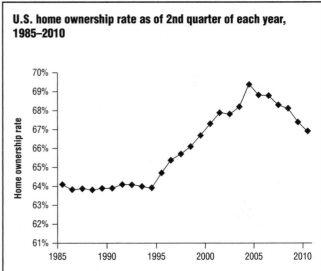

U.S. home ownership rate as of 2nd quarter of each year, 1985–2010

SOURCE: Adapted from "Table 4SA. Homeownership Rates for the United States: 1985 to 2010, Seasonally Adjusted (in Percent)," in *Residential Vacancies and Homeownership in the Second Quarter 2010*, U.S. Department of Commerce, U.S. Census Bureau, July 27, 2010, http://www.census.gov/hhes/www/housing/hvs/qtr210/files/q210press.pdf (accessed July 27, 2010)

Besides the VA, there are several other agencies and organizations that operate under government control or mandate to increase homeownership among Americans, including the FHA, the Federal National Mortgage Association, and the Federal Home Loan Mortgage Corporation.

FEDERAL HOUSING ADMINISTRATION. The FHA was created in 1934 and later placed under the oversight of the U.S. Department of Housing and Urban Development. The FHA provides mortgage insurance on loans made by FHA-approved lenders to buyers of single- and multifamily homes. FHA-insured loans require less cash down payment from the home buyer than most conventional loans. The insurance provides assurances to lenders that the government will cover losses resulting from homeowners who default on their loans.

FEDERAL NATIONAL MORTGAGE ASSOCIATION. The Federal National Mortgage Association (Fannie Mae) was created in 1938. Fannie Mae began buying FHA-insured mortgages from banks and other lenders. It then bundled the mortgages together and sold the mortgage packages as investments on the stock market. In essence, Fannie Mae created the secondary market for home mortgages. Lenders benefit because they receive immediate money that can be lent to new customers, and home buyers benefit from the increased availability of mortgage loans. The mortgage packages have been attractive to investors because the mortgages are backed by FHA insurance. In 1968 Fannie Mae became a private organization and expanded its portfolio beyond FHA-insured mortgages to private-label MBS (i.e., MBS products securitized by nongovernmental businesses, such as banks and financial institutions).

FEDERAL HOME LOAN MORTGAGE CORPORATION. The Federal Home Loan Mortgage Corporation (Freddie Mac) was created by the federal government in 1970 to prevent Fannie Mae's monopolization of the mortgage market. Like Fannie Mae, Freddie Mac is a private organization operating under a government charter and buys and sells home mortgages on the secondary market. Both Fannie Mae and Freddie Mac are shareholder-owned corporations.

The Housing Market Booms and Busts

As noted in Chapter 1, markets sometimes boom (become overly inflated in value) and then bust (lose value suddenly and dramatically). What frustrates investors and analysts alike is that the evidence of a boom is not obvious until after a bust occurs. In other words, most people do not see a bust coming because they are caught up in the excitement of making money and expect the financial windfall to continue indefinitely.

The historically low interest rates during the first half of the first decade of the 21st century spurred demand in the real estate market. For example, sales of newly built single-family homes increased steadily from the late 1990s to 2005, when a record of 1.4 million units were sold. (See Figure 4.5.) Sales of existing homes also grew, but at a less dramatic rate; their sales rate also peaked in 2005 at just over 6 million units.

High demand pushes prices upward. The Federal Housing Finance Agency (FHFA) uses an index called the house price index (HPI) to track home prices for mortgages acquired by Fannie Mae and Freddie Mac. (It should be noted that the HPI covers purchase-only mortgages and not refinanced loans.) The HPI for January 1991 is arbitrarily set at 100. According to Figure 4.6, the HPI increased dramatically through mid-2007, when it peaked above 220. Figure 4.7 shows the quarterly change and four-quarter change in the HPI from the first quarter of 1992 to the first quarter of 2010. The HPI grew by 1% to 2% per quarter from the late 1990s to the end of the fourth quarter of 2004. By the first quarter of 2005 the HPI had increased (appreciated) by 9.3% compared with the year before. (See Figure 4.8.)

The financial company Standard & Poor's (S&P) maintains home price indexes known as the S&P/Case-Shiller indexes. They are named after the economists Karl E. Case and Robert J. Shiller. One of the indexes—the 20-city composite—measures home price changes by compiling and weighting data for 20 major metropolitan areas:

- Atlanta, Georgia
- Boston, Massachusetts
- Charlotte, North Carolina
- Chicago, Illinois
- Cleveland, Ohio
- Dallas, Texas
- Denver, Colorado
- Detroit, Michigan
- Las Vegas, Nevada
- Los Angeles, California
- Miami, Florida
- Minneapolis, Minnesota
- New York City, New York
- Phoenix, Arizona
- Portland, Oregon
- San Diego, California
- San Francisco, California
- Seattle, Washington
- Tampa, Florida
- Washington, D.C.

FIGURE 4.5

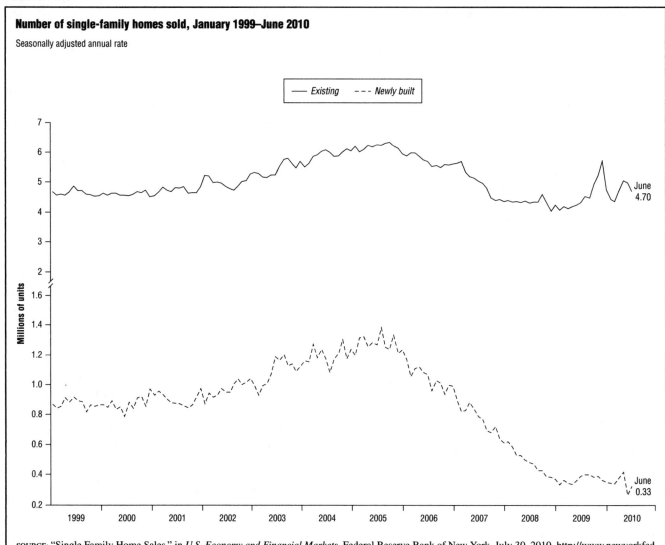

Number of single-family homes sold, January 1999–June 2010

Seasonally adjusted annual rate

SOURCE: "Single Family Home Sales," in *U.S. Economy and Financial Markets*, Federal Reserve Bank of New York, July 30, 2010, http://www.newyorkfed.org/research/directors_charts/econ_fin.pdf (accessed August 2, 2010)

In the press release "For the Past Year Home Prices Have Generally Moved Sideways According to the S&P/Case-Shiller Home Price Indices" (July 27, 2010, http://www.standardandpoors.com/), S&P reports that the 20-city composite index reached its highest point—just over 200—in 2006. The index is benchmarked to a value of 100 that is assigned to January 2000. Thus, the index more than doubled between 2000 and 2006.

During the first half of the first decade of the 21st century homeowner-occupiers and investors became excited about appreciating home prices. The homeowner-occupiers saw their homes quickly increase in value, allowing them to borrow against the rising equity. Investors reaped handsome profits by selling homes relatively quickly for more than what they paid for them. This process became known as "flipping houses."

Huge demand from potential homeowner-occupiers and investors prompted many lenders to relax their under-writing standards and extend loans to borrowers they might have previously rejected. In addition, many lenders greatly expanded their use of creative financing terms, such as ARMs that featured low initial monthly payments. Subprime ARMs became particularly popular. Eric Petroff indicates in "Who Is to Blame for the Subprime Crisis?" (2010, http://www.investopedia.com/articles/07/subprime-blame.asp) that only $35 billion in subprime mortgage loans were initiated in 1994. By 2002 that number had risen to $213 billion. Over the next three years the subprime market skyrocketed. In 2005 subprime lenders originated $665 billion of the risky mortgage loans. The White House notes in *Economic Report of the President* (February 2008, http://www.gpoaccess.gov/eop/2008/2008_erp.pdf) that the percentage of mortgage originations that were subprime increased from 5% in 2001 to over 20% in 2006.

Mortgage originators also greatly relaxed their LTV standards during the housing boom. As noted earlier, a

FIGURE 4.6

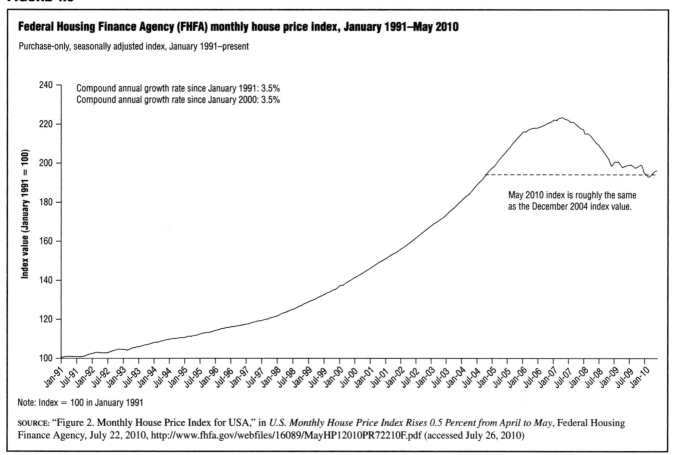

Federal Housing Finance Agency (FHFA) monthly house price index, January 1991–May 2010

Purchase-only, seasonally adjusted index, January 1991–present

Compound annual growth rate since January 1991: 3.5%
Compound annual growth rate since January 2000: 3.5%

May 2010 index is roughly the same as the December 2004 index value.

Note: Index = 100 in January 1991

SOURCE: "Figure 2. Monthly House Price Index for USA," in *U.S. Monthly House Price Index Rises 0.5 Percent from April to May*, Federal Housing Finance Agency, July 22, 2010, http://www.fhfa.gov/webfiles/16089/MayHP12010PR72210F.pdf (accessed July 26, 2010)

low LTV ratio (e.g., less than 0.8 to 0.9) has historically been associated with buyers who are more invested in their properties and less likely to default. Mayer, Pence, and Sherlund find that the median LTV ratio (half of the LTV ratios were higher and half were lower) for subprime mortgages actually increased from 90% in 2003 to 100% in 2005. In other words, many subprime borrowers made no down payment when they purchased their home. In addition. subprime borrowers were regularly put into nontraditional mortgage arrangements, such as ARMs and loans that offered interest-only payments for a short period. These loans featured balloon payments and/or sharp increases in monthly payments at some point during the loan period. The variable interest rates were often tied to economic indexes that can change suddenly and drastically. Mayer, Pence, and Sherlund conclude that "the riskiest borrowers were matched with the most complicated products."

Both the borrowers and lenders of subprime loans expected homes to keep appreciating in value. For homeowners, this appreciation would allow them to refinance their loan and tap into home equity to offset the financial burden of the coming higher monthly payments. Likewise, lenders believed that home appreciation would offset the risk they were taking in lending money to people with poor credit histories or other financial problems.

Thus, like all booms, the housing boom was driven by high expectations that future events would take a favorable path.

Investment companies also drove the housing boom by enthusiastically buying mortgage products on the secondary market. This provided cash to lending companies to underwrite more mortgages. Meanwhile, the stock of banks and other financial institutions providing mortgages greatly rose in value, as investors became excited about the increasing loan portfolios. Construction companies also responded to high housing demand by building more houses. Figure 4.9 shows the number of housing starts in the United States from January 1999 to June 2010. Housing starts is the number of new housing units (or homes) on which construction has begun. The number of housing starts for single-family homes topped 1.8 million units in 2005 and early 2006.

This construction boom resulted in incredibly high employment in the industry. The Bureau of Labor Statistics indicates that the number of workers employed in construction grew dramatically, from 4.6 million workers in 1992 to 7.7 million workers in late 2006 and early 2007. (See Figure 4.10.)

DEFAULTING BEGINS TO GROW. According to Mayer, Pence, and Sherlund, the mortgage market first showed

FIGURE 4.7

Federal Housing Finance Agency (FHFA) house price index, first quarter 1992–first quarter 2010

Seasonally adjusted price change measured in purchase-only index

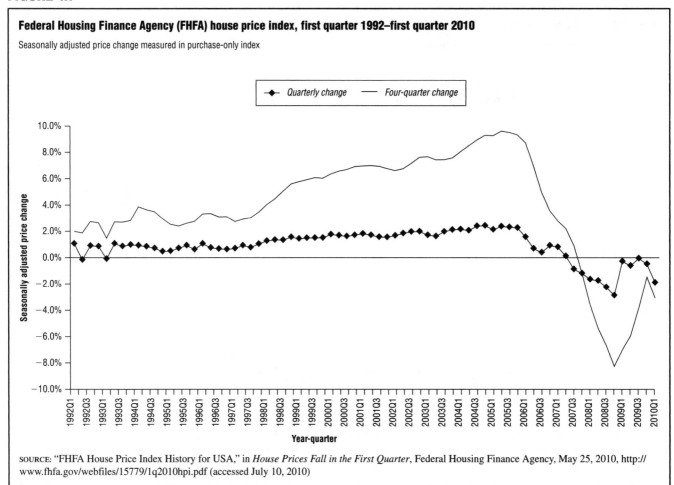

SOURCE: "FHFA House Price Index History for USA," in *House Prices Fall in the First Quarter*, Federal Housing Finance Agency, May 25, 2010, http://www.fhfa.gov/webfiles/15779/1q2010hpi.pdf (accessed July 10, 2010)

signs of trouble in mid-2005, when large lenders noticed a troubling increase in the percentage of their subprime loans that had become "seriously delinquent." Between 2000 and 2004 an average of 1.5% of subprime loans were in default only one year after the loans were originated. In other words, the borrowers stopped making their mortgage payments within months of taking out the loans. Analysts refer to these events as "early payment defaults." By the end of 2005 early payment defaults for subprime loans had climbed to 2.5% and continued to grow, reaching 5% at year-end 2006 and 8% at year-end 2007.

Early payment defaults are particularly troubling because they happen only months after underwriting occurs. Mayer, Pence, and Sherlund note that these loans "may have been underwritten so poorly that borrowers were unable to afford the monthly payments almost from the moment of origination." They also point to evidence suggesting "fraudulent practices by both borrowers and mortgage brokers." These practices may have kept buyers on the secondary mortgage market from realizing the actual riskiness of the investments they were buying. Regardless, Mayer, Pence, and Sherlund maintain that "some of the deterioration in underwriting characteristics should have been apparent to investors in mortgage-backed securities."

In *Economic Report of the President*, the White House notes that between 2004 and 2006 the default rate among homeowners with subprime ARMs was around 6%. By late 2007 the rate had skyrocketed to more than 15%. The default rate for prime mortgage loans also increased during this period, from around 1% to nearly 4%.

Maura Reynolds reports in "Loan Troubles Hit New Heights" (*Los Angeles Times*, March 7, 2008) that the national average foreclosure rate at the end of the fourth quarter of 2007 was the highest in recorded history. Just over 2% of mortgages were in foreclosure at that time. The foreclosure rate was highest in states that had experienced the greatest housing boom (and hence the greatest housing bust): Arizona, California, Florida, and Nevada.

THE ECONOMY SUFFERS. The unusually high default rates caused mounting financial losses for original lenders and MBS investors. The White House states in *Economic Report of the President* that "there were significant disruptions in [the] financial markets in the summer of 2007." In fact, it was the beginning of a vicious downward spiral. As banks, financial institutions, and investment companies reported huge losses, their stock plummeted in value. Some of the companies failed, and many others were in danger of failing.

FIGURE 4.8

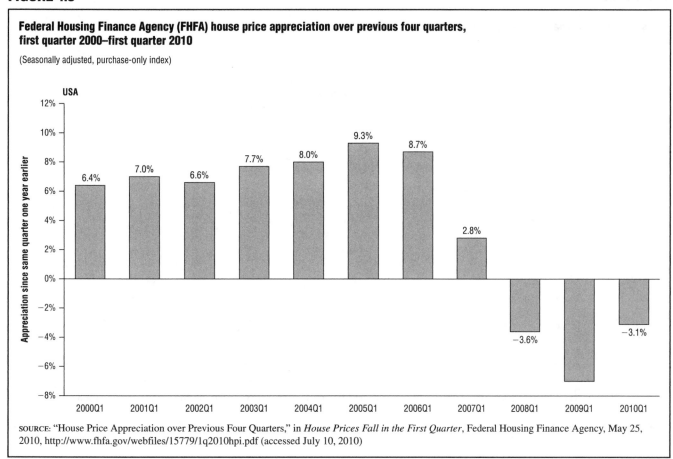

Federal Housing Finance Agency (FHFA) house price appreciation over previous four quarters, first quarter 2000–first quarter 2010

(Seasonally adjusted, purchase-only index)

SOURCE: "House Price Appreciation over Previous Four Quarters," in *House Prices Fall in the First Quarter*, Federal Housing Finance Agency, May 25, 2010, http://www.fhfa.gov/webfiles/15779/1q2010hpi.pdf (accessed July 10, 2010)

By this time many banks and financial institutions had stopped originating new mortgages because they were fearful of experiencing more losses. Meanwhile, the demand for new houses was decreasing rapidly. (See Figure 4.9.) As a result, employment in the construction industry declined. (See Figure 4.10.) Sales of newly built homes also dropped considerably. (See Figure 4.5.) Figure 4.11 shows the median and average sales price of new homes sold in the United States on an annual basis from 1964 to 2009. In 2007 the median price peaked at $247,900, whereas the average price of a new home peaked at $313,600. By 2009 these values had dropped to $216,700 and $270,900, respectively. As shown in Figure 4.7 and Figure 4.8, home prices declined at a record pace. In the first quarter of 2006 home prices based on mortgages acquired by Fannie Mae and Freddie Mac had increased by 8.7% from the year before. Thereafter, first quarter home price appreciation decreased to 2.8% in 2007, to −3.6% in 2008, and to −7% in 2009.

The decline in housing values left many homeowners owing more on their mortgages than their homes were worth in the marketplace. This is called being "upside down" or "underwater" in one's mortgage. Mayer, Pence, and Sherlund report that by mid-2008 more than half of the borrowers in Arizona, California, Florida, and Nevada had negative equity (i.e., they were upside down in their mort-

gages). More than one-third of borrowers in Indiana, Michigan, and Ohio and approximately 10% of borrowers in the rest of the country were upside down in their mortgages.

TROUBLE FOR FANNIE MAE AND FREDDIE MAC. The housing market bust put tremendous financial pressure on Fannie Mae and Freddie Mac. Like many other MBS holders, the two companies suffered huge financial losses due to defaulted loans. By mid-2008 investors were concerned that Fannie Mae and Freddie Mac would be unable to raise sufficient money to cover these losses.

Katie Benner reports in "The $5 Trillion Mess" (CNNMoney.com, July 14, 2008) that shares in Fannie Mae and Freddie Mac dropped in value by 65% and 75%, respectively, during the first half of 2008. At that time the two companies held or guaranteed approximately $5 trillion in mortgage loans.

In July 2008 Congress passed the Housing and Economic Recovery Act (HERA). The act created the Federal Housing Finance Agency (FHFA) and gave it the power to put Fannie Mae and/or Freddie Mac into conservatorship. Mark Jickling of the Congressional Research Service explains in "Fannie Mae and Freddie Mac in Conservatorship" (September 15, 2008, http://fpc.state.gov/documents/organization/110097.pdf) that the FHFA was given "full

FIGURE 4.9

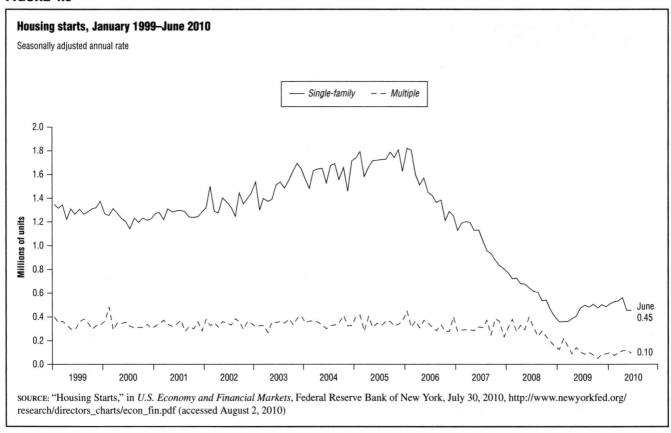

Housing starts, January 1999–June 2010

Seasonally adjusted annual rate

SOURCE: "Housing Starts," in *U.S. Economy and Financial Markets*, Federal Reserve Bank of New York, July 30, 2010, http://www.newyorkfed.org/research/directors_charts/econ_fin.pdf (accessed August 2, 2010)

FIGURE 4.10

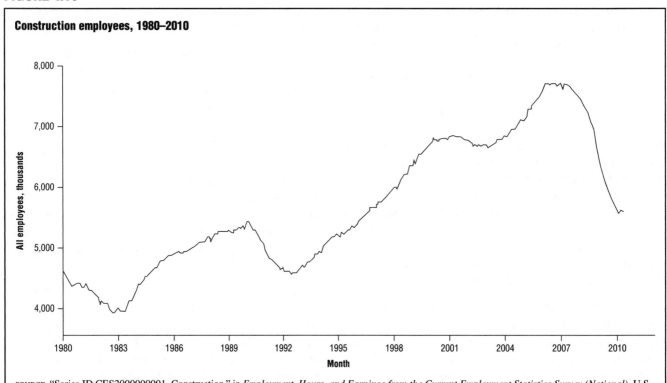

Construction employees, 1980–2010

SOURCE: "Series ID CES2000000001. Construction," in *Employment, Hours, and Earnings from the Current Employment Statistics Survey (National)*, U.S. Department of Labor, Bureau of Labor Statistics, July 7, 2010, http://data.bls.gov/cgi-bin/surveymost?ce (accessed July 7, 2010)

FIGURE 4.11

Median and average sales prices of new homes sold in United States, 1964–2009

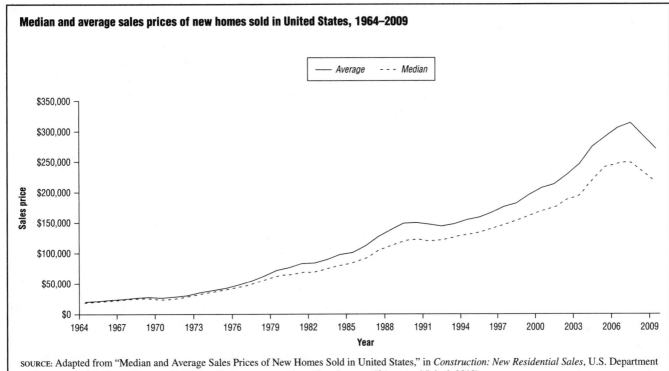

SOURCE: Adapted from "Median and Average Sales Prices of New Homes Sold in United States," in *Construction: New Residential Sales*, U.S. Department of Commerce, U.S. Census Bureau, 2010, http://www.census.gov/const/uspriceann.pdf (accessed July 6, 2010)

powers to control the assets and operations of the firms." A conservatorship for both companies was officially established in September 2008.

Jickling notes that the U.S. Department of the Treasury began investing money into the firms by buying shares of their stock and "newly issued" Fannie Mae and Freddie Mac MBS packages. In addition, the two firms were allowed to get short-term loans from the Treasury Department using MBS as collateral.

Under the HERA, the FHFA must submit an annual report to Congress about the status and financial soundness of Fannie Mae and Freddie Mac. In *Report to Congress, 2009* (May 25, 2010, http://www.fhfa.gov/webfiles/15784/FHFAReportToCongress52510.pdf), the FHFA notes that the main reason the companies were put into conservatorship was because of their investments in private-label MBS. The market value of these investments had declined sharply between 2007 and 2008.

According to the FHFA, Fannie Mae's annual net income was positive in 2005 and 2006. In 2007 the company suffered a loss of around $2 billion. In 2008 and 2009 its annual losses skyrocketed between $60 billion and $70 billion per year. Freddie Mac's financial performance followed a similar pattern. The company had positive net income in 2005 and 2006 and then reported losses of $2 billion in 2007, $50 billion in 2008, and $22 billion in 2009.

At the end of 2009 Fannie Mae and Freddie Mac held or guaranteed nearly half (47%) of the country's outstanding residential mortgage debt. The FHFA reports that the companies have taken a variety of actions since being put into conservatorship to conserve their assets and prevent future losses. These safeguards include higher FICO credit scores for potential borrowers than were required before 2008 and lower average LTV ratios for newly issued mortgages.

Nevertheless, as of May 2010 the FHFA had "critical supervisory concerns" about Fannie Mae and Freddie Mac because both companies were expected to continue to suffer losses from mortgages that had been originated before they went into conservatorship.

GOVERNMENT PROGRAMS. The HERA is only one of many actions that have been taken by the federal government to try to boost the ailing housing market. After taking office in January 2009, President Barack Obama (1961–) pushed for major reforms of the financial markets and set up programs that were designed to help individual homeowners.

The Obama administration's Making Home Affordable plan (August 5, 2010, http://www.makinghomeaffordable.gov/about.html) provides specific programs and measures that are intended to "stabilize the housing market and help struggling homeowners get relief and avoid foreclosure." Some of the major components that make up this plan are:

- Home Affordable Modification Program (HAMP)—homeowners who are struggling to make their monthly payments and who face foreseeable and/or imminent default can have their mortgages restructured to be more affordable. Initially approved homeowners receive trial (temporary) modifications while a more in-depth eligibility analysis is conducted. Homeowners who pass the analysis and successfully make their trial mortgage payments then become eligible to receive HAMP modifications.

- Second Lien Modification Program—homeowners who are approved for a HAMP modification of their first mortgage and who also have a second mortgage (i.e., a home equity loan) may qualify for this program, which allows the terms of the second mortgage to be modified.

- Home Affordable Refinance Program (HARP)—homeowners with mortgages that are owned or guaranteed by Fannie Mae or Freddie Mac may be able to refinance the loans to make the monthly payments more affordable.

- Home Affordable Foreclosure Alternatives (HAFA) Program—HAMP-eligible homeowners facing foreclosure may be able to avoid foreclosure proceedings through alternatives such as a short sale or deed-in-lieu-of-foreclosure. A short sale occurs when a home is sold by a mortgage holder for less than the amount still owed on it by the homeowner. Ordinarily, a mortgage holder can demand payment from the homeowner for the difference, which is called the deficiency. The HAFA Program forbids deficiency collection and provides cash incentives to homeowners and lenders to participate in the program. A deed-in-lieu-of-foreclosure is a similar arrangement in which the homeowner gives up all rights to the property in exchange for being released from the mortgage agreement.

The Departments of Housing and Urban Development and the Treasury report on the status of HAMP in "The Obama Administration's Efforts to Stabilize the Housing Market and Help American Homeowners" (July 2010, http://www.financialstability.gov/docs/JULY_Scorecard _1.10.pdf). According to the report, nearly 1.3 million "distressed" borrowers received HAMP trial modifications between April 2009 and July 2010. However, the report notes that there has been a "high" failure rate for moving borrowers from trial (temporary) modifications to permanent modifications. Only 398,000 people achieved permanent modifications through HAMP between April 2009 and July 2010.

THE HOUSING MARKET IS SLOW TO RECOVER. Figure 4.9 shows that the number of housing starts bottomed out in early 2009 at less than 400,000 units. Housing starts began to climb, reaching nearly 600,000 units by April 2010. However, the number dropped over the following two months. As of June 2010, housing starts totaled 450,000 units. Recent sales of existing single-family homes have also been up and down. (See Figure 4.5.) In late 2009 sales rebounded to near their pre-bust level, but then sagged. Sales of newly built single-family homes stabilized during 2009, showed a brief small upward swing in 2010, and then dropped again.

Home prices tracked by the FHFA have followed a similar pattern. (See Figure 4.7.) Prices made a modest recovery during 2009, but then declined during the first quarter of 2010. Table 4.3 provides a breakdown by state for five-year home appreciation rates as of March 31, 2010. The national average was −2.9%. Nevada, California, Michigan, Florida, and Arizona suffered the highest depreciation in home values. These five states had appreciation rates ranging from −44.7% to −20.5%, which were considerably worse than the national average. However, according to the FHFA, in *House Prices Fall in the First Quarter* (May 25, 2010, http://www.fhfa.gov/webfiles/15779/1q2010hpi .pdf), home prices in California actually appreciated by 2.9% during the one-year period ending March 31, 2010. Even though there was some improvement in that very large market, almost all the other states experienced home price depreciation during the same period. Arizona and Nevada, in particular, had one-year appreciation rates of −13% and −12.1%, respectively, as of March 31, 2010.

According to S&P, in "For the Past Year Home Prices Have Generally Moved Sideways According to the S&P/ Case-Shiller Home Price Indices," the 20-city composite S&P/Case-Shiller Home Price Index plunged below 140 in 2009 (from its record-high value above 200 in late 2006). The index showed only slight improvement throughout 2009 and was hovering just below 150 in early 2010.

Table 4.4 shows the vacancy rates for rental units and owned homes from the first quarter of 1996 to the first quarter of 2010. From the first quarter of 1996 to the third quarter of 2003 the rental vacancy rate remained below 10%. Beginning in the fourth quarter of 2003 the rate rose above 10% and thereafter fluctuated between 9.5% and 11.1%. In the first quarter of 2010 it was 10.6%. In contrast, the homeowner vacancy rate was less than 2% from the first quarter of 1996 to the third quarter of 2005, and then it began to rise. The homeowner vacancy rate peaked in 2008 at 2.9% in both the first and fourth quarters. The rate then declined somewhat, dropping to 2.6% in the first quarter of 2010.

Meanwhile, delinquency and foreclosure data show continuing problems in the housing market. The Mortgage Bankers Association (MBA) reports in "National Delinquency Survey Q1 2010: Data as of March 31, 2010" (May 2010, http://www.mortgagebankers.org/files/ Research/NDSQ110flyer.pdf) that 10.1% of all mortgage loans on one-to-four-unit residential properties were past

TABLE 4.3

Federal Housing Finance Agency (FHFA) house price appreciation, by state, 5-year period ending March 31, 2010

	Five-year house price appreciation rate
Nevada (NV)	−44.73
California (CA)	−31.40
Michigan (MI)	−27.16
Florida (FL)	−25.55
Arizona (AZ)	−20.54
Rhode Island (RI)	−17.68
New Hampshire (NH)	−13.43
Minnesota (MN)	−12.00
Massachusetts (MA)	−10.50
Georgia (GA)	−7.08
Ohio (OH)	−6.91
Maryland (MD)	−5.27
Connecticut (CT)	−4.36
Illinois (IL)	−3.21
USA	−2.85
New Jersey (NJ)	−2.02
Wisconsin (WI)	−1.27
Indiana (IN)	−0.51
Maine (ME)	0.33
Missouri (MO)	1.08
Nebraska (NE)	1.24
Hawaii (HI)	1.67
Virginia (VA)	2.11
Delaware (DE)	2.13
Arkansas (AR)	4.21
New York (NY)	4.56
Colorado (CO)	5.05
Idaho (ID)	6.13
Kansas (KS)	6.14
Kentucky (KY)	6.27
Tennessee (TN)	6.31
Iowa (IA)	6.88
Oregon (OR)	7.35
Mississippi (MS)	7.42
South Carolina (SC)	8.84
West Virginia (WV)	8.94
North Carolina (NC)	9.82
Pennsylvania (PA)	11.28
Alabama (AL)	11.63
Vermont (VT)	13.00
Washington (WA)	13.06
Utah (UT)	13.29
South Dakota (SD)	13.91
Alaska (AK)	13.93
Oklahoma (OK)	15.71
Texas (TX)	16.18
New Mexico (NM)	16.76
Louisiana (LA)	18.69
Montana (MT)	19.42
Wyoming (WY)	21.37
District of Columbia (DC)	22.46
North Dakota (ND)	24.82

SOURCE: Adapted from "House Price Appreciation by State," in *House Prices Fall in the First Quarter*, Federal Housing Finance Agency, May 25, 2010, http://www.fhfa.gov/webfiles/15779/1q2010hpi.pdf (accessed July 10, 2010)

due on payments at the end of the first quarter of 2010. The past due rate for subprime loans was 27.2%—the highest level on record. Just over 13% of FHA loans were past due at the end of the first quarter of 2010. The past due rates were better for VA loans (7.9%) and prime loans (7.3%). The performance of prime loans is of particular interest because these loans are made to people who are considered very creditworthy. The past due rate for prime loans was only 2% to 3% from 2000 to the second quarter of 2007.

However, between the third quarter of 2007 and the first quarter of 2010 the rate more than doubled, from 3.1% to 7.3%.

According to the MBA, 4.6% of all loans were in foreclosure at the end of the first quarter of 2010. Foreclosure rates by loan type were as follows:

- Subprime loans—15.4%
- FHA loans—3.9%
- Prime loans—3.4%
- VA loans—2.6%

The foreclosure rate for prime loans was less than 1% from 2000 to the fourth quarter of 2007.

RealtyTrac is an online marketplace for foreclosure properties. In the press release "1.65 Million Properties Receive Foreclosure Filings in First Half of 2010" (July 15, 2010, http://www.realtytrac.com/) the company reports that nearly 1.7 million U.S. properties were in the foreclosure process during the first half of 2010. This number was down 5% from the last six months of 2009, but up 8% compared with the first half of 2009.

MORTGAGE SUPPLY AND DEMAND. Throughout 2009 and into 2010 interest rates continued to be very low by historical standards. (See Figure 4.2.) Ordinarily, low interest rates spur people to buy new houses, refinance existing mortgage loans, or take out home equity loans. However, as of September 2010 a combination of factors dampened mortgage loan supply and demand. Many mortgage lenders suffered huge financial losses due to rising foreclosure and default rates. As a result, lenders severely tightened their underwriting process to help prevent future losses. In "Analysis: Banks May Not See Hoped-For Refinancing Boom," (September 22, 2010, http://www.cnbc.com/id/39313090), CNBC reports that banks "are extremely wary of taking on new mortgage risk. They are asking for extensive documentation, and turning down a higher percentage of loans."

Furthermore, some homeowners were "under water" in their existing mortgage loans, meaning that they owed more than their home was worth. These people found it extremely difficult, if not impossible, to refinance and take advantage of low interest rates. Analysts also believe that the nation's continuing high unemployment rate reduced mortgage demand. CNBC notes that people who were unemployed or underemployed (working for less money than they ordinarily would because of the poor job market) were not pursuing mortgage loans. The same goes for employed people who were fearful about losing their job.

CONSUMER CREDIT

The Federal Reserve defines the term *consumer credit* as credit extended to individuals that does not

TABLE 4.4

Vacancy rates for rental units and owned homes, first quarter 1996–first quarter 2010

	Rental vacancy rate				Homeowner vacancy rate			
Year	First quarter	Second quarter	Third quarter	Fourth quarter	First quarter	Second quarter	Third quarter	Fourth quarter
2010	10.6				2.6			
2009	10.1	10.6	11.1	10.7	2.7	2.5	2.6	2.7
2008	10.1	10.0	9.9	10.1	2.9	2.8	2.8	2.9
2007	10.1	9.5	9.8	9.6	2.8	2.6	2.7	2.8
2006	9.5	9.6	9.9	9.8	2.1	2.2	2.5	2.7
2005	10.1	9.8	9.9	9.6	1.8	1.8	1.9	2.0
2004	10.4	10.2	10.1	10.0	1.7	1.7	1.7	1.8
2003	9.4	9.6	9.9	10.2	1.7	1.7	1.9	1.8
2002*	9.1	8.4	9.0	9.3	1.7	1.7	1.7	1.7
2002	9.1	8.5	9.1	9.4	1.7	1.7	1.7	1.7
2001	8.2	8.3	8.4	8.8	1.5	1.8	1.9	1.8
2000	7.9	8.0	8.2	7.8	1.6	1.5	1.6	1.6
1999	8.2	8.1	8.2	7.9	1.8	1.6	1.6	1.6
1998	7.7	8.0	8.2	7.8	1.7	1.7	1.7	1.8
1997	7.5	7.9	7.9	7.7	1.7	1.6	1.5	1.7
1996	7.9	7.8	8.0	7.7	1.6	1.5	1.7	1.7

*Revised in 2002 to incorporate information collected in Census 2000.

SOURCE: "Table 1. Rental and Homeowner Vacancy Rates for the United States: 1996 to 2010 (in Percent)," in *Residential Vacancies and Homeownership in the First Quarter 2010*, U.S. Department of Commerce, U.S. Census Bureau, April 26, 2010, http://www.census.gov/hhes/www/housing/hvs/qtr110/files/q110press.pdf (accessed July 6, 2010)

include loans secured by real estate. In other words, mortgages are excluded from consumer credit.

Figure 4.12 shows that the amount of outstanding consumer credit grew relatively slowly during the 1970s and 1980s and then skyrocketed during the 1990s and the first half of the first decade of the 21st century. Consumer credit peaked at nearly $2.6 trillion in late 2008 and then declined. In June 2010 it totaled $2.4 trillion. As shown in Figure 4.12, consumer credit during the 1970s and 1980s consisted almost entirely of nonrevolving debt. Nonrevolving debt includes loans for vehicles, boats, vacations, and student loans. During the 1990s the breakdown began to change with revolving debt accounting for an ever-increasing proportion of consumer debt. Revolving debt consists almost entirely of credit card debt. Of the $2.4 trillion in consumer debt in June 2010, nonrevolving debt accounted for $1.6 trillion (66% of the total) and revolving debt accounted for $819.8 billion (34% of the total). (See Table 4.5.)

Table 4.5 also provides a detailed breakdown of outstanding consumer debt by creditor as of June 2010. Commercial banks held over $1.1 trillion (48% of the total), finance companies held $529 billion (22% of the total), and credit unions held $228.3 billion (9.5% of the total). The remaining balance was held by federal government loan programs, savings institutions, nonfinancial businesses, and pools of securitized assets (bundled debts sold as securities on the stock markets).

Interest Rates on Consumer Loans

Consumer loans are not secured by real estate. Because they have a higher risk of default, consumer loans generally have a higher interest rate than mortgage loans. Table 4.6 lists the average interest rates charged on various kinds of consumer loans from 2005 to June 2010. It should be noted that borrowers with good credit histories would have likely received lower interest rates than these averages and that borrowers with poor credit histories would have been charged higher rates.

New Car Loans

Loans for the purchase of new cars (and other types of vehicles) are secured by the vehicle being purchased. In other words, the creditor can repossess the vehicle if the loan is in default. As a result of this collateral, the interest rates on new vehicle loans tend to be lower than on other types of consumer loans.

In the second quarter of 2010 the average interest rate on a four-year loan from a commercial bank for the purchase of a new car was 6.3%. (See Table 4.6.) The interest rate charged by auto finance companies for a new car loan was lower, at 4.1%. According to the Federal Reserve, the interest rate charged by auto finance companies is based on the rates charged by the finance companies of the "three major U.S. automobile manufacturers." These companies are General Motors Corporation, Ford Motor Company, and Chrysler Group.

The typical loan period reported by the auto finance companies during the second quarter of 2010 was 62.9 months (just over five years). (Table 4.6.) This is much longer than the three-year loan period that was common for new car loans during the mid-1970s. Longer loan periods reflect longer car lifetimes. The average LTV ratio reported by the auto finance companies for the second

FIGURE 4.12

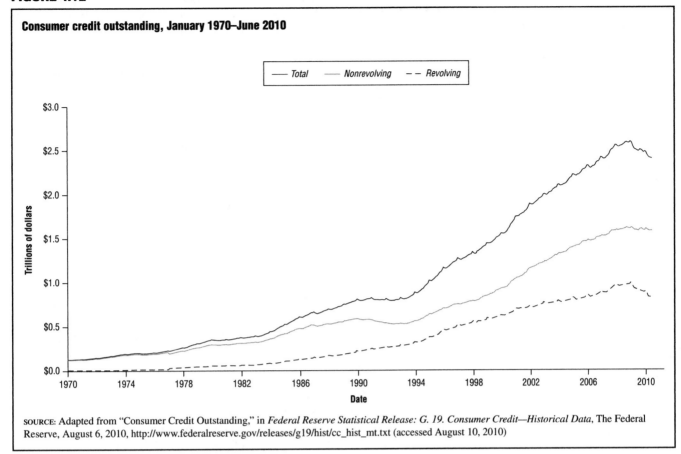

Consumer credit outstanding, January 1970–June 2010

SOURCE: Adapted from "Consumer Credit Outstanding," in *Federal Reserve Statistical Release: G. 19. Consumer Credit—Historical Data*, The Federal Reserve, August 6, 2010, http://www.federalreserve.gov/releases/g19/hist/cc_hist_mt.txt (accessed August 10, 2010)

quarter of 2010 was 87%. This means that the average new car buyer borrowed 87% of the value of the new car being purchased. The remaining 13% was a down payment paid by the buyer in cash or via trade-in of another vehicle. The average amount financed during the second quarter of 2010 for a new car purchase was $27,888.

Personal Loans

Personal loans are generally unsecured loans based on the creditworthiness of the borrower. A lack of collateral makes personal loans more risky from the loaners' viewpoint; thus, interest rates are higher for personal loans than for car loans. In the second quarter of 2010 the average interest rate charged by commercial banks for a 24-month personal loan was 11%. (See Table 4.6.) The rate varied from 11.1% to 12.4% between 2005 and 2009.

Credit Cards

Credit cards have the highest average interest rates of all types of consumer loans. Most credit card loans are unsecured and are granted based on the creditworthiness of the borrower. The higher risk factor for the creditor and the huge demand for credit cards contribute to the high interest rates that are charged.

The average interest rate charged by commercial banks on credit card loans was 14% in the second quarter

of 2010. (See Table 4.6.) The rate varied from 12.1% to 13.4% between 2005 and 2009. However, Liz Pulliam Weston explains in "The World's Worst Credit Cards" (MSN.com, June 4, 2009) that rates charged on credit cards issued by retail stores are typically more than 20%.

REVOLVING CREDIT AND MINIMUM PAYMENTS. Credit card debt is an example of revolving debt, a type of debt that is not amortized. There is no preset schedule of payments that will eliminate the debt within a particular time frame. The creditor grants the borrower a total amount of credit at a particular interest rate. Even though the interest rate may be fixed for a short introductory period, in general, credit card interest rates are variable.

Each month the borrower is billed for the outstanding balance on the credit card, which includes principal plus interest. The borrower can pay off the entire balance or a lesser amount down to the minimum payment required by the credit card issuer. Payment of any amount less than the minimum required will result in additional finance charges on the remaining balance. This is an example of compound interest (interest charged on an amount that already includes built-up interest charges).

When credit cards were first introduced, it was common for creditors to require 5% or more of the balance as a minimum monthly payment. Minimum payment

TABLE 4.5

Major holders and types of outstanding consumer credit, June 2010

[Billions of dollars]

	2010 June
Total	**2,401.0**
Major holders	
Total	**2,401.0**
Commercial banks	1,148.1
Finance companies	529.0
Credit unions	228.3
Federal government[a]	222.6
Savings institutions	74.2
Nonfinancial business	53.0
Pools of securitized assets[b, c]	145.8
Major types of credit	
Revolving	819.8
Commercial banks	622.1
Finance companies	66.2
Credit unions	34.9
Federal government[a]	n.a.
Savings institutions	39.5
Nonfinancial business	8.3
Pools of securitized assets[b, c]	48.9
Nonrevolving	1,581.1
Commercial banks	526.0
Finance companies	462.8
Credit unions	193.4
Federal government[a]	222.6
Savings institutions	34.7
Nonfinancial business	44.7
Pools of securitized assets[b, c]	96.9

Note: Data are preliminary.
[a]Data for the Student Loan Marketing Association (Sallie Mae) are included in the federal government sector until the completion of Sallie Mae's privatization in 2004:Q4 and in the finance company sector thereafter.
[b]Outstanding balances of pools upon which securities have been issued; these balances are no longer carried on the balance sheets of the loan originators.
[c]The shift of consumer credit from pools of securitized assets to other categories is largely due to financial institutions' implementation of the Financial Accounting Standards (FAS) 166/167 accounting rules.

SOURCE: Adapted from "Consumer Credit Outstanding," in *Federal Reserve Statistical Release: G.19. Consumer Credit, June 2010*, The Federal Reserve, August 6, 2010, http://www.federalreserve.gov/releases/g19/Current/g19.pdf (accessed August 10, 2010)

requirements were gradually reduced to 2% by most credit card issuers. Low required minimum payments, high interest rates, and the effect of compounding interest make it difficult for many consumers to pay off credit card debt. The Bankruptcy Abuse Prevention and Consumer Protection Act of 2005 requires creditors to tell borrowers how long it will take to pay off their credit card debt if only minimum payments are made. The Credit CARD Act of 2009 puts limits on when credit card issuers can raise interest rates and bans "unfair or deceptive" billing procedures.

Student Loans

Student loans are loans obtained to pay for educational expenses, primarily at the college level. Even though they are technically consumer loans, student loans are not for consumption purposes. They fund the advancement of skill and knowledge in individuals, likely increasing the potential for higher future income. Thus, student loans are considered a type of "human investment."

Because the federal government encourages secondary education, it plays a major role in ensuring that student loans are available. There are three major types of student loans:

- Low-interest loans provided by the government through the financial aid departments of participating schools; these loans are available to needy students through the Perkins Loan Program

- Loans provided directly to students by the government through the William D. Ford Federal Direct Loan Program

- Loans guaranteed by the federal government but provided to students by private lenders

The National Center for Education Statistics indicates in "Fast Facts" (2010, http://nces.ed.gov/fastfacts/display .asp?id=31) that more than one-third (34.7%) of all undergraduates received federal student loans for the 2007–08 academic school year. The average loan amount was $5,100.

In "William D. Ford Federal Direct Loan Program" (December 14, 2009, http://www2.ed.gov/programs/wdffdl/ funding.html), the U.S. Department of Education reports that the loan volume of the William D. Ford Federal Direct Loan Program totaled an estimated $38.3 billion in fiscal year 2009.

PERSONAL BANKRUPTCIES

The word *bankrupt* is derived from the Italian phrase *banca rotta*, which means "bench broken," referring to the benches or tables that were used by merchants in outdoor markets in 16th-century Italy. Bankruptcy is a state of financial ruin. Under U.S. law people with more debts than they can reasonably hope to repay can file for personal bankruptcy. This results in a legally binding agreement between debtors and the federal government worked out in a federal bankruptcy court. The agreement calls for the debtors to pay as much as they can with whatever assets they have, and after a predetermined amount of time— usually a number of years—the debtors begin again with new credit. Depending on state law, certain belongings may be kept through the bankruptcy.

The American Bankruptcy Institute explains in "General Concepts" (2010, http://consumer.abiworld.org/?q =node/21) that an official declaration of bankruptcy benefits individuals in the short term because it puts a stop to all collection efforts by creditors. An "automatic stay" goes into effect that prevents creditors from calling, writing, or suing debtors covered by a bankruptcy plan.

Figure 4.13 shows the number of nonbusiness (personal) bankruptcy cases per 12-month period ending

TABLE 4.6

Terms of credit at commercial banks and finance companies, 2005–June 2010

Percent except as noted: not seasonally adjusted

Institution, terms, and type of loan	2005	2006	2007	2008	2009	2010 Q1[a]	Q2[b]	April[a]	May[a]	June[b]
Commercial banks										
Interest rates										
48-mo. new car	7.07	7.72	7.77	7.02	6.72	6.45	6.26	n.a.	6.26	n.a.
24-mo. personal	12.06	12.41	12.38	11.37	11.10	10.83	11.00	n.a.	11.00	n.a.
Credit card plan										
All accounts	12.51	13.21	13.30	12.08	13.40	14.26	14.04	n.a.	14.04	n.a.
Accounts assessed interest	14.55	14.73	14.68	13.57	14.31	14.67	14.48	n.a.	14.48	n.a.
New car loans at auto finance companies										
Interest rates	6.02	4.99	4.87	5.52	3.82	4.31	4.09	4.13	4.13	4.02
Maturity (months)	60.0	63.0	62.0	63.4	62.0	62.9	62.9	62.8	62.9	63.1
Loan-to-value ratio	88	94	95	91	90	89	87	88	87	87
Amount financed (dollars)	24,133	26,620	28,287	26,178	28,272	28,444	27,888	27,797	27,886	27,980

Notes: Interest rates are annual percentage rates (APR) as specified by the Federal Reserve's Regulation Z. Interest rates for new-car loans and personal loans at commercial banks are simple unweighted averages of each bank's most common rate charged during the first calendar week of the middle month of each quarter. For credit card accounts, the rate for all accounts is the stated APR averaged across all credit card accounts at all reporting banks. The rate for accounts assessed interest is the annualized ratio of total finance charges at all reporting banks to the total average daily balances against which the finance charges were assessed (excludes accounts for which no finance charges were assessed). Finance company data are from the subsidiaries of the three major U.S. automobile manufacturers and are volume-weighted averages covering all loans of each type purchased during the month.

n.a. = Not available.

[a]Revised.

[b]Preliminary.

SOURCE: "Terms of Credit at Commercial Banks and Finance Companies," in *Federal Reserve Statistical Release: G.19. Consumer Credit, June 2010*, The Federal Reserve, August 6, 2010, http://www.federalreserve.gov/releases/g19/Current/g19.pdf (accessed August 10, 2010)

March 31 of each year from 2001 to 2010. For the 12-month period ending March 31, 2010, there were 1.5 million personal bankruptcy filings. This value was up substantially from the previous three years, but down from levels reported from 2003 to 2006.

There are three types (or chapters) of personal bankruptcy under which individuals may file:

- Chapter 7—a liquidation plan is developed in which the debtor turns over certain assets that are sold and used to pay creditors.

- Chapter 13—a payment plan is developed under which debtors receiving regular income repay their creditors. Liquidation of assets is not required in most cases.

- Chapter 11—while similar to Chapter 13, Chapter 11 is reserved for individuals with substantial debts and assets.

According to the U.S. Courts (2010, http://www.uscourts.gov/uscourts/Statistics/BankruptcyStatistics/BankruptcyFilings/2010/0310_f2.pdf), nearly 1.1 million personal bankruptcy cases were filed under Chapter 7 during the 12-month period ending March 31, 2010. This represented about 72% of the total 1.5 million personal bankruptcy filings. Another 411,000 (28%) filings were under Chapter 13 and the remaining 1,700 (0.1%) were under Chapter 11.

Evolving Bankruptcy Law

The first federal bankruptcy laws were written in the early 1800s but were considered emergency measures to remain in effect for only short periods of time. The first comprehensive federal legislation was the National Bankruptcy Act of 1898, which was extensively amended during the 1930s and later replaced by the Bankruptcy Reform Act of 1978. This law was substantially amended by the Bankruptcy Reform Act of 1994. Major reforms in the law were enacted when the Bankruptcy Abuse Prevention and Consumer Protection Act (BAPCPA) of 2005 went into effect.

Because of different state laws regulating which assets and belongings a person could keep after a Chapter 7 filing, regulators and creditors believed that some people were using bankruptcy as a way to keep possessions without having to pay for them. The BAPCPA instituted measures that were intended to eliminate abuses and loopholes and increased the amount of paperwork and fees required for most filers.

Opponents of the new bill argued that it was designed to make more money for credit card companies and lenders and that it would be detrimental to ordinary people who choose bankruptcy as a last resort.

PREYING ON DEBTORS

Consumer demand for credit has led to enormous growth in businesses engaged in making loans, counseling debtors, and arranging debt management plans. Even though these are legitimate enterprises, some businesses have aroused consumer ire and even run afoul of the law with practices that are considered abusive toward debtors.

FIGURE 4.13

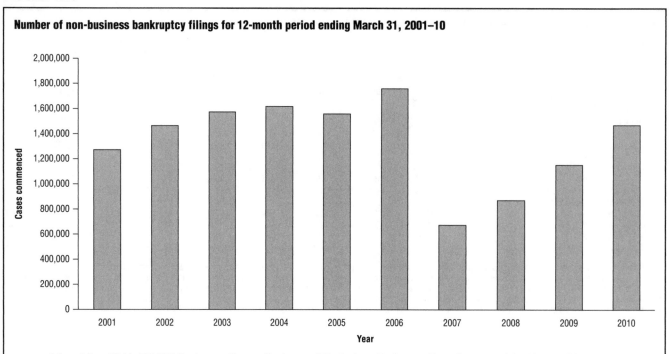

Number of non-business bankruptcy filings for 12-month period ending March 31, 2001–10

SOURCE: Adapted from "Table F-2. U.S. Bankruptcy Courts—Business and Nonbusiness Bankruptcy Cases Commenced, by Chapter of the Bankruptcy Code," in *Bankruptcy Statistics: Filings: 12 Month Period Ending March*, The U.S. Courts, 2010, http://www.uscourts.gov/uscourts/Statistics/BankruptcyStatistics/BankruptcyFilings/1986-2003_Filings_Ending_March.pdf (accessed July 7, 2010)

Predatory Lending?

Most large creditors, such as banks and finance companies, only make consumer loans to applicants who meet stringent requirements for creditworthiness, excluding people with low incomes and poor credit histories. This has led to the growth of subprime lenders—businesses that make consumer loans to customers who are considered undesirable by traditional lenders. Because they are assuming higher risk, subprime lenders charge their customers higher interest rates and fees to loan money to them. Some consumers and legislators have accused these businesses of charging excessive fees and interest rates on consumer loans—a practice called predatory lending. Predatory lenders allegedly victimize poor people by imposing loan terms that are designed to maximize creditor profits and make it difficult for debtors to pay off their debt.

Usury is a word that centuries ago meant "interest" or "the charging of interest." In modern terminology it has come to mean the charging of excessive interest. Even though there are state usury laws against the charging of excessive interest, this issue has not been addressed at the federal level. In fact, most banks are allowed to ignore state usury laws. Other lenders can avoid usury laws through a variety of means, such as by charging large loan fees and forcing borrowers to take out expensive insurance policies.

Two particular types of consumer loans are often called predatory: payday loans and refund anticipation loans (RALs). Borrowers obtain payday loans from establishments that agree to accept and hold personal checks until the borrower receives a paycheck. RALs are also short-term loans that must be paid back within two weeks. Creditors offer RALs to people expecting refunds when their income taxes are filed. Critics complain the loans are targeted at uneducated minority populations who are desperate for quick cash.

Credit Counseling and Debt Management Services

The explosive growth in consumer debt has resulted in many organizations offering credit counseling and debt management services to debtors in financial difficulties. Consumer activists maintain that many of these organizations charge debtors large fees in return for little to no aid. The Permanent Subcommittee on Investigations describes the history of the industry in *Profiteering in a Non-profit Industry: Abusive Practices in Credit Counseling* (April 13, 2005, http://bulk.resource.org/gpo.gov/reports/109/sr055.109.pdf).

The subcommittee explains that credit counseling as an industry began during the 1960s with the help of large creditors, such as banks, that were concerned about rising bankruptcy rates. The early credit counseling agencies (CCAs) were locally based nonprofit organizations with trained counselors who met in person with debtors and provided advice on budgeting and paying off debt. CCAs could also arrange debt management plans for debtors in which creditors agreed to charge lower monthly minimum payments, lower interest rates, and waive outstanding late fees. The CCAs collected the new monthly payments from the debtors and paid the creditors. Creditors supported the CCAs with contributions and participated in debt management plans in hopes that the debtors would avoid filing for bankruptcy. Some CCAs also charged small fees to the debtor for administrative costs. These reputable CCAs were members of the National Foundation for Credit Counseling, an organization known for its focus on standards and ethics.

According to the subcommittee, several of the new CCAs that have entered the industry since the 1990s operate in a much different way. Most are Internet-based, communicate with consumers solely by phone, and focus exclusively on enrolling debtors in debt management plans for large fees. Even though they are officially non-profit organizations, many of these new CCAs have ties to for-profit businesses. The subcommittee concludes that these CCAs engage in deceptive practices and provide no actual counseling services to debtors.

The subcommittee's investigation coincided with a federal crackdown on CCAs. The Internal Revenue Service responded by revoking the tax-exempt status of CCAs that were found to be funneling money to for-profit businesses.

IDENTITY THEFT

Modern technology and compilation of personal and financial information in computer databases has made obtaining loans faster and easier than in the past. No longer are face-to-face meetings required between creditors and borrowers. Loans can be secured through the mail, over the phone, and via the Internet. However, this convenience has a price. It allows unscrupulous people to pretend to be someone else by stealing the identity of people with good credit histories and using it for criminal purposes.

According to the Federal Trade Commission (FTC), in *Consumer Sentinel Network Data Book, for January–December 2009* (February 2010, http://www.ftc.gov/sen tinel/reports/sentinel-annual-reports/sentinel-cy2009.pdf), the number of identity theft complaints reported to the FTC skyrocketed from 31,140 in 2000 to 278,078 in 2009. The FTC notes that the most common form of reported identity theft in 2009 was credit card fraud. Seventeen percent of the complaints filed were associated with credit card fraud. Other significant forms of identity theft were government documents/benefits fraud (16%), phone or utilities fraud (15%), and employment fraud (13%). The FTC reports that Florida had the highest per capita rate for identity theft complaints in 2009, followed by Arizona and Texas.

CHAPTER 5
THE AMERICAN WORKER

When we are all in the business working together, we all ought to have some share in the profits—by way of a good wage, or salary, or added compensation.

—Henry Ford, *My Life and Work* (1922)

The American workforce plays a major role in the U.S. economy. Workers produce goods and provide services, the consumption of which drives the nation's gross domestic product (the total market value of final goods and services produced within an economy in a given year) growth. However, there is an age-old struggle between employers and employees over compensation. Businesses must compensate workers with pay and benefits that are high enough to attract and keep motivated employees, but not so high as to damage the profitability and growth of the business itself. On a macroeconomic scale, gainful employment of large numbers of workers is important to the overall health of the U.S. economy. As noted in Chapter 2, the so-called great recession (December 2007 to June 2009) led to a huge increase in the nation's unemployment rate. High unemployment lingered even after the recession ended and still plagued the country as of September 2010. Unemployment was one of the most devastating effects of the recession on the economic well-being of the American people.

THE EMPLOYMENT SITUATION

The Bureau of Labor Statistics (BLS; August 2010, http://www.bls.gov/ces/) conducts a monthly survey of approximately 140,000 nonfarm businesses and government agencies with around 410,000 worksites around the country. Detailed information on employment, work hours, and payroll are obtained as part of the Current Employment Statistics program. These data are published monthly by the BLS in the news release "The Employment Situation." Also included are data collected by the U.S. Census Bureau from approximately 50,000 households as part of the Current Population Survey.

The BLS defines the civilian labor force as including all civilian noninstitutionalized people (i.e., people not in the military and not in institutions, such as prisons or long-term care facilities) aged 16 years and older who have a job or are actively looking for a job. People are considered to be employed during a given week if they meet any of the following criteria:

- They performed any work that week for pay or profit

- They worked without pay for at least 15 hours that week in a family-operated enterprise

- They had a job but could not work that week due to illness, vacation, personal obligations, leave of absence, bad weather, or labor disputes

People considered not to be in the labor force are those who do not have a job and are not looking for a job. This category includes many students, retirees, stay-at-home parents, the mentally and physically challenged, and people in prison and other institutions, as well as those who are not employed but have become discouraged from looking for work. The unemployed are counted as those who do not have a job but have actively looked for a job during the previous four weeks and are available for work. Also included are people who did not work during a given week due to temporary layoffs.

Employment and Unemployment

The BLS reports in "The Employment Situation—June 2010" (July 2, 2010, http://www.bls.gov/news.release/archives/empsit_07022010.pdf) that the civilian labor force consisted of 153.7 million people in June 2010. Another 83.9 million people were considered to not be in the labor force. The BLS estimates that this number included 1.2 million "discouraged workers."

Figure 5.1 shows monthly changes in nonfarm payroll employment from June 2008 to June 2010. In late 2008 and early 2009 nonfarm payrolls were losing nearly 800,000

FIGURE 5.1

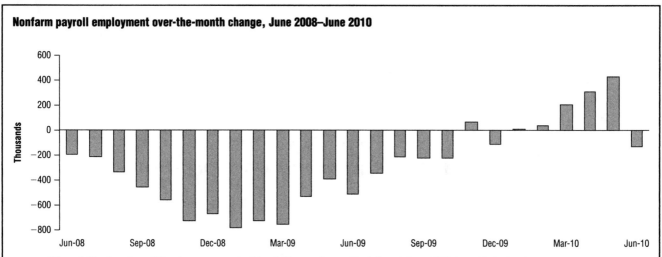

Nonfarm payroll employment over-the-month change, June 2008–June 2010

SOURCE: "Chart 2. Nonfarm Payroll Employment over-the-Month Change, Seasonally Adjusted, June 2008–June 2010," in *The Employment Situation—June 2010*, U.S. Department of Labor, Bureau of Labor Statistics, July 2, 2010, http://www.bls.gov/news.release/archives/empsit_07022010.pdf (accessed July 7, 2010)

FIGURE 5.2

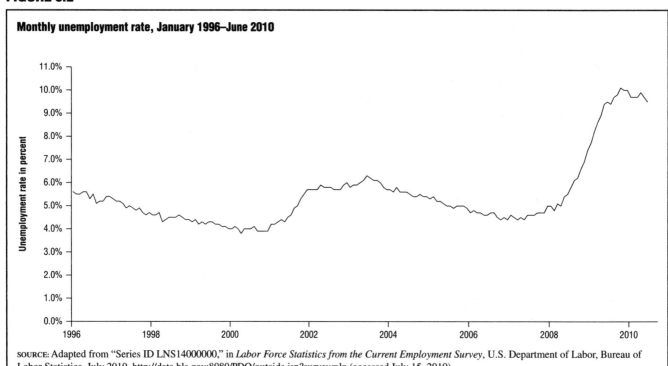

Monthly unemployment rate, January 1996–June 2010

SOURCE: Adapted from "Series ID LNS14000000," in *Labor Force Statistics from the Current Employment Survey*, U.S. Department of Labor, Bureau of Labor Statistics, July 2010, http://data.bls.gov:8080/PDQ/outside.jsp?survey=ln (accessed July 15, 2010)

workers per month. The losses continued through late 2009, before turning around. By mid-2010 payrolls were adding a few hundred thousand workers per month. However, the recovery reversed itself in June 2010, when an estimated 125,000 payroll jobs were lost. (See Table 2.2 in Chapter 2.)

According to the BLS, the breakdown for the civilian labor force in June 2010 was 139.1 million employed and 14.6 million unemployed, giving an overall unemployment rate of 9.5%. This rate was down slightly from October

2009, when it peaked at 10.1%. (See Figure 5.2.) However, the unemployment rate in June 2010 was high by historical standards. Rates above 9% have not been seen since the 1930s, at the height of the Great Depression, and the early 1980s. (See Figure 2.6 in Chapter 2.)

The unemployment rate in June 2010 varied widely according to certain demographic factors. Teenagers aged 16 to 19 years were unemployed at a rate of 25.7%. (See Figure 5.3.) Racial and ethnic differences were also sig-

FIGURE 5.3

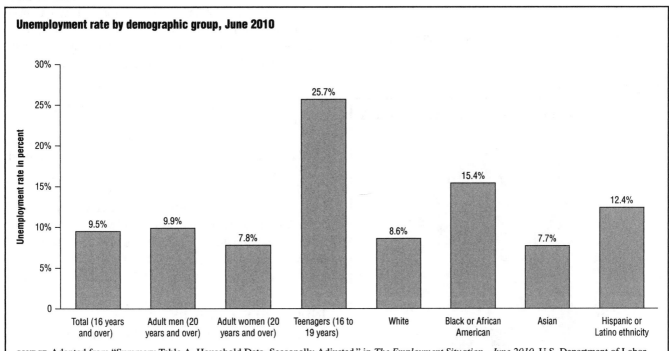

Unemployment rate by demographic group, June 2010

SOURCE: Adapted from "Summary Table A. Household Data, Seasonally Adjusted," in *The Employment Situation—June 2010*, U.S. Department of Labor, Bureau of Labor Statistics, July 2, 2010, http://www.bls.gov/news.release/archives/empsit_07022010.pdf (accessed July 7, 2010)

FIGURE 5.4

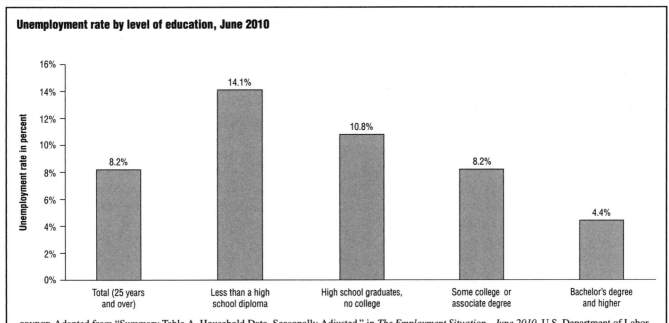

Unemployment rate by level of education, June 2010

SOURCE: Adapted from "Summary Table A. Household Data, Seasonally Adjusted," in *The Employment Situation—June 2010*, U.S. Department of Labor, Bureau of Labor Statistics, July 2, 2010, http://www.bls.gov/news.release/archives/empsit_07022010.pdf (accessed July 7, 2010)

nificant; African-American workers had an unemployment rate of 15.4% and Hispanic or Latino workers had a rate of 12.4%. These values were higher than the 8.6% unemployment rate reported for white workers. However, the rate for Asian-American workers was only 7.7%. There was a small difference in rates by sex among adults; for adult men the rate was 9.9% and for adult women it was 7.8%.

Educational attainment played a major role in unemployment rates in June 2010. (See Figure 5.4.) The rate for all workers aged 25 years and older was 8.2%. Among those with less than a high school diploma the rate was much higher, at 14.1%. High school graduates with no college had an unemployment rate of 10.8%. Workers who had taken some college courses or who had earned an associate degree had a rate of 8.2%. Those with a bachelor's degree or higher had the lowest unemployment rate, at 4.4%.

Figure 5.5 provides a breakdown on the duration of unemployment as of June 2010. Nearly half (45%) of the

unemployed had been unemployed for 27 weeks or more (i.e., roughly six months or more). Another 15% had been unemployed for 15 to 26 weeks, and 21% had been unemployed for five to 14 weeks. The remaining 19% of the unemployed had been unemployed for less than five weeks.

The Gallup Organization conducts regular polls that question Americans about their perceptions of the job situation. In *Americans Slightly Less Negative about Finding Quality Jobs* (June 29, 2010, http://www.gallup.com/poll/141071/Americans-Slightly-Less-Negative-About-Finding-Quality-Jobs.aspx), Dennis Jacobe of the Gallup Organization finds that in June 2010, 85% of those asked thought it was a "bad time" to find a quality job. Only 12% said it was a "good time" to find a quality job. (See Figure 5.6.) This number was down significantly from early 2007, when nearly half of those asked said it was a "good time" to find a quality job.

INDUSTRIES AND JOBS

The federal government broadly characterizes jobs as being in the goods-providing or service-providing categories. Goods-providing industries include businesses engaged in manufacturing, construction, mining, and natural resources. Service-providing industries include businesses whose main function is to provide a professional or trade service, rather than a product. Service-providing industries are extremely diverse and include businesses involved in retail and whole-

FIGURE 5.5

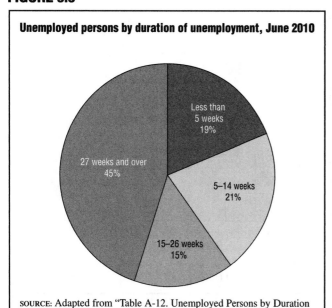

Unemployed persons by duration of unemployment, June 2010

SOURCE: Adapted from "Table A-12. Unemployed Persons by Duration of Unemployment," in *The Employment Situation—June 2010*, U.S. Department of Labor, Bureau of Labor Statistics, July 2, 2010, http://www.bls.gov/news.release/archives/empsit_07022010.pdf (accessed July 7, 2010)

FIGURE 5.6

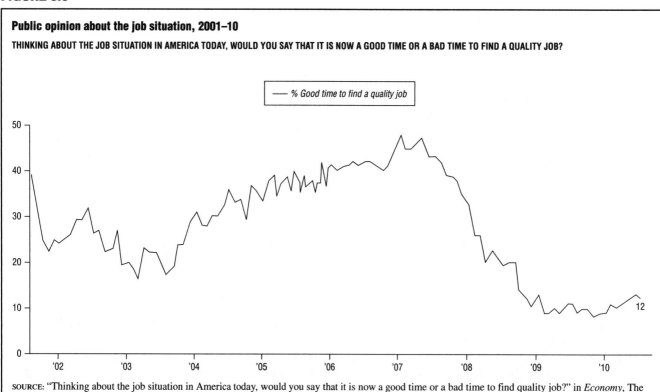

Public opinion about the job situation, 2001–10

THINKING ABOUT THE JOB SITUATION IN AMERICA TODAY, WOULD YOU SAY THAT IT IS NOW A GOOD TIME OR A BAD TIME TO FIND A QUALITY JOB?

— % Good time to find a quality job

SOURCE: "Thinking about the job situation in America today, would you say that it is now a good time or a bad time to find quality job?" in *Economy*, The Gallup Organization, 2010, http://www.gallup.com/poll/1609/Economy.aspx#1 (accessed August 5, 2010). Copyright © 2010 by The Gallup Organization. Reproduced by permission of The Gallup Organization.

The American Economy

FIGURE 5.7

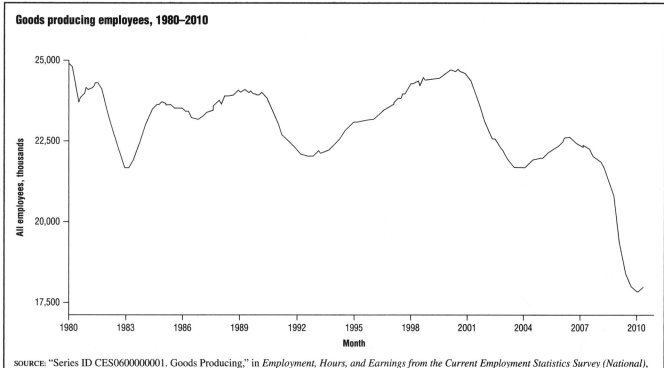

Goods producing employees, 1980–2010

SOURCE: "Series ID CES0600000001. Goods Producing," in *Employment, Hours, and Earnings from the Current Employment Statistics Survey (National)*, U.S. Department of Labor, Bureau of Labor Statistics, July 7, 2010, http://data.bls.gov/cgi-bin/surveymost?ce (accessed July 7, 2010)

sale trade, professional and business services, education and health services, leisure and hospitality, government, and many other services.

Since the mid-20th century the service-providing industries have grown to dominate the U.S. economy. The BLS (August 2010, ftp://ftp.bls.gov/pub/suppl/empsit.ceseeb1.txt) reports that in 1960 goods-producing industries employed 19.2 million people. This value rose and fell over time, and was near 18 million in 2010. (See Figure 5.7.) By comparison, the number of people employed in service-providing industries skyrocketed from 35.1 million in 1960 to approximately 108 million in 2010. Figure 5.8 shows how employment in service-providing industries varied from 1980 to early 2010. The number of employees peaked between 2007 and 2008 in excess of 115 million and then declined as the great recession unfolded.

In June 2010 the number of private service-providing employees on nonfarm payrolls was 89.7 million (See Table 5.1.) The remainder of the service-providing employees (nearly 22.8 million) were on government payrolls. As shown in Figure 5.9, private service-providing companies employed around 50 million people in 1980. By 2008 that number was closer to 95 million. Throughout 2009 employment in these companies declined, dropping below 90 million. In early 2010 employment in this industry began to increase again.

Industry Supersectors

The government categorizes jobs by using the North American Industry Classification System (NAICS). Adopted in 1997, the NAICS was devised by the U.S. Economic Classification Policy Committee in conjunction with Statistics Canada and the Instituto Nacional de Estadística, Geografia e Informática of Mexico and is the standard classification system for businesses throughout North America. There are 11 major so-called supersectors tracked by the BLS that encompass all public and private jobs within the United States and businesses owned by U.S.-based companies operating in other countries.

The 11 supersectors are:

• Construction

• Education and health services

• Financial activities

• Government

• Information

• Leisure and hospitality

• Manufacturing

• Natural resources and mining

• Other services

• Professional and business services

• Trade, transportation, and utilities

Virtually every job can be placed into one of these categories. It should be noted that industry tracking focuses on the core mission of the business rather than on the

FIGURE 5.8

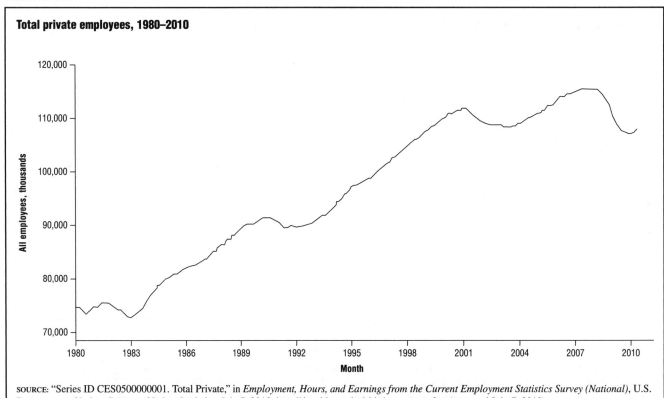

Total private employees, 1980–2010

SOURCE: "Series ID CES0500000001. Total Private," in *Employment, Hours, and Earnings from the Current Employment Statistics Survey (National)*, U.S. Department of Labor, Bureau of Labor Statistics, July 7, 2010, http://data.bls.gov/cgi-bin/surveymost?ce (accessed July 7, 2010)

particular tasks performed by employees. For example, jobs in public schools and government-owned hospitals are considered part of the government supersector rather than part of the education and health services supersector.

Table 5.1 itemizes the number of employees by industry sector as of June 2010. Approximately 130.5 million workers were on nonfarm payrolls that month. The vast majority (107.7 million employees) were in the private (nongovernmental) sector. As shown in Figure 5.10, the number of employees on nonfarm payrolls has grown dramatically since the 1980s. The value peaked between 2007 and 2008 at about 137 million employees, and then declined as the great recession progressed. The number began to grow again in early 2010. A similar pattern is seen in Figure 5.8 for employees in the private sector. Their number peaked between 2007 and 2008 at around 115 million and then decreased as the economy contracted. Employment in the private sector was slowly recovering in early 2010.

Table 5.2 shows the unemployment rates in June 2010 for each supersector and for agricultural and self-employed workers. The highest rate was 20.1% for construction workers. As described in Chapter 4, the housing industry underwent a sharp downturn in the second half of the first decade of the 21st century, leaving millions of construction workers unemployed. Other industries with relatively high unemployment rates in June 2010 were leisure and hospitality (12.3%), agriculture (11.7%), manufacturing of durable goods (10.4%), and professional and business services (10.3%). The workers with the lowest unemployment rates were those in the government supersector (4.4%), self-employed and unpaid family workers (5%), and workers in education and health services (6.2%), financial activities (6.9%), and transportation and utilities (7.2%).

General industry information in the following sections was obtained from the BLS sources *Career Guide to Industries, 2010–11 Edition* (2010, http://www.bls.gov/oco/cg/home.htm) and *Industries at a Glance* (2010, http://stats.bls.gov/iag/iaghome.htm), which profiles U.S. businesses.

CONSTRUCTION. The construction supersector includes all businesses that contribute to the development of land, roads, utilities, buildings and houses, and structures such as bridges and dams. Included are firms that build new projects and those that provide maintenance, repairs, and alterations to existing structures. For the most part, such enterprises are managed from a central location with work performed elsewhere. Construction employment often fluctuates throughout the year, especially in areas of the country that experience severe winter weather.

Figure 4.10 in Chapter 4 shows employment in the construction industry from 1980 to 2010. Employment peaked at around 7.7 million workers between 2006 and 2007 and then plummeted due to the housing market bust. In June 2010 the industry employed nearly 5.6 million workers. As noted

TABLE 5.1

Employees on nonfarm payrolls by job sector, June 2010

[In thousands]

Industry	Seasonally adjusted June 2010*
Total nonfarm	130,470
Total private	107,700
Goods-producing	17,977
Mining and logging	725
Logging	48.0
Mining	676.5
Construction	5,582
Manufacturing	11,670
Durable goods	7,166
Nondurable goods	4,504
Private service-providing	89,723
Trade, transportation, and utilities	24,744
Wholesale trade	5,574.9
Retail trade	14,435.8
Transportation and warehousing	4,177.4
Utilities	556.1
Information	2,715
Financial activities	7,584
Professional and business services	16,709
Education and health services	19,519
Educational services	3,142.7
Health care and social assistance	16,376.6
Leisure and hospitality	13,114
Arts, entertainment, and recreation	1,923.6
Accommodation and food services	11,190.0
Other services	5,338
Government	22,770
Federal	3,208.0
State government	5,159.0
Local government	14,403.0

*Preliminary

SOURCE: Adapted from "Table B-1. Employees on Nonfarm Payrolls by Industry Sector and Selected Industry Detail," in *The Employment Situation—June 2010*, U.S. Department of Labor, Bureau of Labor Statistics, July 2, 2010, http://www.bls.gov/news.release/archives/empsit_07022010.pdf (accessed July 7, 2010)

earlier, the unemployment rate that month for construction workers was 20.1%. (See Table 5.2.) This rate was down from its peak of 27.1% in February 2010, but was still high by historical standards. The BLS (September 14, 2010, http://data.bls.gov/PDQ/servlet/SurveyOutputServlet?series_id=LNU 04032231&data_tool=XGtable) reports that between 2000 and 2007 the average annual unemployment rate in the construction industry was between 6.2% and 9.3%. The rate crept above 10% in 2008 and then mushroomed to 19% in 2009.

Nevertheless, the BLS predicts modest growth for this supersector through 2018. Employment is projected to increase by 1.7% annually. (See Table 5.3.) This is slightly higher than the 1% growth rate expected for the nonfarm industry overall.

EDUCATION AND HEALTH SERVICES. The education and health services supersector includes all instructional and training facilities, including private schools and universities, that are not funded by the government. Nongovernmental organizations that provide child day care,

medical care, and social assistance are also included. Businesses of this type that are government owned (e.g., public schools and hospitals) are considered part of the government supersector.

In June 2010 employment in this supersector was 19.5 million. (See Table 5.1.) The BLS provides in "Employment Situation—June 2010" a breakdown by specific category:

- Health care—13.7 million workers
- Educational services—3.1 million workers
- Social assistance (including child day care)—2.6 million workers

The unemployment rate for this supersector was 6.2% in June 2010. (See Table 5.2.) This value was up substantially from the early part of the decade. According to the BLS (September 14, 2010, http://data.bls.gov/PDQ/servlet/SurveyOutputServlet?series_id=LNU04032240&data_tool=XGtable), between 2000 and 2008 the average annual unemployment rate varied between 2.5% and 3.6%. In 2009 the rate increased to 5.3%.

The BLS projects good employment growth in this supersector through 2018. Employment in educational services is expected to grow at an average annual rate of 2.4% (the highest of any industry sector). (See Table 5.3.) Likewise, health care and social assistance employment is projected to increase by 2.3% annually through 2018.

FINANCIAL ACTIVITIES. The financial activities supersector includes the banking, insurance, and real estate industries, including businesses that, according to the BLS in *Industries at a Glance* (September 9, 2010, http://stats.bls.gov/iag/tgs/iag52.htm), facilitate "transactions involving the creation, liquidation, or change in ownership of financial assets." The real estate sector includes businesses that manage properties for others, appraise real estate, and facilitate property buying, selling, and leasing.

As shown in Table 5.1, the financial activities supersector employed nearly 7.6 million workers in June 2010. In "Employment Situation—June 2010," the BLS notes that 5.6 million of these employees worked in finance and insurance. The remaining 1.9 million were in real estate or rental and leasing services.

The unemployment rate for this supersector was 6.9% in June 2010. (See Table 5.2.) According to the BLS (September 14, 2010, http://data.bls.gov/PDQ/servlet/SurveyOutput Servlet?series_id=LNU04032238&data_tool=XGtable), from 2000 to 2007 the annual unemployment rate for the financial activities supersector was very low, averaging between 2.4% and 3.6%. The housing market boom buoyed the economic performance of the financial industry. However, the resulting bust and associated credit crisis brought instability to many financial institutions. In 2008 the unemployment rate in this supersector began

FIGURE 5.9

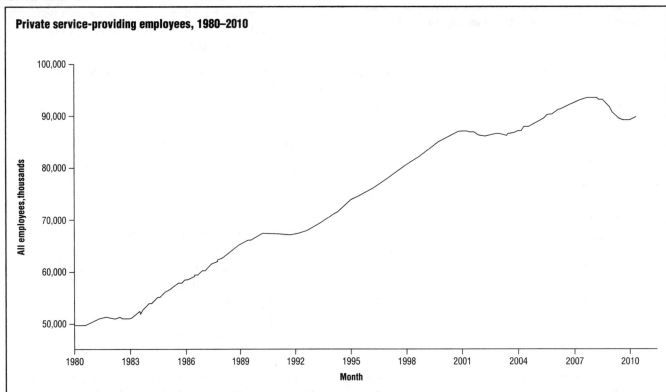

Private service-providing employees, 1980–2010

SOURCE: "Series ID CES0800000001. Private Service-Providing," in *Employment, Hours, and Earnings from the Current Employment Statistics Survey (National)*, U.S. Department of Labor, Bureau of Labor Statistics, July 7, 2010, http://data.bls.gov/cgi-bin/surveymost?ce (accessed July 7, 2010)

FIGURE 5.10

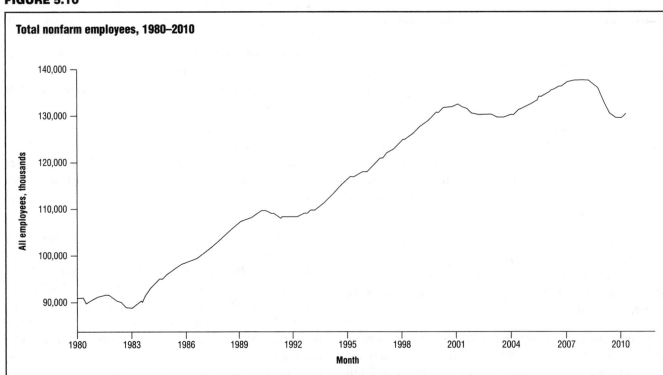

Total nonfarm employees, 1980–2010

SOURCE: "Series ID CES0000000001. Total Nonfarm," in *Employment, Hours, and Earnings from the Current Employment Statistics Survey (National)*, U.S. Department of Labor, Bureau of Labor Statistics, July 7, 2010, http://data.bls.gov/cgi-bin/surveymost?ce (accessed July 7, 2010)

TABLE 5.2

Unemployment rates by industry and class of worker, June 2010

Industry and class of worker	Unemployment rates June 2010
Total, 16 years and over*	9.6
Nonagricultural private wage and salary	
workers	9.7
Mining, quarrying, and oil and gas extraction	8.2
Construction	20.1
Manufacturing	9.9
Durable goods	10.4
Nondurable goods	9.1
Wholesale and retail trade	9.3
Transportation and utilities	7.2
Information	8.8
Financial activities	6.9
Professional and business services	10.3
Education and health services	6.2
Leisure and hospitality	12.3
Other services	8.5
Agriculture and related private wage and	
salary workers	11.7
Government workers	4.4
Self-employed and unpaid family workers	5.0

Note: Updated population controls are introduced annually with the release of January data.
*Persons with no previous work experience and persons whose last job was in the U.S. Armed Forces are included in the unemployed total.

SOURCE: Adapted from "Table A-14. Unemployed Persons by Industry and Class of Worker, Not Seasonally Adjusted," in *The Employment Situation— June 2010*, U.S. Department of Labor, Bureau of Labor Statistics, July 2, 2010, http://www.bls.gov/news.release/archives/empsit_07022010.pdf (accessed July 7, 2010)

increasing. In late 2009 and early 2010 the monthly rate was regularly above 7%.

The BLS predicts that employment in the financial activities supersector will increase on average by 0.7% annually through 2018. (See Table 5.3.) This is less than the 1% growth rate expected for the nonfarm industry overall.

GOVERNMENT. The government supersector encompasses all local, state, and federal government agencies as well as public schools and public hospitals. It also includes law enforcement agencies, courts, and legislative assemblies, but, for the purposes of industry tracking, it does not include military personnel.

The government was the largest employer among all the supersectors in June 2010, employing nearly 22.8 million people (See Table 5.1.) The BLS explains in "Employment Situation—June 2010" that the breakdown by level was as follows:

• Local government—14.4 million

• State government—5.2 million

• Federal government—3.2 million

More than half (8 million) of the local government workers and slightly less than half (2.4 million) of the state government workers were employed in education.

TABLE 5.3

Nonfarm wage and salary employment, by major industry, 2008 and projected for 2018

Industry sector	Employment[a]		Numerical change	Average annual rate of change
	2008	2018	2008–18	2008–18
Total	137,814.8	152,443.5	14,628.7	1.0
Goods producing, excluding agriculture	21,363.1	21,390.4	27.3	0.0
Mining	717.0	613.2	−103.8	−1.6
Construction	7,214.9	8,552.0	1,337.1	1.7
Manufacturing	13,431.2	12,225.2	−1,206.0	−0.9
Service providing	116,451.7	131,053.1	14,601.4	1.2
Utilities	559.5	500.5	−59.0	−1.1
Wholesale trade	5,963.9	6,219.8	255.9	0.4
Retail trade	15,356.4	16,010.4	654.0	0.4
Transportation and warehousing	4,504.9	4,950.4	445.5	0.9
Information	2,996.9	3,115.0	118.1	0.4
Financial activities	8,145.5	8,702.7	557.2	0.7
Professional and business services	17,778.0	21,967.9	4,189.9	2.1
Educational services	3,036.5	3,842.0	805.5	2.4
Health care and social assistance	15,818.7	19,815.6	3,996.9	2.3
Leisure and hospitality	13,458.7	14,601.1	1,142.4	0.8
Other services[b]	6,333.2	7,141.9	808.7	1.2
Federal government	2,764.3	2,859.1	94.8	0.3
State and local government	19,735.2	21,326.7	1,591.5	0.8

[a]Includes nonfarm wage and salary data from the Current Employment Statistics survey and data on private households from the Current Population Survey.
[b]Includes data on private households from the Current Population Survey.

SOURCE: Adapted from Kristina J. Bartsch, "Table 1. Nonfarm Wage and Salary Employment, by Major Industry, 2007, 2008, and Projected 2018," in "The Employment Projections for 2008–18," *Monthly Labor Review*, vol. 132, no. 11, November 2009, http://www.bls.gov/opub/mlr/2009/11/mlr200911.pdf (accessed July 9, 2010)

FIGURE 5.11

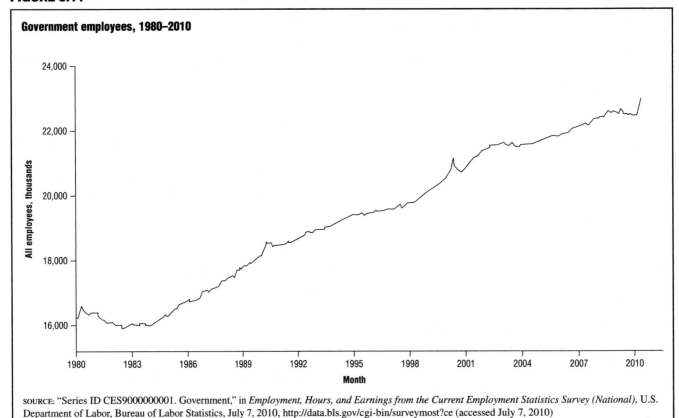

Government employees, 1980–2010

SOURCE: "Series ID CES9000000001. Government," in *Employment, Hours, and Earnings from the Current Employment Statistics Survey (National)*, U.S. Department of Labor, Bureau of Labor Statistics, July 7, 2010, http://data.bls.gov/cgi-bin/surveymost?ce (accessed July 7, 2010)

The total federal workforce of 3.2 million workers included 654,900 employees of the U.S. Postal Service.

The unemployment rate for government workers was only 4.4% in June 2010, the lowest of all the supersectors. (See Table 5.2.)

As shown in Figure 5.11, the total number of people employed in government grew steadily from around 16.3 million in 1980 to 22.1 million in 2007. There was no decrease in employment between 2008 and 2009 as occurred in other supersectors. The BLS predicts small annual growth in government employment through 2018. Employment in the federal government is expected to increase by 0.3% per year and in state and local government by 0.8% per year. (See Table 5.3.) Both values are less than the 1% growth rate expected for the nonfarm industry overall.

INFORMATION. The production and distribution of information falls under the information supersector of the U.S. economy. This supersector includes book and software publishing, Internet service providers, and television broadcasting, as well as the motion picture and sound recording industries.

This supersector employed 2.7 million people in June 2010. (See Table 5.1). In "Employment Situation—June 2010," the BLS explains that the three largest industries were telecommunications (925,300 workers), publishing,

excluding the Internet (760,600 workers), and motion pictures and sound recording (353,200).

As shown in Table 5.2, the unemployment rate for the information supersector was 8.8% in June 2010. According to the BLS (September 14, 2010, http://data.bls.gov/PDQ/servlet/SurveyOutputServlet?series_id=LNU04032237&data_tool=XGtable), unemployment in this industry fluctuated greatly on a monthly and annual basis over the past decade. The average annual unemployment rate grew from 3.2% in 2000 to 6.9% in 2002, but then declined to 3.6% in 2007. The rate for 2008 was up slightly at 5%. Several monthly rates in 2009 soared above 10%. The overall unemployment rate for 2009 was 9.2%.

The BLS expects employment in this supersector to increase by only 0.4% annually through 2018. (See Table 5.3.) This is less than the 1% growth rate expected for the nonfarm industry overall.

LEISURE AND HOSPITALITY. The leisure and hospitality supersector encompasses businesses in the arts, entertainment, recreation, spectator sports, accommodation, and food service industries. It also includes performance venues, gambling outlets, golf courses, amusement parks, arcades, hotels and other lodging sites, food service establishments, and privately funded exhibit spaces and historic sites.

As shown in Table 5.1, just over 13.1 million people worked in leisure and hospitality in June 2010. According to the BLS, in "Employment Situation—June 2010," the vast

FIGURE 5.12

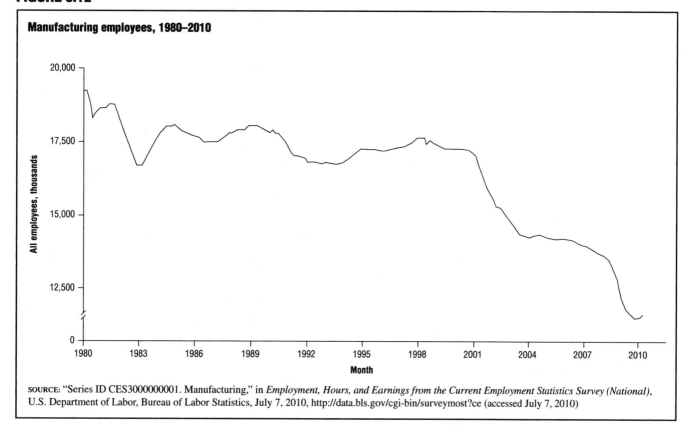

Manufacturing employees, 1980–2010

SOURCE: "Series ID CES3000000001. Manufacturing," in *Employment, Hours, and Earnings from the Current Employment Statistics Survey (National)*, U.S. Department of Labor, Bureau of Labor Statistics, July 7, 2010, http://data.bls.gov/cgi-bin/surveymost?ce (accessed July 7, 2010)

majority (11.2 million employees, or 85% of the total) were employed in accommodations and food services.

The unemployment rate for this supersector was 12.3% in June 2010. (See Table 5.2.) Historical data from the BLS (September 14, 2010, http://data.bls.gov/ PDQ/servlet/SurveyOutputServlet?series_id=LNU04032241 &data_tool=XGtable) indicate that this industry experienced average annual unemployment rates of between 6.6% and 8.7% from 2000 to 2008. These are high rates compared with the other supersectors for the same period. Unemployment in leisure and hospitality was 11.7% in 2009.

The BLS projects that employment in this supersector will grow by 0.8% annually through 2018. (See Table 5.3.) This is slightly less than the 1% growth rate expected for the nonfarm industry overall.

MANUFACTURING. An organization is considered part of the manufacturing supersector if its primary business is to transform raw materials into new products through mechanical, physical, or chemical processes. Manufacturing covers many separate industries and provides products that contribute and support all other economic sectors. The government categorizes manufactured goods as either durable goods or nondurable goods. The BLS (http://www.bls.gov/iag/tgs/ iag423.htm) defines durable goods as "items generally with a normal life expectancy of three years or more." Thus, it can be inferred that nondurable goods are those with a normal life expectancy of less than three years.

In "Employment Situation—June 2010," the BLS lists the following industry sectors as manufacturing durable goods:

- Wood products
- Nonmetallic mineral products
- Primary metals
- Fabricated metal products
- Machinery
- Computer and electronic products
- Electrical equipment and appliances
- Transportation equipment
- Furniture and related products
- Miscellaneous manufacturing

Likewise, the BLS lists the following industry sectors as manufacturing nondurable goods:

- Food manufacturing
- Beverages and tobacco products
- Textile mills
- Textile product mills
- Apparel
- Leather and allied products

- Paper and paper products

- Printing and related support activities

- Petroleum and coal products

- Chemicals

- Plastics and rubber products

Figure 5.12 shows how employment in the manufacturing supersector declined significantly from 1980 to 2010. In 1980 nearly 18 million people were employed in manufacturing. By early 2010 that number was less than 12 million. In June 2010 the manufacturing supersector employed 11.7 million workers. (See Table 5.1.) The BLS indicates that 7.2 million workers were in durable goods. The remaining 4.5 million workers produced nondurable goods.

The unemployment rate for this supersector was 9.9% in June 2010. (See Table 5.2.) Unemployment was slightly higher in the durable goods industries (10.4%) than in the nondurable goods industries (9.1%).

According to the BLS (September 14, 2010, http://data .bls.gov/PDQ/servlet/SurveyOutputServlet?series_id=LNU 04032232&data_tool=XGtable), the manufacturing supersector had average annual unemployment rates of between 3.5% and 6.7% from 2000 to 2008. In 2009 the rate increased to 12.1% as the industry was hit hard by the great recession.

The BLS projects that manufacturing employment will decrease by 0.9% annually through 2018. (See Table 5.3.) This is considerably less than the 1% growth rate expected for the nonfarm industry overall.

NATURAL RESOURCES AND MINING. The natural resources and mining supersector includes all agriculture, forestry, fishing, hunting, and mining enterprises. Farms engaged in growing crops and raising animals are included in this supersector, as are lumber and fishing operations, coal mining, petroleum and natural gas extraction, and other mining and quarrying activities. This supersector also includes heavy truck and tractor-trailer drivers.

In June 2010 employment in the mining and logging industries was 676,500 and 48,000, respectively. (See Table 5.1.) Employment estimates for the agriculture, forestry, fishing, and hunting industries are not included in Table 5.1. Many people engaged in these activities are self-employed, for example, farmers and ranchers. In *Industries at a Glance* (September 9, 2010, http://stats.bls.gov/iag/tgs/iag11.htm), the BLS reports that these industries employed over 228,000 people as laborers, farm hands, supervisors, and equipment operators in 2009. Another 11,900 people worked as truck drivers.

As shown in Table 5.2, the unemployment rate for agriculture and related industries was relatively high at 11.7% in June 2010. The economic performance of the agriculture industry will be examined in more detail in Chapter 6. The BLS predicts that employment in the mining industry will decrease on average by 1.6% annually through 2018. (See Table 5.3.) Employment projections are not provided for other industries within this supersector.

OTHER SERVICES. This supersector includes jobs such as repairing equipment and machinery, promoting or administering religious activities, operating dry cleaning and laundry services, conducting personal care, death care, and pet care services, and supplying photo processing services, temporary parking, and dating services. People who work in grant making and advocacy are also included in this category.

Approximately 5.3 million people were employed in the other services supersector in June 2010. (See Table 5.1.) In "Employment Situation—June 2010," the BLS notes that 2.9 million of these workers were employed by membership associations and organizations. Nearly 1.3 million performed personal and laundry services. The remaining 1.1 million worked in repair and maintenance occupations.

The unemployment rate for this supersector was 8.5% in June 2010. (See Table 5.2.) The BLS (September 14, 2010, http://data.bls.gov/PDQ/servlet/SurveyOutputServlet?series _id=LNU04032242&data_tool=XGtable) reports that the average annual unemployment rates from 2000 to 2008 were relatively low, averaging between 3.9% and 5.7%. In 2009 the rate increased to 7.5%.

The BLS projects that employment in the other services supersector will grow by 1.2% annually through 2018. (See Table 5.3.) This is slightly higher than the 1% growth rate predicted for nonfarm employment overall.

PROFESSIONAL AND BUSINESS SERVICES. The professional and business services supersector includes legal, accounting, architectural, engineering, advertising, marketing, translation, and veterinary services. This supersector also includes those who manage companies and all the administrative support that is needed for a business to operate. In addition, security, surveillance, cleaning, and waste disposal services are tracked in this category.

This large supersector employed more than 16.7 million people in June 2010. (See Table 5.1.) The BLS explains in "Employment Situation—June 2010" that the greatest number of employees (7.4 million) worked in professional and technical services, such as accounting, legal, architectural, engineering, computer system, and management and technical consulting services. Nearly as many (7.1 million) were employed in administrative and support services. Over 1.8 million worked in the management of companies and enterprise. A much smaller number (353,500) were employed in waste management and remediation services.

In June 2010 the unemployment rate for this supersector was 10.3%. (See Table 5.2.) The BLS (September

14, 2010, http://data.bls.gov/PDQ/servlet/SurveyOutput Servlet?series_id=LNU04032239&data_tool=XGtable) indicates that the average annual unemployment rates from 2000 to 2008 varied widely, from a low of 4.8% in 2000 to a high of 8.2% in 2003. The rate in 2009 was 10.8%.

The BLS predicts that employment in this supersector will increase by 2.1% annually through 2018. (See Table 5.3.) This is higher than the rate of 1% projected for nonfarm employment overall.

TRANSPORTATION, WAREHOUSING, AND UTILITIES. The transportation, warehousing, and utilities supersector includes businesses that transport passengers or cargo by air, rail, water, road, or pipeline. The sector also includes businesses that provide storage of goods and that support transportation activities. Also tracked in this sector are private enterprises that generate, transmit, or distribute utilities such as electric power, natural gas, and water.

As shown in Table 5.1, nearly 4.2 million people worked in transportation and warehousing in June 2010. In "Employment Situation—June 2010," the BLS indicates that the largest component (1.2 million) was engaged in truck transportation. Just over 556,100 people were employed by utilities.

The unemployment rate for this supersector was 7.2% in June 2010. (See Table 5.2.) The BLS (September 14, 2010, http://data.bls.gov/PDQ/servlet/SurveyOutput Servlet?series_id=LNU04034171&data_tool=XGtable) reports that unemployment was extremely low in the utilities industry for most of the decade. From 2000 to 2008 the average annual rate was less than 3.1%. In 2009 the rate increased to 4.8%. According to the BLS (September 14, 2010, http://data.bls.gov/PDQ/servlet/SurveyOutputServlet?series_id=LNU04034168&data_tool=XGtable), the transportation and warehousing industry enjoyed relatively low unemployment rates of between 3.8% and 5.7% from 2000 to 2008. In 2009 the rate grew dramatically to 9.7%.

As shown in Table 5.3, employment in transportation and warehousing is expected to increase by an average of 0.9% per year through 2018. This is slightly below the forecasted rate of 1% growth for nonfarm employment overall. The outlook is not as good for utilities. Employment in this industry is projected to decrease on average by 1.1% annually through 2018.

WHOLESALE AND RETAIL TRADE. The wholesale and retail supersector encompasses private businesses that trade in products that they do not produce. Wholesalers buy large quantities of finished goods from manufacturers and sell the goods in smaller lots to businesses that are engaged in retail trade. Retailers then offer the goods for sale to consumers at an increased price, usually figured as a percentage of the wholesale cost. Even though

the traditional notion of a retail establishment includes at least one store location, many retailers in the early 21st century sell their products over the Internet or in catalogs without stores.

As shown in Table 5.1, this supersector employed 14.4 million people in retail trade and 5.6 million people in wholesale trade in June 2010. The BLS explains in "Employment Situation—June 2010" that the largest numbers of retail employees worked in general merchandise stores (2.9 million), food and beverage stores (2.8 million), and motor vehicle and parts dealers (1.6 million).

The overall unemployment rate for this supersector was 9.3% in June 2010. (See Table 5.2.) According to the BLS (September 14, 2010, http://data.bls.gov/PDQ/servlet/SurveyOutputServlet?series_id=LNU04034154&data_tool=XGtable), the unemployment rates in wholesale trade were relatively low from 2000 to 2008, averaging between 3.2% and 5.1% per year. In 2009 the rate climbed to 7.2%. In June 2010 the unemployment rate for wholesale trade was 6.7%. Historically, the unemployment rates in retail have been slightly higher than those in wholesale. The BLS (September 14, 2010, http://data.bls.gov/PDQ/servlet/SurveyOutputServlet?series_id=LNU04034163&data_tool=XGtable) reports that rates on an average annual basis were between 4.6% and 6.4% from 2000 to 2008. The rate in 2009 increased to 9.5%. In June 2010 the unemployment rate in retail was 9.9%.

The BLS predicts that employment in both the wholesale and retail trades will increase at a rate of 0.4% annually through 2018. (See Table 5.3.) This is less than the rate of 1% projected for nonfarm employment overall.

LABOR UNIONS

Even though many historians trace the origins of labor unions to medieval guilds (organized groups of tradespeople and artisans in the Middle Ages), the modern labor movement is more directly linked to the trade unions of the early Industrial Revolution, when working conditions in factories and mines were barely tolerable and employees began to join together to demand reasonable work hours, safe conditions, and decent wages. Since their establishment, unions have had tense relationships with both employers and government; at times, they have been banned altogether, and the struggle between labor and employers has sometimes resulted in violence.

Labor unions have had a significant impact on the U.S. workforce and labor policy. Unions are often able to secure higher wages and increased benefits for their members. The BLS reports in *Union Members—2009* (January 22, 2010, http://www.bls.gov/news.release/pdf/union2.pdf) that 15.3 million wage and salary workers were union members in 2009. This represented 12.3% of all wage and salary workers in the United States. The

FIGURE 5.13

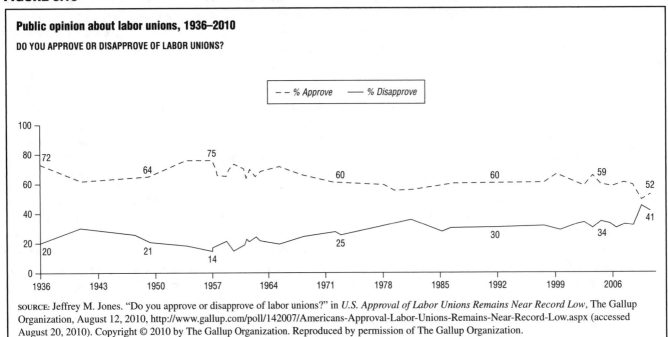

Public opinion about labor unions, 1936–2010

DO YOU APPROVE OR DISAPPROVE OF LABOR UNIONS?

- - - % Approve   ——— % Disapprove

SOURCE: Jeffrey M. Jones. "Do you approve or disapprove of labor unions?" in *U.S. Approval of Labor Unions Remains Near Record Low*, The Gallup Organization, August 12, 2010, http://www.gallup.com/poll/142007/Americans-Approval-Labor-Unions-Remains-Near-Record-Low.aspx (accessed August 20, 2010). Copyright © 2010 by The Gallup Organization. Reproduced by permission of The Gallup Organization.

percentage is significantly lower than the rate of 20.1% reported in 1983 (the first year the BLS tracked union membership). According to the BLS, 37.4% of government workers were unionized in 2009, compared with only 7.2% of private industry workers. Local governments have the most highly unionized employees, particularly teachers, police officers, and firefighters. The highest rates of union membership in the private industries are found in the transportation and utilities, telecommunications, and construction sectors.

Despite their successes on behalf of American workers, contemporary labor unions continue to face opposition from employers, and often from employees, who question whether the benefits of being associated with a union are worth the cost. Union members are required to go on strike when the union has an unresolved grievance against an employer, and striking union members receive only a fraction of their income in strike pay. Workers who are part of a union may also find themselves facing fines for not abiding by the union bylaws.

For employers, unions can pose other problems. Business operations can be greatly interrupted by unresolved negotiations, whether or not they lead to a strike. Furthermore, because of the increased expenses associated with employing union members, a company's products or services might become less competitively priced in the marketplace. If sales are lost to foreign or nonunion competitors, companies may be forced to lay off employees or even go out of business.

The Gallup Organization has polled Americans regarding their opinions about labor unions since the 1930s. The most recent polls were conducted in 2010. As shown in Figure 5.13, approval of labor unions reached its lowest point in 2010. Only 52% of respondents said they approve of labor unions. Historical support for unions was much higher, regularly 60% or greater through 2006. Support was highest during the 1950s, when 75% of those asked approved of unions.

Jeffrey M. Jones of the Gallup Organization notes in *U.S. Approval of Labor Unions Remains Near Record Low* (August 12, 2010, http://www.gallup.com/poll/142007/Americans-Approval-Labor-Unions-Remains-Near-Record-Low.aspx) that in August 2010, 10% of respondents said they belonged to a union. Another 6% of respondents said another household member belonged to a union. Overall, 72% of these respondents approved of unions. By contrast, only 48% of respondents in nonunion households approved of unions. There were wide differences of opinion based on political affiliation: 71% of Democrats, 49% of Independents, and 34% of Republicans approved of labor unions. Jones blames the loss of public support for unions on two factors: the economic downturn that began in late 2007 and opposition from union critics to policies of the administration of President Barack Obama (1961–). Those policies may be seen as unfairly benefiting union members who are employed in education and other government jobs.

COMPENSATION OF AMERICAN WORKERS

Compensation has two components: pay and benefits. Pay includes wages (which is the term used primarily for pay made on an hourly, weekly, or monthly basis) and salaries (which is pay calculated yearly). Benefits provided by employers include paid time off from work,

TABLE 5.4

Personal income, 2006–09, and first and second quarters 2010

[Billions of dollars]

	2006	2007	2008	2009	Seasonally adjusted at annual rates 2010 I	II
Personal income	11,268.1	11,912.3	12,391.1	12,174.9	12,361.8	12,485.7
Compensation of employees, received	7,475.7	7,862.2	8,065.8	7,806.7	7,871.2	7,934.5
Wage and salary disbursements	6,068.9	6,421.7	6,559.0	6,274.1	6,303.7	6,356.1
Private industries	5,033.7	5,332.7	5,415.1	5, 100.5	5,118.2	5,161.6
Goods-producing industries	1,176.0	1,213.4	1,207.6	1,064.0	1,036.1	1,044.4
Manufacturing	738.7	752.2	741.2	661.5	655.8	662.1
Services-producing industries	3,857.8	4,119.3	4,207.4	4,036.6	4,082.1	4,117.2
Trade, transportation, and utilities	996.0	1,045.2	1,050.9	990.5	990.1	999.3
Other services-producing industries	2,861.8	3,074.1	3,156.6	3,046.1	3,092.0	3,117.9
Government	1,035.2	1,089.0	1,144.0	1,173.6	1,185.5	1,194.6
Supplements to wages and salaries	1,406.9	1,440.4	1,506.8	1,532.6	1,567.5	1,578.4
Employer contributions for employee pension and insurance funds	960.1	980.5	1,036.6	1,072.0	1,095.8	1,102.8
Employer contributions for government social insurance	446.7	459.9	470.1	460.6	471.7	475.6

SOURCE: Adapted from "Table 2. Personal Income and Its Disposition (Years and Quarters)," in *Personal Income and Outlays: June 2010; Revised Estimates: 2007 through May 2010*, U.S. Department of Commerce, Bureau of Economic Analysis, August 3, 2010, http://www.bea.gov/newsreleases/national/pi/2010/pdf/pi0610.pdf (accessed August 6, 2010)

various insurance and retirement plans, and other programs that are designed to attract and keep employees.

Table 5.4 shows the wage and salary disbursements and supplements paid by employers from 2006 to 2009 and for the first two quarters of 2010. Approximately $7.8 trillion was paid out in compensation in 2009, down from $8.1 trillion in 2008 and $7.9 trillion in 2007. In addition, more than $1.5 trillion in supplements was estimated to be contributed by employers in 2009, primarily for employee pensions and insurance funds. In 2007 and 2008 these supplements totaled $1.4 trillion and $1.5 trillion, respectively.

Income

In *Income, Poverty, and Health Insurance Coverage in the United States: 2009* (September 2010, http://www.census.gov/prod/2010pubs/p60-238.pdf), Carmen DeNavas-Walt, Bernadette D. Proctor, and Jessica C. Smith of the Census Bureau note that the median U.S. household income (half of all households earned more and half earned less) in 2009 was $49,777. This value was slightly lower than the median income of $50,112 reported in 2008.

Benefits

To attract and keep the best employees and earn a level of loyalty from them, many U.S. employers offer benefits and incentives. As of March 2010, a majority of employees in private industry and in state and local governments had access to retirement benefits, medical care benefits, life insurance, paid sick leave, paid vacation, and paid personal leave. (See Table 5.5.) The take-up rates (the number of employees with access divided by the number of employees participating) were highest for

life insurance benefits (96% of private industry workers and 97% of state and local government workers).

Figure 5.14 compares benefit availability for full-time and part-time workers employed in private industry as of March 2010. Part-time employees had much lower rates of access to employer-provided retirement plans, medical care benefits, life insurance policies, and paid sick leave than did full-time employees. There were also substantial benefit availability differences between workers at the high and low ends of the pay scale. As shown in Figure 5.15, private-industry employees with the highest 10% of earnings had much greater access to benefits than did workers with the lowest 10% of earnings.

MEDICAL INSURANCE. Typically, the total cost of monthly health insurance coverage is split between employers and employees, with employers paying the largest portion. As shown in Table 3.1 in Chapter 3, the price of health care grew at a faster rate from 2002 to 2009 than the overall rate for the urban consumer price index. Because of rising health care costs, medical insurance has become a costly benefit for both employers and employees.

NONTRADITIONAL WORK ARRANGEMENTS
Working at Home

With technological advances such as Internet access, e-mail, and teleconferencing, working at home has become a viable option for many types of jobs. As employees conduct much of their daily work from home offices, employers are able to save on operating costs. Many employers will pay for computers, additional telephone lines, and even utilities to allow their employees to work from home offices. This allows them to reduce office space, which is one of the

TABLE 5.5

Access, participation, and take-up rates in percent for certain employee benefits, March 2010

Benefit	Civilian workers*			Private industry workers			State and local government workers		
	Access	Participation	Take-up rate	Access	Participation	Take-up rate	Access	Participation	Take-up rate
Retirement benefits	69	55	80	65	50	76	90	85	95
Medical care benefits	73	55	75	71	51	73	88	73	83
Life insurance	62	60	96	59	56	96	80	78	97
Paid sick leave	67	NA	NA	62	NA	NA	89	NA	NA
Paid vacation	74	NA	NA	77	NA	NA	60	NA	NA
Paid personal leave	41	NA	NA	37	NA	NA	60	NA	NA

Note: NA = No data available
*Includes workers in the private nonfarm economy except those in private households, and workers in the public sector, except the federal government.

SOURCE: Adapted from "Table 1. Retirement Benefits," "Table 2. Medical Care Benefits," "Table 5. Life Insurance Benefits," and "Table 6. Selected Paid Leave Benefits," in *Employee Benefits in the United States—March 2010*, U.S. Department of Labor, Bureau of Labor Statistics, July 27, 2010, http://www.bls.gov/news.release/pdf/ebs2.pdf (accessed August 6, 2010)

FIGURE 5.14

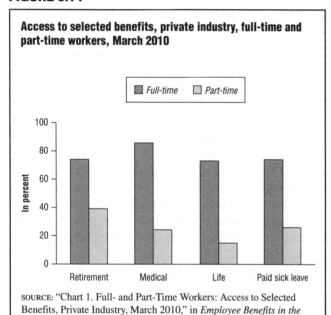

Access to selected benefits, private industry, full-time and part-time workers, March 2010

SOURCE: "Chart 1. Full- and Part-Time Workers: Access to Selected Benefits, Private Industry, March 2010," in *Employee Benefits in the United States—March 2010*, U.S. Department of Labor, Bureau of Labor Statistics, July 27, 2010, http://www.bls.gov/news.release/pdf/ebs2.pdf (accessed August 6, 2010)

FIGURE 5.15

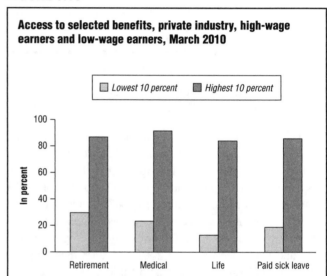

Access to selected benefits, private industry, high-wage earners and low-wage earners, March 2010

SOURCE: "Chart 2. High- and Low-Wage Earners: Access to Selected Benefits, Private Industry—March 2010," in *Employee Benefits in the United States, March 2010*, U.S. Department of Labor, Bureau of Labor Statistics, July 27, 2010, http://www.bls.gov/news.release/pdf/ebs2.pdf (accessed August 6, 2010)

higher costs for an employer, especially in large metropolitan markets.

As of September 2010, the most recent comprehensive data on the number of Americans working at home were collected in May 2004 by the Census Bureau as part of its Current Population Survey. In *Work at Home Summary* (September 22, 2005, http://www.bls.gov/news.release/homey.nr0.htm), the BLS notes that the survey indicated that 20.7 million Americans reported working at home at least once per week as part of their primary job. This number represents about 15% of the total nonagricultural workforce in May 2004. Approximately 30.2% of the people reporting that they regularly work at home described themselves as self-employed.

Self-Employment

Self-employed workers are not on the payroll of a company. They may own or operate small businesses or work under contract arrangements with companies. Detailed information about self-employed business owners is provided in Chapter 6.

FOREIGN WORKERS IN THE UNITED STATES

Relatively high wages and favorable working conditions have attracted workers from around the world to the United States. There are two broad categories of foreign workers: those who have entered the country legally with the proper paperwork to pursue work and those who have entered illegally. Legal workers are tracked by the U.S.

Citizenship and Immigration Service, formerly the U.S. Immigration and Naturalization Service.

Legal Foreign Workers

The U.S. Department of Labor explains in "Guest-worker Programs" (January 7, 2010, http://www.doleta.gov/Business/gw/guestwkr/) that it issues a limited number of certifications to foreign workers to work in the United States on a temporary or permanent basis under the following programs:

- Permanent Labor Certification—allows a foreign worker to work permanently in the United States

- H-1B Specialty (Professional) Workers—temporary certification for workers in occupations requiring highly specialized knowledge with at least a bachelor's degree or equivalent; a subcategory, H-1B1, applies only to H-1B workers from Chile and Singapore

- H-2A Temporary Labor Certification (Seasonal Agricultural)—temporary certification for workers who work for employers anticipating a shortage of U.S. workers in agricultural labor or services of a temporary or seasonal nature

- H-2B Temporary Labor Certification (Nonagricultural)—temporary certification for nonagricultural laborers working for employers anticipating a shortage of U.S. workers; the need can be a one-time occurrence, seasonal, peak load, or intermittent

- D-1 Crewmembers Certification—for longshoremen hired to work at U.S. ports; there are many restrictions, one of which is that there cannot be a strike or lockout ongoing that keeps U.S. longshoremen from working

According to the Department of Labor, "certification may be obtained in cases where it can be demonstrated that there are insufficient qualified U.S. workers available and willing to perform the work at wages that meet or exceed the prevailing wage paid for that occupation in the area of intended employment."

The U.S. Department of Homeland Security's Office of Immigration Statistics tracks the number of foreign workers entering the United States and publishes related data in annual reports. In *Nonimmigrant Admissions to the United States: 2009* (April 2010, http://www.dhs.gov/xlibrary/assets/statistics/publications/ni_fr_2009.pdf), Randall Monger and Macreadie Barr of the Department of Homeland Security note that 936,272 temporary workers and trainees were admitted into the United States in fiscal year 2009 (October 1, 2008, to September 30, 2009). Legal permanent residents are foreigners who have obtained so-called green cards and have been granted permanent residency in the United States. According to Monger, in *U.S. Legal Permanent Residents: 2009* (April 2010, http://www.dhs.gov/xlibrary/assets/statistics/publications/lpr_fr_2009

.pdf), 144,034 foreigners were granted employment-based legal permanent residency in fiscal year 2009.

Temporary foreign workers maintain the citizenship of their native country, and after fulfilling their contracts with U.S. employers they typically return to their country. Immigrant workers are people who have come to the United States through legal channels and intend to become citizens. They obtain jobs while waiting for their naturalization (the process of becoming a U.S. citizen) to be finalized.

Illegal Foreign Workers

The issue of illegal immigration has become a heated topic. Much of the debate centers on the economic effect of undocumented workers (foreign workers who have entered the United States illegally). Some people claim that undocumented workers take jobs away from Americans and place a large burden on government-provided social programs. Others believe that undocumented workers are willing to take jobs that Americans do not want— low paying, labor-intensive jobs with no benefits and little to no chance for advancement.

Frank Newport of the Gallup Organization notes in *Economy Dominates as Nation's Most Important Problem* (July 14, 2010, http://www.gallup.com/poll/141275/Economy-Dominates-Nation-Important-Problem.aspx) that in July 2010 issues related to immigration and illegal aliens were named among the top four problems "facing this country today."

Employers are required by law to verify that new hires are U.S. citizens or foreigners with legal working status who are eligible to work in the United States. Job applicants have to show identification and documentation, including a Social Security card. However, the authenticity of these documents cannot be verified immediately. Thus, well-meaning businesses may unknowingly hire and train illegal workers who use fake documentation to obtain jobs.

There is little doubt that some businesses purposely hire illegal workers or at least ignore questionable paperwork to get inexpensive labor. Many critics maintain that the federal government's focus on terrorism and national security has diminished attention on issues related to undocumented workers. Others believe that businesses willing to hire the workers are to blame. Like many factors in the U.S. economy, the issue of undocumented workers is driven by supply and demand factors.

POLITICAL DEBATE AND PUBLIC PROTEST. Michael Hoefer, Nancy Rytina, and Bryan C. Baker of the Department of Homeland Security indicate in *Estimates of the Unauthorized Immigrant Population Residing in the United States: January 2009* (January 2010, http://www.dhs.gov/xlibrary/assets/statistics/publications/ois_ill_pe_2009.pdf) that there were around 10.8 million illegal immigrants in the United States in January 2009. This number was down from an estimated 11.6 million in January 2008. Many analysts believe job losses and other economic pressures of the great recession are responsible for the decrease.

Illegal immigration has become a politically charged and divisive issue. Some politicians advocate allowing many illegal immigrants already in the country the opportunity to obtain U.S. citizenship under certain conditions. This is called an amnesty provision by its critics and "a conditional pathway to legal status" by its supporters. The gist of the concept was advocated by President George W. Bush (1946–).

As of September 2010, the White House (http://www.whitehouse.gov/issues/immigration) described President Obama's views on the amnesty provision as follows: "President Obama supports a system that allows undocumented immigrants who are in good standing to pay a fine, learn English, and go to the back of the line for the opportunity to become citizens."

In October 2007 Bush signed into law a bill calling for the building of a 700-mile (1,300-km) fence along the U.S.-Mexican border. The article "Footbridges Cut through Mexican Border Fence" (Associated Press, August 20, 2010) reports that as of August 2010 steel fencing covered approximately 600 miles (970 km) of the border along Texas, New Mexico, Arizona, and California. Even though it is commonly referred to as a fence or wall, the structure includes steel fencing in some areas (primarily urban areas) and concrete barriers in other areas. The structure is not continuous.

In August 2010 President Obama signed into law the Southwest Border Security Bill, a $600 million measure to enhance security along the U.S.-Mexican border. In "Obama to Sign $600M Border Security Bill Friday" (Associated Press, August 12, 2010), Jim Abrams notes that the law will fund the hiring of approximately 1,500 agents and officers for federal agencies that are charged with enforcing border security. It also includes funds for new equipment, including unmanned drones to conduct surveillance. These measures are designed to stem the flow of illegal immigrants across the border and to cut down on the smuggling of illegal drugs and human trafficking.

Many state governments have grown frustrated by what they consider to be the failure of the federal government to stem the flow of illegal immigrants into the United States. Since the 1990s hundreds of laws addressing illegal immigration have been passed by state legislators. Some of the laws have not survived court challenges. In "State Laws Related to Immigration and Immigrants" (2010, http://www.ncsl.org/default.aspx?tabid=19897), the National Conference of State Legislatures (NCSL) reports that in 2009, 48 state legislatures enacted 222 laws relating to immigrants and refugees. During the first half of 2010 the NCSL notes that 44 states had enacted 319 additional laws and resolu-

tions dealing with this issue. The most controversial of these laws was Arizona's Senate Bill 1070, which was signed into law in April 2010. Among other provisions, the law gives Arizona law enforcement officials the power to detain anyone they suspect of being in the United States illegally. The constitutionality of the law has been challenged in court by the federal government and by private organizations. As of September 2010, the major provisions of the law had not yet gone into effect due to these challenges.

U.S. JOBS GOING TO FOREIGN COUNTRIES

One consequence of the globalization of U.S. business has been offshoring (the transfer of jobs from the United States to other countries). This can occur when an entire business establishment, such as a factory or service center, is relocated to another nation or when certain jobs within a business are transferred to a foreign company. The latter is also an example of outsourcing (a business practice in which certain tasks within a company are contracted out to another firm; outsourcing may or may not involve sending work to another country). During the 1990s outsourcing became a popular means of reducing costs for some companies. Noncore functions, such as payroll management or housekeeping, are common examples in which outsourcing can be cost effective. However, offshoring is controversial because jobs move outside of the United States, primarily to developing countries, where labor costs are much cheaper.

Critics suggest that offshoring harms the U.S. economy by putting Americans out of work. Others claim that relocation of some operations to foreign countries has a limited effect on domestic employment. They argue that offshoring leads to lower prices for consumer and investment goods, with the ultimate effect of raising real wages (wages that are adjusted for changes in the price of consumer goods) and living standards in the United States.

PROTECTING AMERICAN WORKERS

The United States has enacted comprehensive labor laws to ensure that workplaces are operated safely and that workers are treated fairly. These include relatively strict laws to protect American workers from discrimination on the basis of gender, age, race, ethnicity, religion, sexual orientation, and other factors.

The Fair Labor Standards Act

The Fair Labor Standards Act (FLSA) offers protection for full- and part-time workers in private and government jobs and covers minimum wages, overtime pay, employer record keeping, and child labor. The FLSA also established the standard 40-hour workweek. Local fire and police employees are typically not covered by the FLSA. It was passed in 1938 and has been amended many times over the years.

THE MINIMUM WAGE. The FLSA established a federal hourly minimum wage that U.S. employers must honor for many nonsupervisory, nonfarm, private-sector, and government employees. Most states have their own minimum wage as well. In states with minimum wages that differ from the federal minimum wage, the employer must pay the higher of the two. As of September 2010, the federal minimum wage was $7.25 per hour. This level was set by the Fair Minimum Wage Act of 2007, one of many amendments that have been made to the FLSA.

There are many exceptions to the minimum wage law. Employers may apply for subminimum wage certificates for disabled workers, full-time students, workers under the age of 20 years who are in their first 90 days of employment, workers who receive tips, and student-learners (usually high school students). Lawmakers reason that exempting employers from paying the minimum wage to certain workers (e.g., the disabled and students) encourages them to hire more of those workers who may otherwise be at a disadvantage. Employers may not, however, displace other workers to hire those subject to the subminimum wage. Other workers exempt from the minimum wage include certain professional and administrative employees, certain workers in the fishing industry, certain seasonal employees, babysitters, and certain farm workers.

The BLS tracks the number of hourly wage earners in the United States based on the results of the Current Population Survey. In *Characteristics of Minimum Wage Workers: 2009* (March 1, 2010, http://www.bls.gov/cps/minwage2009.pdf), the BLS indicates that there were 980,000 workers paid the federal minimum wage during 2009. Nearly 2.6 million workers earned less than the minimum wage. The total number of workers earning minimum wage or less accounted for 4.9% of the 72.6 million people earning hourly wages that year.

The minimum wage policy is not without controversy. Advocates for low-income workers believe the minimum wage should be increased regularly to keep up with the effects of inflation. Opponents of the minimum wage assert that wage levels should be determined by market conditions and supply and demand factors. They argue that forcing businesses to pay a higher minimum wage discourages the hiring of low-income workers.

Occupational Safety and Health Administration

The Occupational Safety and Health Administration (OSHA) was formed in 1971 to institute and monitor safety regulations in the workplace. By focusing mainly on industries with high rates of work-related injuries and illnesses, OSHA works directly with employers and employees to ensure that health and safety standards are followed.

Equal Employment Opportunity Commission

The Equal Employment Opportunity Commission (EEOC) enforces federal workplace discrimination laws. It consists of a general counsel and five commissioners who are appointed by the U.S. president and approved by the U.S. Senate. Besides its enforcement role, the EEOC has a training institute to educate employers on workplace discrimination and help them comply with the laws.

CHAPTER 6
U.S. BUSINESSES

*After all, the chief business of the American people is
business.*

—President Calvin Coolidge, January 17, 1925

Businesses are diverse in the United States. They range
in size from the huge multinational corporation employing
thousands of people to the self-employed individual.
They include large and small businesses, home-based
businesses, Internet-based businesses, and corporate and
family farms. Businesses are a vital part of the American
economic engine. They supply goods and services to the
world. The consumption of business output is the primary
driver behind the growth of the nation's gross domestic
product (GDP; the total market value of final goods and
services produced within an economy in a given year).
Businesses also provide opportunities for employment,
wealth-building, and investment.

Capitalism encourages business growth. However,
businesses can become so large and powerful that they
trigger concern about the lack of competition within an
industry. Corporate fraud and accounting scandals have
eroded the public's trust in the integrity of "big business."
These negative feelings deepened during the latter half of
the first decade of the 21st century because many Americans blamed irresponsible behavior by large corporations,
particularly those in the financial industry, for causing the
so-called great recession (December 2007 to June 2009).

HISTORICAL DEVELOPMENTS

When the first colonists arrived in North America, they
traded in furs and food with the native peoples and
exchanged North American resources for goods from other
countries. The primary industries were agriculture, timber
harvesting, and shipbuilding. Manufacturing gradually
grew in importance as the United States became an independent country and underwent the Industrial Revolution.
Agriculture accounted for 22% of the national income in
1869. (See Figure 1.2 in Chapter 1.) Other major sectors

were trade and manufacturing (15% each), services (14%),
and finance, insurance, and real estate (12%). The U.S.
Census Bureau reports in *Historical Statistics of the United
States, Colonial Times to 1970, Bicentennial Edition, Part
1* (September 1975, http://www2.census.gov/prod2/stat
comp/documents/CT1970p1-01.pdf) that by 1929 the
contribution of agriculture to the national income had
shrunk to only 12%, whereas manufacturing had grown to
22%. By the mid-1950s agriculture accounted for only 5%
of the national income, whereas manufacturing had grown
to 31%. (See Figure 1.8 in Chapter 1.)

During the next half-century the United States underwent a gradual change from dependence on manufacturing
as its primary business to reliance on service industries.
Services accounted for only 10% of the national income
during the mid-1950s. (See Figure 1.8 in Chapter 1.) By the
beginning of the 21st century service industries dominated
the American business world.

LEGAL STRUCTURES OF BUSINESSES

For legal and tax purposes, all U.S. businesses must
be structured as one of several legally defined forms: sole
proprietorships, business partnerships, corporations, or
limited liability companies. Each offers both advantages
and disadvantages to the business owner.

Sole Proprietorships

In a sole proprietorship one person owns and operates
the whole business. Because the business and its owner
are considered a single entity under the law, the owner
assumes all the risk but also reaps all the benefits of the
business. If the business fails, the sole proprietor may have
to cover the losses from his or her personal assets, but if
the business succeeds, he or she keeps all the profits. Sole
proprietors typically pay lower taxes than those who head
corporations or other forms of small businesses. Still,
because almost all credit decisions are based on the

owner's assets and credit history, it is often difficult for a business set up under this structure to borrow enough money to expand as rapidly as other kinds of businesses.

Business Partnerships

A business partnership has two or more co-owners. As in a sole proprietorship, members of a business partnership are legally recognized as one and the same with their company, meaning that they are personally responsible for the company's debts and other liabilities. Most partnerships start with the partners signing agreements that specify their duties in the business. Many states allow for silent partners, who invest start-up capital but have little role in the company's day-to-day affairs. (Start-up capital is the money used to start a new business.) A significant drawback to this form of business is that each of the partners is responsible for every other partner's actions. If a partner loses or steals money from the company, the other partners will have a legal responsibility to pay that debt.

There are three kinds of business partnerships: A general partnership is the simplest form, in which profits and liability are equally divided among partners or divided according to the terms of the signed agreement; a limited partnership allows partners to have limited liability for the company but also limited decision-making rights; and a joint venture, which is similar to a general partnership but is used only for single projects or for short periods of time.

Corporations

A corporation is an entity recognized by the state and federal government as entirely separate from its owner or owners. As such, a corporation can be taxed and sued and can enter into contractual agreements. Because it is an individual legal entity, a corporation allows its owners to have less personal liability for debts and lawsuits than a sole proprietorship or business partnership. Owners of corporations are considered shareholders, and they may elect a board of directors to oversee management of the company.

Even though corporations are commonly thought of as large companies with hundreds or thousands of employees and publicly traded stock, this is not always the case. Owners of small businesses frequently incorporate as their business expands. All corporate owners must file "articles of incorporation" with their state government. For smaller businesses these forms are simple to fill out and file. One option is to file with the Internal Revenue Service as a subchapter S corporation. In an S corporation the owner must pay him- or herself wages like any other employee, but the structure also offers substantial tax flexibility. All corporations that are publicly traded have C corporation status. This means they have nearly unrestricted ownership and they are subject to corporate taxes, paying at both the corporate and stockholder levels.

Limited Liability Company

The limited liability company is a combination of a corporation and a partnership in which the owners (or shareholders) have less personal liability for the company's debts and legal issues and have the benefit of simpler tax filings and more control over management issues.

THE ROLE OF SMALL BUSINESS IN A COMPLEX ECONOMY

Many people perceive the U.S. economy as being dominated by large businesses, such as McDonald's and Microsoft. Even though it is true that many of the world's largest companies are headquartered in the United States, small businesses exert enormous influence on the U.S. economy.

The Small Business Administration (SBA) is a federal agency that was created in 1953 with the passage of the Small Business Act. The SBA's purpose is to support small businesses by offering financial and counseling assistance and ensuring that small businesses can compete against large companies in receiving government contracts.

The size of what is considered a small business varies by industry, and official size standards are determined by the SBA's Office of Size Standards, which issues standards according to a business's number of employees or its average annual receipts. However, the more generally accepted definition of a small business is one that employs fewer than 500 people at any one time.

Every five years the Census Bureau conducts an economic census in which it collects detailed data about American businesses. As of September 2010, the most recent economic data were from the 2007 census. Table 6.1 is a compilation of that data for business size, number of firms, establishments, and employees, payroll, and estimated receipts. Note that only employer firms are included, not self-employed individuals. In 2007 there were just over 6 million firms operating. They had more than 7.7 million establishments (facilities) around the country that employed 120.6 million people. The annual payroll of all the businesses was just over $5 trillion. The Census Bureau estimates that the businesses had receipts of $29.7 trillion in 2007.

Small businesses (those with fewer than 500 employees) numbered just over 6 million in 2007, accounting for 99.7% of all firms. (See Table 6.1.) They employed nearly 60 million people, which was half of total business employment. They had an annual payroll of $2.2 trillion, which accounted for 44% of total payroll. The Census Bureau estimates that small businesses had receipts of nearly $11.4 trillion in 2007, which was 38% of total receipts.

Of the 6 million small businesses operating in 2007, the vast majority (5.4 million, or 90%) were firms that employed fewer than 20 people each. (See Table 6.1.)

TABLE 6.1

Business sizes, number of establishments, employment, and annual payrolls, 2007

Employment size of firm	Firms	Establishments	Employment	Annual payroll ($1,000)	Estimated receipts ($1,000)
Total	6,049,655	7,705,018	120,604,265	5,026,778,232	29,746,741,904
0–4*	3,705,275	3,710,700	6,139,463	234,921,325	1,434,680,823
5–9	1,060,250	1,073,875	6,974,591	222,419,546	1,144,930,232
10–14	425,914	444,721	4,981,758	166,162,571	791,709,665
15–19	218,928	237,689	3,674,424	125,925,706	603,788,766
20–24	134,254	152,547	2,928,296	101,579,621	489,530,870
25–29	89,643	106,623	2,405,637	85,593,387	402,007,359
30–34	64,753	81,086	2,063,987	73,717,550	364,392,992
35–39	47,641	62,878	1,754,582	64,092,610	304,339,758
40–44	38,221	51,847	1,600,913	58,993,856	293,476,569
45–49	29,705	43,325	1,391,754	52,128,470	249,407,544
50–74	86,364	139,864	5,195,105	194,613,428	979,545,562
75–99	41,810	85,215	3,582,686	137,827,633	710,220,323
100–149	39,316	102,135	4,749,055	184,445,128	967,245,234
150–199	18,620	66,602	3,205,201	127,511,217	674,337,913
200–299	17,780	87,923	4,309,143	172,915,898	897,848,746
300–399	8,155	55,515	2,808,347	114,914,623	595,711,397
400–499	4,715	43,678	2,101,982	87,075,152	476,906,931
500–749	6,094	71,702	3,695,682	152,059,022	800,475,934
750–999	2,970	45,990	2,561,972	109,833,289	636,199,229
1,000–1,499	2,916	59,311	3,552,259	153,957,992	792,993,702
1,500–1,999	1,542	46,221	2,664,416	120,606,441	695,739,349
2,000–2,499	942	36,388	2,094,728	94,001,450	544,038,807
2,500–4,999	1,920	118,282	6,687,266	320,640,371	1,979,674,138
5,000+	1,927	780,901	39,481,018	1,870,841,946	12,917,540,061
<20	5,410,367	5,466,985	21,770,236	749,429,148	3,975,109,486
<50	5,814,584	5,965,291	33,915,405	1,185,534,642	6,078,264,578
<100	5,942,758	6,190,370	42,693,196	1,517,975,703	7,768,030,463
<500	6,031,344	6,546,223	59,866,924	2,204,837,721	11,380,080,684

*Employment is measured in March, thus some firms (start-ups after March, closures before March, and seasonal firms) will have zero employment and some annual payroll. Excludes farms.

SOURCE: "Employer Firms, Establishments, Employment, and Annual Payroll Small Firm Size Classes, 2007," in *Firm Size Data*, U.S. Small Business Administration, Office of Advocacy, June 29, 2010, http://www.sba.gov/advo/research/us_07ss.pdf (accessed July 8, 2010)

Just over 3.7 million (61%) of all small business firms had four or fewer employees each.

Small businesses are not evenly distributed among all industries. According to the SBA (June 2010, http://www.sba.gov/advo/research/us07_n6.pdf), the five industry sectors with the largest numbers of small business firms in 2007 were:

- Construction—798,708 firms

- Professional, scientific, and technical services—784,075 firms

- Retail trade—710,597 firms

- Other services (except public administration)—676,062 firms

- Health care and social assistance—611,157 firms

As noted in Chapter 5, the other services sector includes jobs such as repairing equipment and machinery, promoting or administering religious activities, operating dry cleaning and laundry services, conducting personal care, death care, and pet care services, and supplying photo processing services, temporary parking, dating services, grant making, and advocacy services.

From an employment standpoint, the health care and social assistance sector employed the most workers (nearly 8 million) in small businesses. However, small businesses engaged in wholesale trade had the largest estimated receipts ($2.5 trillion).

Every year since 1982 the SBA has prepared a report for the U.S. president that summarizes the economic status and impact of small businesses (those with fewer than 500 employees each). As of September 2010, the most recent report was *The Small Business Economy: A Report to the President* (2009, http://www.sba.gov/advo/research/sb_econ2009.pdf), based on 2008 data. As noted earlier, 2008 witnessed the full onset of the great recession. The SBA notes that from the mid-1990s to 2007 small businesses accounted for approximately 60% to 80% of the country's net new jobs each year. However, in 2008 small businesses suffered a net loss of 3.1 million jobs.

The SBA states that "small businesses with fewer than 500 workers account for half of the nation's private, non-farm real gross domestic product." This is based on a 2007 report from Katherine Kobe of the Economic Consulting Services. In *The Small Business Share of GDP, 1998–2004* (April 2007, http://www.sba.gov/advo/research/rs299tot

TABLE 6.2

Employer and nonemployer statistics by industry sector, 2007

2007 NAICS code	Meaning of 2007 NAICS code	Number of employer establishments	Employer sales, shipments, receipts, revenue, or business done ($1,000)	Annual payroll ($1,000)	Number of paid employees for pay period including March 12	Number of nonemployer establishments	Nonemployer sales, shipments, receipts, revenue, or business done ($1,000)
21	Mining, quarrying, and oil and gas extraction	22,667	413,524,731	40,687,472	730,433	101,607	9,012,220
22	Utilities	16,578	584,192,658	51,653,618	637,247	17,573	727,843
23	Construction	729,345	1,731,841,830	331,002,718	7,316,240	2,657,360	159,041,760
31–33	Manufacturing	293,919	5,339,345,058	612,474,100	13,333,390	328,060	16,332,595
42	Wholesale trade	434,983	6,515,708,554	336,206,776	6,227,389	401,863	35,822,540
44–45	Retail trade	1,128,112	3,917,663,456	362,818,687	15,515,396	1,979,576	88,142,918
48–49	Transportation and warehousing	219,706	639,916,407	173,183,073	4,454,383	1,083,139	66,632,938
51	Information	141,566	1,072,342,856	228,836,587	3,496,773	307,143	10,957,788
52	Finance and insurance	501,713	3,669,302,691	502,416,670	6,607,511	763,527	54,351,422
53	Real estate and rental and leasing	384,297	485,058,597	84,764,864	2,188,479	2,327,057	183,264,078
54	Professional, scientific, and technical services	847,492	1,251,003,504	502,074,331	7,870,414	3,028,528	130,386,056
55	Management of companies and enterprises	51,451	104,442,966	249,510,832	2,664,203	Not available	Not available
56	Administrative and Support and Waste Mang and Remediation Srvs	395,292	630,771,091	301,450,047	10,250,955	1,792,523	39,810,944
61	Educational services	61,385	44,980,656	14,259,109	539,951	528,217	7,214,509
62	Health care and social assistance	779,074	1,697,230,614	665,831,857	16,859,513	1,768,093	55,050,044
71	Arts, entertainment, and recreation	124,620	189,416,942	58,359,104	2,061,348	1,119,586	27,356,700
72	Accommodation and food services	634,361	613,795,732	170,826,847	11,600,751	303,482	16,071,088
81	Other services (except public administration)	540,148	405,284,048	99,123,269	3,479,011	2,964,627	80,653,086
		7,306,709	29,305,822,391	4,785,479,961	115,833,387	21,471,961	980,828,529

Note: The data in this file come from separate 2007 Economic Census Industry Series, Geographic Area Series, and Summary Series data files, as well as data files from the 2007 Economic Census of Island Areas and the 2007 Nonemployer Statistics. These files are released on a flow basis from March 2009 through mid-2011. The national data are subject to change; they will be replaced when updated data are added from the Geographic Area Series and Summary Series in 2010 and 2011.

SOURCE: Adapted from "Sector 00: EC0700A1. All Sectors: Geographic Area Series: Economy-Wide Key Statistics: 2007 ," in *American Fact Finder: 2007 Economic Census*, U.S. Department of Commerce, U.S. Census Bureau, July 2, 2010, http://factfinder.census.gov/servlet/IBQTable?_bm=y&-geo_id =01000US&-_skip=0&-ds_name=EC0700A1&-_lang=en (accessed July 8, 2010)

.pdf), Kobe reports that small businesses were responsible for approximately 48% to 51% of the nation's nonfarm, private industry GDP between 1998 and 2004.

Nonemployer Small Businesses

In "Nonemployer Statistics" (June 24, 2010, http://www.census.gov/econ/nonemployer/intro.htm), the Census Bureau defines nonemployer businesses as "businesses that have no paid employees and are subject to federal income tax." It further notes that nonemployers are typically "self-employed individuals operating very small businesses, which may or may not be the owner's principal source of income." The Census Bureau compiles nonemployer statistics using data from the Internal Revenue Service.

Table 6.2 shows employer and nonemployer statistics by industry for 2007. As described in Chapter 5, the government categorizes jobs using the North American Industry Classification System (NAICS). The NAICS is the standard classification system for businesses throughout North America. Table 6.2 provides statistics for 7.3 million employer establishments and 21.5 million nonemployer establishments. The largest numbers of nonemployer establishments were in the following five NAICS categories:

- Professional, scientific, and technical services—3,028,528 establishments

- Other services (except public administration)—2,964,627 establishments

- Construction—2,657,360 establishments

- Real estate and rental and leasing—2,327,057 establishments

- Retail trade—1,979,576 establishments

In 2007 nonemployers reported $980.8 billion in sales, shipments, receipts, revenue, or business done, compared with $29.3 trillion for employers. (See Table 6.2.) Thus, nonemployers make up a large fraction of the number of U.S. businesses, but a small fraction of overall business sales and receipts.

THE ROLE OF BIG BUSINESS IN THE U.S. AND GLOBAL ECONOMIES

Big businesses (those with 500 or more employees) accounted for only 0.3% of all nonfarm firms in the United States in 2007. (See Table 6.1.) However, these 18,311 big firms employed 60.7 million people (just over half of the nation's total nonfarm employees), provided $2.8 trillion in payroll (56% of total annual payroll), and had more than $18.4 trillion in estimated receipts (62% of total receipts).

The business magazine *Forbes* publishes an annual list of the world's 2,000 largest companies. In "The Global 2000" (April 21, 2010, http://www.forbes.com/lists/2010/18/global-2000-10_The-Global-2000_Rank.html), *Forbes* ranks public companies using a composite score based on sales, assets, profits, and market value. The top-10 companies in the 2010 report and their primary areas of business were:

- J.P. Morgan Chase (banking)
- General Electric (conglomerate)
- Bank of America (banking)
- Exxon Mobil (oil and gas)
- ICBC (banking)
- Banco Santander (banking)
- Wells Fargo (banking)
- HSBC Holdings (banking)
- Royal Dutch Shell (oil and gas)
- BP (oil and gas)

Five of the top-10 companies—J.P. Morgan Chase, General Electric, Bank of America, Exxon Mobil, and Wells Fargo—are based in the United States. ICBC is a China-based company. Banco Santander is based in Spain. HSBC Holdings and BP are United Kingdom–based companies. Royal Dutch Shell is based in the Netherlands.

Scott DeCarlo notes in "The Grand Totals" (April 21, 2010, http://www.forbes.com/2010/04/20/global-2000-aggregate-recession-business-global-2000-10-grand-totals.html) that the 2,000 companies employed 76.2 million people and had $124 trillion in assets, $30 trillion in sales, $1.4 trillion in profits, and $31.4 trillion in market value in 2010. Each year between 2004 and 2008 the top 2,000 companies cited by *Forbes* showed year-over-year increases in sales, profits, assets, and market value. However, the economic contraction that began in late 2007 in the United States had a ripple effect throughout the world. The profits and market value of the top 2,000 companies declined significantly in 2009.

According to DeCarlo, sales, profits, and assets in 2010 were down compared with 2009 values. Sales declined by $2 trillion, profits by $200 billion, and assets by $580 billion. Even though market value increased by $11.8 trillion between 2009 and 2010, it was extremely low in 2009 (only $19.6 trillion, compared with $38.6 trillion in 2008).

Six of *Forbes*'s top-10 companies in 2010 were also among the top 10 in 2009 (http://www.forbes.com/lists/2009/18/global-09_The-Global-2000_Rank.html): General Electric (ranked first), Royal Dutch Shell (ranked second), Exxon Mobil (ranked fourth), BP (ranked fifth), HSBC Holdings (ranked sixth), and Banco Santander (ranked ninth). The remaining four companies in the 2010 top-10 list that moved up from their 2009 rankings were ICBC (ranked 12th in 2009), J.P. Morgan Chase (ranked 16th in 2009), Bank of America (ranked 38th in 2009), and Wells Fargo (ranked 51st in 2009).

The four companies that were listed in the 2009 top-10 list but not in the 2010 top-10 list were Toyota Motor (ranked third in 2009), AT&T (ranked seventh in 2009), Wal-Mart Stores (ranked eighth in 2009), and Chevron (ranked 10th in 2009). All but Toyota Motor were among *Forbes*'s top-20 companies in 2010. Toyota Motor took a tremendous fall from number 3 in 2009 to number 360 in 2010. The automaker had to recall millions of its vehicles in late 2009 due to problems with stuck accelerators.

BUSINESS AND POLITICS

Large companies often have strong ties to the government. They have the resources to donate millions of dollars to political campaigns to elect sympathetic lawmakers and to otherwise encourage the passage of pro-business legislation. Likewise, lawmakers, eager to have companies locate facilities in their constituencies to boost local economies, may support policies that favor business interests to the detriment of other programs. Members of Congress may be more inclined to pass pro-business laws if their region has benefited from a large corporation's presence, or if they or their party have received campaign contributions from such a company. This raises concerns that big businesses may be able to convince the government to favor their interests at the expense of the interests of other businesses, or even the population as a whole.

THE FINANCIAL INDUSTRY FALTERS

The U.S. financial industry consists of companies that are engaged primarily in banking, insurance, and investment. Large corporations, in particular, may be involved in a mixture of these enterprises. However, there is an important distinction between commercial banking and investment banking. John Waggoner and David J. Lynch explain in "Red Flags in Bear Stearns' Collapse" (*USA Today*, March 19, 2008) that commercial banks offer products, such as checking and savings accounts, and make loans. They are heavily regulated by the federal government and in most cases the deposits of the banks' customers are insured by the federal government through the Federal Deposit Insurance Corporation (FDIC). In contrast, investment banks facilitate and finance the buying and selling of investments, including stocks and bonds. Investment products are not FDIC insured. The clients of investment banks are mainly companies and government bodies, such as counties and cities. Waggoner and Lynch point out that investment banks receive much less government scrutiny and regulation than commercial banks.

As noted in Chapter 4, investment companies helped drive the housing boom during the first few years of the first decade of the 21st century by buying mortgage-backed securities (MBS) in the secondary mortgage market. The cash inflow allowed lenders to underwrite even more mortgages. At first, MBS were considered a wise investment, and financial institutions saw their stock values rise. However, many of the underlying mortgages were poorly underwritten, meaning that the applicants had not been properly screened by the mortgage companies. In many cases, applicants with poor credit histories were given complex mortgages with fluctuating interest rates and ballooning payments. The result was a recipe for disaster. The housing bubble burst and mortgage default rates skyrocketed. Ever since the bust, economists have argued about whether or not investment companies knew that the products they were buying contained these so-called toxic mortgages.

Credit Default Swaps

Investment always entails a certain amount of risk. The article "Credit Default Swaps" (*New York Times,* May 21, 2010) explains that during the late 1990s the financial industry "invented" a type of insurance contract called the credit default swap (CDS) that was supposed to protect investors "against a default by a particular bond or security." However, CDS products are not technically insurance. The insurance industry is heavily regulated by the federal government. Insurance companies must show that they have the collateral (typically cash or other assets with immediately obtainable and verifiable worth) to cover losses that their clients might suffer.

The *New York Times* article notes that between 2000 and 2008 CDS sales skyrocketed from $900 billion to more than $30 trillion. Unbeknown to the investors, many of these products were "insuring" MBS that contained toxic mortgages. In addition, the swaps were not backed by enough cash collateral. Economists call this being undercapitalized. Some investment companies were even using swaps as collateral for the other swaps they were selling to investors.

In *The U.S. Financial Crisis: The Global Dimension with Implications for U.S. Policy* (January 30, 2009, http://graphics8.nytimes.com/packages/pdf/globalconcrs.pdf), Dick K. Nanto of the Congressional Research Service examines in detail the role of CDSs in the great recession. Nanto points out that investors may have thought that CDSs were safe because the swaps were rated by credit rating firms. Credit rating firms are paid fees to assess the financial soundness of companies and investments. The firms use past historical data and computer models in their assessments. However, Nanto notes that CDSs were rather new in the first decade of the 21st century. In addition, the credit rating firms used computer models that were supplied by the very companies that were issuing the CDSs. Nanto also suspects that the firms were advising clients "how to structure securities in order to receive higher ratings." Nanto concludes that "the large fees offered to credit rating firms for providing credit ratings were difficult for them to refuse in spite of doubts they might have had about the underlying quality of the securities."

Too Big to Fail?

By 2007 the toxic mortgages that had been initiated during the housing boom were going into default in record high numbers. These defaults devastated the value of the MBS. However, the supposed safety net—the CDSs—were too undercapitalized to cover the losses. The resultant effect was disastrous for the financial industry. Companies, many of them large corporations that had been in business for more than a century and that had weathered the Great Depression, were at the brink of failing. In early 2008 the Federal Reserve System, the national bank of the United States, brokered the sale of the investment bank Bear Stearns to J.P. Morgan Chase. Waggoner and Lynch note that the Federal Reserve agreed to cover $30 billion in bad assets held by Bear Stearns. The media called it the government's "too big to fail" approach, meaning that some banks are so vital to the overall success of the nation's financial industry that they cannot be allowed to fail. However, Waggoner and Lynch point out that it is more appropriate to say that some banks are "too interconnected to fail." They note that "Bear Stearns had a web of intertwined [investment] agreements with other banks, investment houses and corporations." Thus, the failure of one party in the web could bring down all the others.

Yalman Onaran notes in "Banks' Subprime Losses Top $500 Billion on Writedowns (Update1)" (Bloomberg.com, August 12, 2008) that by August 2008 banks and securities firms around the world had suffered losses totaling more than $500 billion due to declining MBS values. In September 2008 the investment firm Lehman Brothers declared bankruptcy after the government refused to bail out the company. However, later that month the government did intervene to save American International Group (AIG), a giant insurance corporation. Meanwhile, the administration of President George W. Bush (1946–) proposed a $700 billion bailout fund to rescue other struggling companies in the financial and automotive industries. It was called the Troubled Asset Relief Program (TARP) and was very unpopular politically. According to the article "Credit Crisis—The Essentials" (*New York Times*, July 12, 2010), "many Americans were angered by the idea of a proposal that provided billions of dollars in taxpayer money to Wall Street banks, which many believed had caused the crisis in the first place." Nevertheless, Congress approved the bailout measure. In February 2009 newly inaugurated President Barack Obama (1961–) proposed and Congress passed a $787 billion stimulus package that included funds that could be used to buy up toxic assets from troubled companies.

Throughout 2009 dozens of struggling companies in the financial industry received bailout funds from the federal government. By mid-2010 many of these companies had repaid the government. In *Troubled Assets Relief Program (TARP) Monthly 105(a) Report—August 2010*

(September 10, 2010, http://www.financialstability.gov/docs/105CongressionalReports/August%202010%20105(a)%20Report_final_9%2010%2010.pdf), the U.S. Department of the Treasury reports that more than 75% of the TARP funds provided to companies had been repaid as of August 2010.

Commercial Bank Failures

Commercial banks are heavily regulated by the government. They may be chartered (incorporated and authorized to conduct a certain business) at the state or federal level. The Department of the Treasury's Office of the Comptroller of the Currency (OCC) explains in "Is Your Financial Institution a National Bank" (June 2007, http://www.helpwithmybank.gov/national_banks/index.html) that three federal agencies—the OCC, the Office of Thrift Supervision, and the Federal Reserve—are responsible for supervising and regulating all federally chartered banks and credit unions and some state-chartered banks. The FDIC has regulatory authority for state-chartered banks that are not members of the Federal Reserve System. All state-chartered banks are also supervised by state banking regulators. According to the FDIC, in "Who Is the FDIC?" (August 11, 2010, http://www.fdic.gov/about/learn/symbol/index.html), as of August 2010 the FDIC supervised more than 4,900 banks for "operational safety and soundness." This represented more than half the banks in the United States.

Federal and state regulators closely monitor commercial financial institutions to ensure that they have enough assets to cover their obligations. The regulators close down banks that are in danger of failing and temporarily take over banks that fail. In "When a Bank Fails—Facts for Depositors, Creditors, and Borrowers" (July 7, 2010, http://www.fdic.gov/consumers/banking/facts/index.html), the FDIC explains that it acts as a "receiver" of failed banks, meaning that it takes over "selling/collecting the assets of the failed bank and settling its debts."

Following the Great Depression a number of strict commercial bank regulations were implemented. The direct result was that bank failures became very rare. However, the housing industry bust and the crisis in the financial industry that set off the great recession in late 2007 triggered historically high numbers of bank failures. The FDIC reports in "Failed Bank List" (September 14, 2010, http://www.fdic.gov/bank/individual/failed/banklist.html) the following number of bank failures per year:

- 2001—4 failed banks
- 2002—11 failed banks
- 2003—3 failed banks
- 2004—4 failed banks
- 2005—no failed banks
- 2006—no failed banks
- 2007—3 failed banks
- 2008—25 failed banks
- 2009—140 failed banks

In addition, between January and September 2010 another 120 banks had failed.

The huge increase in bank failures in 2008 and 2009 depleted the FDIC's Deposit Insurance Fund (DIF). The DIF is funded primarily by insurance premiums from FDIC-insured commercial banks. The FDIC reports in "Quarterly Banking Profile, Deposit Insurance Fund Trends Fourth Quarter 2009" (February 23, 2010, http://www2.fdic.gov/qbp/2009dec/qbpdep.html) that the DIF paid out $35.1 billion in 2008 and $38.1 billion in 2009 due to failed banks. At the end of 2009 the fund had a balance of −$20.9 billion. In late 2009 the FDIC required insured financial institutions to prepay 13 quarters' worth of deposit insurance premiums to help build back up the cash reserves of the DIF. By December 30, 2009, $46 billion in prepayments had been collected.

ECONOMIC PERFORMANCE

U.S. businesses produce goods and provide services that are purchased by consumers. The consumption of business output is the major driving force behind the nation's GDP growth.

The U.S. Department of Commerce's Bureau of Economic Analysis (BEA) compiles data on the contributions made to the real GDP by various industries. Figure 6.1 shows the BEA breakdown of real GDP growth per year by private industry category from 1998 to 2009. From 1998 to 2002 the services-producing sector had 3.6% annual growth in the real GDP, compared with 1.9% for the goods-producing sector. From 2002 to 2007 the services-producing sector showed 3.1% annual growth in the real GDP, compared with 2.3% for the goods-producing sector. In 2008 (the first full year of the great recession) the real GDP growth was down significantly—only 0.6% for the services-producing sector and −2.5% for the goods-producing sector. In 2009 both sectors had negative annual growth. The services-producing sector dropped by 1.9%, and the goods-producing sector dropped by 5.3%.

The BEA explains in the press release "2009 Decline Widespread across Industries" (May 25, 2009, http://www.bea.gov/newsreleases/industry/gdpindustry/2010/pdf/gdpind09.pdf) that downturns in durable-goods manufacturing and in the finance and insurance industries (both services-producing industries) were the "leading contributors" to the poor overall GPD performance in 2009.

Another measure of business output is called "real value added." This is defined as gross output minus the consumption of intermediate inputs. For example, the real

FIGURE 6.1

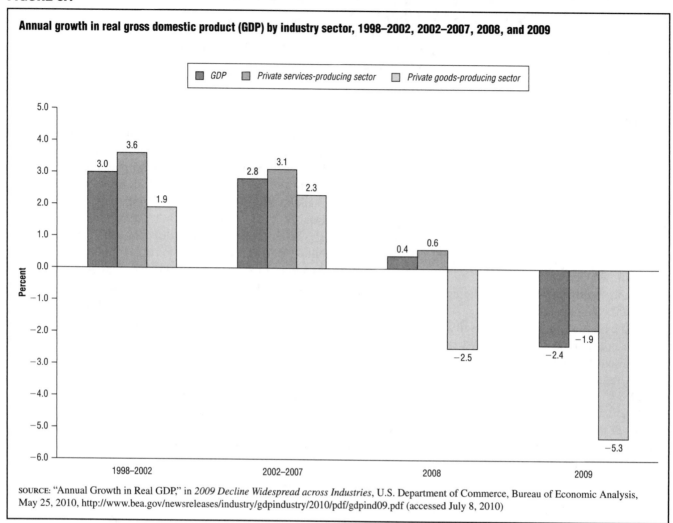

Annual growth in real gross domestic product (GDP) by industry sector, 1998–2002, 2002–2007, 2008, and 2009

SOURCE: "Annual Growth in Real GDP," in *2009 Decline Widespread across Industries*, U.S. Department of Commerce, Bureau of Economic Analysis, May 25, 2010, http://www.bea.gov/newsreleases/industry/gdpindustry/2010/pdf/gdpind09.pdf (accessed July 8, 2010)

value added to the economy by a manufacturer is calculated using the market value of the goods sold minus the cost of producing the goods. Table 6.3 shows the real value added by industry group in 2009. The best performers in 2009 were agriculture, forestry, fishing, and hunting (up 4.6%), mining (up 3.7%), and utilities (up 3.1%). The worst performers were construction (down 9.9%), durable-goods manufacturing (down 7.5%), and administrative and waste management services (down 6.5%).

Agriculture

The U.S. Department of Agriculture's National Agricultural Statistics Service (NASS; http://www.agcensus.usda.gov/) performs a census of agriculture every five years. As of September 2010, the most recent NASS results available were from the 2007 census. According to the NASS, in *2007 Census of Agriculture: Farm Numbers* (February 2009, http://www.agcensus.usda.gov/Publications/2007/Online_Highlights/Fact_Sheets/farm_numbers.pdf), there were 2.2 million farms and ranches operating in 2007. In "Frequently Asked Questions" (December 3, 2008, http://www.agcensus.usda.gov/Help/FAQs/General_FAQs/

index7.asp), the NASS defines a farm/ranch as an establishment "from which $1,000 or more of agricultural products were produced and sold, or normally would have been sold, during the Census year."

As shown in Table 6.4, U.S. farmers sold $297 billion worth of goods in 2007, up 48% from 2002. Farmers received $8 billion in government payments in 2007, compared with $7 billion in 2002. The government issues the payments (called subsidies) to influence the supply—and consequently the prices—of certain farmed goods. Farmers had $75 billion in net cash income in 2007. In *2007 Census of Agriculture: Economics* (April 2009, http://www.agcensus.usda.gov/Publications/2007/Online_Highlights/Fact_Sheets/economics.pdf), the NASS states that net cash income "is the amount an operation receives from sales of agricultural products, government payments, and farm-related income after expenses are subtracted." Production expenses totaled $241 billion in 2007, which was up substantially from $173 billion in 2002. The NASS reports that "steep" cost increases in gasoline, other fuels, and fertilizer were responsible for much of the increase in production prices.

TABLE 6.3

Percent change in real value added by industry group, 2009

	2009
Gross domestic product	−2.4
Private industries	**−2.6**
Agriculture, forestry, fishing, and hunting	4.6
Mining	3.7
Utilities	3.1
Construction	−9.9
Manufacturing	−5.9
Durable goods	−7.5
Nondurable goods	−3.8
Wholesale trade	−1.0
Retail trade	−4.5
Transportation and warehousing	−2.8
Information	1.6
Finance, insurance, real estate, rental, and leasing	−2.4
Finance and insurance	−2.7
Real estate and rental and leasing	−2.3
Professional and business services	−3.0
Professional, scientific, and technical services	−1.8
Management of companies and enterprises	−2.6
Administrative and waste management services	−6.5
Educational services, health care, and social assistance	1.4
Educational services	−1.1
Health care and social assistance	1.7
Arts, entertainment, recreation, accommodation, and food services	−3.1
Arts, entertainment, and recreation	−2.2
Accommodation and food services	−3.4
Other services, except government	−4.5
Government	**1.9**
Federal	5.7
State and local	0.1
Addenda:	
Private goods-producing industries[a]	−5.3
Private services-producing industries[b]	−1.9
Information-communications-technology-producing industries[c]	−0.1

[a]Consists of agriculture, forestry, fishing, and hunting; mining; construction; and manufacturing.
[b]Consists of utilities; wholesale trade; retail trade; transportation and warehousing; information; finance, insurance, real estate, rental, and leasing; professional and business services; educational services, health care, and social assistance; arts, entertainment, recreation, accommodation, and food services; and other services, except government.
[c]Consists of computer and electronic products within durable-goods manufacturing; publishing industries (includes software) and information and data processing services within information; and computer systems design and related services within professional, scientific, and technical services.

SOURCE: "Table 1. Real Value Added by Industry Group," in *2009 Decline Widespread across Industries*, U.S. Department of Commerce, Bureau of Economic Analysis, May 25, 2010, http://www.bea.gov/newsreleases/industry/gdpindustry/2010/pdf/gdpind09.pdf (accessed July 8, 2010)

Corporate Profits

One of the economic indicators tracked by the BEA is corporate profits. This is a measure of the income generated by corporations from the current production of goods and services. Because only current production is counted, corporate profits do not include capital gains, such as inventory profits.

Table 6.5 lists the corporate profits by industry from 2007 to the first quarter of 2010 and the changes per period. Corporate profits totaled $1.3 trillion in 2009, down from $1.4 trillion in 2008 and $1.5 trillion in 2007. In the first quarter of 2010 corporate profits totaled $1.6 trillion. Domestic industries accounted for $1.3 trillion (79%) of the total in

TABLE 6.4

Agricultural sector economic statistics, 2002 and 2007

	2007	2002	% Change
Market value of products sold			
All farms	$297 billion	$201 billion	+48
Average per farm	$134,807	$94,245	+43
Government payments received			
All farms	$8 billion	$7 billion	+22
Average per farm	$9,523	$9,251	+3
Farm-related income			
All farms	$10 billion	$6 billion	+79
Average per farm	$15,133	$9,421	+61
Production expenses			
All farms	$241 billion	$173 billion	+39
Average per farm	$109,359	$81,362	+34
Net cash income			
All farms	$75 billion	$41 billion	+84
Average per farm	$33,827	$19,032	+78

SOURCE: "Untitled," in *Census Fact Sheet: 2007 Census of Agriculture: Economics*, U.S. Department of Agriculture, National Agricultural Statistics Service, May 24, 2010, http://www.agcensus.usda.gov/Publications/2007/Online_Highlights/Fact_Sheets/economics.pdf (accessed July 9, 2010)

the first quarter of 2010. These values included adjustments for inventory valuation and capital consumption.

Figure 6.2 shows the percentage change in quarter-to-year growth in corporate profits from the second quarter of 2006 to the first quarter of 2010. Corporate profits rose and fell by less than 5% from the second quarter of 2006 to the third quarter of 2008, and then nosedived the following quarter, dropping by more than 20%. Quarterly performance improved greatly in 2009 and in the first quarter of 2010, when profits were up around 7%.

Industry Outlook

Table 6.6 lists the industries that are expected to undergo the greatest growth or decline in output through 2018. This list was compiled by the U.S. Bureau of Labor Statistics (BLS) in November 2009. The BLS expects phenomenal growth (a 17% average increase annually) from businesses engaged in the manufacture of computers and peripheral equipment. This industry is expected to increase its output by $766.8 billion between 2008 and 2018. Strong performance is also expected from software publishers, with an increase in output of $334.7 billion during this period and an average growth of 10.5% annually. Likewise, businesses engaged in data processing, hosting, related services, and other information services are expected to increase output by $203.4 billion during this period and have an average growth of 9.3% annually.

Industries that are expected to suffer the largest declines in output between 2008 and 2018 include federal government enterprises, except the U.S. Postal Service and electric utilities. These industries are projected to decrease output on average by 4.7% annually. (See Table 6.6.) Other

TABLE 6.5

Level of corporate profits and change from preceding period, by industry, 2007–first quarter 2010

[Billions of dollars]

| | Level | | | Seasonally adjusted at annual rates | | | | | Change from preceding period | | | | | |
| | | | | 2009 | | | | 2010 | | | 2009 | | | 2010 |
	2007	2008	2009	I	II	III	IV	I*	2008	2009	II	III	IV	I*
Corporate profits with inventory valuation and capital consumption adjustments	1,541.7	1,360.4	1,308.9	1,182.7	1,226.5	1,358.9	1,467.6	1,584.5	−181.3	−51.5	43.8	132.4	108.7	116.9
Domestic industries	1,193.9	983.2	997.1	867.0	925.3	1,035.7	1,160.4	1,251.3	−210.7	13.9	58.3	110.4	124.7	90.9
Financial	347.0	271.6	316.8	237.8	266.3	349.1	414.1	425.3	−75.4	45.2	28.5	82.8	65.0	11.2
Nonfinancial	846.9	711.6	680.3	629.2	659.0	686.6	746.4	826.0	−135.3	−31.3	29.8	27.6	59.8	79.6
Rest of the world	347.8	377.2	311.8	315.8	301.2	323.2	307.1	333.2	29.4	−65.4	−14.6	22.0	−16.1	26.1
Receipts from the rest of the world	504.5	544.2	430.3	402.2	409.9	440.8	468.5	501.0	39.7	−113.9	7.7	30.9	27.7	32.5
Less: Payments to the rest of the world	156.8	167.0	118.5	86.4	108.7	117.6	161.4	167.8	10.2	−48.5	22.3	8.9	43.8	6.4
Corporate profits with inventory valuation adjustment	1,730.4	1,424.5	1,436.7	1,327.6	1,355.1	1,477.8	1,586.3	1,810.7	−305.9	12.2	27.5	122.7	108.5	224.4
Domestic industries	1,382.6	1,047.3	1,124.9	1,011.9	1,053.9	1,154.6	1,279.2	1,477.5	−335.3	77.6	42.0	100.7	124.6	198.3
Financial	367.8	278.9	331.2	253.9	280.7	362.4	427.9	450.5	−88.9	52.3	26.8	81.7	65.5	22.6
Federal Reserve banks	37.7	35.7	50.1	28.8	46.1	57.6	67.9	77.9	−2.0	14.4	17.3	11.5	10.3	10.0
Other financial	330.1	243.2	281.1	225.1	234.6	304.8	359.9	372.5	−86.9	37.9	9.5	70.2	55.1	12.6
Nonfinancial	1,014.9	768.4	793.7	758.0	773.3	792.2	851.4	1,027.1	−246.5	25.3	15.3	18.9	59.2	175.7
Utilities	49.1	40.1	54.1	53.6	53.4	61.5	47.8	69.4	−9.0	14.0	−0.2	8.1	−13.7	21.6
Manufacturing	278.6	175.5	136.0	121.6	132.3	129.7	160.5	207.7	−103.1	−39.5	10.7	−2.6	30.8	47.2
Durable goods	96.1	30.7	14.9	8.0	11.9	6.7	32.9	70.8	−65.4	−15.8	3.9	−5.2	26.2	37.9
Fabricated metal products	21.3	17.6	13.4	19.3	13.7	10.9	10.0	12.5	−3.7	−4.2	−5.6	−2.8	−0.9	2.5
Machinery	19.8	16.1	11.0	12.8	10.4	8.1	12.7	15.3	−3.7	−5.1	−2.4	−2.3	4.6	2.6
Computer and electronic products	11.2	4.7	3.6	3.2	3.9	3.1	4.2	10.6	−6.5	−1.1	0.7	−0.8	1.1	6.4
Electrical equipment, appliances, and components	−1.1	−4.1	−8.5	−6.3	−9.1	−9.6	−9.0	−5.3	−3.0	−4.4	−2.8	−0.5	0.6	3.7
Motor vehicles, bodies and trailers, and parts	−16.4	−47.5	−28.4	−54.8	−38.5	−16.6	−3.7	7.2	−31.1	19.1	16.3	21.9	12.9	10.9
Other durable goods	61.3	43.9	23.8	33.9	31.5	10.8	18.9	30.5	−17.4	−20.1	−2.4	−20.7	8.1	11.6
Nondurable goods	182.6	144.9	121.1	113.6	120.4	122.9	127.6	136.9	−37.7	−23.8	6.8	2.5	4.7	9.3
Food and beverage and tobacco products	30.2	33.7	33.1	34.7	33.1	35.1	29.4	34.1	3.5	−0.6	−1.6	2.0	−5.7	4.7
Petroleum and coal products	77.8	66.5	21.4	29.4	15.2	15.8	25.3	43.4	−11.3	−45.1	−14.2	0.6	9.5	18.1
Chemical products	51.9	31.3	35.9	29.6	39.4	37.4	37.3	29.2	−20.6	4.6	9.8	−2.0	−0.1	−8.1
Other nondurable goods	22.7	13.3	30.7	19.8	32.8	34.5	35.7	30.2	−9.4	17.4	13.0	1.7	1.2	−5.5
Wholesale trade	102.2	75.1	87.9	94.0	87.5	80.6	89.5	105.4	−27.1	12.8	−6.5	−6.9	8.9	15.9
Retail trade	121.6	78.2	91.2	83.1	95.1	98.8	87.8	111.2	−43.4	13.0	12.0	3.7	−11.0	23.4
Transportation and warehousing	30.0	11.4	5.9	6.7	1.3	4.8	10.8	22.4	−18.6	−5.5	−5.4	3.5	6.0	11.6
Information	90.3	84.7	108.9	95.4	99.4	107.0	133.9	129.7	−5.6	24.2	4.0	7.6	26.9	−4.2
Other nonfinancial	343.0	303.4	309.7	303.6	304.2	309.9	321.0	381.3	−39.6	6.3	0.6	5.7	11.1	60.3
Rest of the world	347.8	377.2	311.8	315.8	301.2	323.2	307.1	333.2	29.4	−65.4	−14.6	22.0	−16.1	26.1

*Revised

Note: Estimates in this table are based on the 2002 North American Industry Classification System (NAICS).

SOURCE: "Table 12. Corporate Profits by Industry: Level and Change from Preceding Period," in *Gross Domestic Product: First Quarter 2010 (Third Estimate); Corporate Profits: First Quarter 2010 (Revised Estimate)*, U.S. Department of Commerce, Bureau of Economic Analysis, June 25, 2010, http://www.bea.gov/newsreleases/national/gdp/2010/pdf/gdp1q10_3rd.pdf (accessed June 28, 2010).

FIGURE 6.2

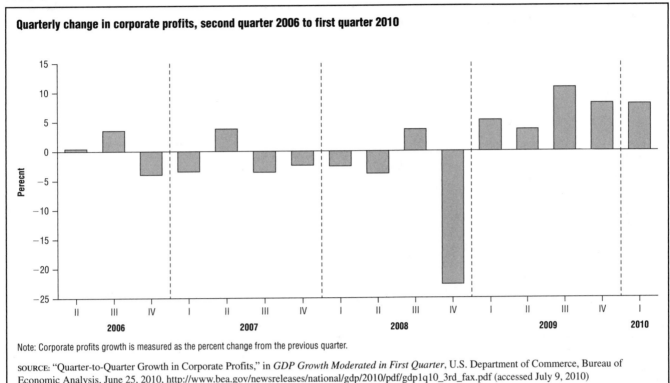

Quarterly change in corporate profits, second quarter 2006 to first quarter 2010

Note: Corporate profits growth is measured as the percent change from the previous quarter.

SOURCE: "Quarter-to-Quarter Growth in Corporate Profits," in *GDP Growth Moderated in First Quarter*, U.S. Department of Commerce, Bureau of Economic Analysis, June 25, 2010, http://www.bea.gov/newsreleases/national/gdp/2010/pdf/gdp1q10_3rd_fax.pdf (accessed July 9, 2010)

industries expected to perform poorly include cut and sew apparel manufacturers, with an average annual decline of 4.1%, and manufacturers engaged in the production and processing of nonferrous metal (except aluminum), with an average decline in output of 4.1% annually.

Table 6.7 lists the industries that the BLS expects will experience the largest average annual growth or decline in wage and salary employment through 2018. Management, scientific, and technical consulting services are projected to add 835,200 jobs for an average annual growth rate of 6.2%. Businesses in the industry called "other educational services" are expected to add 316,000 jobs (up an average of 4.5% annually), and businesses engaged in individual and family services within the health care and social assistance sector are projected to add 530,200 jobs (up an average of 4% annually). The BLS anticipates that offices of health care practitioners will add the most jobs—nearly 1.3 million—between 2008 and 2018.

According to the BLS, the three most rapidly declining industries in terms of employment are expected to be cut and sew apparel manufacturing (down an average of 8.1% annually), apparel knitting mills (down an average of 7.1% annually), and textile and fabric finishing and fabric coating mills (down an average of 7% annually). (See Table 6.7.) The BLS projects that businesses engaged in semiconductor and other electronic component manufacturing will lose the most jobs of any industry. Approximately 145,600 jobs are expected to be lost in this industry between 2008 and 2018.

FEDERAL REGULATION OF BUSINESS

Historically, U.S. economic philosophy has been to let the market operate with a minimum of government interference. This does not mean, however, that U.S. businesses go unregulated. Many local, state, and federal laws exist to protect the public and the economy from dangerous, unfair, or fraudulent activities by businesses. Major federal programs that oversee business activities are:

- Federal Trade Commission (FTC)—created in 1914 with the passage of the Federal Trade Commission Act. Originally intended to combat the rise of business monopolies, the FTC grew to become the U.S. government's consumer protection agency, addressing consumer issues such as identity theft, false advertising, telemarketing and Internet scams, and anticompetition moves by businesses.

- Consumer Product Safety Commission (CPSC)— established in 1973 to protect the American public from unreasonable risks of serious injury or death from consumer products. Through a combination of voluntary and mandatory safety standards, the CPSC tries to prevent dangerous products from entering the market. If a product is found to be dangerous after it has already been sold to consumers, the CPSC has the duty to inform the public and the power to force a recall of the product if it is deemed necessary.

TABLE 6.6

Industries with the fastest growing and most rapidly declining output, 2008–18

| Industry description | Sector | Billions of chained 2000 dollars | | Change | Average annual rate of change |
		2008	2018	2008–18	2008–18
Fastest growing					
Computer and peripheral equipment manufacturing	Manufacturing	200.5	967.3	766.8	17.0
Software publishers	Information	194.9	529.6	334.7	10.5
Data processing, hosting, related services, and other information services	Information	141.9	345.3	203.4	9.3
Audio and video equipment manufacturing	Manufacturing	4.8	10.8	6.0	8.4
Securities, commodity contracts, and other financial investments and related activities	Financial activities	435.5	883.2	447.7	7.3
Medical equipment and supplies manufacturing	Manufacturing	72.1	132.7	60.6	6.3
Scientific research and development services	Professional and business services	159.0	288.5	129.5	6.1
Commercial and industrial machinery and equipment (except automotive and electronic) repair and maintenance	Other services	22.8	40.7	17.9	6.0
Semiconductor and other electronic component manufacturing	Manufacturing	173.4	308.7	135.3	5.9
Other transportation equipment manufacturing	Manufacturing	12.6	21.9	9.3	5.7
Telecommunications	Information	480.3	822.3	342.0	5.5
Management, scientific, and technical consulting services	Professional and business services	171.8	287.2	115.4	5.3
Wholesale trade	Wholesale trade	1,063.5	1,777.0	713.5	5.3
Community and vocational rehabilitation services	Health care and social assistance	24.2	40.3	16.2	5.2
Services to buildings and dwellings	Professional and business services	121.1	197.7	76.6	5.0
Lessors of nonfinancial intangible assets (except copyrighted works)	Financial activities	146.0	235.0	89.0	4.9
Household and institutional furniture and kitchen cabinet manufacturing	Manufacturing	35.6	57.0	21.4	4.8
Waste management and remediation services	Professional and business services	67.0	104.8	37.8	4.6
Outpatient, laboratory, and other ambulatory care services	Health care and social assistance	115.5	180.0	64.5	4.5
Offices of health practitioners	Health care and social assistance	467.9	714.1	246.2	4.3
Management of companies and enterprises	Professional and business services	634.0	964.0	329.9	4.3
Most rapidly declining					
Federal enterprises except the postal service and electric utilities	Federal government	10.9	6.7	−4.2	−4.7
Cut and sew apparel manufacturing	Manufacturing	24.7	16.2	−8.5	−4.1
Nonferrous metal (except aluminum) production and processing	Manufacturing	24.2	15.9	−8.3	−4.1
Apparel knitting mills	Manufacturing	4.6	3.4	−1.2	−3.0
Tobacco manufacturing	Manufacturing	64.8	49.7	−15.2	−2.6
Textile and fabric finishing and fabric coating mills	Manufacturing	8.3	7.1	−1.2	−1.5
Printing and related support activities	Manufacturing	92.2	80.4	−11.9	−1.4
Converted paper product manufacturing	Manufacturing	74.8	66.1	−8.7	−1.2
Death care services	Other services	10.5	9.4	−1.1	−1.1
Fishing, hunting and trapping	Agriculture, forestry, fishing, and hunting	7.1	6.3	−0.8	−1.1
Foundries	Manufacturing	30.3	27.8	−2.5	−0.9
Other textile product mills	Manufacturing	6.4	5.9	−0.5	−0.8
Pulp, paper, and paperboard mills	Manufacturing	66.9	62.2	−4.7	−0.7
Newspaper, periodical, book, and directory publishers	Information	127.0	119.6	−7.3	−0.6
Industrial machinery manufacturing	Manufacturing	33.6	32.1	−1.5	−0.5
Alumina and aluminum production and processing	Manufacturing	41.8	40.0	−1.9	−0.5
Leather and hide tanning and finishing, and other leather and allied product manufacturing	Manufacturing	3.8	3.6	−0.1	−0.4
Personal and household goods repair and maintenance	Other services	14.3	13.7	−0.5	−0.4
Footwear manufacturing	Manufacturing	7.8	7.5	−0.3	−0.4
Oil and gas extraction	Mining	125.6	121.9	−3.7	−0.3
Support activities for mining	Mining	55.7	54.3	−1.4	−0.3

SOURCE: Adapted from Rose A. Woods, "Table 5. Industries with the Fastest Growing and Most Rapidly Declining Output, 2008–18," in "Industry Output and Employment Projections to 2018," *Monthly Labor Review*, vol. 132, no. 11, November 2009, http://www.bls.gov/opub/mlr/2009/11/mlr200911.pdf (accessed July 9, 2010)

- Equal Employment Opportunity Commission (EEOC)—established in 1965, the EEOC is the primary federal agency responsible for preventing discrimination in the workplace. Its original purpose was to investigate violations of the Civil Rights Act of 1964, which prohibited discrimination in the workplace on the basis of race, color, national origin, sex, and religion. Over the years its powers have been expanded and it has been given responsibility to enforce other anti-discrimination laws.

TABLE 6.7

Industries with the fastest growing and most rapidly declining wage and salary employment, 2008–18

Industry description	Sector	Thousands of jobs		Change	Average annual rate of change
		2008	2018	2008–18	2008–18
Fastest growth					
Management, scientific, and technical consulting services	Professional and business services	1,008.9	1,844.1	835.2	6.2
Other educational services	Educational services	578.9	894.9	316.0	4.5
Individual and family services	Health care and social assistance	1,108.6	1,638.8	530.2	4.0
Home health care services	Health care and social assistance	958.0	1,399.4	441.4	3.9
Specialized design services	Professional and business services	143.1	208.7	65.6	3.8
Data processing, hosting, related services, and other information services	Information	395.2	574.1	178.9	3.8
Computer systems design and related services	Professional and business services	1,450.3	2,106.7	656.4	3.8
Lessors of nonfinancial intangible assets (except copyrighted works)	Financial activities	28.2	37.9	9.7	3.0
Offices of health practitioners	Health care and social assistance	3,713.3	4,978.6	1,265.3	3.0
Personal care services	Other services	621.6	819.1	197.5	2.8
Outpatient, laboratory, and other ambulatory care services	Health care and social assistance	989.5	1,297.9	308.4	2.8
Facilities support services	Professional and business services	132.7	173.6	40.9	2.7
Software publishers	Information	263.7	342.8	79.1	2.7
Independent artists, writers, and performers	Leisure and hospitality	50.4	64.8	14.4	2.5
Local government passenger transit	State and local government	268.6	342.6	74.0	2.5
Elementary and secondary schools	Educational services	854.9	1,089.7	234.8	2.5
Scientific research and development services	Professional and business services	621.7	778.9	157.2	2.3
Waste management and remediation services	Professional and business services	360.2	451.0	90.8	2.3
Other miscellaneous manufacturing	Manufacturing	321.0	399.4	78.4	2.2
Community and vocational rehabilitation services	Health care and social assistance	540.9	672.0	131.1	2.2
Most rapidly declining					
Cut and sew apparel manufacturing	Manufacturing	155.2	66.7	−88.5	−8.1
Apparel knitting mills	Manufacturing	26.2	12.5	−13.7	−7.1
Textile and fabric finishing and fabric coating mills	Manufacturing	48.3	23.5	−24.8	−7.0
Fabric mills	Manufacturing	65.4	35.0	−30.4	−6.1
Audio and video equipment manufacturing	Manufacturing	27.0	14.6	−12.4	−6.0
Apparel accessories and other apparel manufacturing	Manufacturing	17.0	9.2	−7.8	−6.0
Fiber, yarn, and thread mills	Manufacturing	37.4	20.7	−16.7	−5.7
Textile furnishings mills	Manufacturing	75.4	41.9	−33.5	−5.7
Railroad rolling stock manufacturing	Manufacturing	28.4	17.5	−10.9	−4.7
Footwear manufacturing	Manufacturing	15.8	10.0	−5.8	−4.5
Pulp, paper, and paperboard mills	Manufacturing	126.1	81.9	−44.2	−4.2
Basic chemical manufacturing	Manufacturing	152.1	99.9	−52.2	−4.1
Semiconductor and other electronic component manufacturing	Manufacturing	432.4	286.8	−145.6	−4.0
Computer and peripheral equipment manufacturing	Manufacturing	182.8	124.7	−58.1	−3.8
Other textile product mills	Manufacturing	72.2	49.4	−22.8	−3.7
Federal enterprises except the postal service and electric utilities	Federal government	63.5	44.9	−18.6	−3.4
Leather and hide tanning and finishing, and other leather and allied product manufacturing	Manufacturing	17.8	13.0	−4.8	−3.1
Cutlery and handtool manufacturing	Manufacturing	49.1	35.9	−13.2	−3.1
Manufacturing and reproducing magnetic and optical media	Manufacturing	34.9	26.0	−8.9	−2.9
Ventilation, heating, air-conditioning, and commercial refrigeration equipment manufacturing	Manufacturing	149.5	112.8	−36.7	−2.8

SOURCE: Adapted from Rose A. Woods, "Table 3. Industries with the Fastest Growing and Most Rapidly Declining Wage and Salary Employment, 2008–18," in "Industry Output and Employment Projections to 2018," *Monthly Labor Review*, vol. 132, no. 11, November 2009, http://www.bls.gov/opub/mlr/2009/11/mlr200911.pdf (accessed July 9, 2010)

- Employment Standards Administration (ESA)—one of the largest branches of the U.S. Department of Labor, the ESA is charged with enforcing a wide variety of labor laws dealing with minimum wage requirements, overtime pay standards, child labor protections, and unpaid leaves of absence. It also provides oversight of federal contractors concerning employment issues.

- U.S. Environmental Protection Agency (EPA)—develops and enforces federal environmental regulations. The EPA keeps track of industrial pollutants and regularly updates its compliance codes for individual sectors and industries.

- U.S. Food and Drug Administration (FDA)—works to ensure that the food, drugs, and cosmetics sold in the United States are safe and effective. It establishes safety and sanitation standards for manufacturers of these goods, as well as quality standards that the goods themselves must meet. The FDA must prove that certain products, especially drugs, are safe and effective before they can be sold in the United States, and it can force products off the market if they are later discovered to be dangerous. In addition, the FDA ensures that the labeling of food, drugs, and cosmetics is complete and truthful.

- Occupational Safety and Health Administration (OSHA)—establishes and enforces workplace safety standards. One or more OSHA standards covers almost every workplace in the United States.

Other Agencies

Besides the previously mentioned agencies, there are a number of other government agencies that regulate specific industries or aspects of the economy. Some of them are well known, whereas many others may be virtually unknown to people outside the fields they regulate. A few examples are:

- Federal Communications Commission—regulates the telecommunications industry, including all television, radio, satellite, cable, and wire services in the United States and its territories

- Federal Energy Regulatory Commission—regulates the national transmission network for oil, natural gas, and electricity

- Federal Maritime Commission—regulates the waterborne foreign commerce of the United States

- National Highway Traffic Safety Administration—regulates automobile design and safety

- Office of Surface Mining—regulates surface coal mining

- Securities and Exchange Commission—regulates the stock market

Government Regulation and Deregulation

Since the late 1970s the federal and many state governments have lessened their restrictions on certain industries. Called deregulation, this process allows industries to set their own standards and control their own systems of pricing and other business functions. For example, beginning in 1938 the airline industry was regulated by a federal body called the Civil Aeronautics Board, which controlled airlines' schedules, flying routes, and prices. To stimulate competition in the industry, Congress passed the Airline Deregulation Act of 1978. The industry experienced a flood of new airlines offering low fares to compete with the established airlines. Even though deregulation has actually caused some problems with larger airlines having too much control of (or monopolizing) the industry and with overly crowded flight routes, most economists agree that the result has been a safer, but cheaper, air transportation system. Other industries that have experienced some degree of deregulation include electric utilities, telephone services, trucking, railroads, and banking.

MARKET POWER: MONOPOLIES AND MONOPSONIES

One of the foundations of a capitalistic economy is competition. Competition for customers among sellers theoretically ensures that buyers receive the lowest price. If an industry becomes dominated by one seller, the lack of competition allows that entity to set prices in the marketplace—a situation known as monopolization. The federal government has long fought against monopolization in most private U.S. industries. In 1890 Congress passed the Sherman Antitrust Act to strengthen competitive forces in the economy. Section 2 of the law states: "Every person who shall monopolize, or attempt to monopolize, or combine or conspire with any other person or persons, to monopolize any part of the trade or commerce among the several States, or with foreign nations, shall be deemed guilty of a felony."

However, the government has allowed monopolies to form in certain industries that are deemed vital to the public interest. Two examples are telephone services and providers of electric power. For nearly 100 years the private company AT&T was allowed to monopolize the telephone services industry in the United States. In 1974 the U.S. Department of Justice filed suit against AT&T, accusing it of using unfair business practices. The suit was finally settled nearly a decade later and resulted in the breakup of the giant company into several smaller business units. Likewise, private utility companies have been permitted by the government to monopolize electric power service in certain geographic areas.

Companies that become hugely successful and powerful in their industry face an increased risk of being accused of using monopolistic practices by their competitors. Dominance also brings more intense scrutiny by federal regulators. During the 1990s and the first decade of the 21st century this was particularly true for two companies: the software giant Microsoft and Google, a provider of Internet services, including the popular Google search engine.

In 1993 the Department of Justice began an investigation of Microsoft based on allegations that the company was engaging in unfair competition. Microsoft's Windows program already dominated the operating systems market. By bundling web browsers and other applications with Windows, Microsoft made it difficult for other companies to compete in the market for these other applications. Throughout the 1990s and the first decade of the 21st century Microsoft fought (and mostly lost) antitrust cases brought against it in the United States and in other countries. The company paid millions of dollars in fines and agreed to stop bundling other products with Windows.

Google came under fire in 2008 when it was accused by competitors of using unfair business practices. James B.

Stewart reports in "Few Match Google; Does That Make It a Monopoly?" (*Wall Street Journal*, May 6, 2009) that in 2008 the federal government had threatened four separate times to bring antitrust cases against Google for various company actions. Stewart describes Google as a "natural monopoly," meaning that the company's dominance has resulted from its business skill, rather than from treating competitors unfairly. He calls the company "a victim of its own success" and asks "why would the U.S. government be so eager to punish the country's most successful and innovative start-up in recent memory?" This opinion is broadly shared by free-trade advocates, who argue that government crackdowns on alleged monopolists are bad for business overall.

In July 2010 the French government announced its intentions to investigate Google for alleged unfair practices. In "France Calls Google a Monopoly" (*New York Times*, July 1, 2010), Floyd Norris explains that French regulators accused Google of holding "a dominant position on the advertising market related to online searches." As of September 2010, no further developments had been reported in the case.

A monopsony is a different situation, in which the power lies with one buyer. This arrangement can occur if one company wields enormous power over the suppliers in that industry. The lack of other customers forces the suppliers to meet the price and quota demands of the monopsonist. Monopsony is an obscure economic concept to most Americans. However, during the first few years of the first decade of the 21st century the megaretailer Wal-Mart was widely accused in the media of practicing monopsonism. In general, the accusations were that the company had so much market power that it pressured suppliers to sell their goods to Wal-Mart at extremely low prices, which hurt the profits of the suppliers. As of September 2010, no formal complaints or government actions had been taken against the retail company.

CORPORATE BEHAVIOR AND RESPONSIBILITY

Businesses play a vital role in the economic well-being of the United States. Besides economic performance, Americans also expect businesses to behave in a legally and socially responsible manner. There is no public or political consensus on the exact social responsibilities of businesses. However, it is recognized that the decisions and practices of company officials, particularly of large corporations, affect not only employees and investors but also the communities in which businesses are located. Fraud and corruption at the corporate level can adversely affect large numbers of people. Likewise, poor performance by businesses in meeting environmental, health, or consumer-protection standards has detrimental effects on society at large.

Big Tobacco: An Industry under Attack

During the 1990s several state governments brought lawsuits against the nation's major tobacco firms to recoup taxpayer money that was spent treating sick smokers under state Medicaid programs. In 1998 a settlement was reached in which the companies agreed to pay a total of $246 billion spread among the governments of all 50 states. The payments are to be made over a 25-year period. The settlement also required the tobacco companies to change their advertising methods and to reduce their political lobbying efforts.

In 1999 the federal government filed its own lawsuit, *United States v. Philip Morris Inc.* (116 F. Supp. 2d 131), against the tobacco companies, alleging that the defendants had engaged in a decades-long scheme to "defraud the American public" regarding the safety of cigarette smoking. The case centered on internal documents obtained from tobacco companies that seemed to demonstrate that the companies were well aware that nicotine was addictive and that cigarette smoking caused lung cancer. The litigation dragged on for seven years. In 2006 Judge Gladys Kessler (1938–) of the U.S. District Court for the District of Columbia ruled that the cigarette companies had committed civil violations of the Racketeer Influenced and Corrupt Organizations Act. However, rulings by other courts during 2005 meant that the government could not receive billions of dollars in penalty fines that it had sought from the tobacco companies. Kessler did issue an injunction ordering the companies to remove terms such as *light* and *ultra light* from cigarette packaging. Both sides filed appeals in the case that proved to be unsuccessful.

Mike Scarcella notes in "DOJ, Tobacco Lawyers Back in Court over Injunction" (*National Law Journal*, September 16, 2010) that in May 2009 the U.S. Court of Appeals for the District of Columbia Circuit Court issued guidance on how the injunction is to be carried out. The tobacco companies petitioned the U.S. Supreme Court to review portions of the original case, but their petitions were denied. According to Scarcella, attorneys for both sides met in September 2010 to begin discussions on implementing the injunction. They were scheduled to meet again in December 2010.

These lawsuits represent an unusual occurrence in U.S. history because the state and federal governments brought financial pressure on an entire industry. In 2009 Congress passed the Family Smoking Prevention and Tobacco Control Act, which gave the FDA regulatory control over cigarettes and other forms of tobacco. According to Duff Wilson, in "Senate Approves Tight Regulation over Cigarettes" (*New York Times,* June 11, 2009), the act does not allow the FDA to ban smoking or nicotine, but only to "set standards that could reduce nicotine content and regulate chemicals in cigarette smoke." However, Wilson notes that industry analysts believe the tobacco companies will continue to prosper because "as long as they have a market of addicted customers, even if that clientele is dwindling, they can raise prices to remain profitable."

Corporate Scandals in the 21st Century

During the first decade of the 21st century some of the largest corporations in the United States suffered scandals that seriously eroded public confidence in big business. Most of the misdeeds involved deceptive accounting practices that enriched a handful of top executives, but hurt thousands of employees and investors. The four most notorious cases were:

- Enron—the corporation was an international broker of commodities such as natural gas, water, coal, and steel. During the early years of the 21st century top executives collaborated with Arthur Anderson, the company's accounting firm, to hide debts to make Enron seem more profitable than it actually was. As the deception unraveled, Enron filed for bankruptcy. Thousands of people lost their jobs, along with their health care, retirement funds, and, in many cases, life savings. Even though investors both in and outside the company lost tens of billions of dollars, Enron wrote $55 million in bonus checks for company executives the day before it declared bankruptcy. Arthur Andersen was found guilty of obstruction of justice. The former Enron executives Jeffrey Skilling (1953–) and Kenneth Lay (1942–2006) and dozens of other people were convicted in the scandal. Lay died of a heart attack before his sentencing hearing. Skilling was sentenced to 24 years in prison, but appealed his conviction. In June 2010 the U.S. Supreme Court ordered a lower court to reconsider some of the charges against Skilling. As of September 2010, a ruling had not been reached by the lower court.

- WorldCom—in 2002 the federal government uncovered an $11 billion accounting scandal at the telecommunications company. Its resulting bankruptcy left its stock worthless and put thousands of employees out of work. They also lost their pensions and benefits. Several company executives were indicted on fraud charges. The former chief executive officer (CEO) Bernard J. Ebbers (1941–) received a sentence of 25 years in prison.

- Tyco International—in 2002 the company became embroiled in scandals involving its CEO, L. Dennis Kozlowski (1946–), and its chief financial officer, Mark H. Swartz (1960–). Both men resigned and were sued by Tyco in connection with $600 million in loans, salary, and fringe benefits they allegedly took from the company without board approval. The men were indicted for grand larceny and securities fraud. In April 2004 the case was declared a mistrial after a juror who was suspected of communicating with defense attor-

neys was named in the media and subsequently received threatening letters and phone calls. In 2005 the men were retried, found guilty, and sentenced to up to 25 years in prison.

- Qwest Communications—the government found that executives overstated the company's earnings by more than $2 billion. By the time the scandal became public in 2002 top Qwest executives had sold millions of dollars in company stock, even though they knew the company was in serious financial trouble. Joseph Nacchio (1949–), the former CEO, was sentenced to six years in federal prison, fined $19 million, and ordered to forfeit $52 million he made from illegal stock sales.

Bailout Bonuses

As noted earlier, beginning in 2008 the government decided to bail out several financial and insurance corporations that were in danger of failing. This decision was widely unpopular with the American public because it believed the great recession had been caused, in large part, by these corporations. Public dissatisfaction continued to grow when many of the rescued corporations decided to pay large bonuses to their executives.

The furor began in late 2008, when the media reported that the insurance giant AIG still planned to pay out more than $150 million in bonuses after receiving a multibillion-dollar bailout package from the government. The decision was widely criticized as rewarding the risky behavior that drove the company to the brink of financial ruin. However, AIG argued that the bonuses had been promised before the financial meltdown began and still had to be paid. In addition, the company feared that its best-performing employees would quit and go to competing firms if AIG ceased its bonus program.

Throughout 2009 several major corporations in the financial industry were bailed out. They also aroused public outrage by continuing to pay very large bonuses. President Obama and many politicians angrily criticized this practice. In December 2009 Obama gave an interview with the CBS show *60 Minutes* (http://www.cbsnews.com/video/watch/?id=5975130n&tag=contentMain;contentBody), in which he denounced the bonuses and famously proclaimed: "I did not run for office to be helping out a bunch of fat cat bankers on Wall Street."

Jonathan Macey of Yale Law School examines the bailout bonus controversy in "Obama and the 'Fat Cat Bankers'" (*Wall Street Journal*, January 12, 2010). Macey admits that "many of the banks that got the most bailout money are paying the biggest bonuses." He notes that as of January 2010 Bank of America, Citigroup, Goldman Sachs, J.P. Morgan Chase, and Morgan Stanley had "allocated about $90 billion for overall compensation, with bonuses comprising more than half." The average bonus was expected to be $500,000; however, some bonuses could

FIGURE 6.3

Public confidence in societal institutions, July 2010

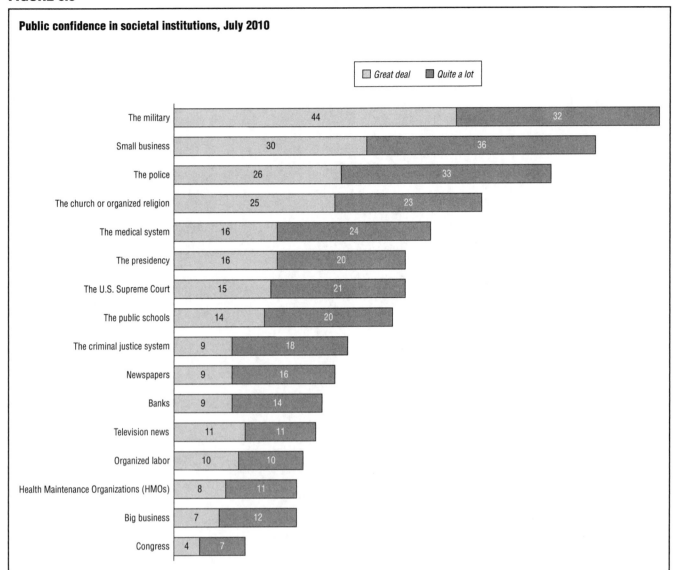

SOURCE: Adapted from "Now I am going to read you a list of institutions in American society. Please tell me how much confidence you, yourself, have in each one—a great deal, quite a lot, some, or very little? First, … Next, [RANDOM ORDER]," in *Gallup News Service: Gallup Poll Social Series: Consumption Habits*, The Gallup Organization, July 8–11, 2010, http://www.gallup.com/poll/File/141515/Confidence_Institutions_July_22_2010.pdf (accessed July 26, 2010). Copyright © 2010 by The Gallup Organization. Reproduced by permission of The Gallup Organization.

be in the millions of dollars. Macey argues that bankers make "relatively modest base salaries," so bonuses for good performance are part of the "basic pay structure" at all major banks, including the bailed-out banks. Macey believes that bank owners and shareholders (which include the federal government and consequently U.S. taxpayers for many of the bailed-out institutions) actually benefit from the bonuses because they are based on performance. In other words, the bonuses reward the employees who make the largest profits for the companies.

Public Perception of Big Business

The Gallup Organization regularly conducts polls that ask respondents about their opinions of various institutions in American society. The results from a July 2010 poll are shown in Figure 6.3. Only 19% of those asked expressed a "great deal" (7%) or "quite a lot" (12%) of confidence in big business. In fact, big business rated 15th out of 16 societal institutions that were listed by Gallup for the public's level of confidence. The only societal institution that was deemed less trustworthy than big business was Congress. The military garnered the highest rating, with 76% of those asked expressing a "great deal" (44%) or "quite a lot" (32%) of confidence. Small business was the second highest, with 66% of respondents providing a favorable opinion (30% had a "great deal" and 36% had "quite a lot" of confidence). Banks (presumably both large and small) received a much lower rating. Only 23% of respondents had a "great deal" (9%) or "quite a lot" (14%) of confidence in banks.

CHAPTER 7
SAVING AND INVESTING

If you would be wealthy, think of saving as well as getting.

—Benjamin Franklin, *The Way to Wealth* (1758)

Saving and investing are two sides of the same coin. The purpose of saving is to put aside money for use in the future. Saved money can actually make money if it is put into a bank account that earns interest. This is basically a low-risk investment with a low rate of return, but it does preserve the money for the future. Investing is another matter. It means exchanging money for assets that may or may not go up in value over time. Investments that go up in value reap profits for the investor, and those profits can be modest or extravagant. Investments that go down in value are another story. Some or even all the original money invested is lost. Thus, investing entails risk, particularly in a market-driven economy where fluctuations in supply and demand determine the profitability of investments. At a macroeconomic level, the U.S. economy thrives on investing—it provides money for business growth and government expenses. From a microeconomic standpoint, Americans are urged to save and/or gainfully invest some of their earnings to ensure that they have a safety net in the event of a personal financial crisis and to sustain them after they retire.

PERSONAL SAVING RATE

The personal saving rate is a government-measured rate that tracks how much money Americans have available for saving and investing. It is calculated by the U.S. Department of Commerce's Bureau of Economic Analysis (BEA) using data from many sources on income, taxes, government revenues and expenses, and personal expenses. The rate is actually a ratio of two BEA measures: disposable personal income (DPI) and personal saving. The DPI is defined as personal income (e.g., wages and salaries) minus tax and nontax payments made to the government. Personal saving is determined by subtracting personal outlays (which are 97% personal consumption expenditures) from the DPI.

Thus, personal saving is the money left over. This value is divided by the DPI to show what percentage of the DPI is available for saving and investing.

Because the personal saving rate is based on so many other calculated variables, any small errors in the dependent variables will be exaggerated in the rate itself. In addition, the BEA excludes from its definition of income certain wealth components such as capital gains (which is an increase in the value of an asset). As a result, the BEA admits that the personal saving rate gives an incomplete picture of household savings behavior. However, it is useful for tracking changes over time.

Disposal Personal Income

Table 7.1 shows the amounts and derivations of personal income from 2006 to 2009 and for the first two quarters of 2010 as calculated by the BEA using the National Income and Product Accounts (NIPAs). As described in Chapter 1, the NIPAs are estimates of national income. The BEA explains how it compiles the NIPAs in *A Guide to the National Income and Product Accounts of the United States* (September 2006, http://www.bea.gov/national/pdf/nipaguid.pdf). It should be noted that the BEA defines "persons" as "individuals, nonprofit institutions that primarily serve households, private noninsured welfare funds, and private trust funds."

As shown in Table 7.1, personal income consists of the following components:

- Compensation of employees—wages, salaries, and supplements

- Proprietors' income—income earned by the proprietors (owners) of unincorporated businesses, such as sole proprietorships, partnerships, and tax-exempt cooperatives

- Rental income—income from rental properties and royalties received by persons from patents, copyrights, and the rights to natural resources

TABLE 7.1

Derivation of personal saving rate, 2006–09, and first and second quarters 2010

[Billions of dollars]

	2006	2007	2008	2009	Seasonally adjusted at annual rates 2010 I	II
Personal income	11,268.1	11,912.3	12,391.1	12,174.9	12,361.8	12,485.7
Compensation of employees, received	7,475.7	7,862.2	8,065.8	7,806.7	7,871.2	7,934.5
Wage and salary disbursements	6,068.9	6,421.7	6,559.0	6,274.1	6,303.7	6,356.1
Private industries	5,033.7	5,332.7	5,415.1	5,100.5	5,118.2	5,161.6
Goods-producing industries	1,176.0	1,213.4	1,207.6	1,064.0	1,036.1	1,044.4
Manufacturing	738.7	752.2	741.2	661.5	655.8	662.1
Services-producing industries	3,857.8	4,119.3	4,207.4	4,036.6	4,082.1	4,117.2
Trade, transportation, and utilities	996.0	1,045.2	1,050.9	990.5	990.1	999.3
Other services-producing industries	2,861.8	3,074.1	3,156.6	3,046.1	3,092.0	3,117.9
Government	1,035.2	1,089.0	1,144.0	1,173.6	1,185.5	1,194.6
Supplements to wages and salaries	1,406.9	1,440.4	1,506.8	1,532.6	1,567.5	1,578.4
Employer contributions for employee pension and insurance funds	960.1	980.5	1,036.6	1,072.0	1,095.8	1,102.8
Employer contributions for government social insurance	446.7	459.9	470.1	460.6	471.7	475.6
Proprietors' income with inventory valuation and capital consumption adjustments	1,133.0	1,090.4	1,102.0	1,011.9	1,030.7	1,049.5
Farm	29.3	37.8	50.8	30.5	36.8	36.6
Nonfarm	1,103.6	1,052.6	1,051.2	981.5	994.0	1,012.9
Rental income of persons with capital consumption adjustment	146.5	143.7	222.0	274.0	292.7	300.9
Personal income receipts on assets	1,829.7	2,057.0	2,109.3	1,919.7	1,911.1	1,915.2
Personal interest income	1,127.5	1,265.1	1,314.7	1,222.3	1,208.7	1,206.0
Personal dividend income	702.2	791.9	794.6	697.4	702.4	709.3
Personal current transfer receipts	1,605.0	1,718.5	1,879.2	2,132.8	2,245.5	2,282.9
Government social benefits to persons	1,583.6	1,687.9	1,842.6	2,096.8	2,208.9	2,245.9
Old-age, survivors, disability, and health insurance benefits	943.3	1,003.2	1,068.3	1,164.5	1,191.3	1,208.1
Government unemployment insurance benefits	29.9	32.3	50.7	128.6	146.1	136.8
Other	610.4	652.4	723.6	803.7	871.5	901.0
Other current transfer receipts, from business (net)	21.4	30.5	36.7	36.0	36.6	37.0
Less: Contributions for government social insurance, domestic	921.8	959.5	987.2	970.3	989.4	997.3
Less: Personal current taxes	1,352.4	1,488.7	1,438.2	1,140.0	1,136.8	1,138.1
Equals: Disposable personal income	9,915.7	10,423.6	10,952.9	11,034.9	11,225.0	11,347.6
Less: Personal outlays	9,680.7	10,208.9	10,505.0	10,379.6	10,603.9	10,640.5
Personal consumption expenditures	9,322.7	9,806.3	10,104.5	10,001.3	10,230.8	10,273.6
Goods	3,221.7	3,357.7	3,379.5	3,230.7	3,380.0	3,377.3
Durable goods	1,133.0	1,159.4	1,083.5	1,026.5	1,060.7	1,075.8
Nondurable goods	2,088.7	2,198.2	2,296.0	2,204.2	2,319.3	3,301.5
Services	6,100.9	6,448.6	6,725.0	6,770.6	6,850.9	6,896.3
Personal interest payments[a]	230.1	260.9	246.2	216.8	203.8	195.9
Personal current transfer payments	128.0	141.7	154.3	161.4	169.2	171.1
To government	76.4	82.4	89.7	95.0	98.5	100.1
To the rest of the world (net)	51.6	59.3	64.6	66.5	70.7	71.0
Equals: Personal saving	235.0	214.7	447.9	655.3	621.1	707.1
Personal saving as a percentage of disposable personal income	2.4	2.1	4.1	5.9	5.5	6.2
Addenda:						
Personal income excluding current transfer receipts, billions of chained (2005) dollars[2]	9,404.8	9,656.5	9,638.5	9,191.1	9,122.1	9,198.9
Disposable personal income:						
Total, billions of chained (2005) dollars[b]	9,650.7	9,874.2	10,042.9	10,099.8	10,121.8	10,231.1
Per capita:						
Current dollars	33,157	34,512	35,931	35,888	36,313	36,638
Chained (2005) dollars	32,271	32,693	32,946	32,847	32,744	33,033
Population (midperiod, thousands)[c]	299,052	302,025	304,831	307,483	309,120	309,723

[a]Consists of nonmortgage interest paid by households.
[b]The current-dollar measure is deflated by the implicit price deflator for personal consumption expenditures.
[c]Population is the total population of the United States, including the armed forces overseas and the institutionalized population. The monthly estimate is the average of estimates for the first of the month and the first of the following month; the annual and quarterly estimates are averages of the monthly estimates.

SOURCE: Adapted from "Table 2. Personal Income and Its Disposition (Years and Quarters)," in *Personal Income and Outlays: June 2010; Revised Estimates: 2007 through May 2010*, U.S. Department of Commerce, Bureau of Economic Analysis, August 3, 2010, http://www.bea.gov/newsreleases/national/pi/2010/pdf/pi0510.pdf (accessed August 6, 2010)

• Receipts on assets—income from interest and dividends; these are payments that persons earn from their assets and investments and will be explained in detail later in this chapter

• Transfer receipts—payments from businesses and the government; for example, government transfers include unemployment benefits and Social Security payments made to persons

- Personal taxes—taxes that persons pay on their income or personal property, for example, cars

The DPI is the sum of the first five components minus personal taxes. Thus, the DPI is the amount of money that persons have available to spend or save. In 2009 the DPI totaled $11 trillion. (See Table 7.1.) In the second quarter of 2010 the DPI totaled $11.3 trillion.

Personal Saving

The BEA explains in *A Guide to the National Income and Product Accounts of the United States* that it calculates personal saving by subtracting personal outlays from the DPI. In other words, personal saving is the amount of money that persons have left over for saving. As shown in Table 7.1, personal outlays consist of three components:

- Personal consumption expenditures (PCE)—PCE is the money spent on certain goods and services; a detailed breakdown for the 2009 PCE total of $10 trillion is provided in Table 3.2 in Chapter 3

- Personal interest payments—nonmortgage interest paid by households

- Personal transfer payments—payments from persons to the government (e.g., fees and fines) and payments from persons to "the rest of the world"

Table 7.1 shows that personal saving totaled $655.3 billion in 2009. This value was up considerably from 2006, when it totaled $235 billion. In the second quarter of 2010 personal saving totaled $707.1 billion.

Personal Saving Rate Trends

The BEA calculates the personal saving rate by dividing the DPI by personal saving. Thus, the personal saving rate shows the percentage of the DPI that persons saved rather than spent. In 2009 the personal saving rate was 5.9%. (See Table 7.1.) This rate was up dramatically from 2006 and 2007, when the rates were 2.4% and 2.1%, respectively. In the second quarter of 2010 the personal saving rate was 6.2%.

Figure 7.1 shows the personal saving rate on a quarterly basis from the first quarter of 2004 to the second quarter of 2010. The rates were regularly less than 2% per quarter from the first quarter of 2005 to the third quarter of 2007. In 2008 the rate began to creep upward. From the first quarter of 2009 to the second quarter of 2010 it was consistently greater than 5%. Analysts believe this rise was driven by fear. The housing market bust in the latter half of the first decade of the 21st century and the economic contraction known as the great recession that began in late 2007 gutted home values and greatly reduced the value of other investments into which Americans had put their money (and faith).

FIGURE 7.1

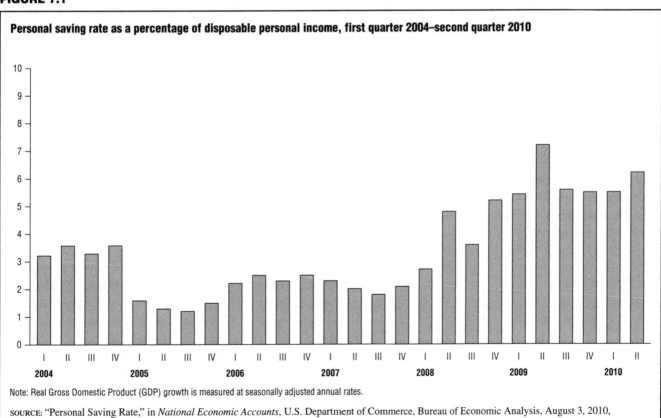

Personal saving rate as a percentage of disposable personal income, first quarter 2004–second quarter 2010

Note: Real Gross Domestic Product (GDP) growth is measured at seasonally adjusted annual rates.

SOURCE: "Personal Saving Rate," in *National Economic Accounts*, U.S. Department of Commerce, Bureau of Economic Analysis, August 3, 2010, http://www.bea.gov/BRIEFRM/SAVING.HTM (accessed August 6, 2010)

FAMILY HOLDINGS

In the broadest sense, any money expenditure that returns a profit is considered an investment. Thus, the cost of a college education can be considered an investment because it will likely increase earnings potential in the future. In this discussion, investments are limited to tangible assets (such as cash or real estate) and intangible financial assets (such as stocks, bonds, and other securities).

The Survey of Consumer Finances (SCF) is conducted every three years by the Federal Reserve System, the national bank of the United States, in cooperation with the Internal Revenue Service, to collect detailed financial information on American families. As of September 2010, the most recent SCF results available were from the 2007 survey. Table 7.2 provides a listing of the percentage of families in 2007 holding particular financial assets (investments with financial value). The table also shows the median value (half of the values were less than the median value and half of the values were greater than the median value) of the holdings for families holding the assets.

SAVINGS ACCOUNTS

Savings accounts are accounts held at financial institutions in which customers can deposit money for safekeeping. Variations on savings accounts include money market deposit accounts (which allow limited withdrawals in some circumstances) and certificates of deposit (CDs). CDs are savings accounts in which money is placed for a predetermined amount of time, commonly one to five years, in exchange for payment of a set interest rate throughout that time period. There are penalties for early withdrawal of the money.

According to the 2007 SCF, 92.1% of U.S. families had transaction accounts in 2007. (See Table 7.2.) Brian K. Bucks et al. of the Federal Reserve report in *Changes in U.S. Family Finances from 2004 to 2007: Evidence from the Survey of Consumer Finances* (February 2009, http://www.federalreserve.gov/pubs/bulletin/2009/pdf/scf09.pdf) that transaction accounts include checking accounts, savings accounts, and money market accounts. The ownership percentages for these types of accounts in 2007 were:

- Checking account—89.7%
- Savings account—47.2%
- Money market account—20.9%

In addition, 16.1% of families held one or more CDs in 2007. (See Table 7.2.) The median value of the transaction accounts was $4,000. The median value of the CDs was $20,000.

In general, savings accounts, money market accounts, and CDs are very low-risk investments. In most cases, deposits up to $250,000 are insured by the Federal Deposit Insurance Corporation (FDIC), an independent government agency. FDIC insurance ensures depositors that their money will be repaid even if the financial institution goes out of business.

GOVERNMENT SECURITIES

The government issues a variety of securities with the purpose of earning revenue. Local and state governments sell bonds to raise funds for public projects, such as road improvement or school construction. A bond is basically an IOU from the government that promises to pay back the borrowed amount plus interest at a specified future date (the maturity date). The federal government also sells bonds (called savings bonds) through the U.S. Department of the Treasury.

As shown in Table 7.2, 14.9% of U.S. families owned savings bonds in 2007. The median value was $1,000.

Savings bonds are not marketable securities. They can only be sold or redeemed by the Treasury Department. Treasury bills (T-bills) are short-term securities that mature within a few days or up to 26 weeks. The customer purchases a T-bill for less than its face value and then receives face value at maturity. For example, a customer might pay $90 upfront for a $100 T-bill. When the T-bill matures, the customer will receive the $100. T-bills can be bought and sold in other markets. Treasury notes (T-notes) have maturity periods lasting two, three, five, and 10 years. They earn a fixed rate of interest every six months. T-notes can be sold by the customer before the maturity date.

Figure 7.2 shows the annual percent yield from 1995 to June 2010 on a 10-year T-note. The interest paid on the 10-year T-note decreased during the late 1990s, rebounded in 1999, and then declined through 2003. After rising for several years, the rate decreased in 2007, before recovering somewhat in 2009 and early 2010.

HOMEOWNERSHIP AS AN INVESTMENT

One of the largest investments made by most Americans is the purchase of a home. Because real estate tends to appreciate (increase in value), buying a home is considered a relatively low-risk investment. However, this conventional wisdom proved faulty when the housing market bust in the latter half of the first decade of the 21st century enveloped the country. As noted in Chapter 4, home prices actually depreciated (decreased in value) throughout 2008 and 2009 and into early 2010. Likewise, historical high foreclosure rates meant that many Americans lost both their home and a substantial investment in their future. As shown in Figure 4.4 in Chapter 4, the nation's homeownership rate peaked at 69.4% in 2004 and then declined to 66.9% by the second quarter of 2010.

TABLE 7.2

Family holdings of financial assets, 2007

Family characteristic	Transaction accounts	Certificates of deposit	Savings bonds	Bonds	Stocks	Pooled investment funds	Retirement accounts	Cash value life insurance	Other managed assets	Other	Any financial asset
						Percentage of families holding asset					
All families	**92.1**	**16.1**	**14.9**	**1.6**	**17.9**	**11.4**	**52.6**	**23.0**	**5.8**	**9.3**	**93.9**
Percentile of income											
Less than 20	74.9	9.4	3.6	*	5.5	3.4	10.7	12.8	2.7	6.6	79.1
20–39.9	90.1	12.7	8.5	*	7.8	4.6	35.6	16.4	4.7	8.8	93.2
40–59.9	96.4	15.4	15.2	*	14.0	7.1	55.2	21.6	5.3	10.2	97.2
60–79.9	99.3	19.3	20.9	1.4	23.2	14.6	73.3	29.4	5.7	8.4	99.7
80–89.9	100.0	19.9	26.2	1.8	30.5	18.9	86.7	30.6	7.6	9.8	100.0
90–100	100.0	27.7	26.1	8.9	47.5	35.5	89.6	38.9	13.6	15.3	100.0
Age of head (years)											
Less than 35	87.3	6.7	13.7	*	13.7	5.3	41.6	11.4	*	10.0	89.2
35–44	91.2	9.0	16.8	0.7	17.0	11.6	57.5	17.5	2.2	9.6	93.1
45–54	91.7	14.3	19.0	1.1	18.6	12.6	64.7	22.3	5.1	10.5	93.3
55–64	96.4	20.5	16.2	2.1	21.3	14.3	60.9	35.2	7.7	9.2	97.8
65–74	94.6	24.2	10.3	4.2	19.1	14.6	51.7	34.4	13.2	9.4	96.1
75 or more	95.3	37.0	7.9	3.5	20.2	13.2	30.0	27.6	14.0	5.3	97.4
Family structure											
Single with child(ren)	84.8	9.6	10.1	*	8.4	9.0	36.1	24.8	*	13.2	88.2
Single, no child, age less than 55	84.3	9.6	9.9	*	14.7	7.7	42.8	11.4	1.6	11.1	86.9
Single, no child, age 55 or more	94.3	23.3	9.9	2.1	13.1	10.4	36.2	23.1	10.8	7.6	96.3
Couple with child(ren)	95.5	15.1	22.8	1.2	20.2	13.6	62.5	27.5	5.3	7.5	96.2
Couple, no child	94.8	17.6	17.1	2.2	21.5	12.9	61.8	26.3	6.3	9.0	96.1
Education of head											
No high school diploma	75.7	9.5	3.4	*	3.9	2.2	21.6	12.6	1.7	7.1	79.7
High school diploma	90.9	14.1	11.5	0.6	9.3	5.8	43.2	22.6	4.2	8.2	93.3
Some college	93.9	14.1	16.4	1.2	17.4	8.9	52.5	23.4	6.6	9.8	95.5
College degree	98.7	21.6	21.6	3.3	31.5	21.4	73.3	27.1	8.5	10.9	98.9
Race or ethnicity of respondent											
White non-Hispanic	95.5	19.4	17.8	2.1	21.4	13.7	58.2	25.3	7.3	9.7	96.8
Nonwhite or Hispanic	83.9	8.2	7.8	0.4	9.4	5.8	39.1	17.6	2.3	8.3	86.7
Current work status of head											
Working for someone else	92.6	13.2	17.0	0.9	17.8	10.4	62.1	20.3	3.7	9.2	94.1
Self-employed	96.9	15.0	15.9	4.2	24.3	21.4	55.3	32.1	6.9	14.8	98.0
Retired	91.6	25.7	10.2	2.3	16.4	11.3	34.2	27.3	11.2	7.0	93.7
Other not working	78.6	5.6	10.7	*	12.8	2.4	22.6	14.5	*	10.6	81.4
Current occupation of head											
Managerial or professional	98.3	18.2	21.1	3.1	28.7	19.7	74.1	24.9	6.7	11.1	98.7
Technical, sales, or services	91.9	11.5	15.0	0.4	14.9	8.8	54.5	21.3	4.0	9.1	94.0
Other occupation	87.9	9.2	13.1	*	9.9	5.4	51.0	19.0	1.1	9.6	90.2
Retired or other not working	89.5	22.5	10.3	2.0	15.8	9.9	32.4	25.3	9.8	7.6	91.8
Region											
Northeast	91.3	18.1	18.9	2.0	21.4	15.5	53.3	23.5	6.4	5.4	92.5
Midwest	93.6	16.8	16.0	1.2	17.9	10.6	57.8	26.6	6.7	9.2	95.4
South	91.3	15.1	12.0	1.7	15.4	9.7	48.8	23.3	5.2	8.6	93.5
West	92.7	15.5	15.0	1.6	19.2	11.5	52.9	18.3	5.5	13.9	93.9
Urbanicity											
Metropolitan statistical area (MSA)	92.8	16.2	15.1	1.8	19.4	12.1	54.8	22.2	5.9	9.5	94.3
Non-MSA	88.7	15.9	13.8	0.8	10.9	7.7	42.0	26.7	5.5	8.6	91.8
Housing status											
Owner	97.3	20.0	18.2	2.2	22.4	15.0	63.3	28.9	7.5	9.4	98.4
Renter or other	80.8	7.7	7.5	0.4	8.1	3.5	29.2	10.1	2.1	9.1	84.0
Percentile of net worth											
Less than 25	76.4	2.5	4.7	*	4.3	*	19.1	7.8	*	7.4	79.6
25–49.9	93.6	9.9	12.3	*	10.2	3.6	48.1	19.7	1.9	8.8	96.4
50–74.9	98.6	19.3	17.5	*	17.3	10.5	62.9	28.5	6.2	8.8	99.5
75–89.9	100.0	32.6	25.9	*	31.6	22.5	77.4	32.1	11.2	9.4	100.0
90–100	100.0	33.0	23.3	11.8	52.3	42.5	84.6	41.9	20.3	16.6	100.0

Home Mortgages

The Federal Reserve compiles home mortgage data on a quarterly and annual basis. These values are published in tabular form in "L.218 Home Mortgages" as part of the *Federal Reserve Statistical Release Z.1: Flow of Funds Accounts of the United States* (http://www.federalreserve.gov/releases/z1/). The Federal Reserve only includes mortgages that are secured by one-to-four

TABLE 7.2

Family holdings of financial assets, 2007 [CONTINUED]

Family characteristic	Transaction accounts	Certificates of deposit	Savings bonds	Bonds	Stocks	Pooled investment funds	Retirement accounts	Cash value life insurance	Other managed assets	Other	Any financial asset
					Median value of holdings for families holding asset (thousands of 2007 dollars)						
All families	4.0	20.0	1.0	80.0	17.0	56.0	45.0	8.0	70.0	6.0	28.8
Percentile of income											
Less than 20	0.8	18.0	0.5	*	3.8	30.0	6.5	2.5	100.0	1.5	1.7
20–39.9	1.6	18.0	1.0	*	10.0	30.0	12.0	5.0	86.0	3.0	7.0
40–59.9	2.7	17.0	0.7	*	5.5	37.5	23.9	5.2	59.0	4.0	18.6
60–79.9	6.0	11.0	1.0	19.0	14.0	35.0	48.0	10.0	52.0	10.0	58.3
80–89.9	12.9	20.0	2.0	81.0	15.0	46.0	85.0	9.0	30.0	10.0	129.9
90–100	36.7	42.0	2.5	250.0	75.0	180.0	200.0	28.1	90.0	45.0	404.5
Age of head (years)											
Less than 35	2.4	5.0	0.7	*	3.0	18.0	10.0	2.8	*	1.5	6.8
35–44	3.4	5.0	1.0	9.7	15.0	22.5	36.0	8.3	24.0	8.0	25.8
45–54	5.0	15.0	1.0	200.0	18.5	50.0	67.0	10.0	45.0	6.0	54.0
55–64	5.2	23.0	1.9	90.8	24.0	112.0	98.0	10.0	59.0	20.0	72.4
65–74	7.7	23.2	1.0	50.0	38.0	86.0	77.0	10.0	70.0	10.0	68.1
75 or more	6.1	30.0	20.0	100.0	40.0	75.0	35.0	5.0	100.0	15.0	41.5
Family structure											
Single with child(ren)	2.4	7.5	1.0	*	13.0	46.0	30.0	5.0	*	5.5	10.3
Single, no child, age less than 55	2.0	5.5	1.5	*	3.8	18.0	20.0	5.2	50.0	3.0	8.9
Single, no child, age 55 or more	2.5	28.0	3.0	50.0	25.0	77.0	45.0	5.0	100.0	3.6	24.4
Couple with child(ren)	5.0	10.0	0.8	530.0	15.0	45.0	52.0	9.0	30.0	10.0	36.3
Couple, no child	6.0	20.0	1.0	80.0	24.0	60.0	55.1	10.0	52.0	10.0	46.1
Education of head											
No high school diploma	1.2	14.0	1.0	*	2.7	64.0	15.0	2.5	30.0	1.5	3.0
High school diploma	2.5	16.0	1.0	46.5	10.0	30.0	28.5	5.2	80.0	5.0	14.2
Some college	2.8	18.0	1.0	50.0	6.0	25.0	32.0	8.0	52.0	4.0	20.0
College degree	10.0	25.0	1.1	100.0	25.0	75.0	75.0	13.0	75.0	10.0	95.7
Race or ethnicity of respondent											
White non-Hispanic	5.1	20.0	1.0	95.9	19.0	64.0	52.7	9.0	70.0	10.0	44.3
Nonwhite or Hispanic	2.0	10.0	1.0	23.1	8.0	30.0	25.4	5.0	30.0	3.0	9.0
Current work status of head											
Working for someone else	3.8	10.0	1.0	46.8	10.5	42.0	40.0	7.5	27.2	5.0	28.5
Self-employed	9.9	25.0	1.0	150.0	60.0	80.0	91.0	24.0	80.0	16.0	54.1
Retired	4.0	30.0	2.5	79.5	28.7	78.2	48.0	5.5	100.0	10.0	29.7
Other not working	1.0	15.0	2.0	*	6.3	50.0	20.8	2.2	*	3.0	3.7
Current occupation of head											
Managerial or professional	8.8	15.0	1.0	80.0	20.0	75.0	72.0	13.0	59.0	10.0	77.0
Technical, sales, or services	3.0	15.0	1.0	123.2	12.0	40.0	30.0	9.0	10.0	5.0	17.6
Other occupation	2.5	10.0	0.7	*	4.0	18.0	24.3	5.0	20.0	5.0	13.8
Retired or other not working	3.3	30.0	2.0	95.9	25.0	78.2	45.0	5.0	100.0	5.5	23.7
Region											
Northeast	5.1	20.0	1.0	114.7	17.9	50.0	57.5	9.0	73.0	10.0	43.8
Midwest	3.8	12.0	1.0	49.3	14.0	37.5	36.0	7.0	67.0	6.0	31.0
South	3.5	20.0	1.2	100.0	17.9	70.0	40.0	8.0	80.0	4.0	20.8
West	4.3	23.0	1.0	60.0	18.0	58.8	45.6	10.0	60.0	6.0	29.1
Urbanicity											
Metropolitan statistical area (MSA)	4.5	20.0	1.0	100.0	19.0	60.0	48.0	9.0	70.0	8.0	32.6
Non-MSA	2.5	10.0	1.2	50.0	11.0	34.0	31.3	5.0	45.0	2.4	15.8
Housing status											
Owner	6.2	20.0	1.0	100.0	20.0	60.0	57.0	10.0	70.0	10.0	54.3
Renter or other	1.2	10.0	0.7	15.0	5.5	40.0	10.0	2.0	54.0	1.8	3.8

family properties, including owner-occupied condominium units. Mortgage types include first and second mortgages, home equity lines of credit, mortgages held by households under seller-financing arrangements, and construction and land development loans that are associated with one-to-four family residences.

Table 7.3 lists outstanding mortgage amounts reported by the Federal Reserve as annual amounts from 2004 to 2008 and from the first quarter of 2009 to the first quarter of 2010. In the first quarter of 2010 outstanding mortgages totaled over $10.7 trillion. The vast majority of this amount—$10.2 trillion, or 95% of the total—was devoted to the household sector. Another $490 billion in mortgages was attributed to nonfarm, noncorporate businesses and $18.4 billion was devoted to nonfinancial corporate businesses. After rising for four consecutive years, from 2004 to 2007, the total amount of home mortgages declined from 2008 to the first quarter of 2010.

TABLE 7.2

Family holdings of financial assets, 2007 [CONTINUED]

Family characteristic	Transaction accounts	Certificates of deposit	Savings bonds	Bonds	Stocks	Pooled investment funds	Retirement accounts	Cash value life insurance	Other managed assets	Other	Any financial asset
	Median value of holdings for families holding asset (thousands of 2007 dollars)										
Percentile of net worth											
Less than 25	0.7	2.0	0.5	*	1.1	*	3.2	1.2	*	1.2	1.4
25–49.9	2.0	7.0	0.7	*	3.0	9.0	15.0	3.0	13.8	3.0	13.2
50–74.9	6.1	15.0	1.2	*	6.0	25.0	48.6	6.5	50.0	10.0	59.6
75–89.9	15.5	25.0	2.0	*	20.0	50.0	117.0	15.0	80.0	20.0	215.0
90–100	46.5	50.0	3.5	150.0	125.0	264.0	314.0	30.0	180.0	50.0	773.0
Memo											
Mean value of holdings for families holding asset	26.4	55.6	6.6	574.3	221.1	309.7	145.8	31.3	248.8	50.3	235.8

*Ten or fewer observations.
Note: For questions on income, respondents were asked to base their answers on the calendar year preceding the interview. For questions on saving, respondents were asked to base their answers on the 12 months preceding the interview. Percentage distributions may not sum to 100 because of rounding. Dollars have been converted to 2007 values with the current-methods consumer price index for all urban consumers.

SOURCE: Brian K. Bucks et al., "Table 6. Family Holdings of Financial Assets, by Selected Characteristics of Families and Type of Asset, 2004 and 2007 Surveys—B. 2007 Survey of Consumer Finances," in *Changes in U.S. Family Finances from 2004 to 2007: Evidence from the Survey of Consumer Finances, Federal Reserve Bulletin*, vol. 95, February 2009, http://www.federalreserve.gov/pubs/bulletin/2009/pdf/scf09.pdf (accessed July 10, 2010)

FIGURE 7.2

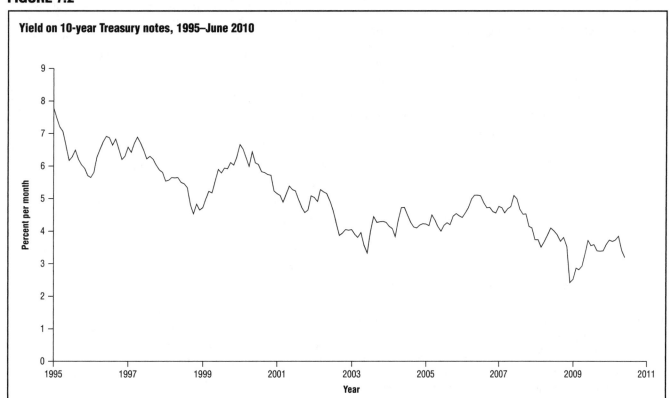

Yield on 10-year Treasury notes, 1995–June 2010

SOURCE: Adapted from "Market Yield on U.S. Treasury Securities at 10-Year Constant Maturity, Quoted on Investment Basis," in *H.15. Selected Interest Rates: Treasury Constant Maturities*, U.S. Federal Reserve, June 2010, http://www.federalreserve.gov/releases/H15/data/Monthly/H15_TCMNOM_Y10 .txt (accessed July 12, 2010)

SECURITIES AND COMMODITIES

Securities markets (stocks, bonds, and mutual funds) and commodities markets (raw materials and foreign currencies and securities) in the United States are used by corporations to raise money for their business operations and by banks and individuals to build wealth and, in some cases, to pay for retirement. These markets have fueled periods of astounding economic growth (called bull markets), but they have also been at the center of downturns (called bear markets) and disastrous economic crashes,

TABLE 7.3

Home mortgages on 1–4 family properties, including farm houses, 2004–first quarter 2010

[Billions of dollars; amounts outstanding at end of period, not seasonally adjusted]

| | 2004 | 2005 | 2006 | 2007 | 2008 | 2009 | | | | 2010 |
						Q1	Q2	Q3	Q4	Q1
Total liabilities	8268.2	9382.4	10455.6	11165.9	11070.6	11059.8	11011.6	10923.5	10858.7	10749.1
Household sector	7835.3	8874.3	9865.0	10538.5	10496.9	10496.6	10461.9	10394.3	10334.4	10240.3
Nonfinancial corporate business	23.5	31.1	39.4	42.2	32.7	30.0	26.8	23.3	20.3	18.4
Nonfarm noncorporate business	409.4	477.0	551.2	585.1	541.0	533.3	523.0	505.8	504.0	490.4

Note: Mortgages on 1–4 family properties including mortgages on farm houses.

SOURCE: Adapted from "L.218. Home Mortgages," in *Federal Reserve Statistical Release Z.1: Flow of Funds Accounts of the United States, Flows and Outstandings, First Quarter 2010*, The Federal Reserve, June 10, 2010, http://www.federalreserve.gov/releases/z1/Current/z1.pdf (accessed July 6, 2010)

creating the need for an extensive regulatory system. Despite regulations, however, the markets occasionally see high-profile scandals involving major figures in the business world.

Securities are financial assets that give holders ownership or creditor rights in a particular organization. The word usually refers to stocks (also sometimes called equities), but there are other types of securities that can be bought and sold on the open market, including bonds and mutual funds. Commodities are typically tangible products (usually raw materials) that are bought and sold in bulk. Financial instruments such as foreign currencies and securities of the U.S. and foreign governments are also called commodities. Commodities can refer either to the material itself or to a contract to buy the item in the future.

Stocks

To raise money to operate and expand a company, its owners will often sell part of the company. A company that wants to raise money this way must first organize itself as a legal corporation. At that time, it creates shares of stock, which are small units of ownership in the company. These shares of stock can then be sold to raise funds for the company. Those who own them are called shareholders in the company. They have the right to attend shareholder meetings, inspect corporate documents, and vote on certain matters that affect the company. Shareholders may also have preemptive rights, which means they are able to buy new shares before they are offered to the public so that existing shareholders can maintain their percentage of ownership in a company.

Not all corporations offer their shares for sale to the public. When a company chooses to do so, its first sale of shares is called an initial public offering (IPO). IPO stock is purchased by investors at a price set by the company. The money paid for each share of stock is then available to the company for its business operations. In return, shareholders can receive benefits in two forms: dividends and appreciation. Dividends are a portion of the company's profits that are distributed to shareholders. Not all companies that issue stock pay dividends. Those that do usually pay them every quarter (a quarter is three consecutive months of the year; there are four quarters in a fiscal year), and, even though each share of stock might earn only a few pennies in dividends, the total amounts to individual or institutional investors who hold large amounts of shares can be enormous. Appreciation is a gradual increase in the value of a share over time. If a corporation prospers, a shareholder can sell his or her share to someone else for a higher price than he or she originally paid for it. There is no guarantee that a stock will appreciate; however, it is quite possible that it will depreciate over time.

PRICING SHARES. When a corporation creates shares, it determines the price per share for the IPO. From then on the price of each share depends on the public's perception of how well the corporation is doing. If a corporation reports higher profits, then the price per share will likely increase. The challenge for investors is that they cannot predict the future, and stock prices tend to fluctuate up and down over time. A variety of events can influence a stock's price, from the release of a popular new product to news that a company's chief executive officer is being investigated for fraud.

The market for stocks sold by shareholders to other shareholders is called the secondary stock market. It would be almost impossible for all shareholders to find buyers for their shares on their own when they choose to sell. To make it easier for shareholders to buy and sell shares, companies affiliate with a particular stock exchange that handles share transactions. The two most prominent exchanges in the United States are the New York Stock Exchange (NYSE) and the National Association of Securities Dealers Automated Quotations (NASDAQ). The NYSE and NASDAQ are themselves publicly traded companies. The United States also hosts the American Stock Exchange in New York City, the Boston Stock Exchange, the Philadelphia Stock Exchange, the Chicago Stock Exchange, and the Pacific Exchange in San Francisco, California. Additionally, there are stock exchanges in most countries throughout the world.

As shown in Table 7.2, 17.9% of U.S. families owned stocks in 2007. The median value was $17,000.

Bonds

Another way for a company to raise money is to borrow it. Companies can borrow from banks, just like individuals, but they can also borrow by issuing bonds, which are written promises to pay the bondholder back with interest. Bonds have a face value, called par, and that amount defines the amount of the debt.

A bond offers returns to holders in two ways. The issuing organization will either make regular interest payments on the bond or initially sell the bond at a much lower price than the face value. After a certain amount of time (often many years), the holder can redeem the bond for face value.

Bonds differ from shares of stock in several important respects. First, any organization can issue bonds, whereas only corporations can issue stock. For that reason, unincorporated businesses and federal, state, and local governments use bonds to raise money. Second, bonds provide no ownership interest in the company. The organization's only obligation to the bondholder is to pay the debt and interest. Third, bonds are usually less risky for the purchaser than stocks because the organization is legally obligated to pay the debt, whereas if a corporation has financial difficulties, it is not permitted to pay anything to shareholders until it has paid off its creditors. However, the rate of return on investment for stocks is generally higher than on bonds to compensate for the higher risk factor. Like stocks, though, bonds are traded by investors for prices that may be different from the par value. Investors who buy bonds are buying the right to receive the interest payments and to redeem the bond.

The price of a bond depends on a number of factors, including the organization's creditworthiness and the interest rate. Generally, the better the organization's credit rating, the higher the price of the bond. If the organization begins to have financial problems that will affect its ability to repay the bonds, the price of those bonds will go down. One of the best-known rating companies for bonds is Standard & Poor's, which rates issuing organizations on a scale ranging from AAA to D. Bonds may be short term or long term. Long-term bonds are riskier than short-term bonds and therefore tend to pay higher interest rates.

In 2007 only 1.6% of U.S. families owned bonds other than savings bonds. (See Table 7.2.) The median value of the bonds was $80,000.

Mutual Funds

Most investors try to diversify investments; that is, they put money into a number of different types of investments, rather than just one or two (a person's total invest-

ments are called his or her portfolio). That way, if one investment loses money, another investment may make enough profit to compensate for the loss.

However, for small investors it can be difficult to diversify. It takes time to evaluate different investments, and small investors may only be able to afford to buy one or two shares of each stock. Most brokers have a minimum purchase requirement that is higher than what the average investor can afford. Mutual funds were developed to solve such problems for small investors. In a mutual fund, the money of multiple investors is pooled and then invested in stocks, bonds, or both. The managers of the mutual fund then buy and sell the stocks and bonds on behalf of the investors. By combining their money, small investors are able to diversify.

Unlike the prices of stocks and bonds, the price of a mutual fund is determined by the fund manager, rather than by the open market. This price, called the net asset value, is based on the fund manager's estimation of the fund's value at a particular time. Mutual funds may be purchased either directly from the fund manager or through a broker or other intermediary. The latter is more expensive because the investor will be required to pay fees. Mutual funds provide income to investors in two ways. First, if the mutual fund sells stocks or bonds at a profit or receives dividends or interest payments on bonds, these gains can be paid to investors as distributions. Second, the price of the mutual fund itself may go up, in which case investors can sell their mutual funds for more than they paid.

Some people are willing to take a fair amount of risk when they invest, hoping that they will make more money. Usually, the riskier the investment is, the higher the potential return. Others would rather get a smaller return but know that their money is invested in a safer vehicle. Different types of mutual funds have been developed to meet the needs of these different types of investors. Mutual funds differ just as investors do in how much risk they want to take. Some mutual funds invest more conservatively than others. The safest type of mutual fund—and the one that pays the lowest interest—is a money-market fund, which invests in short-term bonds such as T-bills.

Commodities

The term *commodity*, in the narrow sense used in this chapter, means a contract to buy or sell something that will be available in the future. (In a broader sense, anything that can be bought or sold is a commodity.) These sorts of agreements are traded in commodities exchanges. Two important exchanges in the United States are the Chicago Board of Trade and the Kansas City Board of Trade.

There are two basic types of commodities. Futures are standardized contracts in which the seller promises to deliver a particular good to the buyer at a specified time in the future, at which point the buyer will pay the seller the price called for in the contract. Options on futures (which are usually simply called options) are more complicated. Depending on their exact terms, they establish the right of the buyer of the option to either buy or sell a futures contract for a specified price. Options that establish the right to buy a futures contract are call options. Those that establish the right to sell a futures contract are put options. In either case, the buyer of the option only has a limited time in which he or she can exercise his or her right, but the buyer is also free not to exercise the right at all.

The meaning of a commodities contract has changed over the years. Raw materials and agricultural commodities have been traded through commodities exchanges since the mid-19th century. More recently, commodities markets have expanded to include trading in foreign currencies, U.S. and foreign government securities, and U.S. and foreign stock indexes.

Because contracts are made before the goods are actually available, commodities are by their very nature speculative. Buyers purchase commodities because they think their value may increase over time, whereas the sellers think their value may decrease. For example, the seller of a grain futures contract may believe there will be a surplus of grain that will drive down prices, whereas the buyer thinks a shortage of grain will drive up prices. It is the speculative nature of commodities that makes them interesting to investors. Even if they have no need for the goods that the commodities contracts represent, speculative investors can make a profit by buying the commodities contracts at low prices and then selling them to others when prices rise. Commodities respond differently than stocks and bonds to market forces such as inflation; therefore, they can be a valuable part of a diversified portfolio. However, they are riskier and more difficult to understand.

INVESTMENT OPTIONS

Thanks to retirement investment options including 401(k) plans (funds that workers can contribute to on a before-tax basis and that grow tax-free until the money is withdrawn), a large percentage of Americans are now stock market investors. Given that Social Security retirement benefits are relatively low compared with a person's career income and that the long-term solvency (the state of having enough money to pay all debts) of Social Security continues to be in question, retirement funds are essential to the baby-boom and later generations as they approach retirement age. (Baby-boomers are people who were born between 1946 and 1964.)

Historically, stocks have appreciated faster than inflation has increased, allowing people to build greater wealth than if they attempted to save money in traditional accounts. Investments can also serve as collateral for certain loans. Therefore, even though Wall Street might seem far away, it provides small investors the opportunity to build wealth and prepare for retirement far more effectively than they otherwise could.

The stock market has also made it easier for employers to contribute to their employees' retirement funds. This is because many employers contribute company stock, instead of cash, to their employees' retirement accounts.

Retirement accounts are the most commonly held type of financial asset. More than half (52.6%) of all families surveyed in 2007 had a retirement account. (See Table 7.2.) The median value was $45,000.

According to the Investment Company Institute (ICI), in *2010 Investment Company Fact Book* (2010, http://icifactbook.org/pdf/2010_factbook.pdf), U.S. retirement assets totaled $16 trillion in 2009, up from $14 trillion in 2008, but down from $18 trillion in 2007. The ICI notes that the largest types of retirement assets in 2009 were individual retirement accounts ($4.2 trillion) and employer-sponsored defined contribution plans ($4.1 trillion).

GOVERNMENT REGULATION OF THE MARKET SYSTEM

Prices of stocks, bonds, and commodities fluctuate naturally, which generally is not cause for concern. However, when fluctuations are created as a result of greed or corruption, or by the creation of artificial and unsustainable conditions, the results can be disastrous. Such was the case in 1929, when the stock market crashed and ushered in the period known as the Great Depression. The exact causes of the 1929 crash and the ensuing depression are complex and reach far beyond U.S. borders. However, certain conditions related to the U.S. stock market were significant contributors to the economic disaster. The federal government under President Franklin D. Roosevelt (1882–1945), who served from 1933 to 1945, passed a number of laws that were designed to prevent the sort of abuses of the market that led to the Great Depression, laws that form the basis for the modern market regulatory system.

An Unregulated System

At the time of the 1929 crash, the stock market was largely unregulated. In the months before the crash, there were signs that the system was beginning to collapse under its own weight, but the industrialists who owned most of the real wealth fed millions of dollars into the market to stabilize it. They were successful for a time, but at last the artificial conditions created through margin buying (the buying of many market shares at a deflated value) and wild speculation brought the whole system down. Most people lost all, or nearly all, of the money they had invested in the stock market.

Regulation of Securities

Beginning in 1933 Congress enacted a series of laws that were designed to regulate the securities markets. The Securities Act of 1933 (sometimes referred to as the Truth in Securities law) was a reaction against the events that led up to the stock market crash of 1929. Its purpose was relatively simple: to protect investors by ensuring that they receive full information on the securities offered for sale to the public and to prohibit fraud in such sales. The Securities Act set up a system whereby most corporations that wanted to offer shares for sale to the public had to register their securities; the registration information was then made available to the public for review. The required registration forms (which are still being used in the 21st century) contained information on the company's management and business structure, its financial statements, and the securities it was offering for sale. This system was intended to protect investors by making available any information they needed to make informed decisions about their investments, although the truth or accuracy of the information was not guaranteed.

With the passage of the Securities Exchange Act in 1934, Congress established the Securities and Exchange Commission (SEC), which regulates the entire U.S. securities industry. The SEC expanded the Securities Act of 1933 to require more stringent reporting of publicly traded companies and all other entities involved in securities transactions, including stockbrokers, dealers, transfer agents, and exchanges. Additionally, large companies with more than $10 million in assets and 500 shareholders are required to file regular reports with the SEC detailing their finances and business dealings. The Securities Exchange Act of 1934 also explicitly outlawed illegal insider trading.

Since the 1930s, additional legislation has been passed to increase oversight of the securities and commodities futures trading industries, to prevent fraud, and to reassure investors.

WEAKNESSES IN THE MARKET SYSTEM

Even with careful oversight, fraudulent activities can occur in the securities industry. Securities fraud and the ensuing scandals are devastating to investors and to the markets as a whole. There were many high-profile instances of accounting scandals and securities fraud during the first decade of the 21st century.

Illegal Insider Trading

Insider trading is the buying or selling of stock by someone who has information about the company that other stockholders do not have. Most often, it refers to directors, officers, or employees buying or selling their own company's stock. Insider trading alone is not illegal, but insiders must report their stock transactions to the SEC. Insider trading becomes illegal when it is not reported to the SEC and breaches a fiduciary duty to the corporation; that is, when it violates a duty to act in the corporation's best interests. Most often, this happens when someone within the company has confidential information and uses it as the basis for a stock transaction. For example, if a company officer knows that the company is going to file for bankruptcy the next day and sells his or her shares of the company's stock because the stock price will likely plummet, the trading is illegal. The same goes for someone who gives the information to an outside stockholder so he or she can act on it.

The best-known case of illegal insider trading during the first decade of the 21st century involved the company ImClone Systems, the media mogul Martha Stewart (1941–), and the stockbroker Peter Bacanovic (1962–). The SEC alleged that Bacanovic passed confidential information to Stewart and that she sold her stock in ImClone because of that information. The SEC also accused Stewart and Bacanovic of trying to cover up the matter afterward by lying to federal investigators. The insider trading charge against Stewart was dropped, but she was convicted of lying to investigators and obstruction of justice. Bacanovic was convicted of most of the charges against him. Stewart and Bacanovic were both sentenced to five months in prison.

Overvaluing and Accounting Scandals

Overvaluing is the overstatement of income by companies with the assistance of their accountants to create an inflated impression of financial success among investors, thereby increasing the value of stock. During the first decade of the 21st century Wall Street experienced many scandals concerning such accounting practices at major corporations. The most egregious and notorious breaches of regulations occurred at three companies: Enron, WorldCom, and Tyco International (see Chapter 6). All three became targets of SEC investigations, with company executives brought up on criminal fraud charges and investors losing billions of dollars.

Ponzi Schemes

A Ponzi scheme is a fraudulent investment deal in which the person perpetrating the scheme convinces potential investors that he or she has special investment know-how and can gain them large returns on their investment. The fraudster collects money from an initial group of investors. He or she then convinces additional people to invest and uses part of their money to pay the dividends that the first group is expecting. The initial investors are so pleased that they invest even more money, and so the scheme continues. The fraudster must continually recruit new investors and/or collect more money from existing investors to keep the scam going.

In "Ponzi Schemes" (February 2, 2003, http://web.archive.org/web/20041001-20051231re_/http://www.ssa.gov/history/ponzi.html), the Social Security Administration (SSA) notes that the scheme is named after Charles Ponzi (1883–1949), an investment broker who conducted such a scam in 1920 in Boston, Massachusetts. Ponzi sold bonds to his investors and promised them a 50% to 100% return on their investments. He managed to maintain his scheme for seven months before being found out by the authorities. During that time he pulled in an estimated $10 million from around 10,000 investors. Ponzi became a near-instant millionaire and bought a large and expensive house for himself. The SSA reports that after seven years of litigation Ponzi's investors each received, on average, 37 cents for each dollar they had invested.

There are many variations of the classic Ponzi scheme. In 2008 the investment broker Bernard Madoff (1938–) confessed to his sons that he had been running a Ponzi-type investment scam for over a decade. Madoff eventually pleaded guilty and in June 2009 was sentenced to 150 years in prison. In "The Madoff Scam: Meet the Liquidator" (September 27, 2009, http://www.cbsnews.com/stories/2009/09/24/60minutes/main5339719.shtml?tag=currentVideoInfo;segmentUtilities), the CBS program *60 Minutes* reports that Madoff had collected nearly $36 billion from thousands of investors. Approximately half of that money went missing (i.e., could not be found in Madoff's company accounts) before the scam collapsed. As of September 2010, Madoff remained in federal prison. His scam is considered to be the largest Ponzi scheme in U.S. history.

CHAPTER 8
WEALTH IN THE UNITED STATES

All communities divide themselves into the few and the many. The first are the rich and the well-born, the other the mass of the people.

—Alexander Hamilton, 1787

Wealth is collected assets: cash, commodities, stocks, bonds, businesses, and properties. In the United States a small percentage of people have enormous wealth and the rest of the population has far less wealth. Is this a natural and acceptable result of capitalism or an economic injustice that must be righted for the good of society? This is a debate that has raged since the nation was founded. Some people believe the accumulation of great wealth is possible for anyone in the United States as the reward for hard work, ingenuity, and wise decision making. However, other people believe American political, business, and social systems are unfairly structured so as to limit wealth building by certain segments of the population.

WEALTH AND NET WORTH

The components of wealth can be divided into two broad categories: tangible assets and intangible assets. Tangible assets are things that have value in and of themselves. Examples include gold, land, houses, cars, boats, artwork, jewelry, and all other durable consumer goods with recognizable value in the marketplace. Intangible assets are financial devices that have worth because they have perceived value. The most obvious examples are stocks and bonds. Other devices often counted as intangible assets include pensions (which are promises of future income), life insurance policies with cash value, and insurance policies on tangible assets because they protect valuable resources.

The federal government does not measure the overall wealth of individual Americans or the population as a whole. However, it does compile data on related economic indicators that include wealth assets. One of these measures is called net worth.

Net Worth

Net worth is the sum of all assets minus the sum of all liabilities (such as debts). The Federal Reserve System, the national bank of the United States, computes the aggregate net worth of households and nonprofit organizations (NPOs) on a quarterly and annual basis. These values are published in tabular form in "B.100 Balance Sheet of Households and Nonprofit Organizations" as part of the *Federal Reserve Statistical Release Z.1: Flow of Funds Accounts of the United States* (http://www.federalreserve.gov/releases/z1/). Table 8.1 shows the net worth data for the first quarter of 2010.

ASSETS. Overall, U.S. households and NPOs had assets of $68.5 trillion at the end of the first quarter of 2010; of this, nearly $23 trillion was in tangible assets and $45.5 trillion was in financial (intangible) assets. (See Table 8.1.) The Federal Reserve includes only four components in tangible assets: real estate held by households ($16.5 trillion), real estate held by NPOs ($1.6 trillion), NPO equipment and software ($218.6 billion), and consumer durable goods ($4.6 trillion). Figure 8.1 shows the breakdown of these assets at the end of the first quarter of 2010. Real estate held by households accounted for the vast majority (72%) of tangible assets, followed by consumer durable goods (20%), real estate held by NPOs (7%), and NPO-owned equipment and software (1%).

Financial assets were much more diverse in type. The largest components of the $45.5 trillion held in financial assets at the end of the first quarter of 2010 were pension fund reserves ($12.3 trillion, or 27% of the total), corporate equities ($7.8 trillion, or 17% of the total), and deposits and currency ($7.7 trillion, or 17% of the total). (See Table 8.1 and Figure 8.2.) Deposits include monies in checking and savings accounts and in money market funds.

Figure 8.3 shows the breakdown of financial and tangible assets for households and NPOs from 2003 to the first quarter of 2010. The total value of assets peaked

TABLE 8.1

Balance sheet of households and nonprofit organizations, first quarter 2010

[Billions of dollars; amounts outstanding at end of period, not seasonally adjusted]

	2010 Q1	
1 Assets	**68,535.8**	1
2 Tangible assets	22,993.6	2
3 Real estate	18,141.8	3
4 Households[a, b]	16,507.2	4
5 Nonprofit organizations	1,634.6	5
6 Equipment and software owned by nonprofit organizations[c]	218.6	6
7 Consumer durable goods[c]	4,633.1	7
8 Financial assets	45,542.2	8
9 Deposits	7,651.6	9
10 Foreign deposits	48.1	10
11 Checkable deposits and currency	195.9	11
12 Time and savings deposits	6,205.9	12
13 Money market fund shares	1,201.8	13
14 Credit market instruments	4,180.2	14
15 Open market paper	4.6	15
16 Treasury securities	795.7	16
17 Savings bonds	190.2	17
18 Other Treasury	605.5	18
19 Agency- and GSE-backed securities	94.3	19
20 Municipal securities	1,020.1	20
21 Corporate and foreign bonds	2,139.8	21
22 Other loans and advances[d]	24.9	22
23 Mortgages	100.8	23
24 Corporate equities[a]	7,793.3	24
25 Mutual fund shares[e]	4,318.7	25
26 Security credit	679.5	26
27 Life insurance reserves	1,255.2	27
28 Pension fund reserves	12,345.4	28
29 Equity in noncorporate business[f]	6,525.3	29
30 Miscellaneous assets	792.9	30
31 Liabilities	**13,970.4**	31
32 Credit market instruments	13,503.1	32
33 Home mortgages[g]	10,240.3	33
34 Consumer credit	2,421.8	34
35 Municipal securities[h]	266.1	35
36 Bank loans n.e.c.	200.8	36
37 Other loans and advances	134.3	37
38 Commercial mortgages[h]	239.8	38
39 Security credit	196.4	39
40 Trade payables[h]	246.3	40
41 Deferred and unpaid life insurance premiums	24.6	41
42 Net worth	**54,565.4**	42
Memo: Replacement-cost value of structures:		
43 Residential	13,538.1	43
44 Households	13,343.0	44
45 Nonprofit organizations	195.1	45
46 Nonresidential (nonprofits)	1,333.5	46
47 Disposable personal income (SAAR)	11,095.9	47
48 Household net worth as percentage of disposable personal income (SAAR)	491.8	48

TABLE 8.1

Balance sheet of households and nonprofit organizations, first quarter 2010 [CONTINUED]

[Billions of dollars; amounts outstanding at end of period, not seasonally adjusted]

	2010 Q1	
49 Owners' equity in household real estate[i]	6,266.9	49
50 Owners' equity as percentage of household real estate[j]	38.0	50

Note: Sector includes farm households and domestic hedge funds.
GSE = Government sponsored enterprise.
SAAR = Seasonally adjusted annual rate.
[a]At market value.
[b]All types of owner-occupied housing including farm houses and mobile homes, as well as second homes that are not rented, vacant homes for sale, and vacant land.
[c]At replacement (current) cost.
[d]Syndicated loans to nonfinancial corporate business by nonprofits and domestic hedge funds.
[e]Value based on the market values of equities held and the book value of other assets held by mutual funds.
[f]Net worth of noncorporate business (table B.103, line 31) and owners' equity in farm business and unincorporated security brokers and dealers.
[g]Includes loans made under home equity lines of credit and home equity loans secured by junior liens, shown on table L.218, line 22.
[h]Liabilities of nonprofit organizations.
[i]Line 4 less line 33.
[j]Line 49 divided by line 4.

SOURCE: Adapted from "B.100. Balance Sheet of Households and Nonprofit Organizations," in *Federal Reserve Statistical Release Z.1: Flow of Funds Accounts of the United States, Flows and Outstandings, First Quarter 2010*, The Federal Reserve, June 10, 2010, http://www.federalreserve.gov/releases/z1/Current/z1.pdf (accessed July 6, 2010)

FIGURE 8.1

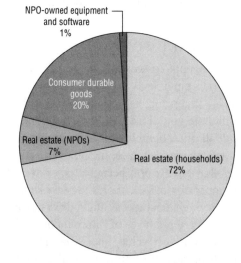

Tangible assets of households and nonprofit organizations at end of first quarter 2010

NPO=Non Profit Organization

SOURCE: Adapted from "B.100. Balance Sheet of Households and Nonprofit Organizations," in *Federal Reserve Statistical Release Z.1: Flow of Funds Accounts of the United States, Flows and Outstandings, First Quarter 2010*, The Federal Reserve, June 10, 2010, http://www.federalreserve.gov/releases/z1/Current/z1.pdf (accessed July 6, 2010)

at year-end 2007 at nearly $78.6 trillion and then plummeted to $65.7 trillion by year-end 2008. Assets grew only slightly in value during 2009 and the first quarter of 2010.

LIABILITIES. Assets alone do not provide an indication of the nation's wealth status. Debts and other obligations, known as liabilities, must be subtracted. These liabilities totaled almost $14 trillion at the end of the first quarter of 2010. (See Table 8.1.) Credit market instruments accounted for the vast majority of this total, at

FIGURE 8.2

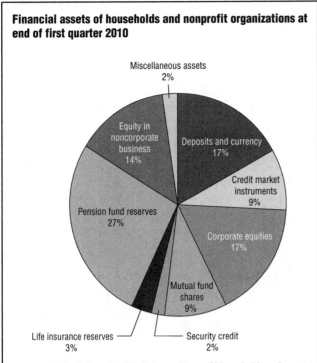

Financial assets of households and nonprofit organizations at end of first quarter 2010

Miscellaneous assets 2%

Equity in noncorporate business 14%

Deposits and currency 17%

Credit market instruments 9%

Pension fund reserves 27%

Corporate equities 17%

Mutual fund shares 9%

Life insurance reserves 3%

Security credit 2%

SOURCE: Adapted from "B.100. Balance Sheet of Households and Nonprofit Organizations," in *Federal Reserve Statistical Release Z.1: Flow of Funds Accounts of the United States, Flows and Outstandings, First Quarter 2010*, The Federal Reserve, June 10, 2010, http://www .federalreserve.gov/releases/z1/Current/z1.pdf (accessed July 6, 2010)

$13.5 trillion. Home mortgages ($10.2 trillion) were the single largest credit market instrument, followed by consumer credit ($2.4 trillion). Both of these liabilities are described in detail in Chapter 7.

TRENDS IN NET WORTH. The net worth of U.S. households and NPOs totaled $54.6 trillion at the end of the first quarter of 2010. (See Table 8.1.) Figure 8.4 compares this value to net worth values calculated by the Federal Reserve from 2003 to the first quarter of 2010. Net worth increased slightly each year, from year-end 2003 to year-end 2006 and then stagnated during 2007. By year-end 2008 net worth declined to $51.3 trillion (a 20% drop from year-end 2007). Net worth grew only slightly during 2009 and the first quarter in 2010.

Personal Income and Income Inequality

The U.S. Department of Commerce's Bureau of Economic Analysis (BEA) collects data on the personal income of Americans. As shown in Table 7.1 in Chapter 7, personal income consists of employee compensation (wages, salaries, and supplements), proprietors' income (income earned by the owners of unincorporated businesses), rental income, income from interest and dividends, and transfer receipts (e.g., unemployment benefits or Social Security benefits). Historically, employee compensation makes up the largest component of personal

FIGURE 8.3

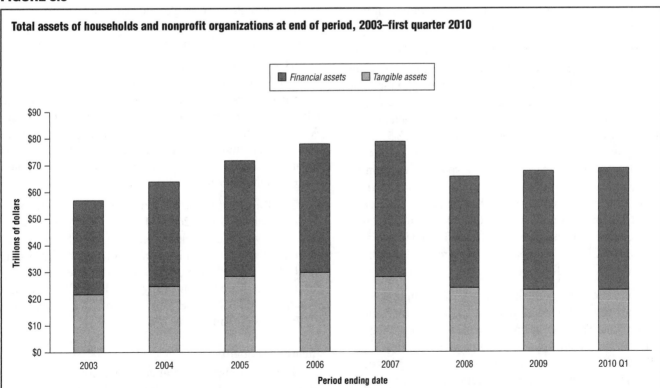

Total assets of households and nonprofit organizations at end of period, 2003–first quarter 2010

■ Financial assets ■ Tangible assets

(Trillions of dollars; x-axis: Period ending date — 2003, 2004, 2005, 2006, 2007, 2008, 2009, 2010 Q1)

SOURCE: Adapted from "B.100.e. Balance Sheet of Households and Nonprofit Organizations with Equity Detail," in *Federal Reserve Statistical Release Z.1: Flow of Funds Accounts of the United States, Flows and Outstandings, First Quarter 2010*, The Federal Reserve, June 10, 2010, http://www.federalreserve .gov/releases/z1/Current/z1.pdf (accessed July 6, 2010)

FIGURE 8.4

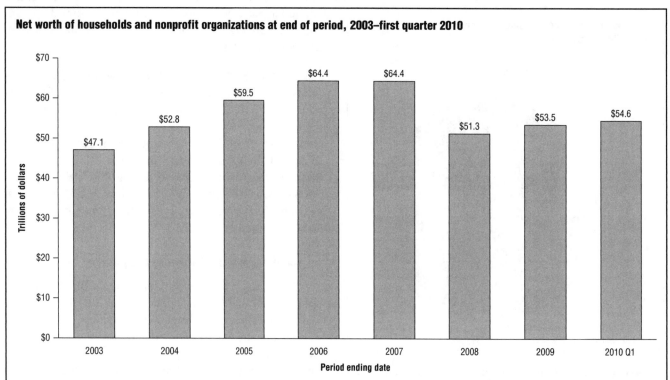

Net worth of households and nonprofit organizations at end of period, 2003–first quarter 2010

SOURCE: Adapted from "B.100. Balance Sheet of Households and Nonprofit Organizations," in *Federal Reserve Statistical Release Z.1: Flow of Funds Accounts of the United States, Flows and Outstandings, First Quarter 2010*, The Federal Reserve, June 10, 2010, http://www.federalreserve.gov/releases/z1/Current/z1.pdf (accessed July 6, 2010)

income. In 2009 employee compensation accounted for $7.8 trillion, or 64% of the nearly $12.2 trillion in personal income. Thus, employment factors are extremely important to a discussion of wealth and its distribution.

DEMOGRAPHICS OF UNEMPLOYMENT. Table 8.2 shows unemployment data and rates by sex, marital status, race, and ethnicity in 2009. The overall unemployment rate among men aged 25 years and older was 8.8%. The rates were much higher for single (never married) men (13.3%) and for widowed, divorced, or separated men (12.5%). The unemployment rate was only 6.5% for men in this age group who were married and had a spouse present in the household. The overall unemployment rate among women aged 25 years and older was 6.9%. Again, the rates were much higher for single women (9.5%) and for widowed, divorced, or separated women (8.9%). The unemployment rate was 5.3% for women who were married and had a spouse present in the household.

On a racial basis the highest rate of unemployment in 2009 among men aged 25 years and older was for African-Americans. The overall unemployment rate for this group was 14.7%. Again, the rate was highest for single men (20.8%). The lowest unemployment rate among African-American men was 10.2% for married men with a spouse present in the household.

The overall unemployment rates were lower for Asian-American men (7.2%), white men (8.1%), and men of Hispanic or Latino ethnicity (10.9%) who were 25 years and older in 2009. In all of these groups, the rates were higher for single and widowed, divorced, and separated men than for men who were married and had a spouse present in the household.

The overall unemployment rates in 2009 among women aged 25 years and older were 10.1% for African-American women, 9.9% for women of Hispanic or Latino ethnicity, 6.4% for white women, and 5.9% for Asian-American women. For all groups, the unemployment rates were higher among single and widowed, divorced, and separated women than for married women with a spouse present in the household.

The Bureau of Labor Statistics reports in *The Employment Situation—June 2010* (July 2, 2010, http://www.bls.gov/news.release/archives/empsit_07022010.pdf) that in June 2010 the overall unemployment rate for people aged 16 years and older was 9.5%. The rate was 25.7% for teenagers aged 16 to 19 years, 15.4% for African-Americans, 12.4% for Hispanics, 8.6% for whites, and 7.7% for Asian-Americans.

Income Inequality

The U.S. Census Bureau collects income data as part of the Current Population Survey Annual Social and Economic Supplement (CPS ASEC), a sample survey of approximately 100,000 U.S. households. Data from 2009 are presented and analyzed by Carmen DeNavas-Walt,

TABLE 8.2

Unemployed persons by demographic group, 2009

Marital status, race, Hispanic or Latino ethnicity, and age	Men		Women	
	Thousands of persons	Unemployment rates	Thousands of persons	Unemployment rates
	2009	2009	2009	2009
Total, 16 years and over	**8,453**	**10.3**	**5,811**	**8.1**
Married, spouse present	3,115	6.6	2,057	5.5
Widowed, divorced, or separated	1,326	12.8	1,330	9.2
Single (never married)	4,011	16.3	2,424	12.0
White 16 years and over	6,421	9.4	4,227	7.3
Married, spouse present	2,498	6.2	1,694	5.4
Widowed, divorced, or separated	1,058	12.4	993	8.8
Single (never married)	2,864	14.8	1,540	10.5
Black or African American, 16 years and over	1,448	17.5	1,159	12.4
Married, spouse present	367	10.3	193	6.6
Widowed, divorced, or separated	205	16.4	257	10.9
Single (never married)	876	25.3	709	17.3
Asian 16 years and over	306	7.9	216	6.6
Married, spouse present	167	6.6	116	5.6
Widowed, divorced, or separated	26	8.2	30	6.2
Single (never married)	112	11.2	70	9.4
Hispanic or Latino ethnicity, 16 years and over	1,670	12.5	1,036	11.5
Married, spouse present	688	9.5	410	9.8
Widowed, divorced, or separated	223	13.3	218	11.1
Single (never married)	759	17.3	408	14.0
Total, 25 years and over	**6,226**	**8.8**	**4,279**	**6.9**
Married, spouse present	3,012	6.5	1,933	5.3
Widowed, divorced, or separated	1,262	12.5	1,263	8.9
Single (never married)	1,952	13.3	1,083	9.5
White, 25 years and over	4,777	8.1	3,157	6.4
Married, spouse present	2,413	6.1	1,589	5.2
Widowed, divorced, or separated	1,007	12.1	947	8.6
Single (never married)	1,358	12.0	621	8.0
Black or African American, 25 years and over	1,022	14.7	809	10.1
Married, spouse present	358	10.2	182	6.5
Widowed, divorced, or separated	197	16.2	239	10.4
Single (never married)	467	20.8	388	13.6
Asian, 25 years and over	253	7.2	176	5.9
Married, spouse present	163	6.5	113	5.6
Widowed, divorced, or separated	26	8.1	29	6.2
Single (never married)	65	9.2	34	6.7
Hispanic or Latino ethnicity, 16 years and over	1,218	10.9	737	9.9
Married, spouse present	655	9.4	374	9.5
Widowed, divorced, or separated	201	12.7	201	10.7
Single (never married)	362	13.8	161	9.9

Notes: Estimates for the above race groups (white, black or African American, and Asian) do not sum to totals because data are not presented for all races. Persons whose ethnicity is identified as Hispanic or Latino may be of any race. Updated population controls are introduced annually with the release of January data.

SOURCE: Adapted from "Table 24. Unemployed Persons by Marital Status, Race, Hispanic or Latino Ethnicity, Age, and Sex," in *Current Population Survey, Tables*, U.S. Department of Labor, Bureau of Labor Statistics, February 24, 2010, http://www.bls.gov/cps/cpsaat24.pdf (accessed July 13, 2010)

Bernadette D. Proctor, and Jessica C. Smith of the Census Bureau in *Income, Poverty, and Health Insurance Coverage in the United States: 2009* (September 2010, http://www.census.gov/prod/2010pubs/p60-238.pdf).

DeNavas-Walt, Proctor, and Smith report that the Census Bureau uses six mathematical and statistical methods to measure income inequality. Three of these methods—mean logarithmic deviation of income, the Theil index, and the Atkinson measure—are complex and not widely used. The remaining three methods and their results are explained in the following sections.

QUINTILE SHARES. The quintile shares method ranks all the households from the lowest to the highest income. The households are divided into five groups of equal population size (i.e., quintiles). The income of each group is then divided by the total income for all groups. If income equality exists, each group will account for 20% of the total income.

Table 8.3 shows quintile shares of income based on CPS ASEC data from 1969, 1979, 1989, 1999, and 2009. In 2009 the lowest quintile of U.S. households accounted for 3.4% of total income, whereas the highest quintile accounted for 50.3% of total income. The lowest quintile lost income share over time, from 4.1% in 1969 to 3.4% in 2009. The second and third quintiles also lost income share. The second quintile fell from 10.9% income share in 1969 to 8.6% income share in 2009. The third quintile decreased from 17.5% income share in 1969 to 14.6% income share in 2009. The fourth quintile increased from 24.5% in 1969 to 24.6% in 1979, but then declined, dropping to 23.2% in 2009. The highest quintile consistently gained income share over the decades, from 43% in 1969 to 50.3% in 2009. As noted in Table 8.3, the mean (average) household

income of the highest quintile in 2009 was $170,844. The mean household income of the lowest quintile in 2009 was $11,552.

GINI INDEX. The Gini index (or Gini coefficient) is a mathematically derived value that is used to describe the inequality in a data distribution. It was developed during the early 1900s by the Italian statistician Corrado Gini (1884–1965). When used to compute income inequality, a value of zero indicates perfect equality, whereas a value of one indicates that all income is made by only one family.

As shown in Table 8.3, in 2009 the Gini index was 0.468. In 1969 it was 0.391. Thus, the Gini index indicates that income inequality increased over these four decades.

TABLE 8.3

Selected measures of household income dispersion, 1969, 1979, 1989, 1999, and 2009

Measures of income dispersion	2009[a]	1999[b]	1989	1979[c]	1969
Measure					
Household income at selected percentiles					
10th percentile limit	12,120	13,318	12,025	11,303	10,221
20th percentile limit	20,453	22,059	20,203	19,274	18,491
50th (median)	49,777	52,388	48,279	45,325	43,391
80th percentile limit	100,000	101,995	89,707	79,851	71,897
90th percentile limit	137,632	138,742	120,178	103,364	91,226
95th percentile limit	180,001	182,795	153,241	129,029	112,759
Household income ratios of selected percentiles					
90th/10th	11.36	10.42	9.99	9.15	8.93
95th/20th	8.80	8.29	7.59	6.69	6.10
95th/50th	3.62	3.49	3.17	2.85	2.60
80th/50th	2.01	1.95	1.86	1.76	1.66
80th/20th	4.89	4.62	4.44	4.14	3.89
20th/50th	0.41	0.42	0.42	0.43	0.43
Mean household income of quintiles					
Lowest quintile	11,552	12,763	11,681	11,031	9,993
Second quintile	29,257	31,339	29,063	27,436	26,979
Third quintile	49,534	52,457	48,311	45,234	43,112
Fourth quintile	78,694	81,644	73,076	66,381	60,388
Highest quintile	170,844	174,106	142,851	119,130	106,138
Shares of household income of quintiles					
Lowest quintile	3.4	3.6	3.8	4.1	4.1
Second quintile	8.6	8.9	9.5	10.2	10.9
Third quintile	14.6	14.9	15.8	16.8	17.5
Fourth quintile	23.2	23.2	24.0	24.6	24.5
Highest quintile	50.3	49.4	46.8	44.2	43.0
Summary measures					
Gini index of income inequality	0.468	0.458	0.431	0.404	0.391
Mean logarithmic deviation of income	0.550	0.476	0.406	0.369	0.357
Theil	0.403	0.386	0.324	0.279	0.268
Atkinson:					
$e=0.25$	0.097	0.092	0.080	0.070	0.067
$e=0.50$	0.190	0.180	0.158	0.141	0.135
$e=0.75$	0.288	0.268	0.239	0.216	0.209

[a]Medians are calculated using $2,500 income intervals. Beginning with 2009 income data, the Census Bureau expanded the upper income intervals used to calculate medians to $250,000 or more. Medians falling in the upper open-ended interval are plugged with "$250,000." Before 2009, the upper open-ended interval was $100,000 and a plug of "$100,000" was used.
[b]Implementation of Census 2000-based population controls.
[c]Implementation of 1980 census population controls. Questionnaire expanded to allow the recording of up to 27 possible values from a list of 51 possible sources of income.

SOURCE: Adapted from Carmen DeNavas-Walt, Bernadette D. Proctor and Jessica C. Smith, "Table A-2. Selected Measures of Household Income Dispersion: 1967 to 2009," in *Income, Poverty, and Health Insurance Coverage in the United States: 2009*, U.S. Department of Commerce, Economics and Statistics Administration, U.S. Census Bureau, September 2010, http://www.census.gov/prod/2010pubs/p60-238.pdf (accessed October 15, 2010)

RATIO OF INCOME PERCENTILES. The top rows in Table 8.3 list household incomes at selected percentiles. Below the rows are listed household income ratios. Each household income ratio is a percentile income limit divided by another percentile income limit; for example, the 95th/50th ratio in 2009 was $180,001 divided by $49,777, which equals 3.62. In other words, the income of households in the 95th percentile was 3.62 times the income of households in the 50th percentile. These ratios are useful for seeing how income inequality changes over time. In 1969 the 95th/50th ratio was 2.60. Thus, the income gap between high-income households and medium-income households widened between 1969 and 2009. The 95th/50th ratio is commonly called the "top half" inequality measure.

QUINTILE MOVEMENT. It is important to remember that the income inequality measures used by the Census Bureau provide only a snapshot of income distribution at a particular time. In reality, many people do not remain in the same quintile continuously, but move up or down depending on their economic circumstances. Quintile movements are tracked by the Census Bureau through the Survey of Income and Program Participation (SIPP). SIPP surveys are conducted monthly and follow the same participants for a multiyear period, called a panel. Each panel typically lasts two to four years. The Census Bureau reports in "SIPP Sample Design and Interview Procedures" (March 15, 2010, http://www.census.gov/sipp/usrguide/ch2_nov20 .pdf) that the 2004 SIPP panel lasted from February 2004 through January 2008. The 2008 panel began in September 2008 and was scheduled to end in December 2012.

As of September 2010, comprehensive SIPP data were available only for the 2004 panel. According to the Census Bureau, in "Overview of the Survey of Income and Program Participation (SIPP)" (May 9, 2006, http://www.census.gov/sipp/overview.html), the panel included 46,500 households.

DeNavas-Walt, Proctor, and Smith note that 30.9% of households in the bottom income quintile in 2004 had moved up to a higher quintile by 2007. Likewise, 32.2% of households in the top income quintile in 2004 had dropped to a lower quintile by 2007. Quintile movement was tied strongly to the educational levels of the survey participants. Households containing participants with lower educational levels were more likely to drop into lower quintiles over time than were households containing participants with higher educational levels.

WEALTH DISTRIBUTION

In *Changes in U.S. Family Finances from 2004 to 2007: Evidence from the Survey of Consumer Finances* (February 2009, http://www.federalreserve.gov/pubs/bull etin/2009/pdf/scf09.pdf), Brian K. Bucks et al. of the Federal Reserve rely on data that were collected for the 2007 Survey of Consumer Finances (SCF). The SCF is a survey that is conducted every three years by the Federal Reserve in cooperation with the Internal Revenue Service (IRS) to collect detailed financial information on American families.

Bucks et al. rank the families by income percentiles. In 2007 the mean income for each percentile was:

- Less than 20 percentile of income—$12,300 income
- 20 to 39.9 percentile of income—$28,300 income
- 40 to 59.9 percentile of income—$47,300 income
- 60 to 79.9 percentile of income—$76,600 income
- 80 to 89.9 percentile of income—$116,000 income
- 90 to 100 percentile of income—$397,700 income

The families were also assessed for net worth (assets minus liabilities). In 2007 the mean net worth for each income percentile was:

- Less than 20 percentile of income—$105,200 net worth
- 20 to 39.9 percentile of income—$134,900 net worth
- 40 to 59.9 percentile of income—$209,900 net worth
- 60 to 79.9 percentile of income—$375,100 net worth
- 80 to 89.9 percentile of income—$606,300 net worth
- 90 to 100 percentile of income—$3,306,000 net worth

Table 8.4 shows the breakdown by income sources for various net worth percentiles in 2007. The data indicate that people at the bottom of the net worth profile (those in the less than 25th percentile) obtained the vast majority (79.9%) of their income from wages. By contrast, people at the upper end of the spectrum (those in the 90th to 100th percentile) obtained only 46.2% of their income from wages. A business, farm, or self-employment provided 24.7% of the income for families in the uppermost percentile. A third major source of income for families in this percentile was capital gains. Capital gains accounted for 14.4% of their income in 2007.

Nonfinancial Assets

Table 8.5 provides a detailed breakdown of the types of nonfinancial assets that were held by families in 2007. Nearly all (92%) the families had at least one nonfinancial asset. The most widely held nonfinancial assets were vehicles (87%) and primary residences (68.6%). Bucks et al. note that housing wealth has historically been a large component of total family wealth. In 2007 primary residences accounted for 31.8% of total family assets.

As shown in Table 8.5, there were substantial differences between net worth percentiles in homeownership and the median values (half of all households were worth more and half were worth less) of their primary residences. Only 13.8% of people in the less than 25th percentile of net worth owned a primary residence in 2007. The

TABLE 8.4

Before-tax family income distributed by income sources and by percentile of net worth, 2007

Income source	Percentile of net worth					All families
	Less than 25	25–49.9	50–74.9	75–89.9	90–100	
2007 Survey of Consumer Finances						
Wages	79.9	79.9	77.8	72.4	46.2	64.5
Interest or dividends	0.1	0.3	0.7	1.9	7.8	3.7
Business, farm, self-employment	1.8	5.3	6.9	7.9	24.7	13.6
Capital gains	0.1	0.4	1.3	2.9	14.4	6.7
Social Security or retirement	9.5	10.9	11.8	14.1	6.2	9.6
Transfers or other	8.6	3.2	1.6	0.8	0.7	1.9
Total	**100**	**100**	**100**	**100**	**100**	**100**

SOURCE: Adapted from Brian K. Bucks et al., "Table 2. Amount of Before-Tax Family Income, Distributed by Income Sources, by Percentile of Net Worth, 2004 and 2007 Surveys," in *Changes in U.S. Family Finances from 2004 to 2007: Evidence from the Survey of Consumer Finances*, Federal Reserve Bulletin, vol. 95, February 2009, http://www.federalreserve.gov/pubs/bulletin/2009/pdf/scf09.pdf (accessed July 10, 2010)

median value of their primary residence was $81,000. In contrast, 96.9% of people in the 90th to 100th percentile of net worth owned a primary residence, and the median value was $550,000. Homeownership rates varied based on demographic qualities, including the age and educational attainment of the head of the household, the family structure, and the race and ethnicity of the respondents. For example, just over three-quarters (75.6%) of non-Hispanic white respondents reported owning a primary residence in 2007, compared with 51.9% of nonwhites or Hispanics.

More recent homeownership data by racial makeup are shown in Figure 8.5. The data were compiled by the Census Bureau. In the second quarter of 2010 the overall homeownership rate in the United States was 67%. The rate was highest (74%) for non-Hispanic white respondents. African-American respondents had a 46% homeownership rate, and Hispanic respondents had a 48% rate. People who described themselves as being of a mixed race or of other races had a homeownership rate of 56%.

Financial Assets

Financial assets include cash, stocks, bonds, and other investments with financial value, such as retirement accounts. Bucks et al. find that 93.9% of all families in 2007 had at least one financial asset. The most widely held financial assets were transaction accounts (92.1%). These include checking accounts, savings accounts, money market deposit accounts, money market mutual funds, and call accounts at brokerages.

Just over half (52.6%) of families had retirement accounts. (It should be noted that this category does not include Social Security benefits and certain employer-sponsored defined benefit plans.) Nearly a quarter (23%) of families had cash value life insurance policies. Smaller percentages of families held stocks (17.9%), certificates of deposit (16.1%), savings bonds (14.9%),

pooled investment funds (11.4%), other managed assets (5.8%), and bonds (1.6%). Approximately 9.3% of families held financial assets of other types.

Overall, Bucks et al. note that families that were the most likely to hold financial assets were those in the highest income brackets, those with a head of household aged 45 years and older, those with a self-employed head of household, and homeowners. Among races, 96.8% of non-Hispanic white families held financial assets in 2007, compared with 86.7% of nonwhite or Hispanic families. The largest difference was in retirement accounts. Nearly six out of 10 (58.2%) non-Hispanic white families had retirement accounts, compared with only four out of 10 (39.1%) nonwhite or Hispanic families.

POVERTY IN THE UNITED STATES

In the United States poverty is officially defined and measured in different ways by various government entities. At the federal level it is measured using two methods: poverty thresholds and poverty guidelines. Poverty thresholds are set by the Census Bureau, which also tracks poverty populations in the United States. The thresholds specify minimum income levels for different sizes and categories of families. For example, the Census Bureau (June 22, 2010, http://www.census.gov/hhes/www/poverty/data/threshld/thresh09.html) notes that in 2009 the poverty threshold for a family of four including two related children in the household was $21,756 per year. Thus, a family matching this description and making less than $21,756 per year in 2009 was considered by the U.S. government to be in poverty.

Poverty guidelines are published by the U.S. Department of Health and Human Services (HHS) for the 50 states and the District of Columbia. According to the HHS, the poverty guidelines are a simplification of the poverty thresholds and are used for administrative purposes, such

TABLE 8.5

Family holdings of nonfinancial assets, 2007

Family characteristic	Vehicles	Primary residence	Other residential property	Equity in nonresidential property	Business equity	Other	Any nonfinancial asset	Any asset
				Percentage of families holding asset				
All families	**87.0**	**68.6**	**13.7**	**8.1**	**12.0**	**7.2**	**92.0**	**97.7**
Percentile of income								
Less than 20	64.4	41.4	5.4	2.5	3.0	3.9	73.4	89.8
20–39.9	85.9	55.2	6.5	3.9	4.5	5.7	91.2	98.9
40–59.9	94.3	69.3	9.9	7.4	9.2	7.4	97.2	100.0
60–79.9	95.4	83.9	15.4	9.4	15.9	7.2	98.5	100.0
80–89.9	95.6	92.6	21.0	13.6	17.0	9.0	99.6	100.0
90–100	94.8	94.3	42.2	21.0	37.5	14.1	99.7	100.0
Age of head (years)								
Less than 35	85.4	40.7	5.6	3.2	6.8	5.9	88.2	97.1
35–44	87.5	66.1	12.0	7.5	16.0	5.5	91.3	96.9
45–54	90.3	77.3	15.7	9.5	15.2	8.7	95.0	97.6
55–64	92.2	81.0	20.9	11.5	16.3	8.5	95.6	99.1
65–74	90.6	85.5	18.9	12.3	10.1	9.1	94.5	98.4
75 or more	71.5	77.0	13.4	6.8	3.8	5.8	87.3	98.1
Family structure								
Single with child(ren)	80.5	53.4	8.9	5.6	5.6	5.8	89.5	95.7
Single, no child, age less than 55	77.0	42.6	6.2	2.9	7.5	7.0	82.5	93.7
Single, no child, age 55 or more	73.9	68.1	11.8	7.3	3.3	5.7	85.1	97.7
Couple with child(ren)	94.0	78.3	14.8	8.4	15.6	8.9	96.9	98.8
Couple, no child	94.6	79.2	18.0	10.8	16.6	7.4	97.3	99.4
Education of head								
No high school diploma	73.7	52.8	5.8	2.6	5.3	2.2	80.9	91.7
High school diploma	87.5	68.9	10.0	7.3	8.7	5.1	92.2	97.7
Some college	86.7	62.3	13.2	6.5	10.7	7.0	91.0	98.5
College degree	91.9	77.8	20.6	11.8	18.2	11.0	96.6	99.6
Race or ethnicity of respondent								
White non-Hispanic	89.6	75.6	15.3	9.0	13.9	8.4	94.6	98.9
Nonwhite or Hispanic	80.9	51.9	10.0	5.9	7.4	4.3	85.8	94.9
Current work status of head								
Working for someone else	91.3	67.2	11.9	7.0	6.3	7.1	94.4	98.6
Self-employed	90.6	82.4	26.5	17.3	68.4	11.0	97.6	99.7
Retired	78.6	72.9	14.6	7.7	3.6	5.4	87.2	96.1
Other not working	69.3	33.3	3.8	4.7	3.6	8.5	74.8	90.0
Current occupation of head								
Managerial or professional	93.1	78.2	20.7	10.8	22.0	9.9	97.2	99.8
Technical, sales, or services	87.4	61.5	10.2	7.3	9.2	7.7	91.6	97.8
Other occupation	92.6	66.3	9.6	6.7	13.6	4.9	95.2	98.5
Retired or other not working	77.1	66.7	12.9	7.2	3.6	5.9	85.2	95.2
Region								
Northeast	75.4	66.1	13.3	5.6	7.8	5.5	84.2	94.6
Midwest	89.5	71.3	13.7	8.4	13.1	6.4	93.4	98.4
South	89.2	70.2	11.3	8.8	11.4	7.2	93.8	98.5
West	90.5	65.4	18.3	8.7	15.3	9.3	94.1	98.4
Urbanicity								
Metropolitan statistical area (MSA)	86.2	68.1	14.2	7.6	12.3	7.6	91.5	97.7
Non-MSA	90.9	71.1	11.7	10.7	10.6	5.1	94.3	97.9
Housing status								
Owner	93.8	100.0	17.5	10.8	15.4	8.0	100.0	100.0
Renter or other	72.3	*	5.6	2.1	4.5	5.3	74.5	92.8
Percentile of net worth								
Less than 25	69.5	13.8	1.2	*	1.3	2.4	71.6	90.9
25–49.9	91.2	72.1	7.1	3.7	6.2	6.5	97.7	100.0
50–74.9	93.3	92.8	11.9	7.7	11.6	7.8	99.5	100.0
75–89.9	94.5	95.3	26.2	16.4	17.9	7.5	99.0	100.0
90–100	93.6	96.9	47.7	27.3	45.1	18.5	99.6	100.0

as determining eligibility for specific federal programs. The most recent guidelines were published in "Annual Update of the HHS Poverty Guidelines" (*Federal Register*, vol. 73, no. 15, January 23, 2009). Ordinarily, the HHS updates the poverty guidelines every year; however, as of September 2010 the HHS (http://aspe.hhs.gov/POVERTY/09exten sion.shtml) indicated that the 2009 guidelines were still being used.

TABLE 8.5

Family holdings of nonfinancial assets, 2007 [CONTINUED]

Family characteristic	Vehicles	Primary residence	Other residential property	Equity in nonresidential property	Business equity	Other	Any nonfinancial asset	Any asset
				Median value of holdings for families holding asset (thousands of 2007 dollars)				
All families	15.5	200.0	146.0	75.0	100.5	14.0	177.4	221.5
Percentile of income								
Less than 20	5.6	100.0	60.0	65.0	100.0	3.0	40.0	23.5
20–39.9	9.2	120.0	57.5	60.0	25.0	6.0	77.2	84.9
40–59.9	14.6	150.0	100.0	40.0	53.7	10.0	139.0	183.5
60–79.9	20.4	215.0	120.0	71.0	81.0	15.0	246.3	342.8
80–89.9	25.4	300.0	175.0	72.0	100.0	20.0	360.1	558.1
90–100	33.9	500.0	324.0	175.0	500.0	75.0	799.9	1,358.4
Age of head (years)								
Less than 35	13.3	175.0	85.0	50.0	59.9	8.0	30.9	38.8
35–44	17.4	205.0	150.0	50.0	86.0	10.0	182.6	222.3
45–54	18.7	230.0	150.0	80.0	100.0	15.0	224.9	306.0
55–64	17.4	210.0	157.0	90.0	116.3	20.0	233.1	347.0
65–74	14.6	200.0	150.0	75.0	415.0	20.0	212.2	303.3
75 or more	9.4	150.0	100.0	110.0	250.0	25.0	157.1	219.3
Family structure								
Single with child(ren)	8.3	165.0	90.0	71.0	100.0	9.0	106.9	116.4
Single, no child, age less than 55	9.8	155.0	120.0	48.8	50.0	9.0	52.0	52.6
Single, no child, age 55 or more	7.4	140.0	80.0	75.0	300.0	10.0	133.0	177.1
Couple with child(ren)	20.8	225.0	133.0	50.0	81.8	12.5	218.0	292.8
Couple, no child	20.6	230.0	165.0	85.0	130.0	20.0	235.6	312.1
Education of head								
No high school diploma	10.4	122.5	65.0	125.0	66.0	13.2	84.4	64.6
High school diploma	13.3	150.0	76.0	50.0	100.0	7.3	137.7	161.8
Some college	14.6	192.0	100.0	52.8	81.2	13.0	157.3	186.3
College degree	19.9	280.0	200.0	90.0	125.4	20.0	289.4	435.4
Race or ethnicity of respondent								
White non-Hispanic	17.1	200.0	136.5	75.0	112.5	15.0	203.8	271.0
Nonwhite or Hispanic	12.0	180.0	175.0	62.7	60.0	8.0	102.0	89.2
Current work status of head								
Working for someone else	17.0	200.0	120.0	52.8	50.0	10.0	167.1	213.3
Self-employed	22.1	300.0	293.0	152.5	150.0	50.0	455.0	543.9
Retired	11.4	155.0	100.0	75.0	212.6	13.2	156.0	203.5
Other not working	6.9	160.0	130.5	48.8	103.1	2.5	29.3	28.9
Current occupation of head								
Managerial or professional	20.2	270.0	200.0	105.0	200.0	20.0	278.9	411.2
Technical, sales, or services	14.4	200.0	125.0	85.0	40.0	15.0	155.0	187.0
Other occupation	16.7	157.9	90.0	37.0	68.6	10.8	135.6	157.6
Retired or other not working	10.4	155.0	100.0	75.0	196.9	12.5	146.7	177.1
Region								
Northeast	14.5	275.0	190.0	112.0	150.0	20.0	250.0	290.4
Midwest	14.6	155.0	110.0	52.8	112.4	10.0	157.5	204.7
South	15.6	160.0	120.0	71.5	93.8	15.0	145.8	180.9
West	17.1	300.0	210.0	90.0	101.4	14.0	251.6	293.2
Urbanicity								
Metropolitan statistical area (MSA)	15.8	220.0	150.0	82.5	105.0	13.5	194.0	243.9
Non-MSA	14.5	115.0	80.0	50.0	100.0	22.0	118.6	149.2
Housing status								
Owner	18.4	200.0	150.0	80.0	113.4	20.0	253.5	344.2
Renter or other	8.6	*	85.0	38.0	50.0	5.4	10.1	13.6

The Poverty Rate

The Census Bureau calculates the number of people in poverty and the poverty rate using the poverty thresholds. The most recent data were collected in 2009 as part of the CPS ASEC and are analyzed by DeNavas-Walt, Proctor, and Smith. As noted earlier, the CPS ASEC surveys around 100,000 U.S. households per year. The data are used to estimate annual poverty levels for the nation as a whole.

According to DeNavas-Walt, Proctor, and Smith, 43.6 million people in the United States lived at or below the federal poverty level in 2009. This represented 14.3% of the total U.S. population and was up from 13.2% in 2008. The number of people in poverty has varied widely over the past few decades. In 1960 approximately 39.9 million people in the United States lived in poverty. This value dropped to fewer than 25 million people during the 1970s and then began increasing, reaching 39 million

TABLE 8.5

Family holdings of nonfinancial assets, 2007 [CONTINUED]

Family characteristic	Vehicles	Primary residence	Other residential property	Equity in nonresidential property	Business equity	Other	Any nonfinancial asset	Any asset
				Median value of holdings for families holding asset (thousands of 2007 dollars)				
Percentile of net worth								
Less than 25	6.9	81.0	12.0	*	4.0	1.3	8.6	8.1
25–49.9	13.1	100.0	30.0	25.0	20.0	7.5	95.8	107.8
50–74.9	17.5	200.0	60.0	38.4	67.6	13.0	229.1	304.3
75–89.9	22.0	317.2	146.0	82.5	125.0	30.0	443.7	687.1
90–100	31.1	550.0	400.0	266.7	690.0	75.0	1,160.0	2,104.0
Memo								
Mean value of holdings for families holding asset	22.0	302.4	335.6	309.4	1071.1	80.7	469.5	668.5

*Ten or fewer observations.
Note: For questions on income, respondents were asked to base their answers on the calendar year preceding the interview. For questions on saving, respondents were asked to base their answers on the 12 months preceding the interview. Percentage distributions may not sum to 100 because of rounding. Dollars have been converted to 2007 values with the current-methods consumer price index for all urban consumers.

SOURCE: Brian K. Bucks et al., "Table 9. Family Holdings of Nonfinancial Assets and of Any Asset, by Selected Characteristics of Families and Type of Asset, 2004 and 2007 Surveys—B. 2007 Survey of Consumer Finances," in *Changes in U.S. Family Finances from 2004 to 2007: Evidence from the Survey of Consumer Finances, Federal Reserve Bulletin*, vol. 95, February 2009, http://www.federalreserve.gov/pubs/bulletin/2009/pdf/scf09.pdf (accessed July 10, 2010)

FIGURE 8.5

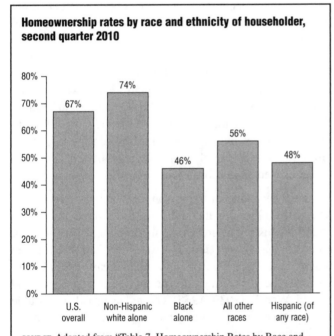

Homeownership rates by race and ethnicity of householder, second quarter 2010

SOURCE: Adapted from "Table 7. Homeownership Rates by Race and Ethnicity of Householder: 2007 to 2010 (in Percent)," in *Residential Vacancies and Homeownership in the Second Quarter 2010*, U.S. Department of Commerce, U.S. Census Bureau, July 27, 2010, http://www.census.gov/hhes/www/housing/hvs/qtr210/files/q210press.pdf (accessed July 27, 2010)

during the early 1990s. The number declined to around 31 million in 2000 and then increased over the ensuing nine years.

The poverty rate was around 22% during the early 1960s, and then it dropped to around 11% during the early 1970s. It topped 15% during the early 1990s and then decreased to around 12% in 2000, before it began to rise again. The 2009 poverty rate was the highest since 1994.

There were dramatic demographic differences in the U.S. poverty rate in 2009. The differences by race and ethnicity were:

- Blacks—25.8%
- Hispanics—25.3%
- Asians—12.5%
- Non-Hispanic whites—9.4%

DeNavas-Walt, Proctor, and Smith note that the 2009 CPS ASEC included native-born Americans, foreign-born naturalized U.S. citizens, and noncitizens. Poverty rate estimates for these groups on a national level were:

- Native-born Americans—13.7%
- Foreign-born naturalized U.S. citizens—10.8%
- Noncitizens—25.1%

Other demographic differences were also significant. The poverty rate in 2009 for those under the age of 18 years was 20.7%, compared with 12.9% for people aged 18 to 64 years and 8.9% for people aged 65 years and older. Among family types, the highest poverty rate was experienced by families headed by unmarried females, at 29.9%. By contrast, the poverty rate for families headed by unmarried males was 16.9% and for those headed by married couples it was only 5.8%.

Poverty rates also differed by work experience. The rate for people who did not work at least one week in 2009 was 22.7%, compared with 14.5% for people who worked part time or part of the year. The rate was 2.7% for those who worked full-time year-round. DeNavas-Walt,

Proctor, and Smith report that 2.6 million people fell into this category.

Temporary and Chronic Poverty

As noted earlier, there is significant movement between income quintiles over time. Likewise, people can slip in and out of poverty over time. DeNavas-Walt, Proctor, and Smith used data from the SIPP 2004 panel (February 2004 to January 2008) to gauge these movements on a month-to-month basis. The results indicate that approximately 31.6% of the U.S. population experienced at least one spell of poverty lasting for at least two months during this period. Only 2.2% of the U.S. population is estimated to have lived in poverty continuously throughout this entire period.

Poverty and Economic Well-Being

The poverty rates calculated by the Census Bureau are based on cash income only. There is widespread agreement that these rates do not adequately characterize the standard of living of the nation's poorest people. DeNavas-Walt, Proctor, and Smith acknowledge that the poverty estimates do not consider the value of noncash benefits. These include government assistance programs, such as Medicare and Medicaid, government subsidies for food and housing, and employer-provided fringe benefits.

The federal government uses other methods to measure what it calls the "economic well-being" of the nation's households. The SIPP surveys described earlier are one of these methods. In "Dynamics of Economic Well-Being" (December 8, 2009, http://www.census.gov/population/www/socdemo/wellbeing.html), the Census Bureau notes that the SIPP data provide a better measure than do income data of the degree to which people are "well off." The SIPP program surveys people about their consumer possessions and seeks to determine if their basic needs are being met for housing and food. As of September 2010, the most recent published SIPP data relevant to "economic well-being" were from 2005. In "Extended Measures of Well-Being: Living Conditions in the United States, 2005" (November 2009, http://www.census.gov/population/www/socdemo/extended-05.html), the Census Bureau includes data tables reflecting SIPP survey results on various topics. For example, in "Table 1. Percent of Households Reporting Consumer Durables, for Householders 15 Years and Older, by Selected Characteristics: 2005," the Census Bureau lists the percentages of households classified as being "in poverty" in 2005 that owned the following consumer goods:

- Refrigerator—98.5%
- Television—97.4%
- Stove—97%
- Microwave—91.2%
- Videocassette recorder—83.6%
- Telephone—79.8%
- Air conditioner—78.8%
- Clothes washer—68.7%
- Clothes dryer—61.2%
- Cellular phone—48.3%
- Computer—42.4%
- Dishwasher—36.7%
- Food freezer—25.1%

In "Table 2. Percent of Households Reporting Favorable Housing Conditions by Selected Characteristics, for Householders 15 Years and Older: 2005," the Census Bureau indicates that 91.1% of "in poverty" households in 2005 expressed "overall satisfaction" with their housing conditions.

WEALTH INEQUALITY: IS IT A PROBLEM?

Even though the data are clear that wealth inequality exists in the United States and has been growing in recent decades, there is contentious debate about whether or not this condition poses a problem to the U.S. economy and society.

Wealth Inequality Seen as Harmful

The debate over wealth inequality has always been a politically partisan issue, with those on the right arguing that the market should be allowed to adjust itself with regard to wages and income and those on the left maintaining that widespread financial inequality causes many social and economic problems.

Paul Krugman of Princeton University is an outspoken critic of wealth inequality in the United States. He examines historical growth in income inequality in "For Richer" (*New York Times*, October 20, 2002). Krugman asserts that wage controls and other measures that were taken by the government during the Great Depression and World War II (1939–1945) created a broad and stable middle class in the United States. An abundance of high-paying unionized manufacturing jobs ensured that less-educated working-class people could maintain a standard of living similar to that of highly educated professionals. Krugman believes that changing social attitudes—a "new permissiveness"—has permitted wealth inequality to grow unchecked since the 1970s. He uses as an example the enormous growth in the salaries of chief executive officers (CEOs) of major corporations. He claims that ideas about corporate responsibility and financial prudence kept CEO salaries in check until the 1970s and 1980s, when a new societal attitude emerged that Krugman describes as "greed is good."

Krugman also suggests that "as the gap between the rich and the rest of the population grows, economic policy increasingly caters to the interests of the elite, while public services for the population at large—above all, public education—are starved of resources. As policy increasingly favors the interests of the rich and neglects the interests of the general population, income disparities grow even wider."

The Institute for Policy Studies (IPS) is a nonprofit organization that champions progressive social causes. Progressivism as a political movement dates back to the late 1800s in the United States and generally promotes social and economic reforms that reduce all forms of inequality, such as racial segregation and wealth inequality. The IPS alleges in "Inequality and the Common Good" (2010, http://www.ips-dc.org/inequality) that growing income inequality in the United States threatens "U.S. democracy, economic health and civic life." The institute operates the website Extremeinequality.org, which highlights studies the IPS claims show that growing wealth inequality (or concentration of wealth among only a few Americans) causes hundreds of specific problems in American society. Examples include worse customer service, less job security, higher credit card interest rates, more overpriced housing, and shorter life expectancies. Like Krugman, the IPS believes that wealth concentration results in the overapplication of resources to matters that are important to the wealthy at the expense of the poorer segments of the U.S. population.

In general, people who consider wealth inequality to be a social and economic wrong believe the government should right the wrong. Progressives support government actions that alleviate wealth inequality, just as the government outlawed racial segregation in schools during the 1950s as a step toward eliminating racial inequality in society at large. Progressives typically advocate "bottom-up" measures, such as raising the minimum wage or improving public education, to "raise the floor" for Americans in the lower- and middle-income classes. Progressives also champion "top-down" measures that shrink the wealth of the higher-income classes to pay for the bottom-up measures. This concept is known as the redistribution of wealth.

Taxation is the primary tool by which the government can and does "redistribute" wealth among Americans. As will be explained in Chapter 9, the U.S. income tax system is called progressive because it taxes individuals with higher incomes at higher rates than individuals with lower incomes. For example, in 2009 the IRS (http://www.irs.gov/pub/irs-drop/rp-09-50.pdf) set tax rates (or brackets) for married individuals filing joint tax returns in 2010 with the following ranges of taxable income:

- Less than or equal to $16,750—10% tax

- $16,751 to $68,000—$1,675 plus 15% of the excess over $16,750

- $68,001 to $137,300—$9,362.50 plus 25% of the excess over $68,000

- $137,301 to $209,250—$26,687.50 plus 28% of the excess over $137,300

- $209,251 to $373,650—$46,833.50 plus 33% of the excess over $209,250

- More than $373,650—$101,085.50 plus 35% of the excess over $373,650

The tax rate applies only to what the IRS defines as "taxable income." The U.S. tax code allows hundreds of deductions and credits that lessen taxable income amounts. The most well-known example is the deduction for mortgage interest. However, critics complain that wealthy individuals and businesses benefit the most from tax deductions and credits that have been built into the tax code over the years.

Many progressives support raising the tax rates and reducing the tax deductions and credits for people in the higher tax brackets. In addition, they advocate eliminating tax deductions, tax credits, and subsidies (government-provided funds) for wealthy private corporations, particularly those in the oil and gas industry. As social activists, progressives typically oppose war and government spending on national defense. For example, in "Mobilizing for Equality" (2008, http://extremeinequality.org/?page_id=12), the IPS promotes "recovering funds from wasteful military ventures."

President Barack Obama (1961–) supports many progressive causes. For example, the White House states in "Taxes" (2010, http://www.whitehouse.gov/issues/taxes) that "for too long, the U.S. tax code has benefited the wealthy and well-connected at the expense of the vast majority of Americans." The White House also complains about "loopholes that prevent wealthy companies and individuals from paying a fair share." Obama's tax policy will be discussed at length in Chapter 9.

Wealth Inequality Seen as Not Harmful

On the other side of this issue are those who believe that wealth inequality does not pose a problem to the U.S. economy and society. This viewpoint is generally associated with conservative political thinking, which holds that market forces must be allowed to adjust themselves without government interference. One idea that is regularly expressed by politicians in this camp is that "what's good for the rich is good for the rest of us." This philosophy was espoused by President Ronald Reagan (1911–2004), who championed a trickle-down economic policy—economic actions (such as tax cuts beneficial to the wealthy) that encourage greater investment in business growth, thus increasing employment, wages, and other benefits to those in the middle and lower classes.

In "Rich Man, Poor Man: How to Think about Income Inequality" (*National Review*, vol. 55, June 16, 2003), Kevin A. Hassett states his belief that the unease over wealth inequality is driven by social views on the "basic justice" of society. However, he argues that there are similarly compelling arguments against taking from the rich to benefit the poor. Hassett notes that taking resources from the rich limits their ability and incentive to start and grow businesses, which will ultimately hurt American workers even more.

This argument is commonly cited by people who oppose wealth redistribution. They also point out that wealth redistribution is an improper term because wealth was not originally "distributed" to its owners, but earned by them.

Public Opinion on Wealth Distribution

The American public has provided conflicting answers in regards to their opinions on wealth distribution. Like polling so often illustrates when it concerns politically charged issues, the answers depend on how the questions are phrased.

In April 2010 the Gallup Organization asked Americans whether certain segments of society "are paying their fair share in federal taxes." In *Taxes* (2010, http://www.gallup.com/poll/1714/Taxes.aspx), Gallup reports that 35% of respondents said "lower-income" people are paying a "fair share." Thirty-nine percent believed this segment pays "too much" in taxes, and 22% believed lower-income people pay "too little" in taxes. Nearly half (49%) of those asked said "middle-income" people pay their "fair share" in taxes. Almost as many (43%) said the segment pays "too much," and 6% thought middle-income people pay "too little" in taxes. Only 26% of respondents said "upper-income" people pay their "fair share" of taxes. Fifteen percent thought this segment pays "too much," and 55% said upper-income people pay "too little" in taxes.

Less than a quarter (22%) of poll participants said corporations pay a "fair share" in taxes. Nine percent thought corporations pay "too much," and 62% said corporations pay "too little" in taxes.

The Gallup Organization did not ask about wealth redistribution in its 2010 poll. Such questioning was performed in April 2008. As part of the *Gallup Poll Social Series: Economy & Personal Finance* (April 2008, http://

brain.gallup.com/documents/questionnaire.aspx?STUDY =P0804015), Gallup pollsters asked Americans to answer two questions about wealth distribution in the United States. The first question asked: "Do you feel that the distribution of money and wealth in this country today is fair, or do you feel that the money and wealth in this country should be more evenly distributed among a larger percentage of the people?" More than two-thirds (68%) of respondents said the nation's money and wealth should be more evenly distributed. Only 27% felt the current distribution "is fair."

In the second question, Gallup asked: "Do you think our government should or should not redistribute wealth by heavy taxes on the rich?" A slim majority (51%) agreed that the government should redistribute wealth via heavy taxes on the rich. Forty-three percent disagreed with this approach.

However, a poll conducted later that year, in June 2008, found different responses when the participants were given two specific choices for how the government should deal with the nation's economic woes. Dennis Jacobe of the Gallup Organization reports in *Americans Oppose Income Redistribution to Fix Economy* (June 27, 2008, http://www.gallup.com/poll/108445/Americans-Oppose-Income-Redistribution-Fix-Economy.aspx) that poll participants were asked to choose between two approaches that the government could "focus on" to "fix the economy":

- "Take steps to distribute wealth more evenly among Americans"

- "Take steps to improve overall economic conditions and the jobs situation"

Only 13% of respondents supported the wealth redistribution measure, compared with 84% who supported overall economic improvement measures.

Jacobe notes that the April 2008 poll showed that "while, in the abstract, many Americans believe that the wealthy do not pay enough taxes, ... there is a strong feeling that taxing one group to give the money to another is not the favored approach to fixing the economy."

CHAPTER 9
THE ROLE OF THE GOVERNMENT

In general, the art of government consists in taking as much money as possible from one party of the citizens to give to the other.

—Voltaire, *Dictionnaire Philosophique* (1764)

The government has many roles in the U.S. economy. Like other businesses, the government spends and makes money, consumes goods and services, and employs people. Federal, state, and local governments raise funds directly through taxes and fees. They often borrow money from the public by selling securities, such as bonds. A bond is an investment in which people lend money to the government for a specified time and interest rate. Governments also disburse money via contracts with businesses or through social programs that benefit the public.

Finally, the federal government is a manipulator of the U.S. economy. It influences macroeconomic factors, such as inflation and unemployment, through fiscal policy and monetary policy. Fiscal policy revolves around spending and taxation. Monetary policy is concerned with the amount of money in circulation and the operation of the nation's central banking system.

FUNDING GOVERNMENT SERVICES

Governments are responsible for providing services that individuals cannot effectively provide for themselves, such as military defense, roads, education, social services, and environmental protection. Some government entities also provide public utilities, such as water, sewage treatment, or electricity. To generate the revenue that is necessary to provide services, governments collect taxes and fees and charge for many services they provide to the public. If these revenues are not sufficient to fund desired programs, governments borrow money.

Taxation

Even before the United States became an independent nation, taxes were a significant issue for Americans.

The Stamp Act of 1765 was the first tax imposed specifically on the North American colonies by the British Parliament and was strongly resisted by the colonists, who maintained that only representative legislatures in each colony possessed the right to impose taxes. The view that "taxation without representation" was tyranny contributed to the opposition to British rule that led to the Revolutionary War (1775–1783). Of course, it was necessary for the newly independent colonies to establish taxes of their own. As Benjamin Franklin (1706–1790) wrote, "In this world nothing can be said to be certain, except death and taxes" (November 13, 1789), and over the next two centuries a complex taxation code was developed at the federal, state, and local levels.

The most common taxes levied by federal, state, and local governments are:

- Income taxes—charged on wages, salaries, and tips

- Payroll taxes—Social Security insurance and unemployment compensation, both of which are withdrawn from payroll checks and paid by employers

- Property taxes—levied on the value of property owned, usually real estate

- Capital gains taxes—charged on the profit from the sale of an asset such as stock or real estate

- Corporate taxes—levied on the profits of a corporation

- Estate taxes—charged against the assets of a deceased person

- Excise taxes—collected at the time something is sold or when a good is imported

- Wealth taxes—levied on the value of assets rather than on the income they produce

Taxes are broadly defined as being either direct or indirect. Direct taxes (such as income taxes) are paid by the entity on whom the tax is being levied. Indirect taxes are passed on from the responsible party to someone else. Examples of indirect taxes include business property taxes, gasoline taxes, and sales taxes, which are levied on businesses but passed on to consumers via increased prices.

When individuals with higher incomes pay a higher percentage of a tax, it is called a progressive tax; when those with lower incomes pay a larger percentage of their income, a tax is considered regressive. The federal income tax is an example of a progressive tax because individuals with higher incomes are subject to higher tax rates. Sales and excise taxes are regressive because the same tax applies to all consumers regardless of income, so less prosperous individuals pay a higher percentage of their income.

Borrowing against the Future

Like many members of the public, government entities sometimes spend more than they make. When cash revenues from taxes, fees, and other sources are not sufficient to cover spending, money must be borrowed. One method used by government to borrow money is the selling of securities, such as bonds, to the public. A bond is basically an IOU that a government body writes to a buyer. The buyer pays money up front in exchange for the IOU, which is redeemable at some point in the future (the maturity date) for the amount of the original loan plus interest. In addition, the federal government has the ability to write itself IOUs—to spend money in the present that it expects to make in the future.

U.S. government bodies borrow money because they are optimistic that future revenues will cover the IOUs they have written. This optimism is based in part on the power that governments have to tax their citizens and to control the cost of provided government services. Even though tax increases and cuts in services can be enacted to raise money, these actions have political and economic repercussions. Politicians who wish to remain in office are reluctant to displease their constituents. Furthermore, the more citizens pay in taxes, the less money they will have to spend in the marketplace or invest in private business, thereby hurting the overall economy. As a result, governments must weigh their need to borrow against the future likely consequences of paying back the loan.

LOCAL GOVERNMENTS

The U.S. Census Bureau performs a comprehensive Census of Government every five years. As of September 2010, the most recent data were from the 2007 census (http://www.census.gov/govs/cog/). In between the censuses, annual surveys are conducted to collect certain data on government finances and employment.

The 2007 Census of Government found that 89,476 local government units were in operation. These units consisted of counties, municipalities, townships, school districts, and special districts. Special district governments usually perform a single function, such as flood control or water supply. For example, Florida is divided into five water management districts, each of which is responsible for managing and protecting water resources and balancing the water needs of other government units within its jurisdiction.

Local Revenues

As of September 2010, the most recent comprehensive data for local government revenues were from 2008. Local governments took in more than $1.5 trillion that year. (See Table 9.1.) Most of the money came from three sources: intergovernmental revenue ($524.7 billion), property taxes ($397 billion), and current charges for services ($222.7 billion). Intergovernmental revenue consists of funds that are transferred to the local governments from the federal and state governments. State funds accounted for the vast majority of intergovernmental transfers in 2008.

Taxes, particularly property taxes, are an important source of revenue for many local governments. Consumption taxes are also collected on sales and gross receipts. This includes selective taxes that are levied against particular goods, such as motor fuels, alcoholic beverages, and tobacco products. Miscellaneous taxes include individual and corporate income taxes, motor vehicle license taxes, and a wide variety of other taxes.

The revenue included in current charges for services comes from many local sources, including hospitals, sewage treatment facilities, solid waste management, parks and recreation areas, airports, and educational facilities (e.g., the sale of school lunches).

Other revenue sources for local governments are miscellaneous general revenue, public utilities, and insurance trusts. Miscellaneous general revenue comes from a variety of sources, including interest payments and the sale of public property. Public utilities primarily supply water, electricity, natural gas, and public transportation (such as buses and trains). Insurance trusts are monies collected from the paychecks of local government employees to pay for worker programs, such as retirement benefits.

PROPERTY TAXES. A property tax is tax levied on the value of land, buildings, businesses, and personal property, including business equipment and automobiles. The U.S. Department of the Treasury explains that property taxes in the United States date back to the Massachusetts Bay Colony in 1646 and that the separate states began imposing property taxes soon after declaring independence from Great Britain. A property tax is an example of an ad valorem tax. Ad valorem is a Latin phrase meaning "according to the value."

TABLE 9.1

Breakdown of local government revenue, 2008

[Dollar amounts are in thousands.]

Description	Local government amount
Revenue*	1,530,813,774
General revenue*	1,401,341,276
Intergovernmental revenue*	524,737,727
From federal government	58,229,585
From state government*	466,508,142
From local governments*	(1)
General revenue from own sources	876,603,549
Taxes	548,764,528
Property	396,994,711
Sales and gross receipts	90,166,095
General sales	63,427,174
Selective sales	26,738,921
Motor fuel	1,424,840
Alcoholic beverage	470,655
Tobacco products	507,538
Public utilities	13,335,881
Other selective sales	11,000,007
Individual income	26,254,751
Corporate income	7,050,511
Motor vehicle license	1,625,537
Other taxes	26,672,923
Charges and miscellaneous general revenue	327,839,021
Current charges	222,667,126
Education	24,960,426
Institutions of higher education	10,247,777
School lunch sales (gross)	6,968,816
Hospitals	61,001,468
Highways	4,748,105
Air transportation (airports)	16,454,763
Parking facilities	1,937,817
Sea and inland port facilities	2,917,089
Natural resources	1,465,443
Parks and recreation	8,026,539
Housing and community development	4,970,076
Sewerage	38,018,858
Solid waste management	14,811,802
Other charges	43,354,740
Miscellaneous general revenue	105,171,895
Interest earnings	46,071,905
Special assessments	6,960,978
Sale of property	3,329,468
Other general revenue	48,809,544
Utility revenue	122,619,919
Water supply	45,177,884
Electric power	58,807,556
Gas supply	8,914,062
Transit	9,720,417
Liquor store revenue	1,114,462
Insurance trust revenue	5,738,117
Unemployment compensation	128,865
Employee retirement	5,609,252
Workers' compensation	—
Other insurance trust revenue	—

*Duplicative intergovernmental transactions are excluded.
—zero or rounds to zero.
(X) not applicable.
Note that data released for assets in Pennsylvania and Kentucky and debt in Wyoming do not meet the Total Quantity Response Rates for the Census Bureau's 70 percent standard. For 2008, the District of Columbia provided detailed administrative records that were not available in previous survey cycles. As a result, data may not be comparable to prior years in certain functions.

SOURCE: Adapted from "Table 1. State and Local Government Finances by Level of Government and by State: 2007–08," in *State and Local Government Finance*, U.S. Department of Commerce, U.S. Census Bureau, July 7, 2010, http://www2.census.gov/govs/estimate/08slsstab1a.xls (accessed July 14, 2010)

Property taxes are generally levied annually and calculated by multiplying the property value by an assessment ratio to obtain a taxable value. Assessment ratios can vary from less than 0.1 (less than 10%) to more than 1 (greater than 100%). The calculated taxable value is multiplied by a tax rate that is typically expressed in tax dollars per hundred or thousand dollars of value. For example, a home valued at $150,000 in an area with an assessment ratio of 0.5 (50%) would have a taxable value of $75,000. Assuming a tax rate of $3 per $1,000 of value, the property tax would be three times $75, or $225. Tax rates based on $1,000 of value are also known as the millage rate.

Government entities at the local and sometimes state level determine the tax rate and the assessment ratio for their area. If permitted by their constituents, governments may choose to increase these values to raise additional revenue. Because real estate generally increases in value over time, property taxes can increase each year even if the tax rate and the assessment ratio remain constant.

RECENT LOCAL TAX DATA. Every quarter the Census Bureau compiles detailed data on local tax collection. Figure 9.1 shows local tax revenue by quarter from the first quarter of 1990 to the first quarter of 2010. Examination of the historical data indicates that local tax revenues peak in the fourth quarter of each year. In the fourth quarter of 2009 local governments collected $194.7 billion in taxes. Collections for the first quarter of 2010 were $134.6 billion. Figure 9.2 provides a breakdown of the tax monies that were collected for the four quarters ending with the first quarter of 2010. Property taxes accounted for the vast majority (79%) of the taxes that were collected over that one-year period.

Local Expenditures

Local governments spent nearly $1.6 trillion on annual expenses in 2008. (See Table 9.2.) Education was the largest single component, accounting for $593.9 billion in spending. Lesser amounts were spent on public health, welfare, and hospitals; utilities; environmental and housing concerns; and public safety (e.g., police and fire).

The Census Bureau (December 2009, http://www2.census.gov/govs/apes/08locus.txt) estimates that in March 2008 local governments employed the equivalent of 12.3 million full-time employees.

STATE GOVERNMENTS

State Revenues

According to the Census Bureau, state governments had revenues just over $1.6 trillion in 2008. (See Table 9.3.) Intergovernmental revenue from the federal government accounted for $423.2 billion of the total. Self-generated

FIGURE 9.1

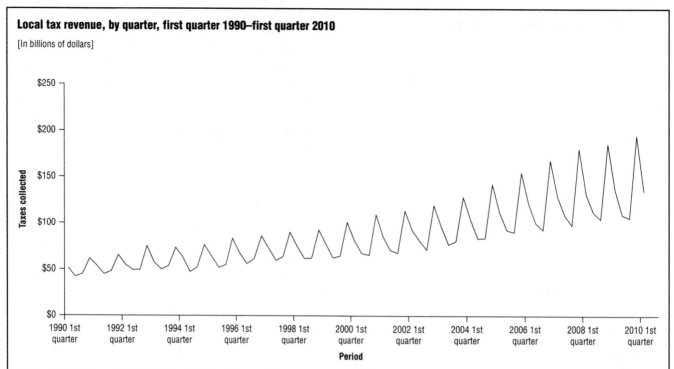

Local tax revenue, by quarter, first quarter 1990–first quarter 2010

[In billions of dollars]

SOURCE: Adapted from "Table 1. National Totals of State and Local Tax Revenue, by Type of Tax," in *Quarterly Summary of State and Local Tax Revenue*, U.S. Department of Commerce, U.S. Census Bureau, June 29, 2010, http://www2.census.gov/govs/qtax/2010/q1t1.pdf (accessed July 14, 2010), and "Table 2. National Totals of State Tax Revenue, by Type of Tax," in *Quarterly Summary of State and Local Tax Revenue*, U.S. Department of Commerce, U.S. Census Bureau, June 29, 2010, http://www2.census.gov/govs/qtax/2010/q1t2.pdf (accessed July 14, 2010)

FIGURE 9.2

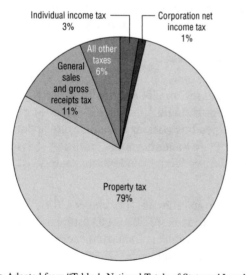

Breakdown of local tax revenue, four quarters ending first quarter 2010

SOURCE: Adapted from "Table 1. National Totals of State and Local Tax Revenue, by Type of Tax," in *Quarterly Summary of State and Local Tax Revenue*, U.S. Department of Commerce, U.S. Census Bureau, June 29, 2010, http://www2.census.gov/govs/qtax/2010/q1t1.pdf (accessed July 14, 2010), and "Table 2. National Totals of State Tax Revenue, by Type of Tax," in *Quarterly Summary of State and Local Tax Revenue*, U.S. Department of Commerce, U.S. Census Bureau, June 29, 2010, http://www2.census.gov/govs/qtax/2010/q1t2.pdf (accessed July 14, 2010)

state revenue totaled nearly $1.1 trillion and consisted largely of collected taxes ($781.6 billion).

STATE TAXES. The Federation of Tax Administrators (FTA) is a nonprofit organization that provides research services for the tax administrators of all 50 states and the District of Columbia. According to the FTA, in "State Sales Tax Rates" (January 1, 2010, http://www.taxadmin.org/fta/rate/sales.html), 45 states and the District of Columbia assessed sales taxes. As of January 2010, the five states without a sales tax were Alaska, Delaware, Montana, New Hampshire, and Oregon.

In "State Individual Income Taxes" (January 1, 2010, http://www.taxadmin.org/fta/rate/ind_inc.html), the FTA provides information on state income tax rates. As of January 2010, 43 states and the District of Columbia imposed income taxes. The states that did not tax income were Alaska, Florida, Nevada, South Dakota, Texas, Washington, and Wyoming. Two additional states, Tennessee and New Hampshire, taxed only personal income derived from dividends and interest.

Figure 9.3 shows state tax revenue by quarter from the first quarter of 1990 to the first quarter of 2010. In general, state tax revenues peak in the second quarter of each year. In the second quarter of 2008 state taxes reached a high of $240.8 billion. However, the economic contraction associated with the so-called great recession

TABLE 9.2

Breakdown of local government spending, 2008

[Dollar amounts are in thousands.]

Description	State government amount
Expenditure*	1,593,087,951
By character and object:	
Intergovernmental expenditure*	15,790,216
Direct expenditure	1,577,297,735
Current operations	1,232,399,387
Capital outlay	235,806,420
Construction	176,230,185
Other capital outlay	59,576,235
Assistance and subsidies	9,387,793
Interest on debt	66,214,107
Insurance benefits and repayments	33,490,028
Exhibit: Salaries and wages	571,073,284
Direct expenditure by function	1,577,297,735
Direct general expenditure	1,375,538,830
Capital outlay	200,389,681
Other direct general expenditure	1,175,149,149
Education services:	
Education	593,850,972
Capital outlay	73,149,943
Higher education	36,463,048
Capital outlay	4,459,024
Elementary & secondary	557,387,924
Capital outlay	68,690,919
Other education	—
Libraries	11,165,862
Social services and income maintenance:	
Public welfare	50,576,147
Cash assistance payments	9,387,793
Vendor payments	5,581,046
Other public welfare	35,607,308
Hospitals	76,915,678
Capital outlay	5,741,483
Health	39,670,896
Social insurance administration	16,829
Veterans' services	—
Transportation:	
Highways	62,870,122
Capital outlay	26,513,027
Air transportation (airports)	19,506,575
Parking facilities	1,594,570
Sea and inland port facilities	3,448,071
Public safety:	
Police protection	77,642,159
Fire protection	39,683,287
Correction	25,665,059
Capital outlay	1,596,336
Protective inspection and regulation	5,638,833
Environment and housing:	
Natural resources	9,974,458
Capital outlay	3,730,534
Parks and recreation	35,135,671
Capital outlay	10,479,272
Housing and community development	40,117,580
Sewerage	45,406,182
Capital outlay	18,175,615
Solid waste management	21,318,335
Capital outlay	2,117,651
Governmental administration:	
Financial administration	17,760,584
Judicial and legal	21,008,774
General public buildings	11,526,329
Other governmental administration	24,599,255
Interest on general debt	55,336,081
General expenditure, n.e.c.:	
Miscellaneous commercial activities	4,008,484
Other and unallocable	81,102,037

TABLE 9.2

Breakdown of local government spending, 2008 [CONTINUED]

[Dollar amounts are in thousands.]

Description	State government amount
Utility expenditure	167,279,888
Capital outlay	35,412,426
Water supply	54,860,453
Electric power	61,226,769
Gas supply	10,515,345
Transit	40,677,321
Liquor store expenditure	988,989
Insurance trust expenditure	33,490,028
Unemployment compensation	97,081
Employee retirement	33,392,947
Workers' compensation	—
Other insurance trust	—

*Duplicative intergovernmental transactions are excluded.
—zero or rounds to zero.
Note that the data released for assets in Pennsylvania and Kentucky and debt in Wyoming do not meet the Total Quantity Response Rates for the Census Bureau's 70 percent standard. For 2008, the District of Columbia provided detailed administrative records that were not available in previous survey cycles. As a result, data may not be comparable to prior years in certain functions.

SOURCE: Adapted from "Table 1. State and Local Government Finances by Level of Government and by State: 2007–08," in *State and Local Government Finance*, U.S. Department of Commerce, U.S. Census Bureau, July 7, 2010, http://www2.census.gov/govs/estimate/08slsstab1a.xls (accessed July 14, 2010)

basis. Figure 9.4 indicates the breakdown by type of state taxes that were collected over four quarters ending with the first quarter of 2010. Individual income taxes (34%) and general sales and gross receipts taxes (32%) were the two largest components of the total collected.

State Expenditures

The Census Bureau reports that state governments had expenditures of more than $1.7 trillion in 2008. (See Table 9.4.) Approximately $477.1 billion of this total was in the form of transfers to other governments, such as local governments within the state. The remainder was devoted to spending priorities at the state level. Public welfare composed the single largest expense at $354 billion, followed by education at $232.2 billion. State spending on education is primarily for higher education, such as colleges and universities.

The Census Bureau (December 2009, http://ftp2.census.gov/govs/apes/08stus.txt) estimates that in March 2008 state governments employed the equivalent of nearly 4.4 million full-time employees.

FEDERAL GOVERNMENT

For accounting purposes, the federal government operates on a fiscal year (FY) that begins in October and runs through the end of September. Thus, FY 2011 covers the period of October 1, 2010, to September 30, 2011. Each year by the first Monday in February the U.S. president must present a proposed budget to the U.S.

(December 2007 to June 2009) dramatically diminished state tax collections. Tax revenues through the first quarter of 2010 were all substantially lower on a year-to-year

TABLE 9.3

Breakdown of state government revenue, 2008

[Dollar amounts are in thousands.]

Description	State government amount
Revenue*	1,619,127,732
General revenue*	1,513,903,945
Intergovernmental revenue*	446,109,032
From federal government	423,150,438
From state government*	—
From local governments*	22,958,594
General revenue from own sources	1,067,794,913
Taxes	781,647,244
Property	12,690,856
Sales and gross receipts	358,522,420
General sales	241,007,659
Selective sales	117,514,761
Motor fuel	36,476,852
Alcoholic beverage	5,292,681
Tobacco products	16,068,075
Public utilities	14,794,363
Other selective sales	44,882,790
Individual income	278,372,654
Corporate income	50,759,081
Motor vehicle license	19,718,724
Other taxes	61,583,509
Charges and miscellaneous general revenue	286,147,669
Current charges	151,001,985
Education	85,551,280
Institutions of higher education	84,416,909
School lunch sales (gross)	30,940
Hospitals	36,268,297
Highways	6,418,714
Air transportation (airports)	1,326,156
Parking facilities	19,103
Sea and inland port facilities	1,221,426
Natural resources	2,543,334
Parks and recreation	1,592,968
Housing and community development	676,338
Sewerage	44,668
Solid waste management	457,149
Other charges	14,882,552
Miscellaneous general revenue	135,145,684
Interest earnings	47,297,876
Special assessments	966,738
Sale of property	1,110,256
Other general revenue	85,770,814
Utility revenue	16,521,947
Water supply	240,277
Electric power	13,861,163
Gas supply	16,289
Transit	2,404,218
Liquor store revenue	6,128,282
Insurance trust revenue	82,573,558
Unemployment compensation	34,359,648
Employee retirement	20,664,213
Workers' compensation	18,695,989
Other insurance trust revenue	8,853,708

*Duplicative intergovernmental transactions are excluded.
—zero or rounds to zero.
Note that the data released for assets in Pennsylvania and Kentucky and debt in Wyoming do not meet the Total Quantity Response Rates for the Census Bureau's 70 percent standard. For 2008, the District of Columbia provided detailed administrative records that were not available in previous survey cycles. As a result, data may not be comparable to prior years in certain functions.

SOURCE: Adapted from "Table 1. State and Local Government Finances by Level of Government and by State: 2007–08," in *State and Local Government Finance*, U.S. Department of Commerce, U.S. Census Bureau, July 7, 2010, http://www2.census.gov/govs/estimate/08slsstab1a.xls (accessed July 14, 2010)

House of Representatives. This is the amount of money that the president estimates will be required to operate the federal government during the next fiscal year.

It can take several months for the House to debate, negotiate, and approve a final budget. The budget must also be approved by the U.S. Senate. This entire process can take many months, and sometimes longer than a year. This means that the federal government can be well into (or beyond) a fiscal year before knowing the exact amount of its budget for that year.

Detailed data on the finances of the federal government are maintained by the Office of Management and Budget (OMB), an executive office of the U.S. president. The OMB assists the president in preparing the federal budget and supervises budget administration. Information on the FY 2011 budget is available at http://www.whitehouse.gov/omb/budget/Overview. Budget documents include historical tables that provide annual data on federal government receipts, outlays, debt, and employment dating back to 1940 or earlier. The FY 2011 budget includes final values for years to 2009 and estimates from 2010 to 2015.

Federal Revenues

According to the OMB, in *Historical Tables: Budget of the U.S. Government, Fiscal Year 2011* (February 2010, http://www.gpoaccess.gov/usbudget/fy11/pdf/hist.pdf), the federal government had revenues (receipts) of $2.1 trillion in FY 2009. As shown in Figure 9.5, the two largest sources of revenue for the federal government in FY 2009 were individual income taxes (43%) and social insurance and retirement receipts (42%).

TAXES ON INCOME. The federal income tax was authorized in 1913 with ratification of the 16th Amendment to the U.S. Constitution: "The Congress shall have power to lay and collect taxes on incomes, from whatever source derived, without apportionment among the several states, and without regard to any census or enumeration." In the United States tax rates are approved by Congress and signed into law by the president; the Internal Revenue Service, a bureau of the Treasury Department, enforces the tax codes and collects tax payments, which are due each year on April 15.

The percentage of an individual's income that he or she pays in federal tax is based on his or her income level, which determines the individual's tax bracket. Tax brackets change as Congress modifies the tax codes, but individuals with higher incomes are always taxed at a higher rate than individuals with lower incomes. Through a variety of tax credits and deductions, individuals can lower the amount of income on which taxes are calculated, thereby lowering the amount of tax they pay.

The federal tax on corporate income has been in effect since 1909. Because corporations are owned, and individuals derive income from them, the potential exists for "double taxation," that is, the same income is taxed twice, once as corporate income and, when the profits have been distributed to shareholders, again as individual

FIGURE 9.3

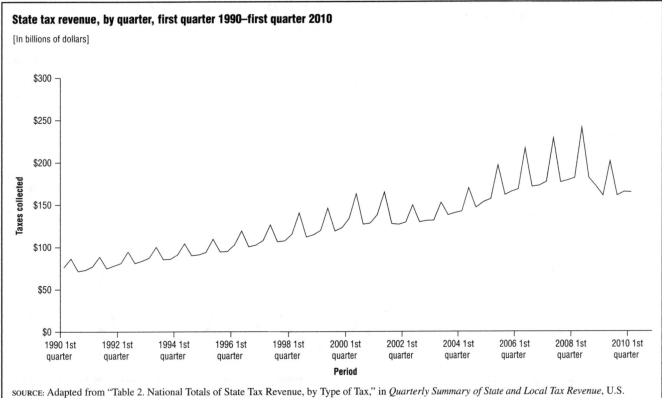

State tax revenue, by quarter, first quarter 1990–first quarter 2010

[In billions of dollars]

SOURCE: Adapted from "Table 2. National Totals of State Tax Revenue, by Type of Tax," in *Quarterly Summary of State and Local Tax Revenue*, U.S. Department of Commerce, U.S. Census Bureau, June 29, 2010, http://www2.census.gov/govs/qtax/2010/q1t2.pdf (accessed July 14, 2010)

FIGURE 9.4

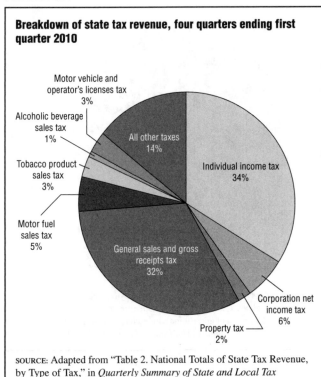

Breakdown of state tax revenue, four quarters ending first quarter 2010

SOURCE: Adapted from "Table 2. National Totals of State Tax Revenue, by Type of Tax," in *Quarterly Summary of State and Local Tax Revenue*, U.S. Department of Commerce, U.S. Census Bureau, June 29, 2010, http://www2.census.gov/govs/qtax/2010/q1t2.pdf (accessed July 14, 2010)

income. To reduce the effects of double taxation, various credits and deductions have been enacted over the decades to allow income to pass through a corporation without being taxed until it reaches the individual. Credits and depreciation schedules reduce the amount of revenue that is subject to tax.

SOCIAL INSURANCE AND RETIREMENT RECEIPTS. Social insurance and retirement receipts are collected to fund specific programs for people who are retired, disabled, unemployed, or poor. The primary programs are Social Security and Medicare. Social Security provides funds to most workers who retire or become disabled. It also pays money to the survivors of workers who die. Medicare is a health insurance program for poor people.

In "Update 2010" (January 2010, http://www.ssa.gov/pubs/10003.html), the Social Security Administration (SSA) explains that as of 2010 the federal government collected money to pay for these two programs as follows:

- Social Security—a tax of 12.4% on earned annual income up to $106,800. In other words, people who earn more than the annual limit pay the tax on $106,800, regardless of how much they earn.

- Medicare—a tax of 2.9% on all earned annual income.

These taxes are known as payroll taxes because they are assessed based on the amounts that businesses pay

TABLE 9.4

Breakdown of state government spending, 2008

[Dollar amounts are in thousands.]

Description	State government amount
Expenditure*	1,733,861,802
By character and object:	
Intergovernmental expenditure*	477,084,924
Direct expenditure	1,256,776,878
Current operations	863,372,166
Capital outlay	113,020,942
Construction	92,067,791
Other capital outlay	20,953,151
Assistance and subsidies	32,572,852
Interest on debt	46,717,232
Insurance benefits and repayments	201,093,686
Exhibit: Salaries and wages	229,818,658
Direct expenditure by function	1,256,776,878
Direct general expenditure	1,024,665,561
Capital outlay	107,057,892
Other direct general expenditure	917,607,669
Education services:	
Education	232,212,206
Capital outlay	24,704,829
Higher education	186,830,495
Capital outlay	22,493,693
Elementary & secondary	8,243,312
Capital outlay	1,591,614
Other education	37,138,399
Libraries	445,608
Social services and income maintenance:	
Public welfare	354,047,572
Cash assistance payments	11,181,193
Vendor payments	296,811,939
Other public welfare	46,054,440
Hospitals	51,937,541
Capital outlay	3,308,414
Health	40,033,167
Social insurance administration	4,071,956
Veterans' services	1,083,098
Transportation:	
Highways	90,644,565
Capital outlay	61,704,878
Air transportation (airports)	1,757,667
Parking facilities	7,909
Sea and inland port facilities	1,492,064
Public safety:	
Police protection	12,034,322
Fire protection	—
Correction	47,239,040
Capital outlay	1,953,631
Protective inspection and regulation	9,297,965
Environment and housing:	
Natural resources	19,942,068
Capital outlay	3,024,353
Parks and recreation	5,509,852
Capital outlay	1,192,486
Housing and community development	10,856,663
Sewerage	1,272,666
Capital outlay	601,440
Solid waste management	2,438,631
Capital outlay	254,823
Governmental administration:	
Financial administration	23,233,998
Judicial and legal	20,442,128
General public buildings	3,565,073
Other governmental administration	4,861,052
Interest on general debt	44,719,371
General expenditure, n.e.c.:	
Miscellaneous commercial activities	1,647,572
Other and unallocable	39,871,807

TABLE 9.4

Breakdown of state government spending, 2008 [CONTINUED]

[Dollar amounts are in thousands.]

Description	State government amount
Utility expenditure	26,072,981
Capital outlay	5,936,015
Water supply	354,255
Electric power	15,439,994
Gas supply	12,107
Transit	10,266,625
Liquor store expenditure	4,944,650
Insurance trust expenditure	201,093,686
Unemployment compensation	35,470,883
Employee retirement	146,664,804
Workers' compensation	12,052,535
Other insurance trust	6,905,464

*Duplicative intergovernmental transactions are excluded.
—zero or rounds to zero.
Note that the data released for assets in Pennsylvania and Kentucky and debt in Wyoming do not meet the Total Quantity Response Rates for the Census Bureau's 70 percent standard. For 2008, the District of Columbia provided detailed administrative records that were not available in previous survey cycles. As a result, data may not be comparable to prior years in certain functions.

SOURCE: Adapted from "Table 1. State and Local Government Finances by Level of Government and by State: 2007–08," in *State and Local Government Finance*, U.S. Department of Commerce, U.S. Census Bureau, July 7, 2010, http://www2.census.gov/govs/estimate/08slsstab1a.xls (accessed July 14, 2010)

FIGURE 9.5

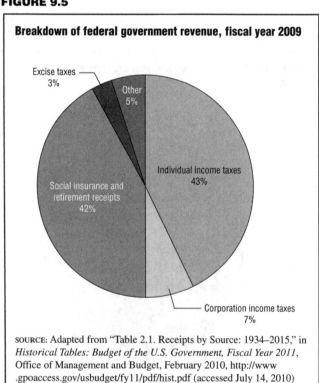

Breakdown of federal government revenue, fiscal year 2009

Excise taxes 3%
Other 5%
Individual income taxes 43%
Social insurance and retirement receipts 42%
Corporation income taxes 7%

SOURCE: Adapted from "Table 2.1. Receipts by Source: 1934–2015," in *Historical Tables: Budget of the U.S. Government, Fiscal Year 2011*, Office of Management and Budget, February 2010, http://www.gpoaccess.gov/usbudget/fy11/pdf/hist.pdf (accessed July 14, 2010)

their workers. Half of the tax (6.2% for Social Security plus 1.45% for Medicare) is paid by wage earners and is deducted from their paychecks; the other half is paid directly by employers. Self-employed people pay the entire tax bill but can deduct half of it as a business expense when they file their income tax.

Unemployment insurance is a joint federal-state program that is funded almost entirely by employers. Employers that meet certain criteria (regarding number of employees and amount of payroll) pay both state and federal unemployment taxes.

SALES AND EXCISE TAXES AND OTHER RECEIPTS. Sales and excise taxes are considered taxes on consumption. Even though there is no federal sales tax, the federal government does levy excise taxes on items such as airplane tickets, gasoline, alcoholic beverages, firearms, and cigarettes. Excise taxes on certain commodities are often hypothecated, meaning they are used to pay for a related government service. For example, fuel taxes are typically used to pay for road and bridge construction or public transportation, or a cigarette excise tax may go to cover government-supported health care programs. Excise taxes can be intended to generate revenue or to discourage use of the taxed product (as in high cigarette taxes that raise the per-pack cost in an attempt to discourage smoking).

The "other" category in Figure 9.5 includes estate and gift taxes and customs duties. Estate and gift taxes are taxes on wealth. Estate taxes are levied against a person's estate after that person dies, whereas gift taxes are levied against the giver while the giver is alive. Estate and gift taxes only apply to amounts over specified limits. Customs duties are taxes charged on goods that are imported into the United States. The taxes vary by product and by exporting nation.

Federal Spending

According to the OMB, the federal government spent just over $3.5 trillion in FY 2009. (See Table 9.5.) The OMB breaks down expenditures into broad categories called superfunctions and narrower categories called functions. Overall, human resources were the largest expenditure for the federal government, accounting for nearly $2.2 trillion in FY 2009. The largest single component of federal spending was for the Social Security program, which accounted for nearly $683 billion of expenditures.

According to the Census Bureau (December 2009, http://www2.census.gov/govs/apes/08fedfun.pdf), the federal government employed nearly 2.8 million civilian (nonmilitary) employees as of December 2008.

Federal Deficits and Surpluses

If the government spends less money than it takes in during a fiscal year, the difference is known as a budget surplus. Likewise, if spending is higher than revenues, the difference is called a budget deficit. A balanced budget occurs when spending and revenue are the same.

Figure 9.6 shows the annual surplus or deficit from 1901 to 2015 as reported in the OMB's FY 2011 budget (2010 to 2015 are estimated). In general, the federal government had a balanced budget for more than half of the 20th century, excluding slight deficits that occurred during

TABLE 9.5

Breakdown of federal government spending, fiscal year 2009

Superfunction and function	2009 In millions of dollars
National defense	661,049
Human resources	2,155,782
Education, training, employment, and social services	79,746
Health	334,327
Medicare	430,093
Income security	533,224
Social security	682,963
Veterans benefits and services	95,429
Physical resources	443,797
Energy	4,749
Natural resources and environment	35,574
Commerce and housing credit	291,535
Transportation	84,289
Community and regional development	27,650
Net interest	186,902
Other functions	162,790
International affairs	37,529
General science, space and technology	29,449
Agriculture	22,237
Administration of justice	51,549
General government	22,026
Allowances	
Undistributed offsetting receipts	−92,639
Total, federal outlays	**3,517,681**

SOURCE: Adapted from "Table 3.1. Outlays by Superfunction and Function: 1940–2015," in *Historical Tables: Budget of the U.S. Government, Fiscal Year 2011*, Office of Management and Budget, February 2010, http://www.gpoaccess.gov/usbudget/fy11/pdf/hist.pdf (accessed July 14, 2010)

World War I (1914–1918) and World War II (1939–1945). Beginning in 1970 the United States had an annual deficit for nearly three decades. The years 1998 to 2001 had budget surpluses. In 2000 the surplus reached a record $236.2 billion. Budget deficits returned during 2002 and reached record lows over the following years. The budget deficit for 2009 was $1.4 trillion. The OMB predicts that the 2010 deficit will exceed $1.5 trillion. Shrinking budget deficits are expected through 2015.

National Debt

Whenever the federal government has a budget deficit, the Treasury Department must borrow money to cover the difference. The total amount of money that the Treasury Department has borrowed over the years is known as the federal debt, or more commonly the national debt. Budget surpluses cause the debt to go down, whereas deficits increase the debt.

The national debt was low until the early 1940s, when it jogged upward in response to government spending during World War II. (See Figure 9.7.) Over the next three decades the debt increased at a slow pace. During the late 1970s the national debt began a steep climb that continued into the first decade of the 21st century. The budget

FIGURE 9.6

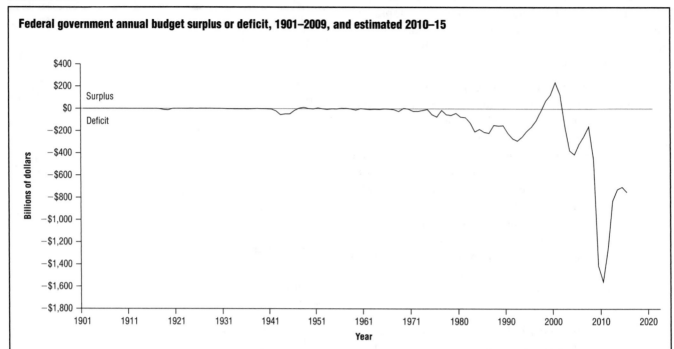

Federal government annual budget surplus or deficit, 1901–2009, and estimated 2010–15

SOURCE: Adapted from "Table 1.1. Summary of Receipts, Outlays, and Surpluses or Deficits (−): 1789–2015," in *Historical Tables: Budget of the U.S. Government, Fiscal Year 2011*, Office of Management and Budget, February 2010, http://www.gpoaccess.gov/usbudget/fy11/pdf/hist.pdf (accessed July 14, 2010)

FIGURE 9.7

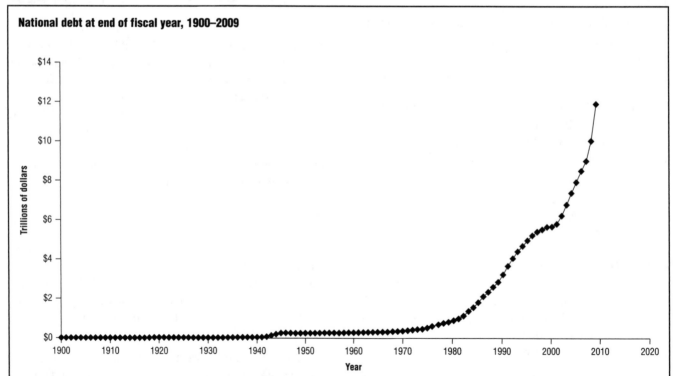

National debt at end of fiscal year, 1900–2009

Note: Fiscal year ended on June 30 from 1900 to 1976 and ended on September 30 from 1977 to 2009.

SOURCE: Adapted from "Historical Debt Outstanding—Annual: 1900–1949," "Historical Debt Outstanding—Annual: 1950–1999," and "Historical Debt Outstanding—Annual: 2000–2009," in *Public Debt Reports*, U.S. Department of the Treasury, Bureau of the Public Debt, March 14, 2007–November 19, 2009, http://www.treasurydirect.gov/govt/reports/pd/histdebt/histdebt.htm (accessed July 14, 2010)

surpluses from 1998 to 2001 had a slight dampening effect on the growth of the debt but did not actually decrease the amount of debt. The budget deficits of the years that followed sent the debt into another rapid incline. By the end of FY 2009 the national debt stood at $11.9 trillion.

BORROWED MONEY AND IOUS. The national debt has two components: money that the federal government has borrowed from the public and money that the federal government has lent itself. The public lends money to the federal government by buying federal bonds and other securities. The government borrows the money with a promise to pay it back with interest after a set term. Some of the most common federal securities sold to the public are Treasury bills, Treasury notes, Treasury bonds, and savings bonds. These vary in value, interest paid, and set terms. Public investors include individuals and businesses (both domestic and foreign) and state and local governments.

The federal government also borrows from itself. This is debt owed by one Treasury account to another. Most of the so-called internal debt involves federal trust funds. For example, if a trust fund takes in more revenue in a year than is paid out, it lends the extra money to another federal account. In exchange, the lending trust fund receives an interest-bearing security (basically an IOU) that is redeemable in the future from the Treasury Department. In "Federal Debt and the Commitments of Federal Trust Funds" (May 6, 2003, http://www.cbo.gov/ftpdocs/39xx/doc3948/10-25-LongRangeBrief4.pdf), the Congressional Budget Office (CBO) explains this accounting procedure in simple terms. The CBO sums up the situation by stating that "what is in the trust funds is simply the government's promise to pay itself back at some time in the future."

On July 31, 2010, the Treasury Department (http://www.treasurydirect.gov/govt/reports/pd/mspd/2010/opds072010.pdf) reported that the national debt was $13.2 trillion, broken down as follows:

- Owed to the public—$8.7 trillion (66% of the total)
- Intragovernmental—$4.5 trillion (34% of the total)

AS A PERCENTAGE OF THE GROSS DOMESTIC PRODUCT. Economists often discuss the national debt in terms of its percentage of the gross domestic product (GDP; the total market value of final goods and services produced within an economy in a given year) because a debt amount alone does not provide a complete picture of the effect of that debt on the one who owes it. According to the Central Intelligence Agency (CIA), in *World Factbook: United States* (September 7, 2010, https://www.cia.gov/library/publications/the-world-factbook/geos/us.html), the U.S. national debt made up an estimated 52.9% of the nation's GDP in 2009.

INTERNATIONAL COMPARISON. In *World Factbook* (2010, https://www.cia.gov/library/publications/the-world-factbook/rankorder/2186rank.html?countryName= United

%20States&countryCode=us&regionCode=na&rank=47#us), the CIA ranks nations of the world in descending order of national debt as a percentage of their GDP in 2009. The United States ranked 47th on this list. The industrialized nation with the largest percentage was Japan (189.3%).

THE BURDEN ON THE ECONOMY. The national debt represents a twofold burden on the U.S. economy. The debt owed to the public imposes a current burden. The federal government pays out interest to investors, and these interest payments are funded by current taxpayers. The debt that the federal government owes to itself is a future burden. At some point in the future the securities issued for intragovernmental debt must be redeemed for cash. The government will have to raise these funds by raising taxes, reducing spending, and/or borrowing more money from the public.

As shown in Table 9.6, a large majority (79%) of respondents in a Gallup Organization poll conducted in May 2010 described the federal debt as an "extremely serious" (40%) or "very serious" (39%) threat to the "future wellbeing" of the United States.

In February 2010 President Barack Obama (1961–) ordered the creation of the bipartisan National Commission on Fiscal Responsibility and Reform to evaluate the administration's options for reducing expected future budget deficits and to make recommendations on which options should be implemented. The commission was tasked to issue its report by December 2010. As of September

TABLE 9.6

Public opinion on the seriousness of various threats to the future well–being of the United States, May 2010

Perceived threats to U.S. future well–being

HOW SERIOUS A THREAT TO THE FUTURE WELLBEING OF THE UNITED STATES DO YOU CONSIDER EACH OF THE FOLLOWING—EXTREMELY SERIOUS, VERY SERIOUS, SOMEWHAT SERIOUS, NOT VERY SERIOUS, OR NOT A THREAT AT ALL? HOW ABOUT__?

	Extremely serious %	Very serious %	Somewhat/ Not very serious/ Not a threat at all %
Terrorism	40	39	21
Federal government debt	40	39	20
Healthcare costs	37	42	21
Unemployment	33	50	17
Illegal immigration	29	34	37
The size and power of the federal government	29	32	38
Having U.S. troops in combat in Iraq/Afghanistan	26	40	31
The environment, including global warming	21	30	49
The size and power of large corporations	21	31	47
Discrimination against minority groups	17	29	53

SOURCE: Lydia Saad, "Perceived Threats to U.S. Future Wellbeing," in *Federal Debt, Terrorism Considered Top Threats to U.S.*, The Gallup Organization, June 4, 2010, http://www.gallup.com/poll/139385/Federal-Debt-Terrorism-Considered-Top-Threats.aspx (accessed July 29, 2010). Copyright © 2010 by The Gallup Organization. Reproduced by permission of The Gallup Organization.

2010, the report had not been issued. Analysts believe that Obama plans to incorporate at least some of the deficit reduction measures into his proposed FY 2012 budget, which will be published in February 2011.

PUBLIC INVESTMENT AND TAXES

To fund itself, the federal government uses the money of its constituents. The buying of federal securities, such as bonds, represents a voluntary investment in the government by the public. Federal securities are considered to be a safe low-risk investment because they are backed by an entity that has been in existence for more than 200 years and has a proven track record of fiscal soundness. However, money invested in government securities is not available for private investment. In general, private investments are seen as more stimulating for the economy because they provide direct funds for growth, such as the building of new factories and the hiring of new workers. Public (government) investment may or may not have a stimulating effect on the economy, depending on how the funds are spent.

Taxes represent an involuntary investment by the public in government. The effect of taxes on the economy is a source of never-ending debate in U.S. politics. Taxing personal income decreases the spending power of the public because people have less money to invest in private enterprise or to use to consume goods and services. Limited taxation is favored by those who believe that workers and companies with more available money to spend will participate to a greater extent in the economy. This, they say, will lead to economic growth. Others observe that cutting taxes without severely reducing government spending leads to large budget deficits and undermines the government programs that provide a social safety net to the disadvantaged.

Tax Breaks

Historically, the federal government has allowed tax breaks (such as deductions) on income or expenses that are related to specific activities. The prime example is mortgage interest. Most taxpayers can deduct the interest they pay each year on their mortgages. The government uses tax breaks to encourage activities it considers good for society in general, such as being a homeowner or donating to charities. However, in "How $1 Trillion Hides in Plain Sight" (CNNMoney.com, March 5, 2010), Jeanne Sahadi explains that all these tax breaks add up to nearly $1 trillion per year in "lost" revenue to the federal government. The two largest components of this "lost" revenue are mortgage interest deductions and the government's failure to tax workers on company-paid health care benefits. According to Sahadi, the number of available tax breaks has quadrupled since the 1970s. The net result is that many individuals and businesses—nearly half by one estimate—wind up paying no federal income tax each year. Sahadi notes that some economists believe that many of the tax breaks should

be streamlined. This would broaden the tax base (spread tax payment among more individuals and businesses) and provide the federal government with revenue that could be used to fund programs or reduce the federal deficit. However, tax deductions are extremely popular with taxpayers, especially those who are able or potentially able to take advantage of them. Thus, eliminating or curtailing tax breaks would be politically unpopular.

Tax Cuts

In general, the Republican Party advocates smaller government and lower taxes. The Economic Growth and Tax Relief Reconciliation Act (EGTRRA) of 2001 was initiated by the first administration of George W. Bush (1946–) and is commonly referred to as the "Bush tax cuts." The EGTRRA instituted a series of tax rate reductions and incentive measures that were phased in over several years. Included in the law were increases in income tax credits for families with children and reductions in estate, gift, and generation-skipping transfer taxes (a special tax on property transfers from grandparents to their grandchildren), but it did not address business taxes. It also called for reductions in the tax brackets. The EGTRRA was designed to expire on January 1, 2011. Even though some of its measures were accelerated or expanded through laws that were passed during Bush's second term in office, as of September 2010 the EGTRRA was still scheduled to expire at the end of the year.

President Obama has publicly stated his support for extending only the EGTRRA provisions that provide tax cuts to the middle class. Sahadi notes in "Obama's $250,000 Mistake" (CNNMoney.com, August 27, 2010) that Obama has vowed not to increase taxes on any individual making less than $200,000 per year or any married couple making less than $250,000 per year. Sahadi estimates that approximately 98% of the nation's taxpayers fall into this range.

According to the White House, in "Taxes" (2010, http://www.whitehouse.gov/issues/taxes), Obama's tax policy has three goals:

- "Restoring fairness" by eliminating provisions of the tax code that benefit "the wealthy and well-connected at the expense of the vast majority of Americans."

- "Supporting the middle class" by extending tax preferences (such as tax credits for education) "that currently benefit only the wealthy."

- "Making taxes consistent and simple" by simplifying the tax code and using the tax system to encourage saving.

In early 2009 Obama ordered the creation of the independent task force called the President's Economic Recovery Advisory Board (PERAB). In August 2010 the PERAB submitted to Obama its analysis of the tax code in *The Report on Tax Reform Options: Simplification,*

Compliance, and Corporate Taxation (http://www.white house.gov/sites/default/files/microsites/PERAB_Tax_Reform _Report.pdf). The PERAB presents dozens of options for simplifying the tax code, preventing tax fraud, and implementing other tax reform measures.

THE FUTURE OF SOCIAL SECURITY AND MEDICARE

Social Security and Medicare are two of the most expensive programs that are operated by the federal government. (See Table 9.5.) Together, they accounted for $1.1 trillion of spending in FY 2009, or 32% of total expenditures.

As of 2010, people born in 1929 or later qualify for retirement benefits once they have worked for 10 years. Benefit amounts are based on wage history; thus, higher-paid workers will have higher retirement benefits than lower-paid workers. The SSA indicates in "Retirement Benefits by Year of Birth" (July 11, 2010, http://www.socialsecurity.gov/retire2/agereduction.htm) the age at which full benefits can be paid:

- People born in or before 1937—aged 65

- People born between 1938 and 1959—sliding age scale ranging from 65 years and 2 months to 66 years and 10 months

- People born in 1960 or after—aged 67

People who have worked for at least 10 years are eligible for permanently reduced retirement benefits starting at age 62. Benefits for widows, widowers, and family members have varying age requirements and other conditions that must be met. Medicare coverage begins at age 65 for everyone except for certain disabled people who can qualify earlier.

Since their inception, the Social Security and Medicare programs have been a source of partisan contention and debate. Much of the debate has centered on how the programs should be funded and the role of government in social welfare. During the 1990s concerns began to arise about how the nation can afford these programs in the future as the population ages and as the number of earners contributing to the plans decreases.

Fewer Contributors, More Beneficiaries

Figure 9.8 shows the percentage of the U.S. population aged 65 years and older from 2000 to 2009 and projected from 2010 to 2035. A huge increase in the aged population is expected to take place after 2015 because of the baby boom that followed World War II. However, as these workers retire, there will be fewer workers contributing to the plan because succeeding generations have been smaller due to declining birth rates. At the same time, life expectancies have been increasing, meaning that elderly people are living longer past retirement age and collecting benefits for more years.

Funding Social Security

In *A Summary of the 2009 Annual Social Security and Medicare Trust Fund Reports* (May 2009, http://www.ssa.gov/OACT/TRSUM/tr09summary.pdf), an annual report on the status of the Social Security trust funds—Old-Age and Survivors Insurance (OASI), Disability Insurance (DI), and Health Insurance (HI)—the Social Security Board of Trustees shows historical trust fund ratios and estimates

FIGURE 9.8

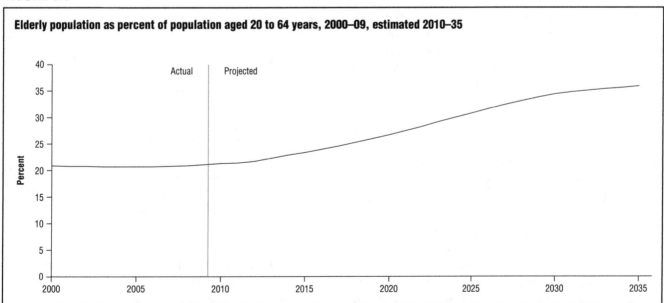

Elderly population as percent of population aged 20 to 64 years, 2000–09, estimated 2010–35

SOURCE: "Figure 3-2. The Population Age 65 or Older As a Percentage of the Population Ages 20 to 64," in *The Long-Term Budget Outlook*, Congressional Budget Office, June 2010, http://www.cbo.gov/ftpdocs/115xx/doc11579/06-30-LTBO.pdf (accessed July 15, 2010)

FIGURE 9.9

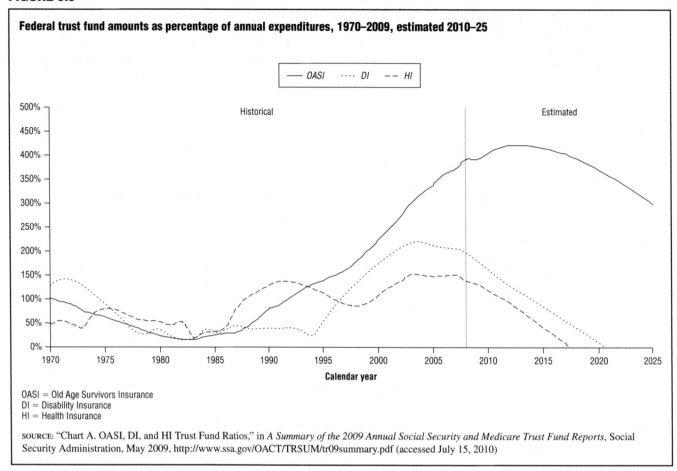

Federal trust fund amounts as percentage of annual expenditures, 1970–2009, estimated 2010–25

OASI = Old Age Survivors Insurance
DI = Disability Insurance
HI = Health Insurance

SOURCE: "Chart A. OASI, DI, and HI Trust Fund Ratios," in *A Summary of the 2009 Annual Social Security and Medicare Trust Fund Reports*, Social Security Administration, May 2009, http://www.ssa.gov/OACT/TRSUM/tr09summary.pdf (accessed July 15, 2010)

future ratios. (See Figure 9.9.) The trustees note that assets as a percentage of annual expenditures peaked for the DI and HI trust funds between 2003 and 2007. The OASI trust fund is projected to peak above 400% during the first half of the second decade of the 21st century and then decline. Table 9.7 shows the first years in which the outgoing amounts from the trust funds will exceed the income into the trust funds (note that the HI trust fund outgoing amount actually exceeded its income beginning in 2008). It also shows the years in which the trust funds will be exhausted. All the trust funds face exhaustion between 2017 and 2039.

FIXING THE PROBLEM. The issue of preparing for future shortfalls in Social Security has become a fierce debate. Republicans generally favor allowing some privatization of the Social Security system, meaning that workers would be able to partially opt out of the Social Security plan and establish their own retirement savings accounts. However, President Obama is against privatization because he believes that such a plan would tie benefits to the stability of the stock market, which has a history of experiencing major fluctuations. Analysts believe that the National Commission on Fiscal Responsibility and Reform will include recommendations for Social Security reform in its report, which was scheduled for release in late 2010.

TABLE 9.7

Key dates for the Social Security and Medicare trust funds, May 2009

	OASI	DI	OASDI	HI
First year outgo exceeds income excluding interest	2017	2005	2016	2008
First year outgo exceeds income including interest	2025	2009	2024	2008
Year trust fund assets are exhausted	2039	2020	2037	2017

OASI = Old Age Survivors Insurance
DI = Disability Insurance
HI = Health Insurance

SOURCE: "Key Dates for the Trust Funds," in *A Summary of the 2009 Annual Social Security and Medicare Trust Fund Reports*, Social Security Administration, May 2009, http://www.ssa.gov/OACT/TRSUM/tr09 summary.pdf (accessed July 15, 2010)

Possible options include increasing the retirement age and/ or decreasing benefits, particularly for wealthier retirees. However, neither of these options would be politically popular with the American public.

FEDERAL GOVERNMENT MANIPULATION OF MACROECONOMICS

The federal government plays a role in the national economy as a tax collector, spender, and employer. Federal policy makers also engage in purposeful manipulation of the U.S. economy at the macroeconomic level—for example, by influencing supply and demand factors. This was not always the case. Before the 1930s the government mostly maintained a hands-off approach to macroeconomic affairs—a tradition that dated back to the founding of the nation. However, the ravages of the Great Depression brought a level of desperation that encouraged leaders to attempt to influence macroeconomic factors. Even though these efforts were largely futile at soothing deep economic depression, they accustomed a generation of Americans to the idea of government interference in economic affairs.

When massive federal spending during World War II helped end the Great Depression, policy makers believed they had discovered a new solution, a government solution, for economic downturns. Government efforts to manage macroeconomic factors became a routine matter over the following decades. These manipulations are commonly divided into two categories: fiscal policy and monetary policy.

Fiscal Policy

The word *fiscal* is derived from the Latin term *fiscalis*, meaning "treasury." It is believed that a fiscalis was originally a woven basket in which money was kept. In modern English, the word *fiscal* has become synonymous with the word *financial*. The federal government's fiscal policy is concerned with the collection and spending of public money so as to influence macroeconomic affairs. Examples of fiscal policy include:

- Increasing government spending to spur businesses to produce more and hire more; this can lower the unemployment rate

- Increasing taxes to pull money out of the hands of consumers; this can lower excessive demand that is driving high inflation rates

- Decreasing taxes to put more money in the hands of consumers; this can increase demand and consequently increase supply (production)

These examples illustrate optimistic outcomes. In reality, the actions of fiscal policy can have complicated (and unforeseen) effects on the U.S. economy. The situation described in the first example can backfire if production does not grow fast enough to satisfy consumer demand. The result will be rising prices and high inflation rates. Likewise, tax increases and decreases can have unexpected and undesirable consequences. The relationships between the major macroeconomic factors—unemployment, inflation, and supply and demand—are complex and difficult to keep in balance.

Fiscal policy is strongly associated with the economist John Maynard Keynes (1883–1946) and is a cornerstone of Keynesian economics.

Monetary Policy

Monetary policy is concerned with influencing the supply of money and credit and the demand for them to achieve specific economic goals. The actions of monetary policy are not as direct and obvious as the tax and spend activities that are associated with fiscal policy. Monetary changes are achieved indirectly through the nation's banking system. The following are some results of monetary policy changes:

- An increase in the amount of money that banks can lend to the public. This leads to greater borrowing, which puts more money into the hands of consumers, increasing the demand for goods and services.

- A decrease in the amount of money that banks can lend to the public. This leads to less borrowing, which slows the growth of the money supply and dampens demand, which can reduce high inflation rates.

- Lower interest rates on loans. This encourages borrowing, which increases the money supply and consumer demand.

- Higher interest rates on loans. This discourages people from borrowing more money, which slows the growth of the money supply and can reduce high inflation rates.

Just as in fiscal policy, it is difficult to achieve the desired results. An oversupply of money and credit will aggravate price inflation if production cannot meet increased consumer demand. Likewise, an undersupply can lower consumer demand too much and stifle economic growth. The challenge for the federal government is deciding when, and by how much, money supply and credit availability should be changed to maintain a healthy economy. These decisions and manipulations are made by the Federal Reserve System, the nation's central bank.

THE FEDERAL RESERVE SYSTEM. In 1913 Congress passed the Federal Reserve Act to form the nation's central bank. The Federal Reserve System was granted power to manipulate the money supply—the total amount of coins and paper currency in circulation, along with all holdings at banks, credit unions, and other financial institutions.

The Federal Reserve includes a seven-member board of governors headquartered in Washington, D.C., and 12 Reserve Banks located in major cities around the country:

- Boston, Massachusetts
- New York City, New York
- Philadelphia, Pennsylvania
- Cleveland, Ohio
- Richmond, Virginia
- Atlanta, Georgia
- Chicago, Illinois

- St. Louis, Missouri

- Minneapolis, Minnesota

- Kansas City, Missouri

- Dallas, Texas

- San Francisco, California

In *The Federal Reserve System: Purposes and Functions* (June 2005, http://www.federalreserve.gov/pf/pdf /pf_complete.pdf), the Federal Reserve explains that it uses three techniques to indirectly achieve "maximum employment, stable prices, and moderate long-term interest rates":

- Open market operations—the Federal Reserve buys and sells government securities on the financial markets. The resulting money transfers ultimately lower or raise the amount of money that banks have available to lend to the public and the associated interest rates.

- Discount rate adjustments—the Federal Reserve raises or lowers the discount rate. This is the rate that it charges banks for short-term loans. In response, the banks adjust the federal funds rate, the rate they charge each other for loans. Then the banks adjust the prime rate, the interest rate they charge their best customers (typically large corporations). In the end, these adjustments affect the interest rates paid by the general public on mortgages, car loans, credit cards, and so on.

- Reserve requirement adjustments—the Federal Reserve raises or lowers the reserve requirement, the amount of readily available money that banks must have to operate. Each bank's reserve requirement is based on a percentage of the total amount of money that customers have deposited at that bank. Money above the reserve requirement can be lent out by the banks. Changes in the reserve requirement influence bank decisions about loans to the public.

CHAPTER 10
INTERNATIONAL TRADE AND THE UNITED STATES' PLACE IN THE GLOBAL ECONOMY

Those who have money go abroad in the world.

—Chinese proverb

Technology has made it easier to go abroad in the world. U.S. companies can sell their goods and services on a global market. Likewise, U.S. consumers can purchase merchandise made around the world—and they do so in large numbers. Global trade is driven by the same forces that control the U.S. market: supply and demand. However, there is the added complication of many very different national governments trying to exert influence over trade and market factors in their favor. The U.S. economy is preeminent in the global economy when it comes to national production. Yet, the United States buys far more from foreign lands than it sells to them. Economists disagree about whether this trade imbalance is good or bad for the U.S. economy.

THE UNITED STATES' PLACE IN THE GLOBAL ECONOMY

The Central Intelligence Agency (CIA) notes in *The World Factbook* (July 2010, https://www.cia.gov/library/publications/the-world-factbook/rankorder/2001rank.html?countryName=UnitedStates&countryCode=us&regionCode=na&rank=2#us) that in 2009 the United States had the largest economy of any single nation ($14.3 trillion), followed by China ($8.8 trillion), Japan ($4.1 trillion), and India ($3.6 trillion). (See Table 10.1.) The combined nations of the European Union (EU) had a gross domestic product (GDP; the total market value of final goods and services produced within an economy in a given year) of $14.5 trillion, putting the EU in a position above the United States in terms of economic strength. The GDP values in Table 10.1 were calculated based on purchasing power parity. This is an accounting method that is useful for comparing different economies. The CIA explains that each non-U.S. GDP listed in Table 10.1 was calculated by valuing that economy's goods and services at the prices prevailing in the United States.

GLOBAL AND U.S. TRADE

In *International Trade Statistics 2009* (2009, http://www.wto.org/english/res_e/statis_e/its2009_e/its2009_e.pdf), the World Trade Organization (WTO) indicates that world trade totaled nearly $18 trillion in 2008. The value of merchandise trade was $15.7 trillion and trade in commercial services was $1.9 trillion.

According to the WTO, the United States was the world's leading importer of goods in 2008, accounting for $2.2 trillion in imports, or 13.2% of the world total. Finishing out the top-five list of importers were Germany ($1.2 trillion, or 7.3% of the world total), China ($1.1 trillion, or 6.9%), Japan ($762.6 billion, or 4.6%), and France ($705.6, or 4.3%). The United States was the third-largest exporter of goods, ranking behind Germany and China. U.S. exports of goods amounted to nearly $1.3 trillion in 2008, accounting for 8% of world merchandise exports. The United States was the top exporter and importer of commercial services in 2008, with $521.4 billion (13.8% of the world total) in exports and $367.9 billion (10.5% of the world total) in imports.

U.S. Trade in Goods and Services

Table 10.2 lists the values of U.S. trade in goods and services for 2008, 2009, and January to May 2010. In 2009 the United States imported over $1.9 trillion in goods and services. The vast majority ($1.6 trillion, or 81%) of the total was in goods. The remaining $370.3 billion (19% of the total) was in services. Overall, U.S. imports were down in 2009 compared with 2008, when they totaled more than $2.5 trillion. U.S. exports totaled $1.6 trillion in 2009. Again, the largest component ($1.1 trillion, or 68%) of the total was in goods. The U.S. exported $502.3 billion (32% of the total) in services.

U.S. Trading Partners

Table 10.3 shows the 20 countries that exported the highest values of goods and services from the United

TABLE 10.1

Gross domestic product (purchasing power parity) for the world's 30 largest economies, 2009

European Union	$14,510,000,000,000
United States	$14,260,000,000,000
China	$8,789,000,000,000
Japan	$4,137,000,000,000
India	$3,560,000,000,000
Germany	$2,811,000,000,000
United Kingdom	$2,149,000,000,000
Russia	$2,116,000,000,000
France	$2,110,000,000,000
Brazil	$2,025,000,000,000
Italy	$1,760,000,000,000
Mexico	$1,482,000,000,000
Spain	$1,368,000,000,000
Korea, South	$1,356,000,000,000
Canada	$1,285,000,000,000
Indonesia	$969,200,000,000
Iran	$876,000,000,000
Turkey	$863,300,000,000
Australia	$824,300,000,000
Taiwan	$717,700,000,000
Poland	$690,100,000,000
Netherlands	$654,900,000,000
Saudi Arabia	$585,800,000,000
Argentina	$558,000,000,000
Thailand	$538,600,000,000
South Africa	$495,100,000,000
Egypt	$471,200,000,000
Pakistan	$449,300,000,000
Colombia	$401,000,000,000
Malaysia	$381,100,000,000

SOURCE: Adapted from "Country Comparison: GDP (Purchasing Power Parity)," in *The World Factbook*, Central Intelligence Agency, July 2010, https://www.cia.gov/library/publications/the-world-factbook/rankorder/2001rank.html?countryName=United States&countryCode=us&regionCode=na&rank=2#us (accessed July 15, 2010)

States in 2009. Canada was the leading export market for U.S. goods and services, accounting for $204.7 billion. Mexico was second with $128.9 billion, and China was third with $69.5 billion. In 2009 the United States imported $296.4 billion of goods and services from China. (See Table 10.4.) Other major exporters to the United States were Canada with $226.2 billion and Mexico with $176.7 billion.

U.S. TRADE BALANCE

The difference between exports and imports over a specific time period is known as the balance of trade (exports − imports = balance of trade). For example, Figure 10.1 shows the U.S. balance of trade in goods and services from May 2008 to May 2010. A positive balance of trade is called a surplus. This is a situation in which the value of exports is greater than the value of imports. A negative balance of trade is called a deficit. This occurs when the value of imports exceeds the value of exports. In May 2010 the United States had a trade deficit of $42.3 billion.

The United States has had a trade deficit for goods every year since 1976, with record levels reached during the first decade of the 21st century. (See Figure 10.2.) In 2009 there was a trade surplus of $132 billion for services. In other words, the value of exported services exceeded the value of imported services by $132 billion. This surplus was more than offset by an enormous trade deficit of $507 billion for goods. In other words, the value of imported goods was $507 billion greater than the value of exported goods. Even though the trade deficit in goods was down significantly in 2009 compared with recent years, it was still high by historical standards.

The historical trade balance in services has been quite different. It has grown from mildly negative numbers during the 1960s to more than $100 billion in the latter half of the first decade of the 21st century. (See Figure 10.2.) From 1996 to 2005 the service trade balance varied only slightly, even as imports and exports increased.

The Trade Deficit and the U.S. Dollar

The trade deficit is directly linked to the value of the U.S. dollar on foreign exchange markets. A dollar can be exchanged for equivalent amounts of any other foreign currency. The exchange rate for any given foreign currency at any given time depends on many complex economic factors, and exchange rates can vary widely over time.

When the U.S. dollar weakens compared with a foreign currency, it means that each dollar buys less of the foreign currency than it did before. Consequently, each dollar buys less goods from that nation. By contrast, each unit of the foreign currency is now worth more in U.S. dollars and has more purchasing power of U.S. goods. For example, when the U.S. dollar weakens compared with the Japanese yen, Japanese goods cost more for Americans, but U.S. goods become cheaper for Japanese consumers. As a result, imports from Japan to the United States are likely to decrease, whereas exports from the United States to Japan are likely to increase.

Likewise, when the U.S. dollar strengthens, it buys more foreign currency and more foreign goods than it did before. Thus, a stronger dollar is associated with higher imports into the United States and fewer exports to foreign lands.

Many economists believe the reduced U.S. trade deficit in goods during the late 1980s and early 1990s was associated with a rapid weakening of the U.S. dollar that occurred at the same time. The trade deficit reduction is evidenced as an upward spike in the bottom line in Figure 10.2 during this period. The trade deficit grew increasingly larger each year between 1980 and 1987 and then suddenly reversed its path for several years. During this time Americans were importing fewer foreign goods than before because foreign goods suddenly cost more.

Cédric Tille, Nicolas Stoffels, and Olga Gorbachev indicate in "To What Extent Does Productivity Drive the Dollar?" (*Current Issues in Economics and Finance*, vol.

TABLE 10.2

U.S. international trade in goods and services, 2008, 2009, and January–May 2010

[In millions of dollars]

Period	Balance			Exports			Imports		
	Total	Goods*	Services	Total	Goods*	Services	Total	Goods*	Services
2008									
Jan.–Dec.	−698,802	−834,652	135,850	1,839,012	1,304,896	534,116	2,537,814	2,139,548	398,266
2009									
Jan.–Dec.	−374,908	−506,944	132,036	1,570,797	1,068,499	502,298	1,945,705	1,575,443	370,262
2010									
Jan.–May	−197,842	−258,292	60,450	739,527	517,099	222,428	937,369	775,391	161,978

*Data are presented on a Balance of Payments (BOP) basis.
Note: Details may not equal totals due to seasonal adjustment and rounding.

SOURCE: Adapted from "Exhibit 1. U.S. International Trade in Goods and Services," in *U.S. International Trade in Goods and Services, May 2010*, U.S. Department of Commerce, Bureau of Economic Analysis, July 13, 2010, http://www.bea.gov/newsreleases/international/trade/2010/pdf/trad0510.pdf (accessed July 15, 2010)

TABLE 10.3

Twenty countries with the highest value of exports from the United States in 2009

[In millions of dollars]

Rank	Nation	Exports from U.S.
1	Canada	$204.7
2	Mexico	$128.9
3	China	$69.5
4	Japan	$51.1
5	United Kingdom	$45.7
6	Germany	$43.3
7	Netherlands	$32.2
8	South Korea	$28.6
9	France	$26.5
10	Brazil	$26.1
11	Singapore	$22.2
12	Belgium	$21.6
13	Hong Kong	$21.1
14	Australia	$19.6
15	Taiwan	$18.5
16	Switzerland	$17.5
17	India	$16.4
18	Italy	$12.3
19	United Arab Emirates	$12.2
20	Saudi Arabia	$10.8

SOURCE: Adapted from "Exhibit 13. Exports, Imports, and Trade Balance by Country and Area: 2009 Annual Totals," in *U.S. International Trade in Goods and Services, Annual Revision for 2009*, U.S. Department of Commerce, U.S. Census Bureau and Bureau of Economic Analysis, June 10, 2010, http://www.bea.gov/newsreleases/international/trade/2010/pdf/trad1310.pdf (accessed July 27, 2010)

TABLE 10.4

Twenty countries with the highest value of imports to the United States in 2009

[In millions of dollars]

Rank	Nation	Imports to U.S.
1	China	$296.4
2	Canada	$226.2
3	Mexico	$176.7
4	Japan	$95.8
5	Germany	$71.5
6	United Kingdom	$47.5
7	South Korea	$39.2
8	France	$34.2
9	Taiwan	$28.4
10	Ireland	$28.1
11	Venezuela	$28.1
12	Italy	$26.4
13	Malaysia	$23.3
14	Saudi Arabia	$22.1
15	India	$21.2
16	Brazil	$20.1
17	Nigeria	$19.1
18	Thailand	$19.1
19	Israel	$18.7
20	Russia	$18.2

SOURCE: Adapted from "Exhibit 13. Exports, Imports, and Trade Balance by Country and Area: 2009 Annual Totals," in *U.S. International Trade in Goods and Services, Annual Revision for 2009*, U.S. Department of Commerce, U.S. Census Bureau and Bureau of Economic Analysis, June 10, 2010, http://www.bea.gov/newsreleases/international/trade/2010/pdf/trad1310.pdf (accessed July 27, 2010)

7, no. 8, August 2001) that the U.S. dollar appreciated by 5.8% against the euro and by 4.8% against the yen on an average annual basis during the 1990s. The relatively strong dollar made foreign goods cheaper for Americans and U.S. goods more expensive for other countries, and unsurprisingly this period coincided with ballooning growth in the U.S. trade deficit. (See Figure 10.2.)

During the first half of the first decade of the 21st century the value of the U.S. dollar began to drop compared with foreign currencies. In contrast to conventional eco-

nomic wisdom, the U.S. trade deficit continued to grow even as the dollar weakened. This contradiction is examined by Peter S. Goodman and Nell Henderson in "Dollar at 20-Month Low vs. the Euro" (*Washington Post*, November 29, 2006). Goodman and Henderson note that other factors allowed the U.S. trade deficit to grow as the dollar was shrinking—primarily huge buys of U.S. government securities by the governments of China and Japan. However, dollar value changes can take many months to several years to be reflected in the U.S. trade balance. Goodman and

FIGURE 10.1

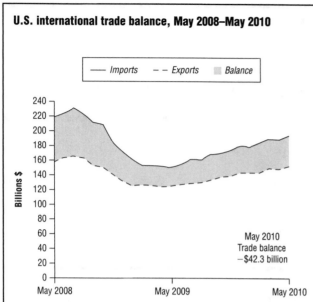

U.S. international trade balance, May 2008–May 2010

Note: Total goods data are reported on a balance of payments basis, unless otherwise specified. Commodity and country detail data for goods are on a census basis. Monthly statistics are seasonally adjusted unless otherwise specified.

SOURCE: "U.S. International Trade in Goods and Services," in *U.S. International Trade in Goods and Services, May 2010*, U.S. Department of Commerce, Bureau of Economic Analysis, July 13, 2010, http://www.bea.gov/newsreleases/international/trade/2010/pdf/trad0510.pdf (accessed July 15, 2010)

Henderson's observation proved to be prophetic as the growth in the U.S. trade deficit was less dramatic between 2005 and 2006 and remained virtually unchanged between 2006 and 2008. (See Figure 10.2.)

The dramatic reduction in the goods trade balance between 2008 and 2009 is attributed to the poor state of the U.S. economy. (See Figure 10.2.) The so-called great recession that began in late 2007 and ended in mid-2009 severely dampened imports as U.S. companies and families spent less money on goods.

Is the Trade Deficit Good or Bad?

The United States' enormous trade deficit is a subject of great debate among economists and politicians. Some believe the deficit is bad for the U.S. economy, particularly the country's manufacturing sector, and that steps should be taken by the government to correct the imbalance. Others contend the deficit is a natural consequence of a strong U.S. economy and should not be an issue of concern.

In "The U.S. Trade Deficit: Causes, Consequences, and Cures" (January 25, 2008, http://italy.usembassy.gov/pdf/other/RL31032.pdf), Craig K. Elwell of the Congressional Research Service (CRS) outlines the perceived good and bad effects of a large trade deficit. As noted earlier, there is a direct link between the trade deficit and

FIGURE 10.2

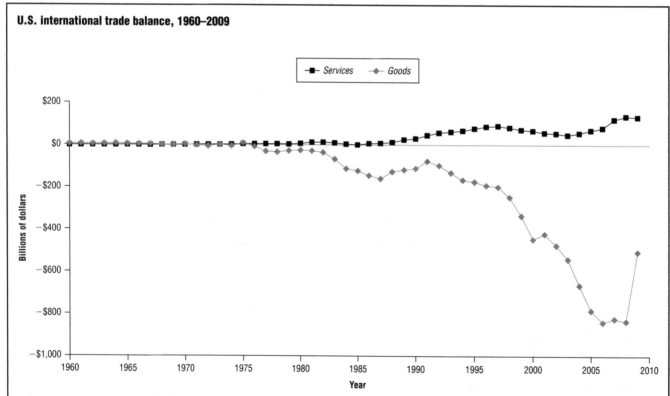

U.S. international trade balance, 1960–2009

SOURCE: Adapted from "Table 1. U.S. International Transactions ," in *U.S. International Transactions Accounts Data*, U.S. Department of Commerce, Bureau of Economic Analysis, June 17, 2010, http://www.bea.gov/international/bp_web/simple.cfm?anon=90730&table_id=1&area_id=3 (accessed July 15, 2010)

the flow of capital. As Americans buy more foreign goods, foreigners have more money to invest in U.S. financial instruments (e.g., stocks, bonds, and Treasury notes). On the plus side, these investments indicate strong foreign confidence in the security and future growth of the U.S. economy. Also, much of the money flowing into the country has been invested in productive capital—that is, invested in growing U.S. industry. However, in many cases these purchases represent debt obligations that the United States will have to pay in the future. In essence, the United States is becoming indebted to foreign nations. Elwell states that "borrowing from abroad allows the United States to live better today, but the payback must mean some decrement to the rate of advance of U.S. living standards in the future."

In a broader sense, large capital inflows demonstrate that Americans prefer spending their money on foreign imports rather than investing it in domestic financial instruments. Put simply, Americans prefer spending to saving. Elwell explains that "so long as domestic saving in the United States falls short of domestic investment and an inflow of foreign saving is available to fill all or part of the gap, the United States will run a trade deficit."

Many critics of the trade deficit claim it hurts the U.S. economy overall, particularly by raising unemployment. Elwell disputes this claim, explaining that the dramatic growth of the trade deficit during the 1990s and the first decade of the 21st century coincided with a generally healthy U.S. economy and relatively low unemployment rates. However, Elwell acknowledges that extensive foreign imports have hurt some U.S. manufacturing industries, particularly textiles, apparel, and steel.

FREE TRADE AGREEMENTS

The U.S. government has long been part of free trade agreements with other individual countries (known as bilateral agreements) and with groups of countries (known as trading blocs). As of July 2010, the United States had free trade agreements with 17 countries. (See Table 10.5.)

In this context, free trade means the ability to buy and sell goods across international borders with a minimum of tariffs or other interferences. Tariffs (import taxes) are fees charged by a country to import goods into that country.

Priorities regarding trade policy have shifted over the years according to the state of the economy. During the recession of the late 1970s, U.S. producers called for the government to institute measures—such as high tariffs—to protect them from international competition. During the growth period of the 1980s, however, the focus of companies turned to their own international expansion, and by the 1990s a push for free trade had gained increased momentum.

TABLE 10.5

Countries with which the United States has free trade agreements as of July 2010

Australia
Bahrain
Canada
Chile
Costa Rica
Dominican Republic
El Salvador
Guatemala
Honduras
Israel
Jordan
Mexico
Morocco
Nicaragua
Oman
Peru
Singapore

The United States has signed free trade agreements with Colombia, Korea, and Panama, but Congress must enact legislation to approve and implement each individual agreement in order for them to go into effect.

SOURCE: Adapted from "Free Trade Agreements," in *Trade Agreements*, U.S. Treasury Department, July 2010, http://www.ustr.gov/trade-agreements/free-trade-agreements (accessed July 15, 2010)

According to Bruce Arnold of the Congressional Budget Office, in *The Pros and Cons of Pursuing Free-Trade Agreements* (July 31, 2003, http://www.cbo.gov/showdoc.cfm?index=4458&sequence=0), opponents to trading blocs argue that when countries with strong economies—such as the United States, Japan, and the countries of the EU—negotiate agreements, smaller nations with developing economies are left at an unfair disadvantage because they are excluded from the favorable terms of the agreement.

North American Free Trade Agreement

The United States, Canada, and Mexico implemented the North American Free Trade Agreement (NAFTA) in January 1994. A primary objective of NAFTA has been the complete elimination of barriers to trade among the three signing countries. Many tariffs were dropped immediately, and others were scheduled to be phased out over time. Agricultural products were an integral part of NAFTA and had some of the longest phase-out schedules. All agricultural provisions of NAFTA were implemented by January 2008.

NAFTA was very controversial in the United States when it was first implemented. Critics claimed that the agreement would encourage U.S. companies to move their manufacturing facilities to Mexico to take advantage of lower labor costs and less government regulation. In "The High Price of 'Free' Trade" (November 17, 2003, http://www.epinet.org/content.cfm/briefingpapers_bp147), Robert E. Scott of the Economic Policy Institute estimates that between 1994 and 2002, 879,280 U.S. jobs (mostly high-paying manufacturing industry positions) had been displaced as a result of NAFTA's removal of trade barriers. However, the Office of the United States Trade Representative (USTR) disputes the idea that NAFTA has caused a loss of U.S. jobs. In "NAFTA—Myth vs. Facts" (March 2008, http://www.ustr.gov/sites/default/files/NAFTA-Myth-versus-Fact.pdf), the USTR notes that employment in the United States increased by 24% between 1993 and 2007. In addition, the U.S. unemployment rate averaged 7.1% annually from 1980 to 1993 (before NAFTA) and averaged 5.1% annually from 1994 to 2007.

General Agreement on Tariffs and Trade and the WTO

One of the most historically notable trade agreements is the General Agreement on Tariffs and Trade (GATT), which was first signed by the United States and 22 other countries in 1947. This agreement dealt primarily with industrial products and marked a trend toward the increasing globalization of the world economy. The agreement reduced tariffs, removed other obstacles to international trade, and clarified rules surrounding barriers to free trade. For the most part, agriculture was kept out of the initial negotiations. By the end of the 1980s, over 100 countries had ratified GATT.

A series of GATT negotiations that concluded in 1994 created the WTO, which replaced GATT. The WTO now functions as the principal international body that is charged with administering rules for trade among member countries. The new agreements that have been established by the WTO cover a range of topics, including agriculture, food safety, animal and plant health regulations, technical standards (testing and certification), import licensing procedures, trade in services, intellectual property rights (including trade in counterfeit goods), as well as rules and procedures for settling disputes. As of May 2010, the WTO (http://www.wto.org/english/theWTO_e/whatis_e/tif_e/org6_e.htm) consisted of 153 member countries, including the United States.

EUROPEAN UNION

In 1957 six European countries signed the Treaty of Rome, which established the European Economic Community. In 1992 the Maastricht Treaty was signed, which officially established the EU. The leaders of European countries hoped that by engaging in commerce they could create long-term stability and enforce the rule of law in cooperative democratic societies. The EU, which is one of the most important trading partners of the United States, expanded in 2004 from 15 nations to 25, creating the largest trading bloc in history.

According to the EU, in "The Member Countries of the European Union" (http://europa.eu/about-eu/27-member-countries/index_en.htm), in 2010 the EU consisted of 27 member countries: Austria, Belgium, Bulgaria, Cyprus, the Czech Republic, Denmark, Estonia, Finland, France, Germany, Greece, Hungary, Ireland, Italy, Latvia, Lithuania, Luxembourg, Malta, the Netherlands, Poland, Portugal, Romania, Slovakia, Slovenia, Spain, Sweden, and the United

Kingdom. Candidate countries for admission to the EU in the future included Croatia, Iceland, Turkey, and the former Yugoslav Republic of Macedonia.

INTERNATIONAL MONETARY FUND

The International Monetary Fund (IMF), a global financial system, was established in July 1944, during the United Nations (UN) Monetary and Financial Conference (more commonly known as the Bretton Woods conference because it took place in Bretton Woods, New Hampshire). The IMF extends short-term loans to members experiencing economic instability. As a condition of receiving its credit assistance, the IMF requires the debtor country to enact significant reform of its economic structure, and often of its political structure as well. The conditions for being granted a loan can include drastic cuts in government spending; privatizing government-owned enterprises, such as railroads and utilities; establishing higher interest rates; increasing taxes; and eliminating subsidies on necessities such as food and fuel.

Supporters of the IMF indicate that these reforms oftentimes eliminate corruption and help establish effective institutions such as courts. In contrast, critics argue that for some countries, these reforms can have devastating social consequences, including severe unemployment, crippling price increases in the cost of basic goods, and political instability resulting from widespread dissatisfaction. Despite this criticism, the IMF membership has grown considerably since its founding. In 1944 it had 45 members. By 2010 the IMF (http://www.imf.org/external/about.htm) consisted of 187 member countries, including the United States.

WORLD BANK

At the same conference that created the IMF in July 1944, the International Bank for Reconstruction and Development (IBRD) was established. In 1960 the International Development Association (IDA) was created. The IBRD and the IDA are commonly known as the World Bank. The World Bank is not a bank in the traditional sense of the word but an agency of the UN. The World Bank works to combat world poverty by providing low-interest loans, interest-free credit, and grants to developing countries. According to the World Bank (http://go.worldbank.org/Y33OQYNE90), in 2010 the IBRD and the IDA consisted of 187 and 170 member countries, respectively.

In its early days, the World Bank often participated in large projects such as dam building. During the first decade of the 21st century it supported the efforts of governments in developing countries to build schools and health centers, provide water and electricity, fight disease, and protect the environment. It is one of the world's largest sources of development assistance. The World Bank notes in *The World Bank Annual Report, 2009: Year in Review* (2009, http://go.world bank.org/Y57CT67Q30) that since 1944 it has provided $479 billion in loans to developing countries worldwide.

GLOBALIZATION AND THE ANTIGLOBALIZATION MOVEMENT

The move toward global free trade, or globalization, has generated intense controversy. Proponents maintain that globalization can improve living standards throughout the world. Their arguments include the following:

- Countries and regions will become more productive by concentrating on industries in which they have a natural advantage and trading with other nations for goods in which they do not have an advantage.

- Multinational corporations will be able to realize economies of scale—that is, operate more economically because they are buying in bulk, selling to a much larger market, and utilizing a much larger labor pool. This will increase productivity and lead to greater prosperity.

- Free trade will lead to faster growth in developing countries.

- Increased incomes and the development of job-related skills among the citizens of poorer nations will foster the spread of information, education, and, ultimately, democracy.

Critics of globalization point out the negative effects that multinational corporations have on people in the developing world. They argue that:

- Most of the profits from free trade flow to the United States and to other industrialized countries.

- Local industries can be destroyed by competition from wealthier nations, causing widespread unemployment and social disruption.

- Centuries of cultural tradition can be quickly obliterated by the influence of international companies.

- Multinational corporations often impinge on national sovereignty to protect their profits.

Critics also note that the free trade policies are often applied unfairly, as the United States insists that other countries open their markets to U.S. goods while it protects its own producers from competition. For example, the U.S. government has established many tariffs and regulations that raise the prices of imported food products, denying poor farmers in the developing world access to the lucrative U.S. market. In addition, opponents of globalization point out that the spread of multinational corporations can be detrimental to workers in industrialized nations by exporting high-paying jobs to countries with lower labor costs, and that international competition in the labor market could actually lead to lower living standards in the industrialized world.

The antiglobalization movement is not an organized group but an umbrella term for many independent organizations that oppose the pursuit of corporate profits at the expense of social justice in the developing world. These groups often protest the actions of organizations such as the WTO, the IMF, and the World Bank for their perceived bias toward corporations and wealthy nations. For example, in 1999 a WTO conference in Seattle, Washington, drew more than 40,000 protestors in a massive demonstration that generated intense media attention and completely overshadowed the meeting itself.

ECONOMIC AND TRADE SANCTIONS

The United States uses economic and trade sanctions (stopping some or all forms of financial transactions and trade with a country) as a political tool against countries that are thought to violate human rights, tolerate drug trafficking, support terrorism, and produce or store weapons of mass destruction. Sanctions are enforced by the Treasury Department's Office of Foreign Assets Control (OFAC). As of September 2010, the OFAC (http://www.ustreas.gov/offices/enforcement/ofac/programs/index.shtml) listed economic and/or trade sanctions against dozens of countries, including Cuba, Iran, and North Korea.

The Trade Act of 1974 allowed the United States to impose sanctions on countries with unfair trade policies. The Jackson-Vanik amendment to this legislation required annual certification for communist countries, including China, and barred the president from granting favorable trade status to countries that limited emigration. This amendment was repealed in 2000, marking a major step in the restoration of relations between China and the United States. In December 2001 China was admitted as a member of the WTO. The Chinese market presents an enormous opportunity for U.S. exports. As noted in Table 10.3, the United States exported $69.5 billion of goods and services to China in 2009. China ranked third for U.S. exports that year behind Canada ($204.7 billion) and Mexico ($128.9 billion).

THE CHANGING FACE OF FREE TRADE
Parity in Labor Standards and Environmental Laws

Discrepancies in labor and environmental regulations among trading nations have formed another barrier to free trade. The administration of President Bill Clinton (1946–) pushed to impose the same labor and environmental standards on trading nations that the United States imposes on itself. The move was designed to discourage trading partners from exploiting workers and abusing the environment to keep capital costs lower and prices down, thus making their goods and services more competitive than U.S. goods in the global market. Before NAFTA was signed, the United States insisted on assurances from Canada and Mexico that they would enforce labor and environmental laws before ratifying the agreement.

Intellectual Property

Technological advancements have posed new challenges to world trade. As private-sector investment in information technology continues, world economies are becoming even more interconnected. Proponents of free trade, including the United States, have pushed for more protection of intellectual property rights, abuse of which poses a major barrier to world trade. As defined by the UN in the Convention Establishing the World Intellectual Property Organization (May 25, 2007, http://www.wipo.int/treaties/en/convention/trtdocs_wo029.html), which was signed on July 14, 1967, and amended on September 28, 1979, intellectual property includes:

- Literary, artistic, and scientific works

- Performances of performing artists, phonograms, and broadcasts

- Inventions in all fields of human endeavor

- Scientific discoveries

- Industrial designs

- Trademarks, service marks, and commercial names and designations

- Protection against unfair competition and all other rights resulting from intellectual activity in the industrial, scientific, literary, or artistic fields

WORLD INTELLECTUAL PROPERTY ORGANIZATION. Challenges for the international community include establishing minimum standards for protecting intellectual property rights and procedures for enforcement and dispute resolution. These challenges are not new. The World Intellectual Property Organization (WIPO) explains in "Major Events 1883 to 2002" (July 4, 2007, http://www.wipo.int/treaties/en/general/) that as early as 1883, with the founding of the 14-member Paris Convention for the Protection of Industrial Property, countries recognized the special nature of creative works, including inventions, trademarks, and industrial designs. In 1886 the Berne Convention for the Protection of Literary and Artistic Works extended the model of international protection to copyrighted works such as novels, poems, plays, songs, operas, musicals, drawings, paintings, sculptures, and architectural works.

In 1893 the Paris Convention and the Berne Convention combined to form the United International Bureaus for the Protection of Intellectual Property, which maintained its headquarters in Berne, Switzerland. This organization eventually evolved into the WIPO, located in Geneva, Switzerland, which carries out a program that is designed to:

- Harmonize national intellectual property legislation and procedures

- Provide services for international applications for industrial property rights

- Exchange intellectual property information

- Provide legal and technical assistance to developing and other countries

- Facilitate the resolution of private intellectual property disputes

- Marshal information technology as a tool for storing, accessing, and using valuable intellectual property information

As of September 2010, the WIPO (http://www.wipo.int/members/en/) consisted of 184 member nations, including the United States.

INTERNATIONAL INVESTMENT

International investment involves the buying and selling of foreign investments (such as stocks, bonds, and other financial instruments) and the investment of cash directly in foreign companies. Also included are investment assets such as foreign-owned gold and foreign currencies.

International investment data are collected by the Bureau of Economic Analysis (BEA), the U.S. Department of the Treasury, and the Federal Reserve System. The two primary types of international investments that they track are financial investments and direct investments. In *Direct Investment Positions for 2009* (July 2010, https://www.bea.gov/scb/pdf/2010/07%20July/0710_dip.pdf), Marilyn Ibarra-Caton of the BEA explains that a direct investment is an investment in which a resident of one country "obtains a lasting interest in, and a degree of influence over the management of a business enterprise in another country." Legally, a resident can be a person or other entity, such as a corporation or government body. The U.S. government defines a direct investment as ownership or control of at least 10% of a foreign business enterprise.

U.S. Investment in Foreign Assets

The BEA reports in the press release "U.S. Net International Investment Position at Yearend 2009" (June 25, 2010, https://www.bea.gov/newsreleases/international/intinv/2010/pdf/intinv09.pdf) that U.S.-owned assets abroad totaled $18.4 trillion at year-end 2009. This value was down from $19.2 trillion at year-end 2008. U.S. ownership of foreign securities (bonds and corporate stocks) totaled $5.5 trillion and direct investments totaled $4.1 trillion at year-end 2009.

Foreign Investment in U.S. Assets

The United States has historically allowed and often encouraged foreign investment in U.S. assets. The U.S. Government Accountability Office (GAO) states in *Sovereign Wealth Funds: Laws Limiting Foreign Investment Affect Certain U.S. Assets and Agencies Have Various Enforcement Processes* (May 2009, http://www.gao.gov/new.items/d09608.pdf) that "the United States has an overall policy of openness to foreign investment through policy statements and treaties and international agreements addressing investment." However, the GAO explains that there are federal laws that limit or otherwise restrict the amount of foreign ownership or control in certain industries—specifically the transportation, energy, natural resources, banking, agriculture, and national defense industries.

Foreign-Owned Assets in the United States

In "U.S. Net International Investment Position at Year-end 2009," the BEA reports that foreign-owned assets in the United States totaled $21.1 trillion at year-end 2009. This value was down from $22.7 trillion at year-end 2008.

It should be noted that the purchase of U.S. assets by foreign entities is funded in large part by U.S. imports. When Americans buy more foreign goods and services, more U.S. dollars flow into foreign countries. This provides greater opportunities for foreigners to invest in U.S. assets. As described earlier, U.S. imports were down substantially in 2009. Thus, fewer U.S. dollars flowed into foreign countries and were available for investment in 2009.

FOREIGN HOLDINGS OF U.S. FINANCIAL ASSETS. Every five years the U.S. government conducts a comprehensive survey called a full benchmark survey to measure foreign holdings of U.S. securities. As of September 2010, the most recent data available were published in *Report on Foreign Portfolio Holdings of U.S. Securities as of June 30, 2009* (April 2010, http://www.ustreas.gov/tic/shl2009r.pdf) by the Treasury Department. It should be noted that securities include stocks (also known as equities), bonds, and other financial instruments (such as U.S. Treasury bills and notes) and securities sold by U.S. agencies (such as the Federal National Mortgage Association and the Federal Home Loan Mortgage Corporation).

As of June 2009, foreign holdings of U.S. securities totaled $9.6 trillion. (See Table 10.6.) The vast majority of the holdings ($8.5 trillion) consisted of long-term securities (securities with maturity time more than one year). A much smaller value ($1.1 trillion) of short-term debt was in foreign hands.

As shown in Table 10.6, foreign holdings of U.S. securities grew from $4.3 trillion in June 2002 to $10.3 trillion in June 2008. However, by June 2009 foreign holdings had decreased to $9.6 trillion. The Treasury Department notes that this decline "reflects asset price changes and portfolio movements resulting from the financial crisis in the second half of 2008 and early 2009."

Overall foreign ownership of U.S. financial assets grew dramatically during the first decade of the 21st century. This trend is of major concern to some analysts and politicians, who fear that the United States has become too dependent on foreign money. The danger to the U.S. economy as a whole lies in the possibility that foreigners might suddenly decide to pull out of U.S. financial assets. This could destabilize the financial market and harm U.S. economic growth.

The Treasury Department estimates ownership by country of foreign-owned U.S. securities. However, it warns that these estimates should be viewed as "rough indicators" because the underlying data are imperfect and are muddied by the complexities of the modern financial system. Certain countries, such as Luxembourg and Switzerland, contain major financial industries that manage or hold securities for residents of other countries. These securities are reported to the U.S. government as owned by Luxembourg and Switzerland, when in fact they are owned by other foreigners. In addition, certain types of securities are allowed to be unregistered as to country of

TABLE 10.6

Foreign holdings of U.S. securities as of June 2002–June 2009

[Billions of dollars]

Type of security	June 2002	June 2003	June 2004	June 2005	June 2006	June 2007	June 2008	June 2009
Long-term securities	**3,926**	**4,503**	**5,431**	**6,262**	**7,162**	**9,136**	**9,463**	**8,492**
Equities*	1,395	1,564	1,930	2,144	2,430	3,130	2,969	2,252
Debt	2,531	2,939	3,501	4,118	4,733	6,007	6,494	6,240
U.S. Treasury	908	1,116	1,426	1,599	1,727	1,965	2,211	2,604
U.S. agency	492	586	619	791	984	1,304	1,464	1,196
Corporate	1,130	1,236	1,455	1,729	2,021	2,738	2,820	2,440
Short-term debt	**412**	**475**	**588**	**602**	**615**	**635**	**858**	**1,149**
U.S. Treasury	232	269	317	284	253	229	379	862
U.S. agency	88	97	124	150	147	109	174	90
Corporate	92	110	147	168	215	297	306	197
Total long-term and short-term	**4,338**	**4,979**	**6,019**	**6,864**	**7,778**	**9,772**	**10,322**	**9,641**

*"Equities" includes both common and preferred stock as well as all types of investment company shares, such as open-end, closed-end, and money market mutual funds.
Note: Components may not sum to totals because of rounding.

SOURCE: "Table 1. Foreign Holdings of U.S. Securities, by Type of Security, As of Selected Survey Dates," in *Report on Foreign Portfolio Holdings of U.S. Securities as of June 30, 2009*, U.S. Treasury Department, Federal Reserve Bank of New York, and Board of Governors of the Federal Reserve System, April 2010, http://www.ustreas.gov/tic/shl2009r.pdf (accessed July 15, 2010)

ownership. With these caveats, the Treasury Department estimates that the following 10 countries held the highest value of U.S. securities as of June 30, 2009:

- China (mainland)—$1.4 trillion
- Japan—$1.3 trillion
- United Kingdom—$788 billion
- Cayman Islands—$650 billion
- Luxembourg—$578 billion
- Belgium—$415 billion
- Middle East oil-exporting countries—$353 billion
- Ireland—$348 billion
- Canada—$337 billion
- Switzerland—$328 billion

China's large holdings of U.S. securities are of particular concern to some analysts. As noted earlier, a country or countries holding large amounts of U.S. securities could, in theory, severely disrupt the U.S. economy by suddenly selling those securities. The probability and consequences of this possible event are examined regularly by the CRS. In *Foreign Ownership of U.S. Financial Assets: Implications of a Withdrawal* (March 9, 2010, http://assets.opencrs .com/rpts/RL34319_20100309.pdf), James K. Jackson of the CRS explains that a sudden sell-off of foreign-owned U.S. securities could, in theory, cause a dramatic spike in interest rates in the United States. However, Jackson explains that this scenario is highly unlikely because the financial industry responds quickly to market fluctuations. As such, any attempted sell-off would lead to a sudden increase in supply, which would drive down the price of the securities and cause the seller or sellers to lose huge amounts of money. In addition, Jackson notes that the Federal Reserve would not "stand idly by" in such a circumstance, but would act quickly in cooperation with other national banks to stabilize credit markets.

FOREIGN DIRECT INVESTMENT IN THE UNITED STATES. As noted earlier, foreign direct investment entails foreign ownership or control of at least 10% of a U.S. business enterprise. Ibarra-Caton reports that foreign direct investment totaled $2.3 trillion at year-end 2009. This value was up from $2.2 trillion at year-end 2008.

The 10-largest holders of foreign direct investments in the United States at year-end 2009 were:

- United Kingdom—$453.9 billion
- Japan—$264.2 billion
- The Netherlands—$238 billion
- Canada—$225.8 billion
- Luxembourg—$127.8 billion
- Australia—$45.7 billion
- Spain—$43.9 billion
- Sweden—$38.9 billion
- Switzerland—$18.4 billion
- France—$18.3 billion

For comparison, China had only $791 million in direct investment in the United States at year-end 2009.

Growth in foreign direct investment in the United States during 2008 and 2009 was extremely low by historical standards due to the effects of the great recession. According to Ibarra-Caton, foreign direct investment grew by 5% in 2008 and by 7% in 2009. This compares to a 12% annual average growth rate from 1997 to 2007.

IMPORTANT NAMES
AND ADDRESSES

Agency for Healthcare Research and Quality
540 Gaither Rd.
Rockville, MD 20850
(301) 427-1364
URL: http://www.ahrq.gov/

American Bankruptcy Institute
44 Canal Center Plaza, Ste. 400
Alexandria, VA 22314
(703) 739-0800
FAX: (703) 739-1060
E-mail: Support@abiworld.org
URL: http://www.abiworld.org/

Bureau of Economic Analysis
1441 L St. NW
Washington, DC 20230
(202) 606-9900
E-mail: CustomerService@bea.gov
URL: http://www.bea.gov/

Bureau of Labor Statistics
Postal Square Building
2 Massachusetts Ave. NE
Washington, DC 20212-0001
(202) 691-5200
URL: http://www.bls.gov/

Commodities Futures Trading Commission
Three Lafayette Centre
1155 21st St. NW
Washington, DC 20581
(202) 418-5000
FAX: (202) 418-5521
E-mail: Questions@cftc.gov
URL: http://www.cftc.gov/

Congressional Budget Office
Ford House Office Bldg., Fourth Floor
Washington, DC 20515-6925
(202) 226-2602
E-mail: communications@cbo.gov
URL: http://www.cbo.gov/

Consumer Federation of America
1620 I St. NW, Ste. 200
Washington, DC 20006
(202) 387-6121
E-mail: cfa@consumerfed.org
URL: http://www.consumerfed.org/

Economic Policy Institute
1333 H St. NW, Ste. 300, East Tower
Washington, DC 20005-4707
(202) 775-8810
FAX: (202) 775-0819
E-mail: researchdept@epi.org
URL: http://www.epi.org/

Federal Communications Commission
445 12th St. SW
Washington, DC 20554
1-888-225-5322
FAX: 1-866-418-0232
E-mail: fccinfo@fcc.gov
URL: http://www.fcc.gov/

Federal Home Loan Mortgage Corporation
8200 Jones Branch Dr.
McLean, VA 22102-3110
(703) 903-2000
URL: http://www.freddiemac.com/

Federal National Mortgage Association
3900 Wisconsin Ave. NW
Washington, DC 20016-2806
(202) 752-7000
URL: http://www.fanniemae.com/

Federal Reserve System, Board of Governors
20th St. and Constitution Ave. NW
Washington, DC 20551
URL: http://www.federalreserve.gov/

Federal Trade Commission
600 Pennsylvania Ave. NW
Washington, DC 20580
(202) 326-2222
URL: http://www.ftc.gov/

Federation of Tax Administrators
444 N. Capitol St. NW, Ste. 348
Washington, DC 20001
(202) 624-5890
URL: http://www.taxadmin.org/

Internal Revenue Service
1111 Constitution Ave. NW
Washington, DC 20224
1-800-829-1040
URL: http://www.irs.gov/

International Monetary Fund
700 19th St. NW
Washington, DC 20431
(202) 623-7000
FAX: (202) 623-4661
URL: http://www.imf.org/

Investment Company Institute
1401 H St. NW, Ste. 1200
Washington, DC 20005
(202) 326-5800
URL: http://www.ici.org/

Office of Federal Housing Enterprise Oversight
1700 G St. NW, Fourth Floor
Washington, DC 20552
E-mail: FHFAinfo@FHFA.gov
URL: http://www.fhfa.gov/

Office of Management and Budget
725 17th St. NW
Washington, DC 20503
(202) 395-3080
FAX: (202) 395-3888
URL: http://www.whitehouse.gov/omb/

Organisation for Economic Cooperation and Development
2 rue André Pascal, F-75775
Paris, Cedex 16 France
(011-33) 1-45-24-82-00
FAX: (011-33) 1-45-24-85-00
URL: http://www.oecd.org/home/

Social Security Administration
Windsor Park Bldg.
6401 Security Blvd.
Baltimore, MD 21235
1-800-772-1213
URL: http://www.ssa.gov/

U.S. Census Bureau
4600 Silver Hill Rd.
Washington, DC 20233
(301) 763-4636
E-mail: pio@census.gov
URL: http://www.census.gov/

U.S. Consumer Product Safety Commission
4330 East-West Hwy.
Bethesda, MD 20814
(301) 504-7923
FAX: (301) 504-0124
URL: http://www.cpsc.gov/

U.S. Department of Commerce
1401 Constitution Ave. NW
Washington, DC 20230
(202) 482-2000
E-mail: webmaster@doc.gov
URL: http://www.commerce.gov/

U.S. Department of Health and Human Services
200 Independence Ave. SW
Washington, DC 20201
1-877-696-6775
URL: http://www.hhs.gov/

U.S. Department of Housing and Urban Development
451 Seventh St. SW
Washington, DC 20410

(202) 708-1112
URL: http://www.hud.gov/

U.S. Department of Labor
Frances Perkins Building
200 Constitution Ave. NW
Washington, DC 20210
1-866-487-2365
URL: http://www.dol.gov/

U.S. Department of the Treasury
1500 Pennsylvania Ave. NW
Washington, DC 20220
(202) 622-2000
FAX: (202) 622-6415
URL: http://www.treasury.gov/

U.S. Equal Opportunity Employment Commission
131 M St. NE
Washington, DC 20507
(202) 663-4900
1-800-669-4000
E-mail: info@eeoc.gov
URL: http://www.eeoc.gov/

U.S. Government Accountability Office
441 G St. NW
Washington, DC 20548
(202) 512-3000
E-mail: contact@gao.gov
URL: http://www.gao.gov/

U.S. International Trade Commission
500 E St. SW
Washington, DC 20436

(202) 205-2000
URL: http://www.usitc.gov/

U.S. Securities and Exchange Commission
100 F St. NE
Washington, DC 20549
(202) 942-8088
URL: http://www.sec.gov/

U.S. Small Business Administration
409 Third St. SW
Washington, DC 20416
1-800-827-5722
URL: http://www.sba.gov/

World Bank
1818 H St. NW
Washington, DC 20433
(202) 473-1000
FAX: (202) 477-6391
URL: http://www.worldbank.org/

World Intellectual Property Organization
34, chemin des Colombettes, CH-1211
Geneva 20 Switzerland
(011-41-22) 338-9111
FAX: (011-41-22) 733-5428
URL: http://www.wipo.int/

World Trade Organization
Centre William Rappard
Rue de Lausanne 154, CH-1211
Geneva 21, Switzerland
(011-41-22) 739-5111
FAX: (011-41-22) 731-4206
E-mail: enquiries@wto.org
URL: http://www.wto.org/

RESOURCES

Several government agencies provided invaluable economic data and information for this book: the U.S. Department of Commerce's Bureau of Economic Analysis (BEA), the U.S. Census Bureau, the U.S. Department of Labor's Bureau of Labor Statistics (BLS), and the Federal Reserve System.

The BEA compiles the *National Income and Product Accounts*, which include detailed financial information on gross domestic product, personal income and outlays, saving, corporate profits, and international trade and balance of payments.

The BLS publishes statistical data on wages, benefits, and income; inflation and economic indexes; employment and unemployment; industries and occupations; employment demographics; and worker health and safety standards. In addition, the BLS posts many of its publications online, including *Employment Situation*, *Occupational Outlook Handbook*, *Monthly Labor Review*, and *Occupational Outlook Quarterly*.

The Census Bureau provides comprehensive economic and demographic data. Particularly useful for the study of the U.S. economy are the census publications *Historical Statistics of the United States, Colonial Times to 1970, Bicentennial Edition, Part 1* (September 1975), *Income, Poverty, and Health Insurance Coverage in the United States: 2009* (Carmen DeNavas-Walt, Bernadette D. Proctor, and Jessica C. Smith, September 2010), the *American Fact Finder: 2007 Economic Census*, and *Statistical Abstract of the United States: 2010* (2010).

The Federal Reserve System publishes economic data and papers on a variety of economic subjects, including housing, consumer spending, interest rates, consumer credit, net worth, wealth distribution, and debt. Especially useful is the series *Federal Reserve Statistical Release*.

Other government agencies and offices consulted during the compilation of this book include the U.S. Government Accountability Office, the Congressional Research Service, the Social Security Administration, and the White House. The latter provided budgetary information and the annual *Economic Report of the President*.

Important information was also obtained from the U.S. Federal Trade Commission; the Commodities Futures Trading Commission; the U.S. Departments of Energy, Health and Human Services, Education, Housing and Urban Development, Agriculture, and the Treasury; the U.S. International Trade Commission; the U.S. Department of Homeland Security's Office of Immigration Statistics; the Internal Revenue Service; the Congressional Budget Office; the Office of Management and Budget; the Office of Federal Housing Enterprise Oversight; the Central Intelligence Agency; and the U.S. Small Business Administration.

International organizations that provided input include the Organisation for Economic Co-operation and Development, the World Trade Organization, the International Monetary Fund, the World Bank, and the World Intellectual Property Organization.

A number of independent, nonpartisan think tanks and private organizations were consulted to obtain various points of view on socioeconomic issues. These organizations include the American Bankruptcy Institute, the Center for Corporate Policy, the Center for a New American Dream, the Center for Responsive Politics, the Consumer Federation of America, the Dollars & Sense Collective, the Economic Policy Institute, the Levy Economic Institute of Bard College, the Tax Foundation, and United for a Fair Economy.

Finally, the Gallup Organization was the source for numerous public opinion polls that were conducted to gauge American attitudes on economic topics.

INDEX